MW00737110

The Family 09/10

Thirty-Fifth Edition

EDITOR

Kathleen R. Gilbert
Indiana University

Kathleen Gilbert is an associate professor in the Department of Applied Health Science at Indiana University. She received a BA in Sociology and an MS in Marriage and Family Relations from Northern Illinois University. Her PhD in Family Studies is from Purdue University. Dr. Gilbert's primary areas of interest are loss and grief in a family context, trauma and the family, family process, and minority families. She has published several books and articles in these areas.

McGraw Hill **Higher Education**

Boston   Burr Ridge, IL   Dubuque, IA   New York   San Francisco   St. Louis
Bangkok   Bogotá   Caracas   Kuala Lumpur   Lisbon   London   Madrid   Mexico City
Milan   Montreal   New Delhi   Santiago   Seoul   Singapore   Sydney   Taipei   Toronto

The McGraw·Hill Companies

Higher Education

ANNUAL EDITIONS: THE FAMILY, THIRTY-FIFTH EDITION

1 2 3 4 5 6 7 8 9 0 QPD/QPD 0 9 8

ISBN 978–0–07–351637–0
MHID 0–07–351637–6
ISSN 1092–4876

Managing Editor: *Larry Loeppke*
Senior Managing Editor: *Faye Schilling*
Developmental Editor: *Dave Welsh*
Editorial Coordinator: *Mary Foust*
Editorial Assistant: *Nancy Meissner*
Production Service Assistant: *Rita Hingtgen*
Permissions Coordinator: *DeAnna Dausener*
Senior Marketing Manager: *Julie Keck*
Marketing Communications Specialist: *Mary Klein*
Marketing Coordinator: *Alice Link*
Project Manager: *Sandy Wille*
Design Specialist: *Tara McDermott*
Senior Production Supervisor: *Laura Fuller*
Cover Graphics: *Kristine Jubeck*

Compositor: Laserwords Private Limited
Cover Image: Photodisc (inset); Steve Cole/Getty Images (background)

Library in Congress Cataloging-in-Publication Data
Main entry under title: Annual Editions: The Family. 2009/2010.
  1. The Family—Periodicals. I. Gilbert, Kathleen R., *comp.* II. Title: The Family.
658'.05

www.mhhe.com

Editors/Advisory Board

Members of the Advisory Board are instrumental in the final selection of articles for each edition of ANNUAL EDITIONS. Their review of articles for content, level, currentness, and appropriateness provides critical direction to the editor and staff. We think that you will find their careful consideration well reflected in this volume.

Preface

In publishing ANNUAL EDITIONS we recognize the enormous role played by the magazines, newspapers, and journals of the public press in providing current, first-rate educational information in a broad spectrum of interest areas. Many of these articles are appropriate for students, researchers, and professionals seeking accurate, current material to help bridge the gap between principles and theories and the real world. These articles, however, become more useful for study when those of lasting value are carefully collected, organized, indexed, and reproduced in a low-cost format, which provides easy and permanent access when the material is needed. That is the role played by ANNUAL EDITIONS.

The purpose of *Annual Editions: The Family 09/10* is to bring to the reader the latest thoughts and trends in our understanding of the family, to identify current concerns as well as problems and potential solutions, and to present alternative views of family processes. The intent of this anthology is to explore intimate relationships as they are played out within the family and, in doing this, to reflect the family's evolving function and importance.

The articles in this volume are taken from professional journals as well as other professionally oriented publications and popular lay publications aimed at both special populations and a general readership. The selections are carefully reviewed for their currency and accuracy. In some cases, contrasting viewpoints are presented; in others, articles are paired in such a way as to personalize more impersonal scholarly information. In the current edition, a number of new articles have been added to reflect reviewers' comments on the previous edition. As the reader, you will note the tremendous range in tone and focus of these articles, from first-person accounts to reports of scientific discoveries as well as philosophical and theoretical writings. Some are more practical and applications-oriented, while others are more conceptual and research-oriented.

This anthology is organized to address many of the important aspects of family and family relationships. The first unit takes an overview perspective and looks at varied perspectives on the family. The second unit examines the beginning steps of relationship building as individuals go through the process of exploring and establishing connections. In the third unit, means of finding and maintaining a relationship balance, romantic as well as for other intimate relationships, are examined. Unit 4 is concerned with crises and ways in which these can act as challenges and opportunities for families and their members. Finally, the fifth unit takes an affirming tone as it looks at family strengths and ways of empowering families.

Annual Editions: The Family 09/10 is intended to be used as a supplemental text for lower-level, introductory marriage and family or sociology of the family classes, particularly when they tie the content of the readings to essential information on marriages and families, however they are defined. As a supplement, this book can also be used to update or emphasize certain aspects of standard marriage and family textbooks. Because of the provocative nature of many of the essays in this anthology, it works well as a basis for class discussion about various aspects of marriages and family relationships.

This edition of *Annual Editions: The Family* contains *World Wide Web* sites that can be used to further explore topics addressed in the articles. These sites are cross-referenced by number in the *topic guide*.

I would like to thank everyone involved in the development of this volume. My appreciation goes to those who sent in *article rating forms* and comments on the previous edition as well as those who suggested articles to consider for inclusion in this edition. To all of the students in my Marriage and Family Interaction class who have contributed critiques of articles, I would like to say thanks.

Anyone interested in providing input for future editions of *Annual Editions: The Family* should complete and return the postage-paid *article rating form* at the end of this book. Your suggestions are much appreciated and contribute to the continuing quality of this anthology.

Kathleen R. Gilbert
Editor

Contents

UNIT 1
Evolving Perspectives on the Family

UNIT 2
Exploring and Establishing Relationships

The concepts in bold italics are developed in the article. For further expansion, please refer to the Topic Guide.

UNIT 3
Family Relationships

The concepts in bold italics are developed in the article. For further expansion, please refer to the Topic Guide.

The concepts in bold italics are developed in the article. For further expansion, please refer to the Topic Guide.

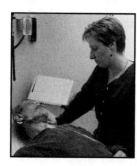

UNIT 4
Challenges and Opportunities

The concepts in bold italics are developed in the article. For further expansion, please refer to the Topic Guide.

The concepts in bold italics are developed in the article. For further expansion, please refer to the Topic Guide.

UNIT 5
Families, Now and into the Future

The concepts in bold italics are developed in the article. For further expansion, please refer to the Topic Guide.

The concepts in bold italics are developed in the article. For further expansion, please refer to the Topic Guide.

Correlation Guide

The *Annual Editions* series provides students with convenient, inexpensive access to current, carefully selected articles from the public press. **Annual Editions: The Family 09/10** is an easy-to-use reader that presents articles on important topics such as *family composition, love and sex, procreation, committed relationships between mates and between parents and their children, family stressors,* and many more. For more information on *Annual Editions* and other *McGraw-Hill Contemporary Learning Series* titles, visit www.mhcls.com.

This convenient guide matches the units in **Annual Editions: The Family 09/10** with the corresponding chapters in two of our best-selling McGraw-Hill Marriage, Family, and Intimacy textbooks by Olson et al. and Miller et al.

Annual Editions: The Family 09/10	Marriages and Families: Intimacy, Diversity, and Strengths, 6/e by Olson et al.	Intimate Relationships, 5/e by Miller et al.
Unit 1: Evolving Perspectives on the Family	**Chapter 1:** Perspectives on Intimate Relationships **Chapter 2:** Cultural Diversity: Family Strengths and Challenges **Chapter 3:** Understanding Marriage and Family Dynamics **Chapter 11:** Marriage: Building a Strong Foundation **Chapter 12:** Parenthood: Choices and Challenges **Chapter 15:** Divorce, Single-Parent Families, and Stepfamilies **Chapter 16:** Strengthening Marriages and Families	**Chapter 3:** Attraction **Chapter 13:** The Dissolution and Loss of Relationships **Chapter 14:** Maintaining and Repairing Relationships
Unit 2: Exploring and Establishing Relationships	**Chapter 1:** Perspectives on Intimate Relationships **Chapter 4:** Communication and Intimacy **Chapter 6:** Sexual Intimacy **Chapter 9:** Friendship, Intimacy, and Singlehood **Chapter 10:** Date, Mate Selection, and Living Together **Chapter 13:** Midlife and Older Couples	**Chapter 1:** The Building Blocks of Relationships **Chapter 2:** Research Methods **Chapter 3:** Attraction **Chapter 4:** Social Cognition **Chapter 5:** Communication **Chapter 6:** Interdependency **Chapter 7:** Friendships **Chapter 8:** Love **Chapter 9:** Sexuality **Chapter 10:** Stresses and Strains **Chapter 11:** Conflict **Chapter 13:** The Dissolution and Loss of Relationships **Chapter 14:** Maintaining and Repairing Relationships
Unit 3: Family Relationships	**Chapter 1:** Perspectives on Intimate Relationships **Chapter 2:** Cultural Diversity: Family Strengths and Challenges **Chapter 3:** Understanding Marriage and Family Dynamics **Chapter 4:** Communication and Intimacy **Chapter 5:** Conflict and Conflict Resolution **Chapter 6:** Sexual Intimacy **Chapter 7:** Gender Roles and Power in the Family **Chapter 8:** Managing Economic Resources **Chapter 9:** Friendship, Intimacy, and Singlehood **Chapter 10:** Date, Mate Selection, and Living Together **Chapter 12:** Parenthood: Choices and Challenges **Chapter 14:** Stress, Abuse, and Family Problems **Chapter 15:** Divorce, Single-Parent Families, and Stepfamilies **Chapter 16:** Strengthening Marriages and Families	**Chapter 1:** The Building Blocks of Relationships **Chapter 9:** Sexuality **Chapter 11:** Conflict **Chapter 14:** Maintaining and Repairing Relationships
Unit 4: Challenges and Opportunities	**Chapter 1:** Perspectives on Intimate Relationships **Chapter 5:** Conflict and Conflict Resolution **Chapter 6:** Sexual Intimacy **Chapter 8:** Managing Economic Resources **Chapter 9:** Friendship, Intimacy, and Singlehood **Chapter 12:** Parenthood: Choices and Challenges **Chapter 13:** Midlife and Older Couples **Chapter 14:** Stress, Abuse, and Family Problems **Chapter 15:** Divorce, Single-Parent Families, and Stepfamilies **Chapter 16:** Strengthening Marriages and Families	**Chapter 9:** Sexuality **Chapter 10:** Stresses and Strains **Chapter 11:** Conflict **Chapter 12:** Power and Violence **Chapter 13:** The Dissolution and Loss of Relationships **Chapter 14:** Maintaining and Repairing Relationships
Unit 5: Families, Now and Into the Future	**Chapter 1:** Perspectives on Intimate Relationships **Chapter 7:** Gender Roles and Power in the Family	**Chapter 14:** Maintaining and Repairing Relationships

Topic Guide

This topic guide suggests how the selections in this book relate to the subjects covered in your course. You may want to use the topics listed on these pages to search the Web more easily.

On the following pages a number of Web sites have been gathered specifically for this book. They are arranged to reflect the units of this Annual Edition reader. You can link to these sites by going to *http://www.mhcls.com/online/*.

All the articles that relate to each topic are listed below the bold-faced term.

Abuse
18. Do We Need a Law to Prohibit Spanking?
19. Prickly Père
26. Recognizing Domestic Partner Abuse
27. The Myths and Truths of Family Abduction

Adoption
11. Adopting a New American Family

Affiliative families
23. Aunties and Uncles

Aging
24. Roles of American Indian Grandparents in Times of Cultural Crisis
25. Aging Japanese Pen Messages to Posterity
36. Caring for the Caregiver

Bereavement
25. Aging Japanese Pen Messages to Posterity
37. Bereavement after Caregiving
38. Terrorism, Trauma, and Children

Biology
4. This Thing Called Love
8. A New Fertility Factor
10. Breeder Reaction
28. Children of Alcoholics

Caregiving
34. Partners Face Cancer Together
35. A Guide for Caregivers
36. Caring for the Caregiver
37. Bereavement after Caregiving

Childcare
3. Children as a Public Good

Children
2. Interracial Families
3. Children as a Public Good
10. Breeder Reaction
11. Adopting a New American Family
17. Kaleidoscope of Parenting Cultures
18. Do We Need a Law to Prohibit Spanking?
22. Being a Sibling
27. The Myths and Truths of Family Abduction
28. Children of Alcoholics
38. Terrorism, Trauma, and Children
46. Sustaining Resilient Families for Children in Primary Grades

Communication
5. Pillow Talk
6. How to Talk about Sex
7. On-Again, Off-Again
30. Love but Don't Touch

34. Partners Face Cancer Together
43. Get a Closer Look
44. Spirituality and Family Nursing
45. The Joy of Rituals
48. Sparking Interest in Nature—Family Style

Dating
7. On-Again, Off-Again
12. Free As a Bird and Loving It

Divorce
1. Marriage and Family in the Scandinavian Experience
27. The Myths and Truths of Family Abduction
39. A Divided House
40. Civil Wars
41. Stepfamily Success Depends on Ingredients

Emotions
5. Pillow Talk
37. Bereavement after Caregiving
44. Spirituality and Family Nursing
45. The Joy of Rituals

Family and marriage
1. Marriage and Family in the Scandinavian Experience
2. Interracial Families
3. Children as a Public Good
14. Two Mommies and a Daddy
15. Marriage at First Sight
23. Aunties and Uncles
41. Stepfamily Success Depends on Ingredients
42. The 3rd National Family History Initiative

Family interaction
19. Prickly Père
22. Being a Sibling
39. A Divided House
41. Stepfamily Success Depends on Ingredients
42. The 3rd National Family History Initiative
43. Get a Closer Look
44. Spirituality and Family Nursing
45. The Joy of Rituals
46. Sustaining Resilient Families for Children in Primary Grades
48. Sparking Interest in Nature—Family Style

Finances, family
1. Marriage and Family in the Scandinavian Experience
21. Last Hope in a Weak Economy?
32. Becoming Financial Grown-ups
33. Making Time for Family Time
35. A Guide for Caregivers
41. Stepfamily Success Depends on Ingredients
47. The Consumer Crunch

Gay marriage
1. Marriage and Family in the Scandinavian Experience
13. Gay Marriage Lite

Gender roles
1. Marriage and Family in the Scandinavian Experience
34. Partners Facing Cancer Together

Internet References

The following Internet sites have been selected to support the articles found in this reader. These sites were available at the time of publication. However, because Web sites often change their structure and content, the information listed may no longer be available. We invite you to visit http://www.mhcls.com for easy access to these sites.

Annual Editions: The Family 09/10

General Sources

AARP (American Association of Retired Persons)
http://www.aarp.org

This major advocacy group for older people includes among its many resources suggested readings and Internet links to organizations that deal with social issues that may affect people and their families as they age.

Encyclopedia Britannica
http://www.britannica.com

This huge "Britannica Internet Guide" leads to a cornucopia of informational sites and reference sources on such topics as family structure, the family cycle, forms of family organization, and other social issues.

Planned Parenthood
http://www.plannedparenthood.org

Visit this well-known organization's home page for links to information on the various kinds of contraceptives (including outercourse and abstinence) and to discussions of other topics related to sexual and reproductive health.

Social Science Information Gateway
http://sosig.esrc.bris.ac.uk/

This is an online catalog of Internet resources relevant to social science education and research. Sites are selected and described by a librarian or subject specialist.

Sympatico: HealthyWay: Health Links
http://www1.sympatico.ca/Contents/health/

This Canadian site, which is meant for consumers, will lead you to many links that are related to sexual orientation. Sympatico also addresses aspects of human sexuality as well as reproductive health over the life span.

UNIT 1: Evolving Perspectives on the Family

American Studies Web
http://www1.georgetown.edu/departments/american_studies/

This site provides links to a wealth of resources on the Internet related to American studies, from gender to race and ethnicity to demography and population studies.

Anthropology Resources Page
http://www.usd.edu/anth/

Many cultural topics can be accessed from this site from the University of South Dakota. Click on the links to find comparisons of values and lifestyles among the world's peoples.

UNIT 2: Exploring and Establishing Relationships

Bonobo Sex and Society
http://songweaver.com/info/bonobos.html

This site, accessed through Carnegie Mellon University, contains an article explaining how a primate's behavior challenges traditional assumptions about male supremacy in human evolution. This interesting site is guaranteed to generate much spirited debate.

Go Ask Alice!
http://www.goaskalice.columbia.edu/index.html

This interactive site of the Columbia University Health Services provides discussion and insight into a number of personal issues of interest to college-age people—and those younger and older.

The Kinsey Institute for Research in Sex, Gender, and Reproduction
http://www.indiana.edu/~kinsey/

The purpose of this Kinsey Institute Web site is to support interdisciplinary research in the study of human sexuality.

Mysteries of Odor in Human Sexuality
http://www.pheromones.com

This is a commercial site with the goal of selling a book by James Kohl. Look here to find topics of interest to nonscientists about pheromones. Check out the diagram of "Mammalian Olfactory-Genetic-Neuronal-Hormonal-Behavioral Reciprocity and Human Sexuality" for a sense of the myriad biological influences that play a part in sexual behavior.

The Society for the Scientific Study of Sexuality
http://www.sexscience.org

The Society for the Scientific Study of Sexuality is an international organization dedicated to the advancement of knowledge about sexuality.

UNIT 3: Family Relationships

Child Welfare League of America
http://www.cwla.org

The CWLA is the largest U.S. organization devoted entirely to the well-being of vulnerable children and their families. This site provides links to information about such issues as teaching morality and values.

Coalition for Marriage, Family, and Couples Education
http://www.smartmarriages.com

CMFCE is dedicated to bringing information about and directories of skill-based marriage education courses to the public. It hopes to lower the rate of family breakdown through couple-empowering preventive education.

The National Academy for Child Development
http://www.nacd.org

The NACD, dedicated to helping children and adults reach their full potential, presents links to various programs, research, and resources into a variety of family topics.

Internet References

National Council on Family Relations

http://www.ncfr.com

This NCFR home page leads to valuable links to articles, research, and other resources on issues in family relations, such as stepfamilies, couples, and children of divorce.

Positive Parenting

http://www.positiveparenting.com

Positive Parenting is an organization dedicated to providing resources and information to make parenting rewarding, effective, and fun.

SocioSite

http://www.pscw.uva.nl/sociosite/TOPICS/Women.html

Open this site to gain insights into a number of issues that affect family relationships. It provides wide-ranging issues of women and men, of family and children, and more.

UNIT 4: Challenges and Opportunities

Alzheimer's Association

http://www.alz.org

The Alzheimer's Association, dedicated to the prevention, cure, and treatment of Alzheimer's and related disorders, provides support to afflicted patients and their families.

Caregiver's Handbook

http://www.acsu.buffalo.edu/~drstall/hndbk0.html

This site is an online handbook for caregivers. Topics include medical aspects and liabilities of care giving.

National Crime Prevention Council

http://www.ncpc.org

NCPC's mission is to enable people to create safer and more caring communities by addressing the causes of crime and violence and reducing the opportunities for crime to occur.

Widow Net

http://www.widownet.org

Widow Net is an information and self-help resource for and by widows and widowers. The information is helpful to people of all ages, religious backgrounds, and sexual orientation who have experienced a loss.

UNIT 5: Families, Now and into the Future

National Institute on Aging

http://www.nih.gov/nia/

The NIA presents this home page that will take you to a variety of resources on health and lifestyle issues that are of interest to people as they grow older.

UNIT 1

Evolving Perspectives on the Family

Unit Selections

1. **Marriage and Family in the Scandinavian Experience,** David Popenoe
2. **Interracial Families,** Carol Mithers
3. **Children As a Public Good,** Myra H. Strober

Key Points to Consider

- How do marriages and families compare in Sweden and the United States? Do you see trends they share in common?

- What are your views on the changing nature of the American family? What are your thoughts on interracial families?

- What are your expectations for the family as an institution? How do personally held views of family influence policy? What might be the effect of this?

Student Web Site

www.mhcls.com/online

Internet References

American Studies Web
http://www1.georgetown.edu/departments/american_studies/
Anthropology Resources Page
http://www.usd.edu/anth/

Our image of what family is and what it should be is a powerful combination of personal experience, family forms we encounter or observe, and attitudes we hold. Once formed, this image informs decision making and interpersonal interaction throughout our lives, and has far-reaching effects: on an intimate level, it influences individual and family development as well as relationships both inside and outside the family; on a broader level, it affects legislation as well as social policy and programming.

In many ways, this image can be positive. It can act to clarify our thinking and facilitate interaction with like-minded individuals. It can also be negative, because it can narrow our thinking and limit our ability to see that other ways of carrying out the functions of family have value. Their very differentness can make them seem "bad." In this case, interaction with others can be impeded because of contrasting views.

This unit is intended to meet several goals with regard to perspectives on the family: (1) to sensitize the reader to sources of beliefs about the "shoulds" of the family—what the family should be and the ways in which family roles should be carried out, (2) to show how different views of the family can influence attitudes toward community responsibility and family policy, and (3) to show how views that dominate one's culture can influence awareness of ways of structuring family life.

In the first reading, "Marriage and Family in the Scandinavian Experience," David Popenoe explores the differences and similarities in marriage and family experiences in the United States and Sweden. These comparisons provide information that may surprise the reader. The nature of "Interracial Families" and children of these families is explored in the next reading. The level of responsibility a society should take for the care and well-being of children is explored in the next reading, "Children As a Public Good."

Marriage and Family in the Scandinavian Experience

DAVID POPENOE

Many Americans have long had a ready answer to America's family problems: We should become more like Scandinavia. Whether the issues are work-family, teen sex, child poverty, or marital break-up, a range of Scandinavian family and welfare policies is commonly put forth with the assertion that, if only these could be instituted in America, family life in our nation would be improved significantly. But what can we in the United States really learn from Scandinavia? The Scandinavian nations are so small and demographically homogeneous that the idea of simply transferring their social policies to this country must be viewed as problematic. Sweden, for example, the largest Scandinavian nation and the one featured in this essay, has only 9 million people compared to our population of nearly 300 million. And how well have these policies actually worked in Scandinavia? As this essay will make clear, some of the Scandinavian family policies have, indeed, been quite successful on their own home ground. Yet aside from the potential non-transferability of these policies, by focusing so much attention on them we may be overlooking some even more important aspects of the Scandinavian family experience.

Sweden and the United States

It is now well known that there has been a weakening of marriage and the nuclear family in advanced, industrialized societies, especially since the 1960s. What is not well known is the surprising fact that the two nations that lead in this weakening are Sweden and the United States—two nations that stand at almost opposite extremes in terms of their socioeconomic systems. Let us look at one telling statistical measure. Defining the nuclear family as a mother and father living together with their own biological children, a good measure of nuclear familism in a society is the percentage of children under the age of 18 who live with both biological parents. This percentage for the United States is 63, the lowest among Western industrialized nations. The second from lowest is Sweden, at 73!

How is this possible? At the one socioeconomic extreme, Sweden has the strongest public sector, the highest taxes, and is the most secular. At the other, the United States has the weakest public sector, the lowest taxes, and is the most religious. Could these fundamental factors be mostly irrelevant to family change? And if so, what key factors are involved? As we shall see, the answer to this intellectual puzzle is to be found largely in the realm of a postmodern trend shared by both nations. But first we need to consider other family differences between the two nations. Two key differences stand out: in the United States more people marry, but they also divorce in large numbers; in Sweden, fewer people marry, but the Swedish divorce rate is a little lower than in the United States.

Here is the recent statistical record, beginning with Sweden. The Swedish marriage rate by the late 1990s was *one of the lowest in the world;* indeed, one of the lowest marriage rates ever recorded and considerably lower than the rates of other Western European nations. (Number of marriages per 1000 unmarried women in 2002—Sweden: 17.5; U.S.: 43.4. Unless otherwise noted, all statistics in this essay were gathered or computed by the National Marriage Project from official statistical sources in each nation.) If this rate holds, only about 60 percent of Swedish women today will "ever marry," compared to over 85 percent in the United States. This is a quite recent development. Not so long ago the two nations were quite similar: For the generation marrying in the 1950s, the figure for Sweden was 91 percent and for the United States 95 percent.

Sweden's low marriage rate does not mean that Swedes are living alone; rather, they are living together outside of marriage—another area in which Sweden has been in the vanguard. In fact, Sweden leads the Western nations in the degree to which nonmarital cohabitation has replaced marriage. The United States, on the other hand, has a lower rate of nonmarital cohabitation than all but the Catholic nations of southern Europe. About 28 percent of all couples in Sweden are cohabiting, versus 8 percent of all American couples. In Sweden, virtually all couples live together before marriage, compared to around two-thirds of couples currently in America. Many couples in Sweden don't marry even when they have children. In a recent opinion poll, Swedish young adults were asked whether it was OK to cohabit even after having children; 89 percent of women and 86 percent of men answered "yes."

Why is the Swedish marriage rate so low relative to other nations? In brief, because religion there is weak, a left-wing political ideology has long been dominant, and almost all governmental incentives for marriage have been removed. First, the religious pressure for marriage in Sweden is all but gone (although of the marriages that do occur, many are for vague religious reasons). Any religious or cultural stigma in Sweden against cohabitation is no longer in evidence; it is regarded as irrelevant to question whether a couple is married or just living together. Second, the political left wing throughout Europe has generally been antagonistic to strong families, based on a combination of feminist concerns about patriarchy and oppression, an antipathy toward a bourgeois social institution with traditional ties to nobility and privilege, and the belief that families have been an impediment to full equality. Finally, unlike in the United States, all government benefits in Sweden are given to individuals irrespective of their intimate relationships or family form. There is no such thing, for example, as spousal benefits in health care. There is also no joint-income taxation for married couples; all income taxation is individual.

Turning to the United States, if Sweden stands out for having the lowest marriage rate, the United States is notable for having the world's highest divorce rate. Given the divorce rates of recent years, the risk of a marriage ending in divorce in the United States is close to 50 percent, compared to a little over 40 percent in Sweden. Why is the American divorce rate so high relative to other nations? Mainly because of our relatively high ethnic, racial and religious diversity, inequality of incomes with a large underclass, and extensive residential mobility, each of which is associated with high divorce rates. Revealingly, if one looks at the divorce rate of the relatively homogeneous and Scandinavian-settled state of Minnesota, it is only slightly higher than that of Sweden. (Number of divorces per 1000 married women in 2002—Sweden: 13.7; Minnesota: 14.7; United States: 18.4.)

Another big divorce risk factor in America is marrying at a young age; the average U.S. ages of first marriage today are 25 for women and 27 for men, versus 31 and 33 in Sweden. As a more consumer-oriented and economically dynamic society, in addition, there is probably something about this nation that promotes a more throw-away attitude toward life. And let us not overlook the dominant influence of Hollywood and pop culture in general, with their emphasis on feel good and forget the consequences.

Of course, if people don't marry, they can't divorce. And that is one reason why, by certain measures, Sweden has a lower divorce rate. But if couples just cohabit they certainly can break up, and that is what Swedish nonmarital couples do in large numbers. It is estimated that the risk of breakup for cohabiting couples in Sweden, even those with children, is several times higher than for married couples. By one indication, in the year 2000 there were two-and-one-half separations or divorces per 100 children among married parents, almost twice that number among unmarried cohabiting parents living with their own biological children, and three times that number among cohabiting couples living with children from a previous relationship. (A recent study found that 50 percent of children born to a cohabiting couple in the United States see their parents' union end by age five, compared to only 15 percent of children born to a married couple. [Wendy D. Manning, Pamela J. Smock, and Debamm Majumdar, "The Relative Stability of Cohabiting and Marital Unions for Children," *Population Research and Policy Review* 23 (2004): 135–159].)

Already one of the highest in Western Europe, the Swedish divorce rate has been growing in recent years, while the U.S. rate has been declining. If we consider this convergence of divorce rates, and count both cohabiting couples and married couples, *the total family breakup rate in the two nations today is actually quite similar.*

So why, in view of the similarity of overall family breakup rates, are more Swedish than American children living with their biological parents? This is especially surprising in view of the fact that the Swedish nonmarital birth percentage is much higher than that of the United States (56 percent in Sweden vs. 35 percent in the U.S.). The main reason is that far more nonmarital births in Sweden, about 90 percent, are actually to biological parents who are living together but have not married, compared to just 40 percent in the United States. The great majority of nonmarital births in the U.S., 60 percent, are to truly single, non-cohabiting mothers. This discrepancy reflects the far higher rate of births in the United States to teenagers, the stage of life at which the father is least likely to remain involved with the mother and child. (Births per 1000 girls ages 15–19 in 2002—United States: 43; Sweden: 5.) The relatively high U.S. teen birthrate, in turn, is commonly accounted for by more teen sexual activity combined with less use of contraceptives. There is also a discrepancy between the two countries in that the United States has about twice Sweden's rate of "unwanted" children.

Having sketched out these noteworthy differences in family structure between the United States and Sweden, together with some causal explanations for the differences, what are some reasonable conclusions that can be drawn from the Scandinavian family experience?

The Decline of Marriage

If a society deinstitutionalizes marriage, as Sweden has done through its tax and benefit policies and the secularization of its culture, marriage will weaken. In addition, because most adults still like to live as couples, human pair-bonding doesn't disappear when this happens. Rather, the institution of marriage is replaced by nonmarital cohabitation—marriage lite. Then, if one institutionalizes nonmarital cohabitation in the laws and government policies, as Sweden has also done, making it the virtual equivalent of marriage, marriage will decline still further.

In the modern world, people are reluctant to make strong commitments if they don't have to; it's easier to hang loose. The problem is that society ends up with adult intimate relationships that are much more fragile. It is, indeed, surprising that Sweden has such a high level of couple breakup, because it is the kind of society—stable, homogeneous, and egalitarian—where one would expect such breakups to be minimal. Yet the high breakup level is testimony to the fragility of modern marriage in which most of the institutional bonds have been stripped away—economic dependence, legal definitions, religious sentiments, and family pressures—leaving marriage and other pair-bonds held together solely by the thin and unstable reed of affection.

The losers in this social trend, of course, are the children. They are highly dependent for their development and success in life on the family in which they are born and raised, and a convincing mass of scientific evidence now exists pointing to the fact that not growing up in an intact nuclear family is one of the most deleterious events that can befall a child. In Sweden, just as in the United States, children from non-intact families—compared to those from intact families—have two to three times the number of serious problems in life. We can only speculate about the extent of psychological damage that future generations will suffer owing to today's family trends. That the very low marriage rate and high level of parental breakup are such non-issues in Sweden, something which few Swedes ever talk about, should be, in my opinion, a cause there for national soul searching.

All that said, however, there are other important conclusions one can draw from the Scandinavian family experience. What most Americans don't realize is that, in a strict comparison, Scandinavia is probably preferable to the United States today as a place to raise young children. In other writings I have suggested that the ideal family environment for raising young children has the following traits: an enduring two-biological-parent family that engages regularly in activities together, has developed its own routines, traditions and stories, and provides a great deal of contact time between adults and children. Surrounded by a community that is child friendly and supportive of parents, the family is able to develop a vibrant family subculture that provides a rich legacy of meaning and values for children throughout their lives. Scandinavians certainly fall short on the enduring two-biological-parent part of this ideal (yet even there they are currently ahead of the United States), but on the key ingredients of structured and consistent contact time between parents and their children in a family-friendly environment, they are well ahead of us.

In America today, the achievement of this ideal family environment requires what many parents are coming to consider a Herculean countercultural effort, one that involves trying to work fewer hours and adopting the mantra of "voluntary simplicity" for those who can afford it; turning off the TV set and avoiding popular culture; seeking employment in firms that have family-friendly policies such as flexible working hours; and residing in areas that are better designed for children and where the cost of living is lower. Families in Scandinavia need not be so countercultural to achieve these goals because the traits of the ideal childrearing environment are to a larger degree already built into their societies.

The Scandinavian societies tend to be "soft" or low-key, with much more leisure time and not so much frantic consumerism and economic striving as in the United States. Perhaps one could even say that they practice "involuntary simplicity." The average American would probably find life in Scandinavia rather uncomfortable due to high taxes, strict government regulation, limited consumer choice, smaller dwelling units, social conformity, and a soft work ethic, not to mention possible boredom. There are also growing concerns about the quality of education in Scandinavia. Moreover, the Scandinavian system may ultimately prove to be so counterproductive for economic growth that it becomes unsustainable. At any one time more than 20 percent of working-age Swedes are either on sick leave, unemployed, or have taken early retirement, and the nation has recently sunk to one of the lowest per capita income levels in Western Europe! (Reported in Sweden's leading newspaper, *Dagen's Nyheter,* on August 23, 2004.) But in the meantime, and compared to other modern nations, the system seems particularly good for the rearing of young children.

The Scandinavian childrearing advantage is probably as much cultural as governmental, as much due to the way Scandinavians think about children as to specific welfare state policies (although the two are, of course, interrelated.) Scandinavian culture has always been more child centered than the more individualistic Anglo societies. The emphasis in Scandinavian culture on nature and the outdoor environment, conflict-aversion, and even social conformity happens to be especially child friendly. Children benefit from highly structured, stable, and low-conflict settings. There are in Scandinavia many statues of children and mothers in public parks (in place of war heroes!), and planned housing environments are heavily oriented to pedestrian access and children's play. Scandinavian children even have their own Ombudsmen who represent them officially in the government and monitor children's rights and interests. Interestingly, Minnesota—the most Scandinavian-settled U.S. state—was recently ranked the number one state in the nation for child well-being by the Kids Count Data Book. (Annie E. Casey Foundation, 2004, Baltimore, MD)

Scandinavian Family Policies

The Scandinavian concern for children, sometimes even smacking of "traditional family values," is expressed in some areas that should surprise those Americans who think only of "decadent welfare states." For example, all Swedish married couples with children aged 16 and younger, should they want a divorce, have a six-month waiting period before a divorce becomes final. Most American states make no distinction in their divorce laws between couples with children and those without. In vitro fertilization in Sweden can be performed only if the woman is married or cohabiting in a relationship resembling marriage, and completely anonymous sperm donations are not allowed, whereas the practice of "assisted reproduction" in America goes virtually unregulated. And no Swedish abortion can take place after the 18th week of pregnancy, except under special circumstances and only with permission from the National Board of Health. The laws permitting abortion are much more liberal in the United States. Some of these positions are made possible, of course, by the fact that the Scandinavian societies are more homogeneous, unified, and less rights-oriented than the United States.

Just as in the United States at least up until welfare reform, welfare policies in Scandinavia have not been drawn up with an eye toward encouraging marriage and limiting family breakup, a very serious problem as noted above. There are relatively few economic disincentives to becoming a single parent in Sweden, in fact probably fewer than in any other society in the world. Nevertheless, many Scandinavian welfare-state policies have brought significant benefits to children and to childrearing families. Scandinavian family leave policies, especially, seem highly desirable for young children. Almost all mothers in Sweden, for example, and far more than in the United States, are at home with their infants up until age one—which is the critical year for mother-child connection. They have one year off from their jobs at 80 percent or more of their salary (and an additional six months at reduced salary), with a guarantee of returning to their old jobs or an equivalent when they reenter the labor force. Recently, two months leave has been set aside solely for fathers to take; if they don't take it, the benefit is lost. Because of these family-leave policies very few Swedish infants under the age of one are in day care or other out-of-home child care arrangement, a quite different situation from the United States. In addition, to help defray the expenses of childrearing, all Swedish parents receive a non-means-tested child allowance and there is also a means-tested housing allowance.

Beyond these benefits, Scandinavian mothers and fathers have far more flex-time from their work to be home with children during the growing-up years, and most women with young children work just part time. There are certainly fewer full-time, non-working, stay-at-home mothers in Sweden than in the United States, in fact almost none because it is economically prohibitive. But in actual parenting time—although good comparative data are unavailable—Sweden may well be in the lead. The larger number of stay-at-home moms in the United States is off-set by the larger number of full-time working mothers, many of whom return to work during their child's first year. It is of interest to note that many fewer Swedish women have top positions in the private sector than is the case in the United States, and this has long been a bone of contention for American feminists when they look at Sweden. By one recent analysis, only 1.5 percent of senior management positions are filled by women in Sweden, compared to 11 percent in the United States. The amount of time that Swedish mothers devote to child care clearly has affected their ability to rise in the private sector hierarchy of jobs, although this is off-set in some degree by their much stronger status in the public sector where a high percentage of the jobs are located.

As a result of welfare state policies child poverty in Sweden is virtually nonexistent (for the 1990s, 1 percent compared to 15 percent in the United States) and all children are covered by health insurance. These and related factors are doubtless of importance in placing Sweden at the top of the list of the best places in the world to live, surpassed only by Norway according to the Human Development Index prepared by the United Nations Development Program (2004), and based on income, life expectancy and education. The United States ranks well down the list, in eighth place, no doubt due in part to the fact that we have a different population mix than other nations.

Again, the two societies are such polar opposites, at least among Western nations, as we have indicated, that it is a mistake to think that what works in Sweden could necessarily be transplanted to the United States. Up to now, at least, the Scandinavian nations have had that strong sense of "brotherhood" or "sisterhood" that is required for a strong welfare state. The common sentiment has been that the high taxes are going for a good cause, "my fellow Swede." Indeed, the lack of outcry against high taxation in Scandinavia comes as a shock to most visiting Americans. To suggest that this communal spirit and attitude toward government and taxation could ever exist in the United States, with all its diversity and individualism, is to enter the realm of utopian thinking. Thus, it is unclear how many of these family policies could be implemented in the United States, and what their actual effect would be if they were.

This leaves us with a final conclusion from the Scandinavian family experience, a more general one. The fact that family breakdown has occurred so prevalently in both the United States and Scandinavia, two almost opposite socio-economic systems, suggests that the root cause lies beyond politics and economics and even national culture in an overarching trend of modernity that affects all advanced, industrial societies. Basic to this trend is the growth of a modern form of individualism, the single-minded pursuit of personal autonomy and self-interest, which takes place at the expense of established social institutions such as marriage. It shows up in low marriage and high cohabitation rates in the Scandinavian societies, even though they are relatively communitarian. And it is expressed in high divorce and high solo parenting rates in the United States, despite our nation's relatively religious character.

One paramount family goal for modern societies today, put forward by many experts, is to create the conditions whereby an increasing number of children are able to grow up with their own two married parents. If this is a worthy goal, both Scandinavia and the United States have failed badly, and millions of children have been hurt. If we are to take seriously the record of recent history in these nations, the market economy on its own, no matter how strong, is unlikely to be of much help in achieving this goal. The wealthier we become, the weaker the family. But neither helpful, apparently, are the many governmental policies of the welfare state. They may help to soften the impact of family breakup, but the state appears relatively powerless to contain family decline and often even contributes to it. What we must look for, are ways to curtail the growth of modern individualism. While in Scandinavia the main thrust of such efforts probably should focus on resisting the anti-marriage influences of political ideologies and social policies, in the United States the issue is to find better ways to insulate marriage and the family from the pernicious effects of a self-interested market economy that is tethered increasingly to a coarsening popular culture.

DAVID POPENOE is co-director of the National Marriage Project at Rutgers, The State University of New Jersey. He is author of *War Over the Family, Disturbing the Nest* and *Private Pleasure, Public Plight* all available from Transaction.

Interracial Families

Marriages between people of different races have mushroomed in the last three decades, and the children of these unions have a whole new point of view.

CAROL MITHERS

The growth of mixed-race marriage: According to the most recent Census figures, the percentage of couples who are interracial increased sevenfold from 1970 to 2000, and the number of children in interracial families quadrupled to 3.4 million. The most prevalent pairing is white men and Asian women. Among people under 30, interracial couples are at least 30 percent more common.

Changing attitudes: More than 300 years ago, Maryland was the first state to outlaw interracial marriage. In 1967 the Supreme Court ruled such laws unconstitutional but many states kept their statutes. Alabama didn't remove its law until 2000. Yet a 2003 poll showed that 86 percent of blacks, 79 percent of Latinos and 66 percent of whites would accept a child marrying someone of a different race.

Tracking the trend: In 2000 Americans could check more than one box for ethnicity and race, and about 7 million did. Estimates put the multiracial population even higher.

Representative family: Sandra and Steven Stites, of Kansas City, Missouri. Married 19 years, both are 46-year-old doctors with three children.

For the Stites children, an interracial life "is all they've ever known," says Sandra, and they are perfectly comfortable with it. Ailea says her friends have affectionately labeled her "halfrican." Her younger sister, Sierra, has dubbed herself a "wack," short for white-black.

Sandra and Steven became friends in 1982 when they were lab partners in an anatomy class at the University of Missouri-Columbia. "We met over a cadaver," Steven jokes. They didn't expect to marry. Steven had grown up in virtually all-white Independence, Missouri. Sandra's Kansas City neighborhood was black but she went to a mostly white private school and briefly dated a white boy. Still, after her first date with Steven, she told a friend, "He's perfect, except he's white."

"Once you learn that people aren't as different as you think they are, the fear goes away."

The couple dated for four years. "It was important to me that we both loved the outdoors and musical theater," Steven says. "We had common ground, even if it didn't include race."

Sandra had concerns, however. "If we had kids, would they be accepted?" she remembers thinking at the time. "Would we be accepted?" They kept their relationship secret for two months. Once they went public, Sandra's fears were realized. Some classmates avoided them. Steven's father said that marrying Sandra would limit his career. Sandra's parents worried "because Steven was 'different.'"

By the time Sandra and Steven married, their parents had come around. "My father got to know Sandra," says Steven. "Most racism is based on a fear of difference. Once you learn that people aren't as different as you think, the fear goes away."

Sandra's family, too, discovered that Steven was less "different" than they'd thought. "His mother was from the South," says Sandra. "My grandfather would prepare food like collard greens and say, 'That boy won't eat this!' But this was food Steven knew."

When Ailea was born, in 1990, Steven and Sandra had already agreed they wanted their children to recognize their dual heritage. The children have contact with white culture in their neighborhood and school, and they are close to Sandra's parents, who live near the Stiteses' home, as well as her extended family in Dallas. "We want the kids to understand the struggles," says Sandra.

Not everyone is on board, though. Steven has an uncle who refuses to let the couple in his house. And while nobody looks twice at the Stites family in Kansas City, in the suburban malls, "we get what we call 'the triangle look,'" says Sandra. "Eyes go to Steven, then me, then the kids. And salespeople don't see us as a couple. Sometimes we pretend we're not together and then say, 'Your name is on my checkbook! How did that happen?'"

"What really rankles are the thoughtless remarks from strangers who see Sandra with her children. "They'll ask, 'Are you the nanny?'" Sandra says.

The Stiteses send their kids to a private school, though they picked one that is 17 percent nonwhite. When the children classified themselves on school forms, Ailea wrote "multiracial," Sierra picked "other," and James chose both African-American and white.

"Their generation doesn't see color the way it used to be seen," says Sandra. "When Ailea describes a guy she likes, she mentions the color of his eyes and skin and hair. She describes his looks, but it never occurs to her to mention his race at all."

Children as a Public Good

Myra H. Strober

Whose responsibility are children? In twenty-first-century America, the answer too often is "their parents." Although politicians and pundits frequently make pious pronouncements calling children "our best hope," "our future," and "our nation's most valuable resource," mouthing such sentiments is a far cry from taking collective responsibility. In the current election season, one listens in vain for concrete proposals from candidates to improve the lives of children. The United States lags behind all other western democracies in providing for their needs. We have to revise the national mindset, visible on the left as well as the right, that puts sole responsibility for children in the hands of individual families, many of whom are ill-equipped to give them the care and opportunities necessary to provide for the citizens, workers, and human beings we wish to develop. Further, instead of viewing parents with professional careers as irresponsible workaholics, we should appreciate the incredibly hard work that parents do when they are simultaneously holding jobs and raising children.

Certainly, parents have primary responsibility for meeting the needs of their children; the argument here is that meeting children's needs should be a collective responsibility as well. Although parents reap the rewards of well-reared children (emotional rather than economic rewards in this day and age), children whose needs have been met confer benefits as well on society as a whole. We need to make a reality of the rhetoric that sees children as our most valuable asset.

As an economist, I argue that children must be considered a public good whose welfare and education need to be addressed collectively. In other words, it really does take a village to raise a child. A public good is one whose provision confers externalities—benefits beyond those accruing to the direct beneficiaries. Public schooling confers such externalities; the public as well as individual students and parents benefit when its citizens are literate and numerate, and when they understand the benefits of democracy. This is how the state justifies taxing the public to provide for children's schooling.

The notion that children are a private good leads to the conclusion that their economic and emotional care is the sole responsibility of their parents. This philosophy was most clearly articulated by President Richard Nixon, when he vetoed the Child Development Act of 1971: "For the Federal Government to plunge headlong financially into supporting child develop-

ment would commit the vast moral authority of the National Government to the side of communal approaches to child rearing over against [sic] the family-centered approach." There was no sense that parents and the federal government might engage in a partnership for child care, no sense that there were public benefits to be gained from federal involvement in improving the child care system. Or, consider the case of the city of Fremont, California, which defeated a 1989 measure asking taxpayers to approve a $12 per year property tax levied on all residential dwelling units to pay for childcare services. An exit poll found that 88 percent of the three-fourths of the electorate that had voted against the measure agreed with the statement, "Child care should be paid for by parents, not by the whole community."

If, instead, we thought of children as public goods, we would behave far differently toward their economic and emotional needs. And we would seek collective solutions for their care. I want to spell out several critical areas in which children's needs are not being met and argue for public investment to remedy that situation. This is not a new argument on the left, but it is one rarely articulated these days.

Freedom from Poverty

What are we doing about child poverty? What are we doing about the fact (published by our own government) that 12.9 million children under the age of eighteen—17.6 percent of all children—live in poverty, that they go hungry, have inadequate clothing and shelter, and are ill-equipped for the education they need? Among white children, 14.3 percent live in poverty, but among black children, an astounding 34.1 percent are poor. Although children under eighteen represent about one-quarter of the total population, they are more than one-third of those in poverty. Similarly, in 2000, families with children under eighteen accounted for 36 percent of Americans who were homeless.

Not only does poverty affect children's economic well-being, it is also associated with poorer performance in school, in part because children in poor neighborhoods go to schools with lower per-pupil expenditures. Data from the National Assessment of Educational Progress (NAEP) indicate that in tests of children in the fourth and eighth grades, those who live in poverty (as measured by being eligible for the National School

Lunch Program) score lower in several subjects as compared to better-off children. NAEP data for twelfth-grade students show that Title I Schools (those with the highest levels of poverty) have a much higher proportion of students who score below basic skill levels in reading, writing, and civics, and especially in math and science.

Let us compare children's poverty in the United States and other developed countries in the late 1990s and 2000. Data from the Luxembourg Income Study show that if we use 50 percent of median adjusted disposable income for all persons in a family as the measure of poverty, 22 percent of all U.S. children are in poverty, one of the highest percentages in the study. Among the 25 countries surveyed, the percentage of all children in poverty ranged from a low of 3 percent in Finland to a high of 24 percent in Russia. The only other country with a rate higher than 20 percent was Italy.

Living with a single mother increases children's chances of being in poverty in all the countries in the Luxembourg study. In some countries, the probabilities triple or quadruple. For example, in Finland, the probability of being in poverty in 2000 was 2 percent for children in two-parent families, but 8 percent for children with a single mother. In the United States, the probability of being in poverty in 2000 was 15 percent for children in two-parent families, but almost 50 percent for children in single-mother families.

Child Care

I won't focus here on the timeworn debate about whether mothers of young children should work outside the home. Others in this series will discuss the rhetoric and sentiments associated with the changing norms of motherhood and their intensive demands. It is enough to say that mothers are in the workforce by economic necessity and seek an income so that they can improve their lives and the lives of their families. For the vast majority of families, the division of emotional and housekeeping labor and income-producing labor between men and women is no longer an option. One could also argue that child care outside the home may offer benefits not to be found in the home—also the topic of another discussion.

But let us consider the pressing needs of families today for quality, affordable, collective child care. Depending on the ages of their children, between 55 percent and 80 percent of mothers are employed. According to the Bureau of Labor Statistics, in 1999, the labor-force participation rate of mothers with school-age children, six to seventeen, was 79 percent; among mothers with children ages three to five, it was 72 percent; among those with children under three, the rate was 61 percent. In 2000, among mothers with infants, the labor-force participation rate was 55 percent, down slightly from 59 percent two years earlier.

These figures represent a sea change from the situation in 1966, when the BLS first began publishing data on mothers' labor-force participation by age of child. In 1966, only about one-fifth of married mothers with a child under age three, and only about 40 percent of widowed and divorced mothers with children under three, were in the labor force.

The role of wives in providing for the money income needs of their families has become exceedingly important. In dual-earner families, wives provide about 40 percent of family income, and in about 25 percent of those families, wives earn more than their husbands. Moreover, in recent years, while men's average earnings have failed to grow (not even keeping up with a modest rate of inflation), women's average earnings have grown, so that the increases in average family income are attributable to women's earnings.

Because mothers now provide for their children's need for emotional and physical care *and* their need for money income (including, often, access to employer-sponsored health insurance), families face serious issues about how to meet these two sets of needs. Because children are considered a private good and child-rearing a private activity, they get little assistance from either employers or the government.

Mothers balance the needs of their children for care and income by using child-care services—either informal (unpaid) or formal (paid). A report by the Urban Institute, based on the 1999 Survey of America's Families, provides information about the primary child-care arrangements for children under the age of thirteen while the adults "most responsible for their care" (most often their mothers) were employed.

Among preschoolers, age zero to four, there were three equally prevalent types of care, which together accounted for slightly more than 80 percent of all the primary-care arrangements of preschoolers: center-based care, care by a parent, and care by a relative. Care by a parent means care by the parent who is not at the place of employment during the time of child care; in two-parent families, it generally means that the parents split shifts. In addition, 14 percent of preschoolers were cared for in family child care, and 4 percent were cared for primarily by a nanny or babysitter.

Among five-year-olds, 40 percent were cared for at centers, 19 percent by a parent, 19 percent by a relative, 11 percent in family child care, 8 percent in before- and after-school programs, and 3 percent by a nanny or babysitter. Among school-age children, ages six to twelve, 41 percent were cared for by a parent, 23 percent by a relative, 15 percent in before- and after-school programs, 10 percent by the child him or herself, 7 percent in family child care, and 4 percent by a nanny or babysitter.

A recent book by Suzanne Helburn and Barbara Bergmann underscores the problems with our current child-care system (or lack thereof). Child care in a center is expensive, and many families cannot afford it; it costs between $5,000 and $10,000 per year per child, depending on the age of the child (infant care costs more) and the geographic location. In some areas, it is even more expensive than $10,000 per year. Median household income in the United States in 2000 was $42,178; the median income for families with four persons was $62,228. Using either measure, child-care costs for two children represent a significant fraction of income.

The second (related) problem with child care is its quality. The Cost, Quality, and Childhood Outcomes Study (CQO) looked at a hundred randomly selected centers in 1993. Although it found that the majority of classrooms provided minimally adequate care, only about 25 percent of preschool care and less than 10 percent of toddler care was rated as "good" or "developmentally appropriate." The highest quality centers were run by public agencies, private schools and colleges, and employers.

Determining the quality of care in family-child-care homes is difficult, because so many are unlicensed. Studies of family-child-care homes find that their quality is more variable than that in centers. In some cases, these homes provided care on par with centers, but particularly in unlicensed homes, care was often found to be poor. Quality control, as currently practiced, has more to do with the child's physical safety than with the emotional or educational skills of the provider or the content of the program.

The search costs of finding good quality child care are high, particularly because parents are generally not well informed about what to look for when they interview potential providers. Parents report that their primary considerations when purchasing child care are location and convenience, the hours of service provided, their child's safety and well-being, and cost. Absent public subsidies, they may not be able to spend enough to assure the high quality of their children's child care.

Policies that Would Help

Helping children in poverty requires more than simply transferring resources to them, although that is certainly important. It requires helping their parents, and particularly their mothers, earn higher incomes. Much of the research on the effects of the recent Temporary Aid to Needy Families (aka "welfare reform") legislation indicates that women are not being trained for the higher paying jobs—that is, for jobs that traditionally have been filled by men only. Women who have been on welfare need training for those jobs if they are to keep their children out of poverty. At the same time, because most poor women will continue to do women's jobs, it is important to raise their wages. In recent years, there has been little progress on the matter of pay equity (paying women the same as men for jobs requiring the same education and experience). Mothers of children in poverty are in dire need of pay equity.

There needs to be national recognition of the service that parents are providing to the society as a whole—and some kind of reimbursement for their efforts. In other countries, most notably Japan, Spain, and Italy, people have reacted to the unwillingness of employers and the government to help parents combine work with child-rearing by not having children or by having only one. The birth rates in these countries are now below replacement. Although Americans have not (yet) taken that tack, government and employers should act now to enable us to meet the emotional, physical, and economic needs of future citizens and workers.

A change in the national mindset about the value of children would lead government, private businesses, and nonprofit organizations to develop policies to assist parents in meeting their child-rearing responsibilities. We might begin by providing par-

tially paid leave to parents during the first year after the birth of their child. We are one of the few industrialized countries that do not provide such leave.

We could also stop discriminating against part-time workers, paying them less per hour than employees who do the same work full time, and often offering them no benefits. Working part time is one of the ways that mothers balance raising children and earning money. We should stop punishing them for working part time. Legislation prohibiting discrimination against part-time workers is long overdue. It would be easy to add a prohibition against discrimination in earnings and benefits for part-time workers to the Fair Labor Standards Act. This would be expensive for employers, and so it might result in less part-time work. On balance, however, the prohibition would be beneficial. The European Union has already begun to move in this direction.

Jerry Jacobs has suggested that we deal with the extraordinary demands for long work hours for highly educated professionals and managers in certain industries by amending the Fair Labor Standards Act so that currently exempted workers are covered. If that were done, employers who wanted their professional and managerial workers to put in more than forty hours a week would have to pay time and a half for overtime and double time for weekends. Jacobs suspects, as I do, that under those circumstances, employers would get the same work done by hiring more employees and helping current employees to work more efficiently. If such a penalty for long hours were enacted, children might well get to see more of their highly educated parents and, presumably, the public interest would be better served.

Lotte Bailyn has done research on firms that have changed their professional structures to allow parents (and others) to work on more reasonable schedules. She has found that such changes produce win-win situations. Not only do employees experience reduced stress, higher morale, and a greater ability to respond to their family's needs, but employers gain increased productivity.

Finally, we must mend our child-care system so that all children who need it get quality care. Helburn and Bergmann estimate (without even considering that child-care workers need higher wages), that the United States would have to spend an additional $26 billion a year on child care. We could afford it, if we didn't spend it elsewhere—or if we stopped reducing taxes. Having a good child-care system simply requires a collective will to spend tax revenues for that purpose.

How will these changes come about? Children are one of the few groups that have not yet created a social movement to improve their situation. Such a movement may one day emerge, but one problem with childhood as a basis for a social movement is that people grow out of it rather quickly. A second problem is that children don't vote. It needs to be adults who lead the way in a movement on children's behalf. There are of course several well-known child advocacy groups, but because they have not been successful in getting Americans to change the way in which we view children, they have not been successful in winning over policymakers. Most child advocates, coming from an equity perspective, argue that treating children well is the right thing to do. This argument has had little traction in our increasingly selfish world. I argue that treating children well is the right thing to do from a self-interest perspective. Collectively meeting the needs of children enhances the well-being of each of us. To get the change we need, children should be viewed as a public good.

Sources of Statistics Cited

Ed Source, "NAEP Results Consistently Show Achievement Gaps Nationally," 2003. http://www.edsource.org/sch_naep03.cfm

Luxembourg Income Study, "Poverty Rates for Children by Family Type," 2000. http://www.lisproject.org/keyfigures/childpovrates.htm

National Education Association, "America's Top Education Priority: Lifting Up Low-Performing Schools," February 2001. http://www.nea.org/lac/bluebook/priority/html

Freya L. Sonenstein, et al., "Primary Child Care Arrangements of Employed Parents: Findings from the 1999 National Survey of America's Families," Occasional Paper No. 59. Washington, D.C.: The Urban Institute, May 2002.

U.S. Bureau of Labor Statistics, "Report on the American Workforce," 1999.

U.S. Dept. of Labor, Bureau of Labor Statistics, "Current Population Survey," 2002. Washington, D.C., U.S. Government Printing Office, 2000. http://ferret.bls.census.gov/macro/032002/pov/new01_001.htm

U.S. Census Bureau, Census of Population, 2000. Washington, D.C.: U.S. Government Printing Office, 2000. http://www.census.gov/population/www/cen2000/phc-t9.html

U.S. Census Bureau, Income 2000 (Income of Households by State). http://www.census.gov/hhes/income/income00/statemhi.html

U.S. Census Bureau, Current Population Reports, pp. 60–226, "Income, Poverty, and Health Insurance Coverage in the United States, 2003," Washington, D.C.: U.S. Government Printing Office, 2004. http://www.census.gov/prod/2004pubs/p60-226

U.S. Census Bureau, Median Family Income for Families with Four Persons, http://www.census.gov/hhes/income/4person.html

U.S. Census Bureau, "Labor Force Participation for Mothers with Infants Declines for First Time," Census Bureau Reports, Press Release, October 18, 2001. http://www.census.gov/Press-Release/www/2001/cb01-170.html

U.S. Dept. of Labor, Bureau of Labor Statistics, "Working in the Twenty-First Century," 1999. http://www.bls.gov/0pub/working/home.html

MYRA H. STROBER is a labor economist and professor of education and business at Stanford University.

UNIT 2

Exploring and Establishing Relationship

Unit Selections

Key Points to Consider

- What are key components to this thing we call "love"? What do you look for in a mate? Do you seem to struggle with lasting relationships? Why do you think this is so?

- Do you see children as a part of your life? Why or why not? At what age do you think one should stop considering having a child? What should be the determining factor? How would you respond if you learned you could not have children? Would you consider adoption?

Student Web Site
www.mhcls.com/online

Internet References

Bonobo Sex and Society
   http://songweaver.com/info/bonobos.html
Go Ask Alice!
   http://www.goaskalice.columbai.edu/index.html
The Kinsey Institute for Research in Sex, Gender, and Reproduction
   http://www.indiana.edu/~kinsey/
Mysteries of Odor in Human Sexuality
   http://www.pheromones.com
The Society for the Scientific Study of Sexuality
   http://www.sexscience.org

By and large, we are social animals, and as such, we seek out meaningful connections with other humans. John Bowlby, Mary Ainsworth, and others have proposed that this drive toward connection is biologically based and is at the core of what it means to be human. However it plays out in childhood and adulthood, the need for connection, to love and be loved, is a powerful force moving us to establish and maintain close relationships.

As we explore various possibilities, we engage in the complex business of relationship building. In doing this, many processes occur simultaneously: messages are sent and received; differences are negotiated; assumptions and expectations are or are not met. The ultimate goals are closeness and continuity.

How we feel about others and what we see as essential to these relationships play an important role in our establishing and maintaining relationships. In this unit, we look at factors that underlie the establishment of relationships as well as the beginning stages of relationships.

The first subsection takes a broad look at factors that influence the building of meaningful connections and at the beginning stages of adult relationships. The first essay, "This Thing Called Love" takes a cross-cultural perspective on the nature of romantic love. Among its interesting and controversial suggestions is that passionate love has a natural lifespan and shares characteristics with obsessive compulsive disorder. "Pillow Talk" documents a conversation with Stephen and Andrea Levine about love and lust, the nature of marriage, and of true intimacy. The next essay goes on to discuss "How to Talk about Sex" with one's partner, especially when the couple has varying levels of interest in and need for sex.

In the second subsection, an aspect of the choice of a mate is examined. "On-Again, Off-Again" examines a number of explanations for why some couples break up and make up, over and over again. Why does this happen and what can they do to break the cycle?

The third subsection looks at pregnancy and the next generation. "A New Fertility Factor" discusses the growing controversy over the use of high technology to allow couples to conceive children. Injections of fertility drugs are expensive and have some health risks, as are in vitro fertilization and other clinical manipulations of egg, sperm, and uterine tissue. "Starting the Good Life in the Womb" addresses important behaviors that

BananaStock/PictureQuest

pregnant women can engage in to improve their baby's chances of growing into healthy adults. The following article, "Breeder Reaction," extends the discussion of the right to reproduce to one about whether or not this is, in fact, a right for all. It goes on to discuss who should fund high-technology interventions for individuals who would like to have a child but are unable to do so without intervention. In "Adopting a New American Family," the evolving nature of adoption in the U.S., with increasing use of international adoptions and open adoption, in which birth parents and adoptive parents maintain contact after the adoption, are chronicled.

This Thing Called Love

LAUREN SLATER

My husband and I got married at eight in the morning. It was winter, freezing, the trees encased in ice and a few lone blackbirds balancing on telephone wires. We were in our early 30s, considered ourselves hip and cynical, the types who decried the institution of marriage even as we sought its status. During our wedding brunch we put out a big suggestion box and asked people to slip us advice on how to avoid divorce; we thought it was a funny, clear-eyed, grounded sort of thing to do, although the suggestions were mostly foolish: Screw the toothpaste cap on tight. After the guests left, the house got quiet. There were flowers everywhere: puckered red roses and fragile ferns. "What can we do that's really romantic?" I asked my newly wed one. Benjamin suggested we take a bath. I didn't want a bath. He suggested a lunch of chilled white wine and salmon. I was sick of salmon.

What can we do that's really romantic? The wedding was over, the silence seemed suffocating, and I felt the familiar disappointment after a longed-for event has come and gone. We were married. Hip, hip, hooray. I decided to take a walk. I went into the center of town, pressed my nose against a bakery window, watched the man with flour on his hands, the dough as soft as skin, pushed and pulled and shaped at last into stars. I milled about in an antique store. At last I came to our town's tattoo parlor. Now I am not a tattoo type person, but for some reason, on that cold silent Sunday, I decided to walk in. "Can I help you?" a woman asked.

"Is there a kind of tattoo I can get that won't be permanent?" I asked.

"Henna tattoos," she said.

She explained that they lasted for six weeks, were used at Indian weddings, were stark and beautiful and all brown. She showed me pictures of Indian women with jewels in their noses, their arms scrolled and laced with the henna markings. Indeed they were beautiful, sharing none of the gaudy comic strip quality of the tattoos we see in the United States. These henna tattoos spoke of intricacy, of the webwork between two people, of ties that bind and how difficult it is to find their beginnings and their elms. And because I had just gotten married, and because I was feeling a post wedding letdown, and because I wanted something really romantic to sail me through the night, I decided to get one.

"Where?" she asked.

"Here," I said. I laid my hands over my breasts and belly.

She raised her eyebrows. "Sure," she said.

I am a modest person. But I took off my shirt, lay on the table, heard her in the back room mixing powders and paints. She came to me carrying a small black-bellied pot inside of which was a rich red mush, slightly glittering. She adorned me. She gave me vines and flowers. She turned my body into a stake supporting whole new gardens of growth, and then, low around my hips, she painted a delicate chain-linked chastity belt. An hour later, the paint dry, I put my clothes back on, went home to film my newly wed one. This, I knew, was my gift to him, the kind of present you offer only once in your lifetime. I let him undress me.

"Wow," he said, standing back.

I blushed, and we began.

We are no longer beginning, my husband and I. This does not surprise me. Even back then, wearing the decor of desire, the serpentining tattoos, I knew they would fade, their red-clay color bleaching out until they were gone. On my wedding day I didn't care.

I do now. Eight years later, pale as a pillowcase, here I sit, with all the extra pounds and baggage time brings. And the questions have only grown more insistent. Does passion necessarily diminish over time? How reliable is romantic love, really, as a means of choosing one's mate? Can a marriage be good when Eros is replaced with friendship, or even economic partnership, two people bound by bank accounts?

Let me be clear: I still love my husband. There is no man I desire more. But it's hard to sustain romance in the crumb-filled quotidian that has become our lives. The ties that bind have been frayed by money and mortgages and children, those little imps who somehow manage to tighten the knot while weakening its actual fibers. Benjamin and I have no time for chilled white wine and salmon. The baths in our house always include Big Bird.

If this all sounds miserable, it isn't. My marriage is like a piece of comfortable clothing; even the arguments have a feel of fuzziness to them, something so familiar it can only be called home. And yet . . .

In the Western world we have for centuries concocted poems and stories and plays about the cycles of love, the way it morphs and changes over time, the way passion grabs us by our flung-back throats and then leaves us for something saner.

If *Dracula*—the frail woman, the sensuality of submission—reflects how we understand the passion of early romance, the *Flintstones* reflects our experiences of long-term love: All is gravel and somewhat silly, the song so familiar you can't stop singing it, and when you do, the emptiness is almost unbearable.

We have relied on stories to explain the complexities of love, tales of jealous gods and arrows. Now, however, these stories—so much a part of every civilization—may be changing as science steps in to explain what we have always felt to be myth, to be magic. For the first time, new research has begun to illuminate where love lies in the brain, the particulars of its chemical components.

Anthropologist Helen Fisher may be the closest we've ever come to having a doyenne of desire. At 60 she exudes a sexy confidence, with corn-colored hair, soft as floss, and a willowy build. A professor at Rutgers University, she lives in New York City, her book-lined apartment near Central Park, with its green trees fluffed out in the summer season, its paths crowded with couples holding hands.

Fisher has devoted much of her career to studying the biochemical pathways of love in all its manifestations: lust, romance, attachment, the way they wax and wane. One leg casually crossed over the other, ice clinking in her glass, she speaks with appealing frankness, discussing the ups and downs of love the way most people talk about real estate. "A woman unconsciously uses orgasms as a way of deciding whether or not a man is good for her. If he's impatient and rough, and she doesn't have the orgasm, she may instinctively feel he's less likely to be a good husband and father. Scientists think the fickle female orgasm may have evolved to help women distinguish Mr. Right from Mr. Wrong."

One of Fisher's central pursuits in the past decade has been looking at love, quite literally, with the aid of an MRI machine. Fisher and her colleagues Arthur Aron and Lucy Brown recruited subjects who had been "madly in love" for an average of seven months. Once inside the MRI machine, subjects were shown two photographs, one neutral, the other of their loved one.

What Fisher saw fascinated her. When each subject looked at his or her loved one, the parts of the brain linked to reward and pleasure—the ventral tegmental area and the caudate nucleus—lit up. What excited Fisher most was not so much finding a location, an address, for love as tracing its specific chemical pathways. Love lights up the caudate nucleus because it is home to a dense spread of receptors for a neurotransmitter called dopamine, which Fisher came to think of as part of our own endogenous love potion. In the right proportions, dopamine creates intense energy, exhilaration, focused attention, and motivation to win rewards. It is why, when you are newly in love, you can stay up all night, watch the sun rise, run a race, ski fast down a slope ordinarily too steep for your skill. Love makes you bold, makes you bright, makes you run real risks, which you sometimes survive, and sometimes you don't.

I first fell in love when I was only 12, with a teacher. His name was Mr. McArthur, and he wore open-toed sandals and sported a beard. I had never had a male teacher before, and I thought it terribly exotic. Mr. McArthur did things no other teacher dared to do. He explained to us the physics of farting. He demonstrated how to make an egg explode. He smoked cigarettes at recess, leaning languidly against the side of the school building, the ash growing longer and longer until he casually tapped it off with his finger.

What unique constellation of needs led me to love a man who made an egg explode is interesting, perhaps, but not as interesting, for me, as my memory of love's sheer physical facts. I had never felt anything like it before. I could not get Mr. McArthur out of my mind. I was anxious; I gnawed at the lining of my cheek until I tasted the tang of blood. School became at once terrifying and exhilarating. Would I see him in the hallway? In the cafeteria? I hoped. But when my wishes were granted, and I got a glimpse of my man, it satisfied nothing; it only inflamed me all the more. Had he looked at me? Why had he not looked at me? When would I see him again? At home I looked him up in the phone book; I rang him, this in a time before caller ID. He answered.

"Hello?" Pain in my heart, ripped down the middle. Hang up.

Call back. "Hello?" I never said a thing.

Once I called him at night, late, and from the way he answered the phone it was clear, even to a prepubescent like me, that he was with a woman. His voice fuzzy, the tinkle of her laughter in the background. I didn't get out of bed for a whole day.

Sound familiar? Maybe you were 30 when it happened to you, or 8 or 80 or 25. Maybe you lived in Kathmandu or Kentucky; age and geography are irrelevant. Donatella Marazziti is a professor of psychiatry at the University of Pisa in Italy who has studied the biochemistry of lovesickness. Having been in love twice herself and felt its awful power, Marazziti became interested in exploring the similarities between love and obsessive-compulsive disorder.

She and her colleagues measured serotonin levels in the blood of 24 subjects who had fallen in love within the past six months and obsessed about this love object for at least four hours every day. Serotonin is, perhaps, our star neurotransmitter, altered by our star psychiatric medications: Prozac and Zoloft and Paxil, among others. Researchers have long hypothesized that people with obsessive-compulsive disorder (OCD) have a serotonin "imbalance." Drugs like Prozac seem to alleviate OCD by increasing the amount of this neurotransmitter available at the juncture between neurons.

Marazziti compared the lovers' serotonin levels with those of a group of people suffering from OCD and another group who were free from both passion and mental illness. Levels of serotonin in both the obsessives' blood and the lovers' blood were 40 percent lower than those in her normal subjects. Translation: Love and obsessive-compulsive disorder could have a similar chemical profile. Translation: Love and mental illness may be difficult to tell apart. Translation: Don't be a fool. Stay away.

Of course that's a mandate none of us can follow. We do fall in love, sometimes over and over again, subjecting ourselves, each time, to a very sick state of mind. There is hope, however, for those caught in the grip of runaway passion—Prozac. There's nothing like that bicolored bullet for damping down the sex drive and making you feel "blah" about the buffet. Helen

Fisher believes that the ingestion of drugs like Prozac jeopardizes one's ability to fall in love—and stay in love. By dulling the keen edge of love and its associated libido, relationships go stale. Says Fisher, "I know of one couple on the edge of divorce. The wife was on an antidepressant. Then she went off it, started having orgasms once more, felt the renewal of sexual attraction for her husband, and they're now in love all over again."

Psychoanalysts have concocted countless theories about why we fall in love with whom we do. Freud would have said your choice is influenced by the unrequited wish to bed your mother, if you're a boy, or your father, if you're a girl, Jung believed that passion is driven by some kind of collective unconscious. Today psychiatrists such as Thomas Lewis from the University of California at San Francisco's School of Medicine hypothesize that romantic love is rooted in our earliest infantile experiences with intimacy, how we felt at the breast, our mother's face, these things of pure unconflicted comfort that get engraved in our brain and that we ceaselessly try to recapture as adults. According to this theory we love whom we love not so much because of the future we hope to build but because of the past we hope to reclaim. Love is reactive, not proactive, it arches us backward, which may be why a certain person just "feels right." Or "feels familiar." He or she is familiar. He or she has a certain look or smell or sound or touch that activates buried memories.

Love and obsessive-compulsive disorder could have a similar chemical profile. Translation: Love and mental illness may be difficult to tell apart. Translation: Don't be a fool. Stay away.

When I first met my husband, I believed this psychological theory was more or less correct. My husband has red hair and a soft voice. A chemist, he is whimsical and odd. One day before we married he dunked a rose in liquid nitrogen so it froze, whereupon he flung it against the wall, spectacularly shattering it. That's when I fell in love with him. My father, too, has red hair, a soft voice, and many eccentricities. He was prone to bursting into song, prompted by something we never saw.

However, it turns out my theories about why I came to love my husband may be just so much hogwash. Evolutionary psychology has said good riddance to Freud and the Oedipal complex and all that other transcendent stuff and hello to simple survival skills. It hypothesizes that we tend to see as attractive, and thereby choose as mates, people who look healthy. And health, say these evolutionary psychologists, is manifested in a woman with a 70 percent waist-to-hip ratio and men with rugged features that suggest a strong supply of testosterone in their blood. Waist-to-hip ratio is important for the successful birth of a baby, and studies have shown this precise ratio signifies higher fertility. As for the rugged look, well, a man with a good dose of testosterone probably also has a strong immune system and so is more likely to give his partner healthy children.

Perhaps our choice of mates is a simple matter of following our noses. Claus Wedekind of the University of Lausanne in Switzerland did an interesting experiment with sweaty T-shirts. He asked 49 women to smell T-shirts previously worn by unidentified men with a variety of the genotypes that influence both body odor and immune systems. He then asked the women to rate which T-shirts smelled the best, which the worst. What Wedekind found was that women preferred the scent of a T-shirt worn by a man whose genotype was most different from hers, a genotype that, perhaps, is linked to an immune system that possesses something hers does not. In this way she increases the chance that her offspring will be robust.

It all seems too good to be true, that we are so hardwired and yet unconscious of the wiring. Because no one to my knowledge has ever said, "I married him because of his B.O." No. We say, "I married him (or her) because he's intelligent, she's beautiful, he's witty, she's compassionate." But we may just be as deluded about love as we are when we're *in* love. If it all comes down to a sniff test, then dogs definitely have the edge when it comes to choosing mates.

Why doesn't passionate love last? How is it possible to see a person as beautiful on Monday, and 364 days later, on another Monday, to see that beauty as bland? Surely the object of your affection could not have changed that much. She still has the same shaped eyes. Her voice has always had that husky sound, but now it grates on you—she sounds like she needs an antibiotic. Or maybe you're the one who needs an antibiotic, because the partner you once loved and cherished and saw as though saturated with starlight now feels more like a low-level infection, tiring you, sapping all your strength.

Studies around the world confirm that, indeed, passion usually ends. Its conclusion is as common as its initial flare. No wonder some cultures think selecting a lifelong mate based on something so fleeting is folly. Helen Fisher has suggested that relationships frequently break up after four years because that's about how long it takes to raise a child through infancy. Passion, that wild, prismatic insane feeling, turns out to be practical after all. We not only need to copulate; we also need enough passion to start breeding, and then feelings of attachment take over as the partners bond to raise a helpless human infant. Once a baby is no longer nursing, the child can be left with sister, aunts, friends. Each parent is now free to meet another mate and have more children.

Biologically speaking, the reasons romantic love fades may be found in the way our brains respond to the surge and pulse of dopamine that accompanies passion and makes us fly. Cocaine users describe the phenomenon of tolerance: The brain adapts to the excessive input of the drug. Perhaps the neurons become desensitized and need more and more to produce the high—to put out pixie dust, metaphorically speaking.

Maybe it's a good thing that romance fizzles. Would we have railroads, bridges, planes, faxes, vaccines, and television if we were all always besotted? In place of the ever evolving technology that has marked human culture from its earliest tool use, we would have instead only bonbons, bouquets, and birth control. More seriously, if the chemically altered state induced by romantic love is akin to a mental illness or a drug-induced euphoria, exposing yourself for too long could result in psychological damage. A good sex life can be as strong as Gorilla Glue, but who wants that stuff on your skin?

Once upon a time, in India, a boy and a girl fell in love without their parents' permission. They were from different castes, their relationship radical and unsanctioned. Picture it: the sparkling sari, the boy in white linen, the clandestine meetings on tiled terraces with a fat, white moon floating overhead. Who could deny these lovers their pleasure, or condemn the force of their attraction?

Their parents could. In one recent incident a boy and girl from different castes were hanged at the hands of their parents as hundreds of villagers watched. A couple who eloped were stripped and beaten. Yet another couple committed suicide after their parents forbade them to marry.

Anthropologists used to think that romance was a Western construct, a bourgeois by-product of the Middle Ages. Romance was for the sophisticated, took place in cafés, with coffees and Cabernets, or on silk sheets, or in rooms with a flickering fire. It was assumed that non-Westerners, with their broad familial and social obligations, were spread too thin for particular passions. How could a collectivist culture celebrate or in any way sanction the obsession with one individual that defines new love? Could a lice-ridden peasant really feel passion?

Easily, as it turns out. Scientists now believe that romance is panhuman, embedded in our brains since Pleistocene times. In a study of 166 cultures, anthropologists William Jankowiak and Edward Fischer observed evidence of passionate love in 147 of them. In another study men and women from Europe, Japan, and the Philippines were asked to fill out a survey to measure their experiences of passionate love. All three groups professed feeling passion with the same searing intensity.

But though romantic love may be universal, its cultural expression is not. To the Fulbe tribe of northern Cameroon, poise matters more than passion. Men who spend too much time with their wives are taunted, and those who are weak-kneed are thought to have fallen under a dangerous spell. Love may be inevitable, but for the Fulbe its manifestations are shameful, equated with sickness and social impairment.

In India romantic love has traditionally been seen as dangerous, a threat to a well-crafted caste system in which marriages are arranged as a means of preserving lineage and bloodlines. Thus the gruesome tales, the warnings embedded in fables about what happens when one's wayward impulses take over.

Today love marriages appear to be on the rise in India, often in defiance of parents' wishes. The triumph of romantic love is celebrated in Bollywood films. Yet most Indians still believe arranged marriages are more likely to succeed than love marriages. In one survey of Indian college students, 76 percent said they'd marry someone with all the right qualities even if they weren't in love with the person (compared with only 14 percent of Americans). Marriage is considered too important a step to leave to chance.

Studies around the world confirm that, indeed, passion usually ends. No wonder some cultures think selecting a lifelong mate based on something so fleeting is folly.

Renu Dinakaran is a striking 45-year-old woman who lives in Bangalore, India. When I meet her, she is dressed in Western-style clothes—black leggings and a T-shirt. Renu lives in a well-appointed apartment in this thronging city, where cows sleep on the highways as tiny cars whiz around them, plumes of black smoke rising from their sooty pipes.

Renu was born into a traditional Indian family where an arranged marriage was expected. She was not an arranged kind of person, though, emerging from her earliest days as a fierce tennis player, too sweaty for saris, and smarter than many of the men around her. Nevertheless at the age of 17 she was married off to a first cousin, a man she barely knew, a man she wanted to learn to love, but couldn't. Renu considers many arranged marriages to be acts of "state-sanctioned rape."

Renu hoped to fall in love with her husband, but the more years that passed, the less love she felt, until, at the end, she was shrunken, bitter, hiding behind the curtains of her in-laws' bungalow, looking with longing at the couple on the balcony across from theirs. "It was so obvious to me that couple had married for love, and I envied them. I really did. It hurt me so much to see how they stood together, how they went shopping for bread and eggs."

Exhausted from being forced into confinement, from being swaddled in saris that made it difficult to move, from resisting the pressure to eat off her husband's plate, Renu did what traditional Indian culture forbids one to do. She left. By this time she had had two children. She took them with her. In her mind was an old movie she'd seen on TV, a movie so strange and enticing to her, so utterly confounding and comforting at the same time, that she couldn't get it out of her head. It was 1986. The movie was *Love Story*.

"Before I saw movies like *Love Story,* I didn't realize the power that love can have," she says.

Renu was lucky in the end. In Mumbai she met a man named Anil, and it was then, for the first time, that she felt passion. "When I first met Anil, it was like nothing I'd ever experienced. He was the first man I ever had an orgasm with. I was high, just high, all the time. And I knew it wouldn't last, couldn't last, and so that infused it with a sweet sense of longing, almost as though we were watching the end approach while we were also discovering each other."

When Renu speaks of the end, she does not, to be sure, mean the end of her relationship with Anil; she means the end of a certain stage. The two are still happily married, companionable, loving if not "in love," with a playful black dachshund they bought together. Their relationship, once so full of fire, now seems to simmer along at an even temperature, enough to keep them well fed and warm. They are grateful.

"Would I want all that passion back?" Renu asks. "Sometimes, yes. But to tell you the truth, it was exhausting."

From a physiological point of view, this couple has moved from the dopamine-drenched state of romantic love to the relative quiet of an oxytocin-induced attachment. Oxytocin is a hormone that promotes a feeling of connection, bonding. It is released when we hug our long-term spouses, or our children. It is released when a mother nurses her infant. Prairie voles, animals with high levels of oxytocin, mate for life. When scientists block oxytocin receptors in these rodents, the animals don't form monogamous bonds and tend to roam. Some researchers speculate that autism, a disorder marked by a profound inability to forge and maintain social connections, is linked to an oxytocin deficiency. Scientists have been experimenting by treating autistic people with oxytocin, which in some cases has helped alleviate their symptoms.

In long-term relationships that work—like Renu and Anil's—oxytocin is believed to be abundant in both partners. In long-term relationships that never get off the ground, like Renu and her first husband's, or that crumble once the high is gone, chances are the couple has not found a way to stimulate or sustain oxytocin production.

"But there are things you can do to help it along," says Helen Fisher. "Massage. Make love. These things trigger oxytocin and thus make you feel much closer to your partner."

Well, I suppose that's good advice, but it's based on the assumption that you still want to have sex with that boring windbag of a husband. Should you fake-it-till-you-make-it?

"Yes," says Fisher. "Assuming a fairly healthy relationship, if you have enough orgasms with your partner, you may become attached to him or her. You will stimulate oxytocin."

This may be true. But it sounds unpleasant. It's exactly what your mother always said about vegetables: "Keep eating your peas. They are an acquired taste. Eventually, you will come to like them."

But I have never been a peas person.

It's 90 degrees on the day my husband and I depart, from Boston for New York City, to attend a kissing school. With two kids, two cats, two dogs, a lopsided house, and a questionable school system, we may know how to kiss, but in the rough and tumble of our harried lives we have indeed forgotten how to *kiss*.

The sky is paved with clouds, the air as sticky as jam in our hands and on our necks. The Kissing School, run by Cherie Byrd, a therapist from Seattle, is being held on the 12th floor of a run-down building in Manhattan. Inside, the room is whitewashed; a tiled table holds bottles of banana and apricot nectar, a pot of green tea, breath mints, and Chapstick. The other Kissing School students—sometimes they come from as far away as Vietnam and Nigeria—are sprawled happily on the bare floor, pillows and blankets beneath them. The class will be seven hours long.

Byrd starts us off with foot rubs. "In order to be a good kisser," she says, "you need to learn how to do the foreplay before the kissing." Foreplay involves rubbing my husband's smelly feet, but that is not as bad as when he has to rub mine. Right before we left the house, I accidentally stepped on a diaper the dog had gotten into, and although I washed, I now wonder how well.

"Inhale," Byrd says, and shows us how to draw in air.

"Exhale," she says, and then she jabs my husband in the back. "Don't focus on the toes so much," she says. "Move on to the calf."

Byrd tells us other things about the art of kissing. She describes the movement of energy through various chakras, the manifestation of emotion in the lips; she describes the importance of embracing all your senses, how to make eye contact as a prelude, how to whisper just the right way. Many hours go by. My cell phone rings. It's our babysitter. Our one-year-old has a high fever. We must cut the long lesson short. We rush out. Later on, at home, I tell my friends what we learned at Kissing School: We don't have time to kiss.

A perfectly typical marriage. Love in the Western world.

Luckily I've learned of other options for restarting love. Arthur Aron, a psychologist at Stony Brook University in New York, conducted an experiment that illuminates some of the mechanisms by which people become and stay attracted. He recruited a group of men and women and put opposite sex pairs in rooms together, instructing each pair to perform a series of tasks, which included telling each other personal details about themselves. He then asked each couple to stare into each other's eyes for two minutes. After this encounter, Aron found most of the couples, previously strangers to each other, reported feelings of attraction. In fact, one couple went on to marry.

Novelty triggers dopamine in the brain, which can stimulate feelings of attraction. So riding a roller coaster on a first date is more likely to lead to second and third dates.

Fisher says this exercise works wonders for some couples. Aron and Fisher also suggest doing novel things together, because novelty triggers dopamine in the brain, which can stimulate feelings of attraction. In other words, if your heart flutters in his presence, you might decide it's not because you're anxious but because you love him. Carrying this a step further, Aron and others have found that even if you just jog in place and then meet someone, you're more likely to think they're attractive. So first dates that involve a nerve-racking activity, like riding a roller coaster, are more likely to lead to second and third dates. That's a strategy worthy of posting on Match. com. Play some squash. And in times of stress—natural disasters, blackouts, predators on the prowl—lock up tight and hold your partner.

In Somerville, Massachusetts, where I live with my husband, our predators are primarily mosquitoes. That needn't stop us from trying to enter the windows of each other's soul. When I propose this to Benjamin, he raises an eyebrow.

"Why don't we just go out for Cambodian food?" he says.

"Because that's not how the experiment happened."

As a scientist, my husband is always up for an experiment. But our lives are so busy that, in order to do this, we have to make a plan. We will meet next Wednesday at lunchtime and try the experiment in our car.

On the Tuesday night before our rendezvous, I have to make an unplanned trip to New York. My husband is more than happy to forget our date. I, however, am not. That night, from my hotel room, I call him.

"We can do it on the phone," I say.

"What am I supposed to stare into?" he asks. "The keypad?"

"There's a picture of me hanging in the hall. Look at that for two minutes. I'll look at a picture I have of you in my wallet."

"Come on," he says.

"Be a sport," I say. "It's better than nothing."

Maybe not. Two minutes seems like a long time to stare at someone's picture with a receiver pressed to your ear. My husband sneezes, and I try to imagine his picture sneezing right along with him, and this makes me laugh.

Another 15 seconds pass, slowly, each second stretched to its limit so I can almost hear time, feel time, its taffy-like texture, the pop it makes when it's done. Pop pop pop. I stare and stare at my husband's picture. It doesn't produce any sense of startling intimacy, and I feel defeated.

Still, I keep on. I can hear him breathing on the other end. The photograph before me was taken a year or so ago, cut to fit my wallet, his strawberry blond hair pulled back in a ponytail. I have never really studied it before. And I realize that in this picture my husband is not looking straight back at me, but his pale blue eyes are cast sideways, off to the left, looking at something I can't see. I touch his eyes. I peer close, and then still closer, at his averted face. Is there something sad in his expression, something sad in the way he gazes off?

I look toward the side of the photo, to find what it is he's looking at, and then I see it: a tiny turtle coming toward him. Now I remember how he caught it after the camera snapped, how he held it gently in his hands, showed it to our kids, stroked its shell, his forefinger moving over the scaly dome, how he held the animal out toward me, a love offering. I took it, and together we sent it back to the sea.

Pillow Talk

A conversation with Stephen and Ondrea Levine about lust, the meaning of marriage, and true intimacy.

NINA UTNE

What is a good long-term relationship? *When we asked the question around the office and among our friends, we heard a lot of fear and even more relief. Fear because asking questions inevitably rocks the boat of marriage and family. Relief because after we admit that there are few long-term relationships to emulate, we can begin an honest exploration of how to do it differently. Stephen and Ondrea Levine, with three marriages behind them, have made their marriage work for 26 years and have raised three children. They work as counselors and writers, with a focus on death and dying as well as relationship issues. Good relationships are entirely idiosyncratic, they say, but self-respect, clarity of intent, and commitment to growth are the key elements. Ondrea says each of us has to start by answering the question "What do you want out of this very short life?" But ultimately, Stephen says, it's about "when you get to just loving the ass off that person and you still don't know what love means."*

Nina: We hear a lot about how relationships begin, and plenty about how they end. But there's not a lot of honest talk about how to make them last—or, for that matter, why they should.

Ondrea: Once the lust of the first couple of years wears off, once the other person is off the pedestal, and you're off the pedestal, and you're facing each other and you see each other's craziness, frailties, vulnerabilities—that's when the work really starts. The initial intensity of the passion cools, and love comes to a middle way, a balance. You have to have something more than the fact that you're in love to keep it going and keep it growing.

Nina: And what is that something?

Stephen: I think relationships persevere because you're interested in what's going to happen the next day and your partner is an interesting person to share it with.

O: Also, the people with the best relationships often have some kind of practice. It can be religious practice, love practice, nature practice, whatever, but they have something that's so essentially helpful in their growth that it keeps the relationship going.

S: People who get into a relationship who don't already have something that's more important to them than themselves—generally spiritual practice and growth, or maybe service work—are less liable to stay with the process when the relationship doesn't give them exactly what their desire system wishes for.

N: Someone wrote that 35 percent of his relationship comes from the fact that he brings his wife a cup of coffee in bed every morning.

S: What a weak relationship! Boy, that's a miserable relationship. This guy better get himself another hobby!

O: I was just thinking how very thoughtful that is. Serving each other is exceptionally important.

S: Growth. Growth is also important.

O: Yes, various levels of growth, but certainly heart expansion. Everybody would define growth so differently, but love has to grow, your heart has to open more, you have to get clearer about your intentions, clearer about what you really want out of this very short life.

And it's so individual; it depends so much on life experience. Love and simple human kindness are of huge value to me, and I find that I'm drawn to people who are thoughtful and kind. I used to be drawn to people who were only wise.

N: It seems like the bottom line is the level of consciousness and openheartedness that we bring to a long-term relationship.

S: In a relationship, we're working on a mystical union. That's a term that came from the Christian tradition, but it's part of almost all devotional traditions. And it means uniting at a level way beyond our separation. After 26 years, the line between Ondrea and the Beloved is very, very blurred. In that context, you may ask what happens when two people's goals change. Well, if they're working on becoming whole human beings, they'll change in a whole way, whether it means being together or separate.

N: **Growth and service and practice are important. But what happens if you have those intentions but there are kids and hectic lives and petty annoyances and betrayals? How does mystical union accommodate that?**

S: But that's what everybody has to work with. I mean, if you can't get through that stuff, there is no mystical union. If only mystical union were so easy—if people could just lean into each other's soul space, as it were. In fact, people think they're doing that, and it's actually lust, generally. We say that love is as close as you get to God without really trying. When people live together, maybe they do feel each other's soul, maybe they do feel the Beloved, maybe they both enter the Beloved. But mind arises, preference arises, attitude arises, inclination arises.

O: We raised three kids, and we certainly had our share of times when our hearts were closed to each other and we felt separate, but our commitment was to work on that and to work with it by trying to stay open, trying to understand the other person's conditioning, because our conditionings were so different.

For instance, what you might think of as betrayal I might not think is betrayal, so all of that has to be defined in a relationship. How I might work with betrayal, you might not be willing to, and that's part of what you have to work out with your partner. Some levels of betrayal are workable, and some are not worth putting in the energy for some relationships. There's no right way other than your way.

S: And *betrayal* is a loaded word. A lot of people naturally feel resentment in a relationship because there are two people with two desire systems. Sometimes they're complementary and sometimes contradictory. And when someone doesn't get what he or she wants—it can be something so simple, like not enough gas in the car, little things—the feeling of betrayal may arise. Now, sexual betrayal, that's something else entirely.

N: **What do you think about the possibility of open marriages?**

S: Raging bullshit. Well, it's fine for young people who don't want a committed relationship. But you might as well kiss your relationship good-bye once you open it. I don't think there is such a thing. People who open their relationships open them at both ends. The relationship becomes something you're just passing through. There's no place for real trust. There's no place where you're concerned about the other person's well-being more than your own, which is what relationship is, which is what love is. I've never, ever seen it work, and we've known some extremely conscious people.

N: **But when I look at the carnage in so many marriages, I think maybe we need to step back and look at the whole agreement. There are many, many different kinds of love, and maybe we're just being too narrow.**

O: We've known a couple of people who have had multiple relationships within their marriage and it's worked out for them, but it takes a certain inner strength and a depth of self-trust. Part of why marriage has been set up is because of trust, and keeping track of lineage and money and paternity and all that stuff. I think it's all based on trust, and we don't seem to have the capacity to trust deeply unless it's just one other person.

S: Then again, for some, sexual betrayal is like an active catapult. It can throw them right into God. It can clarify their priorities.

N: **So you're saying that an open arrangement undercuts intimacy?**

O: So many people nowadays run to divorce court because it's easier than trying to work it through. And it's so exciting to go on to that next new relationship, where someone really loves you and doesn't know your frailties. I know many people who keep going from relationship to relationship because it's easier. Although they wouldn't say that. They wouldn't even think of the children. They would only think of themselves, and that's okay too, but I don't think you get as much growth.

S: That sex thing, that's way overrated. Way, way overrated. Because if two people love each other, the part that becomes most interesting in sex is the part that may be the least interesting in the beginning. It's the quality of taking another person internally. I don't think people realize, with our loose sexual energy, the enormity of letting someone inside your aura, so to speak. To let someone closer to you than a foot and a half, you are already doing something that is touching on universal wonders and terrors.

As the intimacy becomes more intimate, though the sex may not be as hot, the intimacy becomes much hotter. Much more fulfilling. Sexual relationships actually become more fulfilling the longer they go on if you start getting by all the hindrances to intimacy—all your fears, your doubts, your distrust. Sex has an exquisite quality to support a relationship, not because of the skin sensory level, but because of heart sensory level.

N: **What significance is there in the formality of marriage? The contract?**

O: That depends on your conditioning. For us, marriage meant that we were going to work as hard as we could. But we both said that if the other person wanted to go another way or had a major epiphany or wanted a change in life, we would honor that.

The contract gives you a sense of security that both people are willing to work as hard as they can. I certainly don't know that the marriage contract is for everyone, although I think it can be helpful with kids. Then again, I'm 60, and that's an old style of thinking. That's why I think nowadays maybe a six-month marriage contract might be more skillful. The most important thing is to be honest about how you see your relationship: Do you see it as 'til death do you part, do you see it as until you just can't stand each other, do you see it as until the kids are 18? Anything is workable.

N: I'm thinking about children, this container we call family. For me, there's a certain mystical union in families. Sometimes "staying together for the sake of the children" is actually about honoring this idea of family.

O: Of course we didn't stay together for the children, because we're both divorced and had children.

S: It's only my third marriage . . . I'm working at it!

O: I got married for the old reason that many women in my generation did. I was pregnant. I didn't really want to get married, but I would've been a *puta,* a prostitute—looked at as a lesser woman in those days.

  I think that it mostly is an empty relationship when you're staying together for the kids, but we have known some people whose love for their kids was so great that they became more brotherly and sisterly, and it worked very well for them, but that's pretty rare.

S: And usually when people are in that kind of disarray, the children do not benefit from their staying together.

N: Are there other options than the train wreck to divorce?

S: Depends on the individuals. It depends on their spiritual practice. I think it has a lot to do with their toilet training.

O: Oh, we're screwed.

S: What I mean is that our earliest self-esteem and self-image comes into play. The most beautiful thing about love—and the most difficult—is that it makes us go back to our unfinished places and relationships and, maybe, finish them. Your partner is the person who helps you do that, not by serving you, but by serving as a mirror for you, by his or her own honesty. By observing our partners' struggle to be honest we learn to be honest ourselves.

N: I just see so many people who are either rushing to divorce or living in dead marriages. They seem afraid to ask these deep kinds of questions and have these kinds of conversations.

O: I have worked with thousands of people who are dying, and I have heard several common complaints on the deathbed. The first was: "I wish I had got a divorce." Mostly it was fear: They didn't want to start all over again with someone else. Oh, some people were happy. They said marriage was the most wonderful ride of their lives. But many were unhappy. They wished that they hadn't let fear get in the way. But, you know, to wait until you're on your deathbed to start reflecting on what your needs are—it's not too late, but it's awfully late.

N: That's a lot of procrastination.

To learn more about the ideas of counselors, teachers, and writers Stephen and Ondrea Levine, visit their website at www.warmrocktapes.com.

How to Talk about Sex

Whether you have minor problems in bed or a love life dusty with disuse, here's the secret to connecting.

Heidi Raykeil

Ten years ago, before kids and mortgages and All That, my husband and I were experts in the language of love. If sex is a form of communication, well, back then we were on the unlimited calling plan. We may not have always verbally expressed ourselves, but we always conveyed what we meant, physically or emotionally.

Then we had a baby.

Suddenly, I was not only uninterested in sex, I was also strangely confused about how to tell my husband. So while in some ways our daughter's birth brought us closer than ever, in other ways we started to grow apart.

I just didn't know how to explain to J.B. how tired I was, how my body hurt from being pinched and pulled by our baby, and how by the end of the day I couldn't imagine sharing it with anyone else. We both became prickly and defensive: I was sure that when J.B. wrapped his leg over mine at night it meant he was coming on to me (again); when I turned my back and pretended to be asleep, he assumed I no longer found him attractive. Bye-bye, language of love.

Whether it's right after the birth of a baby or a few years down the line, it seems like lots of happily married couples hit the sexual skids when they become parents. And most of them have heard sex therapists on TV and read articles and books, and know they should talk it out.

But there's the rub. Sex is a socially charged and highly personal issue that remains a bit taboo despite our seeming openness. And talking about not having sex? Chances are, the subject comes up when one of you wants it and the other doesn't. Bad time to talk. And who wants to crack open that can of worms later on when it's over? Besides, isn't sex supposed to be fun and spontaneous—like it used to be? Won't talking about it spoil the magic?

"Where's the magic if you're not having sex?" says Valerie Raskin, M.D., author of *Great Sex for Moms: Ten Steps to Nurturing Passion While Raising Kids.* But how do you start talking? What do you say? And how do you say it so you don't end up bruising egos or booting one of you to the couch? My husband and I started by paying attention to the distinction between how we talked about sex and the details of what we were talking about. To begin:

How to Talk
Just Leap In

Nichole Cook, of Pittsburgh, mom of Eleanor, 8, Odessa, 7, and Izabelle, 6, was embarrassed into silence not long after Eleanor was born: One time during sex she squirted breast milk all over her husband. "I was mortified. I thought it was gross—and totally not normal." Rather than telling him how she felt, though, Cook simply avoided sex altogether for the next couple of weeks.

While talking about sex can be awkward, no one yet has actually died of embarrassment. Dr. Raskin suggests breaking the ice simply by acknowledging how hard it is.

That's what Cook did, a few weeks later. "I was really nervous, but I finally just said, 'That was really embarrassing for me.'" As it turned out, her husband hadn't even noticed and didn't think it was a big deal anyway. "After that, we just made sure we had a towel handy. Now it's something we laugh about."

Rather than letting things build up, talking about it now makes room for more openness later.

Choose the Right Place and Tone

One of the worst fights J.B. and I had about sex was right after a failed attempt at it. I really wanted to be in the mood—even though I wasn't at all—so we got partway into the act before I admitted that things weren't working. We lay in bed trying to "talk" about what had happened. But we were so upset that we ended up blaming, and J.B. stormed angrily out of the room.

Thus, we discovered the importance of environment for having a fruitful discussion of our sex life. Choose a night when nothing else is planned and wait until the kids are asleep. Turn off the TV and the phone. This isn't an inquisition. It's an opportunity to reconnect with each other, to steal an intimate moment in a chaotic life. It's about how you show and share love, about something that should be fun and pleasurable.

What Is the Biggest Problem in Your Sex Life Right Now?

- 43% He wants sex more often than I do
- 34% We're both too tired and busy to be in the mood
- 12% Nothing
- 11% A lot about our sex life has changed and we're having trouble adjusting

—*Parenting*'s MomConnection poll

J.B. and I have had some of our best talks late at night on our front stoop. We turn off the porch light, pour some wine, and sit side by side. There's something about not looking directly at each other (and the wine, maybe) that lets things flow. It may cut awkwardness to merge your heart-to-heart with an activity—try talking while hiking, or walking, or sorting through your penny jar.

Acknowledge the Problem

This is not the same as agreeing on the cause of the problem. It's just a way to get the conversation rolling. Dr. Raskin calls this "outing the secret—even though it's not really a secret." Begin by stating the obvious: "I know things aren't like they used to be," or "I know we haven't been having sex very much lately." Often, acknowledging this reality, without judgment, can bring a couple closer.

After that big fight, I realized that my husband and I had let things go far too long. While Ramona was napping the next day, I simply said: "I'm having a hard time with sex these days. I hate the way it's come between us, and it must really suck for you, too." The fact that I wasn't trying to deny or make excuses helped J.B. feel comfortable.

After listening to J.B., I realized he wasn't as angry about the situation as I'd thought. It annoyed him that I'd initiated sex when I didn't really want it, but he'd needed to leave the room to cool down because he simply couldn't change gears and talk rationally while he was still aroused. This not only helped me understand why he became so agitated but also made it easier for me to talk about what I was experiencing physically.

Asking and listening without getting defensive is an important part of this process. Repeat what your partner's saying and ask if you're understanding correctly. Ask, "is there more you want me to know?"

Look Forward, Not Back

Agree to make a fresh start. Don't pull out old fights; avoid generalizing or labeling. Saying things like "You never want sex" or "You're a sex fiend!" is just talking negatively about the past. We all say dumb things; don't waste time fighting about whether they're true.

It's also a bad idea to compare yourself to other couples. What's right for them isn't necessarily what's right for you. When Holly Wing's husband saw a poll in a magazine that claimed most of its readers had sex a lot more often than they

did each month, he kept referring to it—comparing their own not-nearly-so-much stats. Wing, a Berkeley mom of 2-year-old Clio, then started to counter with her own statistics, and before long they were locked in battle. "Instead of solving any problems, we were just getting really good at fighting!"

So stick to what you're feeling ("I feel sad that we're having trouble finding the time to make love") rather than accusations about how you measure up to others.

Stay Positive

"I don't want to talk about sex we haven't had anymore," Wing told her husband after another fight. "If you want to have sex seventeen times a month, well, then, let's go for it!" she said, naming his wildly optimistic ideal. Of course they didn't meet the goal, but the effort did help. Wing felt that her husband realized how hard it is to make time for (and want) frequent sex rather than just complaining about it. And he appreciated her willingness to give it a try.

Shooting for high numbers may not be your solution, but the attitude is admirable. Remind each other that you'll get through this and that you both want to work it out. Instead of saying, "You never woo me anymore," try "Remember that poem you wrote me on our honeymoon? That got me hot!" And if your conversation falls apart and you revert to blaming—stop. Don't try to win. Just end it and try again later when you've both cooled down.

What to Talk about
That There's Love behind Your Lovemaking

If you state explicitly, right up front, that you love and respect each other, and that in talking about this you're only talking about the way you show your love, you're both likely to feel more comfortable expressing your feelings. And keep reminding each other of your love and your mutual desire for each other's happiness—that should be the backdrop to your conversation.

The Meaning of Sex

You can't figure out how to fix your love life if you don't know what you want it to be. So discuss what physical intimacy represents to yourselves and in your relationship.

Women, for instance, often misunderstand the ways in which sex is important for many men. It's not just a matter of stereotypical gotta-have-it male urges but can be a critical form of emotional expression. For whatever combination of reasons, many men feel and express love physically, so they may experience a lack of sex as rejecting not only them but their offering of love as well.

The Definition of Sex

It's a good idea to talk openly about what actually constitutes "sex" to each of you. Is it only intercourse, or does it include other kinds of touching? A husband whose sex drive is at low ebb may be delighted to find that his wife will think him no less a man if he gives her a massage—with or without "extras"—instead of a more "demanding" service.

What's the Hardest Thing to Talk about, Sexually?

- 35% Our different levels of interest in sex
- 33% Something specific I'd like him to do differently or improve
- 18% How often we should have sex
- 14% Other

—Parenting's MomConnection poll

For Cook and her husband, sharing an understanding that she no longer felt sexual about her breasts was a breakthrough. "I felt like they were just for my kids, not him," she says. With that off the table, they were able to talk about what did still work for both of them.

That It's Not Him. Or You

Many factors mess with parents' love life, only rarely sexual skills or prowess. The list includes exhaustion, a light-sleeping child, hormones, embarrassment about weight gain, lack of time, difficulty shifting gears from parent to lover.

When Heidi Johnecheck, of Petosky, Michigan, mother of Max, 4, and Jaxon, 2, found a magazine article that listed ten reasons it's physically hard for moms to have sex—everything from vaginal dryness to sheer exhaustion—she tore it out and gave it to her husband. "As much as I'd tried to tell him, he just couldn't comprehend what 'I don't feel like it' meant," she says, and he took it personally. "But the article showed that it wasn't just me or just him."

Specific Ways to Make Things Better

Johnecheck and her husband decided to tackle one simple problem head-on: They made a kid-free visit to a local sex shop to buy some lubricants. "We actually made a date together,"

Johnecheck says, "and decided to just be silly and have fun with it."

Brainstorming about what might help you get back in the swing of things is a great way to move things forward. At the top of the list for most couples? "More private time," says Dr. Raskin. And while scheduling "date night" can help, think about it broadly. If nights out are expensive and infrequent, what about finding time in the mornings (when women's testosterone levels are highest, resulting in higher libido)? What about Saturday-afternoon naptime (when you'll both be less tired than at night)?

Technique

This is not the time to be shy or coy. Be specific about yourself ("I'm finding that it takes me a lot longer to get excited lately"). If you want more mood setting than "Okay, the baby's asleep. Let's do this," ask for it: "First I'd like you to sit through a chick flick with me and hold my hand."

Your body and your life have changed since you had a child. Maybe there's something in particular that you do want that you never did before. Just say it: harder, softer, faster, slower, touch me here. And if you say what you do want your husband to do instead of just what you don't, he'll likely be turned on, too.

For me and J.B., when I finally could say "Not tonight" without worrying it would turn into a fight, a funny thing happened. It became easier for me to say yes. Because once I knew he understood my feelings, we started to address some of the underlying issues: I needed more time for myself, more romance, and more help with our daughter.

Those first years after the birth of Ramona were tough. But four years later I now see talking about sex as just another opportunity for expanding our intimacy—in and out of the bedroom.

HEIDI RAYKEIL's book about her and her husband's romantic life as parents, *Confessions of a Naughty Mommy: How I Found My Lost Libido,* was just published by Seal Press.

On-Again, Off-Again

What drives couples to repeatedly break up and then make up?

Elizabeth Svoboda

For Laura, a 35-year-old corporate recruiter from New York City, dating had always felt like a Ferris wheel ride. When a relationship started to feel wrong, she'd leave to get a new vantage point on things, but as the pain of singleness set in, she retreated to her former partner for comfort, ending up back where she started. She'd repeat the cycle several times before breaking things off permanently. "It became this crazy pattern," she says. "They weren't good guys at all, but whenever something in my life was difficult, I would go back."

Laura's longtime boomeranging habit puts her in good company. The dynamic is quite common. University of Texas communications professor René Dailey found that 60 percent of adults have ended a romantic relationship and then gotten back together, and that three-quarters of those respondents had been through the breakup, makeup cycle at least twice. But embarking on this bumpy relational road takes an emotional toll: On-off couples have more relational stress than non-cyclical couples, she found.

Given the obvious costs, why do couples keep dancing the on-and-off tango? Many who seesaw from freeze-outs to fervent proclamations of love know deep down that the relationship probably isn't right, says psychologist Steven Stosny. But when couples are faced with the loneliness and low self-esteem that accompany a breakup, they continually fall back on the temporary relief of reconciliation.

It's often the fleeting high points of a fundamentally rocky relationship that convince embattled partners to keep coming back for more, spurring a tortuous dynamic with no end in sight. "Often there is something that works very well for you about this person," says Gail Saltz, a Manhattan-based psychiatrist and author of *Becoming Real*. But when your mate's dreamy qualities are accompanied by deal-breaker ones like dishonesty or irresponsibility, it can be difficult to make a clear-headed assessment of whether to stay or leave.

Many couples with a boomeranging habit know deep down that the relationship probably isn't right.

While problem behaviors may prompt a periodic hiatus, on-again, off-again couples continue to reunite out of a persistent hope that the moments of happiness and fulfillment they've known will someday constitute the entire relationship. "People say, 'I can fix this other part of my partner,'" Saltz says, even though efforts at "remodeling" a mate are typically useless. The self-deprecating internal monologues that serial on-off artists conduct after a breakup—"What was I thinking? I'll never meet

---

Breaking the Breakup Cycle

On-again, off-again couples often find themselves caught between their desire for freedom and their fear of regret. Here's how to decide whether to sign on for the long haul or get out for good.

- **Adopt a worst-case-scenario** mindset. Many perpetual boomerangers keep returning because they assume they can change their partner's worst habits. But that's wishful thinking, psychotherapist Toni Coleman says. "You have to assume that the behaviors you see will get *more* entrenched and worse over time. Ask yourself, 'If that turns out to be the case, would I still want to be in this relationship?'"

- **Seek advice from** a trusted third party. Therapists fill the bill nicely, but family and friends can be just as helpful. Because they don't have as much invested in your partner as you do, they can provide unbiased opinions as to whether smooth sailing is in your relationship's future.

- **Take a time-out.** In an on-again, off-again pairing, hiatuses are par for the course. But resolve to make this one different. Use the emotional distance to think clearly about what you want from a long-term relationship. Make a list if it helps you organize your thoughts. If your partner doesn't measure up, make the hiatus permanent.

someone as funny, smart, and attractive ever again!"—can also lead to repeated reconciliations.

While periodic estrangement is painful, some couples see a silver lining. By experiencing life without their significant others for a while, they come away with a deeper understanding of the value of their bond, even if the romance doesn't always have storybook qualities.

But this kind of "pruning" is no panacea. Virginia psychotherapist Toni Coleman warns couples to steer clear of the false epiphanies making up and breaking up can encourage. After an emotion-filled reunion, it's tempting to assume your partner has permanently changed for the better. But underlying conflicts that simmered before the breakup will resurface—just ask consummate on-off artists Pamela Anderson and Tommy Lee, who married and divorced twice before breaking up for good. "Things will change only if both people commit to working on the big issues," says Coleman.

Saltz recommends veterans of the breakup, makeup carousel take time to think about why they've been there so long in the first place. "The key is in recognizing that there is a pattern," she says. "You need to elucidate what the draw of this relationship really is for you." Some on-off cyclists, she explains, repeatedly return to partnerships with flaws that mirror those in their own parents' marriage, which they've unconsciously internalized as fundamental to any relationship. If your mother took her cheating partner back over and over again, you maybe inclined to do the same. "Just the awareness of that can help you step out: 'Oh, my gosh, this is really me being my mother, and I don't want to recapitulate her love story,'" says Saltz.

Another way to decide whether to fish or cut bait for good, Coleman says, is to take as long a view as possible. By forcing partners to consider the implications of "forever," so-called fast-forwarding scenarios may make them less likely to acquiesce to the temporary high of being "on" again with a problematic mate.

Since casting aside her most recent drama-ridden relationship, Laura has decided to steer clear of the dating world for a while. She sees her new freedom as a chance to step back and contemplate how to avoid the trap in the future. "The whole love industry makes you feel like you have to be in a relationship all the time, but right now I'm just taking some time to figure things out," she says. "I truly am happy on my own."

ELIZABETH SVOBODA is a freelance writer in San Jose, California.

A New Fertility Factor

Stress is just one of many obstacles to pregnancy, but it's one you can control.

ALICE D. DOMAR, PHD

Melissa was 33 when I met her, and she'd been trying to get pregnant for more than two years. Fertility tests had found nothing wrong with her or her husband. Yet all she had gained from two cycles of injected fertility medication was some extra weight. And though she was running 20 miles a week to reduce stress, the experience had left her feeling overwhelmed and isolated. Melissa was crying almost every day when she joined the 10-week mind-body program I oversee in Boston, but she soon realized that she was neither helpless nor alone. Supported by peers and counselors, she dialed back on her running regimen (excessive exercise can hamper fertility), gave up caffeine and alcohol, and started practicing relaxation techniques. After five weeks she resumed fertility-drug injections and conceived on her next cycle. Her daughter arrived nine happy months later.

There are many myths about becoming pregnant. In truth, deciding to adopt a child doesn't boost the odds of conception. Nor does taking a vacation, having a glass of wine before sex or trying an unusual new position. But frustrated couples shouldn't assume that mind-body medicine is irrelevant to their quest for pregnancy. Studies are now confirming what Melissa's experience implies. Distress can hamper fertility—and relieving distress can help improve your chances of conceiving. Though practices like meditation and yoga certainly can't guarantee pregnancy, they have now established their place along with high-tech medicines and procedures.

What do we really know about fertility and the mind? For starters, we know that infertility is stressful. Women who have difficulty conceiving suffer as much anxiety and depression as women with heart disease or cancer. A recent study found that 40 percent of them were anxious or depressed. This shouldn't be surprising. Procreation is one of the strongest instincts in the animal kingdom. Males will die fighting for a chance to mate, and females will die to protect their young. Moreover, most people assume they are fertile. When you've spent your adult life taking precautions to *avoid* pregnancy, it's a shock to discover that you can't make it happen at will. Treatment can add to the anguish. You get poked, prodded, injected, inspected and operated on, and you have mechanical sex on schedule.

Going Beyond Inspections and Injections

High-tech fertility treatments may work better when patients receive emotional support as well.

- Psychotherapy: Helps turn negative thoughts ("I'll never get pregnant") into positive ones ("I'm doing everything I can").
- Relaxation: Healthy approaches such as yoga and meditation can help prevent dependence on caffeine and alcohol, which decrease fertility.
- Group support: Shifts patients' focus from getting pregnant to getting on with life. Opens other paths to parenthood.

No one has proved that feelings of distress actually cause infertility, but there are good reasons to think so. Women with a history of depression are twice as likely to suffer from the problem—and research has shown that distressed women are less responsive to treatment. In one recent trial, high-tech fertility procedures were 93 percent less effective in highly distressed women than in those reporting less emotional upset.

Can mind-body medicine counter these effects? The first mind-body fertility program started in 1987 at Boston's Deaconess Hospital. Thousands of patients have since participated, and the results have been encouraging. Approximately 45 to 50 percent become pregnant within six months (success rates are closer to 20 percent when patients lack psychological support), and most participants experience a significant reduction in both physical and psychological symptoms. My own research supports these observations. With funding from the National Institute of Mental Health, I conducted a controlled clinical trial comparing women in mind-body programs with those receiving only routine medical care. Pregnancy and delivery rates were nearly three times higher among the women who got the additional support. In yet another study,

Turkish researchers found that couples attempting in vitro fertilization achieved a 43 percent pregnancy rate when their treatment included psychological help, but only a 17 percent success rate when it didn't.

Women with fertility problems suffer as much distress as women with heart disease or cancer

Mind-body fertility programs vary, but the ones I have led share several key features. Besides practicing relaxation techniques, participants learn to cut back on caffeine and alcohol, and they use cognitive behavioral therapy to transform negative thoughts ("I will never have a baby") into positive ones ("I am doing everything I can to try to get pregnant"). Indeed, our programs focus less on getting pregnant than on getting your life back—and thinking about all the possible paths to parenthood, including adoption and egg or sperm donation. Similar programs are taking shape in many parts of the world, and their patients are enjoying similar benefits: less distress, higher pregnancy rates and a better quality of life.

Adapted from "6 Steps to Increased Fertility" by Robert L. Barbieri, MD; Alice D. Domar, PhD, and Kevin R. Loughlin, MD (*Fireside,* 2001). For more information about mind-body techniques and fertility go to health.harvard.edu/Newsweek.

Starting the Good Life in the Womb

Pregnant women who eat right, watch their weight and stay active can actually improve their unborn babies' chances of growing into healthy adults.

W. ALLAN WALKER, MD AND COURTNEY HUMPHRIES

Most pregnant women know they can hurt their babies by smoking, drinking alcohol and taking drugs that can cause birth defects. But they also may be able to "program" the baby in the womb to be a healthier adult. New research suggests that mothers-to-be can reduce the risk of their babies developing obesity, high blood pressure, heart disease and diabetes by monitoring their own diet, exercise and weight.

The science behind this is relatively new and still somewhat controversial. In the late 1980s, a British physician and epidemiologist named David Barker noticed that a group of Englishmen who were born small had a higher incidence of heart disease. Studies showed that rates of obesity, high blood pressure and diabetes—illnesses that often are associated with heart disease—are higher in men born small. Barker proposed that poor nutrition in the womb may have "programmed" the men to develop illness 50 years or more later.

The "Barker Hypothesis" is still hotly debated, but it is gaining acceptance as the evidence builds. Because organs develop at different times, it appears that the effects of too little food during pregnancy vary by trimester. One example comes from study of the Dutch Hunger Winter, a brief but severe famine that occurred during World War II. Pregnant women who didn't get enough to eat in their first trimester had babies who were more likely to develop heart disease. If they were in their second trimester, their babies were at risk for kidney disease. A poor diet in the last three months led to babies who had problems with insulin regulation, a precursor of diabetes.

More-recent research has focused on the negative effects of too much food during pregnancy. Women who gain excessive weight during pregnancy are more likely to have babies who are born large for their age and who become overweight in childhood. A recent study from the National Birth Defect Prevention Study found that obesity in pregnancy also increases a baby's risk for birth defects, including those of the spinal cord, heart and limbs.

A mother's nutrition and exercise patterns during pregnancy influence the long-term health of the baby by shaping her baby's metabolism. "Metabolism" includes everything that allows your body to turn food into energy—from the organ systems that process food and waste to the energy-producing chemical reactions that take place inside every cell. It is the collective engine that keeps you alive.

A mother's body may influence her baby's metabolism on many levels: the way organs develop, how appetite signals get released in the brain, how genes are activated, even the metabolic chemistry inside the baby's cells. Research now shows that the environment of the womb helps determine how a baby's metabolism is put together, or "programs" it for later health. The science of fetal programming is still new; it will be a long time before we have all the answers, since these health effects emerge over a lifetime. But several principles already are clear for a pregnant woman.

The first is to get healthy before pregnancy. Weighing too little or too much not only hampers fertility but can set the stage for metabolic problems in pregnancy. Doctors used to think of body fat as nothing more than inert insulation, but they know now that fat is an active tissue that releases hormones and plays a key role in keeping the metabolism running. Women should also eat a balanced diet and take prenatal vitamins before pregnancy to ensure that their bodies provide a good environment from the beginning.

The amount of weight gain is also critical. Women who gain too little weight during pregnancy are more likely to give birth to small babies, while women who gain too much weight are likely to have large babies. Paradoxically, both situations can predispose a child to metabolic disease. The weight gain should come slowly at first—about two to eight pounds in the first trimester, and one pound per week after that for normal-weight women. Obese women (with a body-mass index, or BMI, higher than 29) should gain no more than 15 pounds.

Pregnancy Pounds

Putting on too much or too little weight during pregnancy can predispose the baby to metabolic disorders. The right amount to gain:

Body-mass index (BMI) before pregnancy	Recommended weight gain
Less than 19.8 (underweight)	28–40 lb.
19.8–25 (normal weight)	25–35
26–29 (overweight)	15–25
Greater than 29 (obese)	No more than 15

Source: "Programming Your Baby for a Healthy Life" by W. Allan Walker, M.D., and Courtney Humphries

During pregnancy, women are already more susceptible to metabolic problems such as gestational diabetes and preeclampsia (high blood pressure), so choosing foods that help your metabolism run smoothly is important. Eating whole grains and foods rich in protein and fiber while avoiding foods high in sugar can help even out rises and falls in blood sugar. Pregnant women should eat about 300 extra calories per day while they're pregnant. But, as always, the quality of the calories matters even more. It's important to eat a diet rich in nutrients, since a lack of specific nutrients in the womb can hamper a baby's long-term health. A clear example is folic acid, without which the brain and spinal cord do not develop properly. But new research is uncovering other nutrients that may have subtler but long-lasting effects on health.

Studies suggest that women could benefit from taking omega-3 fatty-acid supplements, particularly those containing docosahexaenoic acid (DHA, for short), a type of fat that has been shown to help prevent prematurity and contribute to healthy brain development. A recent study found that women with more vitamin D in their bodies have children with stronger bones; adequate vitamin D is also needed for organ development.

Women may have different nutrient needs because of genetic differences, but to be safe every woman should take a daily prenatal vitamin before and during pregnancy. But supplements, whether in the form of a pill, a fortified shake or energy bar, don't replace the nutrients found in fruits, vegetables, low-fat meats, whole grains and other foods.

The energy you expend is as important as what you take in. Regular activity helps keep a woman's metabolism running smoothly and offsets problems of pregnancy like varicose veins, leg cramps and lower back pain. Pregnant women should avoid high-impact activities, especially late in their pregnancies.

All this may sound daunting, but most of the changes are simple ones that will improve a mother's long-term health as well as her children's.

W. ALLAN WALKER MD, the Conrad Taff Professor of Pediatrics at Harvard Medical School, and **COURTNEY HUMPHRIES**, a science writer, have written "The Harvard Medical School Guide to Healthy Eating During Pregnancy." For more information, go to health.harvard.edu/newsweek.

Breeder Reaction

Does everybody have the right to have a baby? And who should pay when nature alone doesn't work?

ELIZABETH WEIL

G uadalupe Benitez and her partner, Joanne Clark, had been buying frozen sperm at a bank in Los Angeles and trying to get pregnant at home for two years when Benitez finally sought out the services of a fertility specialist. Not at all uncommon—infertility affects more than 6 million Americans, and about 20 percent of them seek help through assisted reproductive technology, or ART. At that point, 1999, Benitez was 27 years old, Clark was 40 years old, and the couple had been together for eight years, since Benitez emigrated from Culiacán, Mexico. Benitez, a medical assistant, had some infertility benefits at a nearby OB/GYN clinic, the North Coast Women's Care Medical Group. There, Dr. Christine Brody put Benitez on a hormonal drug called Clomid, to treat her polycystic ovarian syndrome, and also told her that she was willing to oversee her treatment but not to perform inseminations because, as a Christian, she disapproved of lesbians having children.

"When she said that," Benitez told me, "I was so upset, but she made it better by saying the other doctors would do it for us." Benitez and Clark tried home inseminations for a few more months, and Brody even did some exploratory surgery. But when the time came to schedule a more effective in utero insemination—a procedure that involves injecting sperm directly into the uterus—an assistant from North Coast Women's Care called to inform Benitez that no one in the practice would do the procedure, nor would they refill her prescriptions. Benitez demanded to speak with the head of the clinic, who responded by telling her that he, too, objected to helping lesbians have children and would not further her care. "They had just lied and lied to me, trying to brush me aside to do inseminations at home as some form of excuse. But once they found themselves against the wall, they had no choice but to tell me they flat-out wouldn't do it." So Benitez sued.

Benitez's is far from the only case brought by a woman turned down for fertility services. Kijuana Chambers, a single blind woman living in Denver, Colorado, was eventually

> Amount that Americans spend each year on assisted reproductive technology: $4 billion.
>
> Chances that ART will be successful: 1 in 3.
>
> Average cost of a single cycle of in vitro fertilization: $12,400.
>
> Average amount spent per baby born through IVF in the United States: $100,000.

turned away from her fertility clinic. Among the reasons cited at trial by one of the clinic's doctors: She was prone to emotional outbursts; she had dirty underwear. Chambers lost her trial in the U.S. District Court in Denver in November 2003. Last summer, the 10th Circuit Court of Appeals declined to rehear her case.

Screening at fertility clinics is not just a concern for gays, lesbians, and the disabled. Women over 39 and women with severely compromised fertility are commonly turned down for services or told they won't be treated unless they agree to use donor eggs. This is largely a matter of economics. Assisted reproduction is a $4 billion-a-year business. The average cost of a single cycle of in vitro fertilization, including medications, egg retrieval, sperm washing, fertilization, incubation, and embryo transfer, is $12,400. Given all the failures and repeat attempts, the average amount spent per baby born through IVF in the United States is much higher: $100,000. Few insurance companies pick up the tab, so patients themselves decide where to spend their considerable money, and they do this largely based on a clinic's success rate. As a result, many doctors try to game the system, producing high "live birth" success rates by cherry-picking patients. Before being accepted by a clinic, a woman must submit to a battery of tests to determine things like the level of follicle-stimulating hormone on day three of her menstrual cycle. Get a number over 12, and she's out of luck.

According to Dr. Geoffrey Sher, founder and medical director of the Sher Institute of Reproductive Medicine, the largest chain of privately owned fertility clinics in the world, almost any clinic that can afford to turn down patients does. "I'd like to think most doctors try to be honest. The problem is, you're confronted with the reality that if you don't get high success rates, patients don't come to you."

"How much selecting is going on?" I asked.

"A lot."

"How much is a lot?"

"A *lot.*"

The practice of screening at fertility clinics poses a simple yet difficult-to-answer question: Should there be a right to reproductive assistance? The very fact that we're asking this question shows how radically things have changed. Up until the birth of Louise Brown, the first test-tube baby, in 1978, if you couldn't reproduce, you couldn't reproduce. You adopted or went childless or spent a lot of time with other people's kids, and that was the end of that. Now, of course, if you want children and they aren't happening naturally, there are many procedures to try: in vitro fertilization, blastocyst transfer, gestational surrogates, donor eggs, donor sperm, donated embryos—the list goes on and on. In recent years, our legal system has had to grapple with such novel, ART-related issues as the parenting rights of the egg donor who is also the ex-live-in lover of the birth mom, the gestational surrogate who refuses to give up the baby, and the couple who refuses to take the delivery of twins from the surrogate. Embryos have been implanted in and carried by the wrong mothers—who gets to bring up the resulting children? In one very sad case, a bachelor hired a gestational surrogate. After delivery, the baby cried an awful lot. The father killed the child in just six weeks.

Amazingly, in the United States, almost no public policy exists around assisted reproduction: what procedures should be legal, how many babies a woman should be allowed to carry at one time, how old is too old for a woman to conceive. The Vatican, on grounds that creating a baby outside of a woman's body is playing God, opposes all IVF. In Europe, the enterprise of technology-enhanced baby-making is subsidized and also well regulated. (Different countries stipulate different benefits: A woman is entitled to two cycles of IVF, a woman is entitled to four cycles of IVF, a doctor will implant one embryo, a doctor will implant up to four.) But the U.S. government has neglected to impose even the most basic medical regulations, in part because politically ART is impossible to touch. Who would possibly stand in the way of families having babies? Yet many procedures, most notably IVF, require producing excess embryos. And if it's unconscionable to create embryos for stem cell research, how can we countenance the thousands being created daily (most of which are ultimately discarded) for couples trying to have kids?

So far in this country no rules have been set. Literally, the only thing you can't do is use embryos created since 2001 for stem cell research in a lab that receives any federal funding. Other than that, anything goes. Women in their 60s have been assisted in having children. Semen has been extracted, without prior consent, from men who've died. In some states, embryos are treated as material possessions and deemed transferable as part of one's estate; in others, they're treated almost as children and cannot be harmed or destroyed, and, if abandoned, can be implanted by doctors in surrogates' wombs. Regularly the news is filled with stories: first surviving set of septuplets! Woman gives birth to two sets of identical twins! (Miracle, multiple ART births have become so common that just this spring a Missouri couple perpetrated the first sextuplet hoax, soliciting donations of cash, gift cards, a washer and dryer, and a van.) A new technology called PGD—preimplantation genetic diagnosis—allows doctors to test for genetic defects just three days after fertilization, when the conceptus, not yet technically an embryo, is still in a petri dish. And that's going to pose a whole new set of moral quandaries: Is it acceptable to screen against cystic fibrosis? What about mild disabilities, say, dyslexia? And what about sex? "To face this issue frontally and regulate," says Northeastern University legal scholar Wendy Parmet, "we first, as a society, need to come to terms and acknowledge the practice, and say, 'IVF and any of the ART procedures are okay except when . . . .' We haven't done that, nor are we aided by the fact that so much of the fertility industry takes place outside the centrifugal force of insurance." So, for now, the particularities around the right to give birth, like the particularities around the right to die, are contested and ill defined. "What we've got," says Parmet, "is a lot of talking and debate going on in professional societies, and not a lot of law."

The level of public debate about ART is so far behind the technology that we haven't even decided who should be deciding what's legal and just: the government, doctors, or patients themselves. Lawyers and bioethicists are fond of explaining that there are positive rights, known as entitlements, and negative rights, known as liberties. With regard to baby-making, a negative right is the right to do as you please, as long as it's consensual. No matter how poor an idea, no one will stop you from a drunken dalliance and parenting the child who may result. But there is no entitlement to have a baby. It goes without saying: The state will not furnish anybody a child. Nobody can demand a spouse for the purpose of creating a child, and, in this country at least, even if you do have a spouse, that spouse is not required by law to reproduce. All we seem to have agreed upon as a society is that reproducing is deeply meaningful and important, and that any attempts to keep people from doing so—i.e., forced sterilization—are abhorrent and illegal. (The 1942 case of *Skinner v. Oklahoma* struck down compulsory sterilization even for

In a Survey of Fertility Clinic Directors:

59% agreed that everyone has the right to have a child.

44% believe that fertility doctors don't have the right to decide who is a fit parent.

48% said they were very or extremely likely to turn away a gay couple seeking a surrogate.

38% would turn away a couple on welfare who wanted to pay for ART with Social Security checks.

20% would turn away a single woman.

17% would turn away a lesbian couple.

13% would turn away a couple in which the woman had bipolar disorder.

9% would turn away a couple who wanted to replace a recently deceased child.

5% would turn away a biracial couple.

repeat sex offenders on the grounds that reproduction is "one of the basic civil rights of man.") Internationally, Article 16 of the United Nations Universal Declaration of Human Rights includes "the right to found a family." The International Covenant on Economic, Social, and Cultural Rights states that everybody has the right to enjoy the benefits of scientific progress. But legally this does not add up to a positive, enforceable right to access reproductive technologies. In the United States, there is not even a positive right to basic health care.

Which raises an interesting question: Should infertility be viewed as a medical problem? Says University of Wisconsin Law School bioethicist Alta Charo, "For many years infertility was not regarded as something sufficiently serious that it necessitated care. Treatment was discretionary, not necessary." RESOLVE and other infertility rights groups have worked hard to change this, as have ART clinics. Yet defining ART as a medical treatment is a bit forced, because "if you use the classic situation of a fertile woman with an infertile male spouse, she never had a fertility problem to begin with," notes Charo. A more logical line of reasoning might be to view her as having a social, not a medical, dilemma. She does not want to have sex outside her marriage—that's why she can't get pregnant. Should society step in to help her? Should this be covered by insurance?

To get around this dilemma, those in favor of greater access to ART like to position infertility as a disease of a couple—a rather unconventional diagnosis. But even if "an infertile couple" gets under the umbrella of medicine, there's no guarantee of particular services. "You have to start with the fact that in the United States of America, in terms of health care, with certain limited exceptions, you have a right to nothing," says Parmet. "If I want a hip replacement and I don't have the money"—be it through insurance or otherwise—"I don't get a hip replacement." And, except for "certain no-no reasons," Parmet notes, all doctors, including fertility clinicians, are free to choose whom they want to treat. "Anybody can deny me care because my name is Wendy, but they can't deny me care because of my religion or my race."

In some states, like California, where Benitez was seeking care, doctors also cannot turn patients away due to sexual orientation, even if the doctor's objection stems from her own religious beliefs. (Perhaps because of this, when North Coast Women's Care challenged the initial ruling favoring Benitez, Dr. Brody claimed she refused to treat Benitez not because Benitez is a lesbian but because she's unmarried, as marital status is not a protected category. North Coast won this round of appeals.) Says Jennifer Pizer, senior counsel at Lambda Legal and Benitez's lawyer, "The courts say that the religious believer must pick a way to make a living that doesn't put them in conflict with society's rules." In other words, a fertility doctor can choose not to treat a patient for many reasons—the patient is not a good candidate for the procedure, the patient is a jerk, the doctor is too busy—but not because of the patient's race, religion, sexual orientation, or country of origin. And while a doctor can abstain from doing a particular procedure—say, in utero inseminations or IVF—across the board, such a doctor would presumably have a hard time practicing infertility medicine.

Some conservative legislators are trying to restrict access to fertility services for certain kinds of patients—most notably, single women and gays—and limit what can be done with embryos that result from IVF. Virginia tried to prohibit doctors and other health care professionals from helping single women get pregnant. (The law didn't pass.) Arizona has attempted to ban the sale of human eggs. (A bill is pending.) Louisiana has succeeded in making embryos "juridical persons," meaning they cannot be intentionally destroyed, and if they are abandoned, the clinician has discretion over what to do with them. Using ART regulation as a backdoor attack on abortion rights is a worrisome trend, says reproductive legal scholar Susan Crockin. "We're starting to hear a lot of talk about embryo adoptions even though very few are actually happening. This way, in the public's mind, you elevate embryos to fetuses, and fetuses to children, and then you can't do things with embryos."

After Benitez severed ties with the North Coast Women's Care Medical Group, she also switched jobs, because her old one required her to be in contact with North Coast and, she told me, she "couldn't handle seeing and hearing about things that they were doing for other couples that they wouldn't do for me." She fell into a depression, in part from worrying whether or not she and Clark should spend their limited earnings on ART.

> Approximately 1 in 3 births that result from IVF involve "multiples," or more than one baby.
>
> In the general population, only 3% of births involve multiples.
>
> Babies born as twins are hospitalized twice as long as singletons, and over the first five years of life, their medical costs are three times as high.
>
> Babies born as triplets have a significantly greater number of cognitive delays. The average cost of a triplet birth exceeds $500,000.
>
> For women under 36, a single embryo transfer is just as likely to result in a live birth as is transferring multiple embryos.
>
> Only 15 states mandate insurers or HMOs pay for any form of infertility treatment. Only 7 states insist insurers pay for at least one cycle of IVF. Of those, 2 states mandate the IVF benefit only if a spouse's sperm is used to fertilize his wife's egg.

Still, she did not give up on her dream of having a child. Benitez grew up in a family with 9 siblings, and never imagined not having kids. She got referred to another ART practice. Her treatments were no longer covered, but she and Clark decided to pay out of pocket for in utero insemination, twice. When Benitez still failed to get pregnant, they stepped up to pay for IVF. Luckily, Benitez conceived on her first IVF try. The couple's first child, Gabriel Benitez-Clark, is now age four.

For patients like Benitez, the best and worst thing about seeking fertility services in the United States is that ART is regulated, such as it is, by the free market, and while not every doctor will treat a nontraditional client, for the right price somebody probably will. That somebody, in fact, is frequently Geoffrey Sher, a man whose operation is so big and whose reputation is so well established he can afford not to manipulate his success rates. Sher's website, have-ababy.com, receives more than 1 million hits a month. His institute, composed of 10 franchises, offers a popular "outcome-based" fee structure, allowing any woman up to the age of 42 to pay a lump sum up front and receive a percentage back if she fails to have a baby—not just get pregnant, have a live baby—after three tries.

Sher is a wildly charismatic man, with a sturdy build, thinning dark hair, and a thick South African accent. The morning I met him, at his headquarters in Las Vegas, he was wearing jeans, sneakers, and a white lab coat and feeling full of his powers as a baby-maker. "Ten transfers today!" he announced, as he sat down in a windowless office with walls of white boards for a working lunch with his longtime business partner, Dr. Ghanima Maassarani. Sher believes every person who's medically fit has the right to access his services. In his 24 years of operation, he's turned down only a few patients for nonmedical reasons—one being a woman who wanted to harvest her eggs, fertilize them, freeze the embryos, have a sex change,

find a woman to marry, and then have his wife carry his babies. Sher came to his open-door philosophy in the early 1990s after a 51-year-old woman approached him with her 43-year-old husband. The woman wanted to get pregnant with a donated egg, and Sher told her she was too old. Maassarani retold the story: "She turned around and said, 'But who are you to judge? If my husband were 51 and I were 43, you would not have said that.' We learned a lesson: Don't make any judgments. As long as the woman is healthy, as long as she has medical clearance, as long as she can hold and carry on a pregnancy, why not?"

Other doctors take differing views. In 2005, *Fertility and Sterility* published a study concerning the screening practices in ART programs. Many clinics have been reluctant to discuss screening because, the authors wrote, "well-intended efforts to prevent the birth of a baby to a parent with a known history of violence against children could perhaps slide into discriminatory or eugenic practices." According to the study, 59 percent of ART program directors agreed that everyone has the right to have a child, yet only 44 percent agreed that fertility doctors don't have the right to decide who is a fit parent. Forty-eight percent of responding directors said they were very or extremely likely to turn away a gay couple seeking a surrogate, 38 percent said they would turn away a couple on welfare who wanted to pay for ART with Social Security checks, 20 percent said they would turn away a single woman, 17 percent would turn away a lesbian couple, 13 percent said they would turn away a couple in which the woman had bipolar disorder, 9 percent said they would turn away a couple who wanted to replace a recently deceased child, 5 percent said they would turn away a biracial couple. Are fertility clinic directors really the best people to decide who will be a good parent?

Given such a paternalistic stance, one might assume that fertility doctors would undertake only those procedures that ensure healthy outcomes, but many do not. In the early days of IVF, most doctors' approach to embryo implantation was, as Sher puts it, "Throw a bunch of spaghetti against the wall and see what sticks." In 1998, for instance, Merryl Fudel, a single, five-times-divorced, part-time airline reservations agent, 55 years old, sought and procured fertility services (IVF with donor eggs) and gave birth to quadruplets. This seems like a miracle, until you learn that the babies were born three months premature, one died eight days after birth, the others will likely have ongoing medical problems, and the hospital bill, largely footed by the state, topped $2 million in the babies' first four months.

In 2004, a review of scientific literature conducted by Johns Hopkins, the American Academy of Pediatrics, and the American Society for Reproductive Medicine found that the biggest risk of IVF is the one we're all aware of anecdotally: multiple births. More than 32 percent of IVF births involve "multiples," or more than one baby, compared to 3 percent in the general population. Nearly anything that can go wrong with a pregnancy goes wrong more often with "higher order births"—and the more babies a woman is carrying, the more frequently things go wrong. Babies born as twins are hospitalized twice as long as singletons, and over the first five years of life, their medical costs are three times as high. Babies born as triplets have a significantly greater number of cognitive delays. The average cost of a triplet birth exceeds $500,000.

Within academic medicine it is widely accepted that in most instances clinics should be practicing "single embryo transfer"—that is, placing only one embryo in a prospective mother's uterus instead of two, three, or more. Single embryo transfer is mandatory for most women in many European countries. The practice is voluntary and unpopular in the United States.

Why? Because by definition when a woman arrives in a fertility clinic, she very much wants to have a baby and has not had an easy time doing so. Since most families are paying for IVF out of pocket, if a woman wants more than one kid, there's a big economic incentive to go for two at once. ("They all want twins," says Rene Danford, patient coordinator for the Sher Institute. "Boy-girl twins. That's what they want. You're done!") And while multiple embryo transfer is no more likely to result in a baby for women under 36—it's just more likely to result in multiples—for older women it raises what can be pretty bleak odds, making the client happy and bolstering the clinic's success rates. The same is true of using donor eggs. In our pay-to-procreate system, the fertility doctor is also a businessman. Sher, arguably the best fertility businessman out there, speaks for many when he says, "My philosophy is it's not our job to tell people what to do. If someone says, 'I want four babies,' the answer is no. If someone says, 'I want three babies,' the answer is no. If someone says, 'I want two babies' and she has half a uterus because she was born that way, the answer is no. But if somebody says, 'I want to have twins' and she's healthy and I see no reason why she'll have a particularly complicated pregnancy, the answer is, 'Okay, I can do that.'"

To goose success rates, clinics encourage multiple embryo transfers and donor eggs, especially for older women. Among patients using their own eggs, the chances per IVF cycle of having a live birth are about:

37% for women age 34 and younger.

30% for women 35 to 37.

20% for women 38 to 40.

11% for women 41 to 42.

4% for women 43 and older.

But among women using donor eggs and fresh (non-frozen) embryos, the live birth rate is 49% whether the patient is 45 or only 32.

Were ART covered by insurance, insurers could pressure doctors into lowering the multiple birth rate, and everyone would save money—including insurers, because ART is relatively cheap compared with births of multiples. It would also help mitigate against the biggest injustice in the American ART system: the fact that if you are wealthy and infertile you are much more likely to have a baby (or two, or three) than if you are infertile and poor. But presently only 15 states mandate group insurers or HMOs pay for any form of ART; of those only 7 insist insurers pay for at least some IVF, and of those 2 mandate the IVF benefit only if a spouse's sperm is used to fertilize his wife's egg—no donated egg or sperm, lesbians or singles need not apply.

European governments have stepped in and regulated, to mixed results. In 2003, Italy enacted Europe's most restrictive policy, stipulating that only long-term heterosexual couples have a right to access IVF, no more than three eggs can be fertilized at any one time, and all fertilized eggs must be transferred to the uterus simultaneously. Italy has since seen pregnancy rates for women utilizing IVF drop from 38 to 30 percent. In 2004, England began limiting all doctors in all cases to implanting only two embryos. Zero women over 44 gave birth in England last year.

To skirt such rules, a Danish company plans to build a fertility ship, sailing in international waters, where people could sidestep their own country's regulations and pay for the services they want—be it transfer of multiple embryos or insemination with anonymous sperm. Fertility tourism already exists—middle-class Americans go to Israel, where services are cheaper; wealthy Europeans come here, where more treatment options are available.

None of this, however, answers the question: Is there, or should there be, a right to reproduce? Though perhaps thinking in terms of rights is not the best way to frame the problem. As Mary Warnock, former chair of the Committee of Enquiry Into Human Fertilization and Embryology in the United Kingdom, points out in her book *Making Babies: Is There a Right to Have Children?,* deep wishes easily slip into the language of rights, and patients who feel themselves to have rights over their doctors fundamentally change the doctor-patient relationship. Our system is already plenty skewed by the idea that if you throw enough money at your infertility problem, you will conceive and the problem will go away. "The patient becomes a client, the doctor obliged to provide what the patient wants. The doctor becomes more like, say, a hairdresser," Warnock writes. "People may well listen to the advice of their hairdressers, and will certainly rely on their hairdresser's skill, which they do not themselves possess. But in the last resort the hairdresser is the servant of the client."

Benitez's case is again on appeal and could reach the California State Supreme Court this fall. Lead counsel Pizer sees the case as seeking to establish a seemingly simple point: that the same framework used to protect people from discrimination in all public settings should also be used to protect people from discrimination in a fertility clinic. Yet at the heart of the case is a more emotional question: "Who is deemed acceptable to be a parent?" asks Pizer.

Benitez views her own case in less theoretical terms. "I want to make sure that these doctors can't do this to anybody else. It was horrible." She is not looking forward to taking the stand, nor to seeing Dr. Brody's face. But for now, at least, she has little time to worry. Ten months ago she gave birth to Shane and Sophia Benitez-Clark, a pair of twin girls conceived through IVF.

ELIZABETH WEIL is fascinated by the ways we build our families in the United States, and the general lack of public discussion surrounding them. A contributing writer for the *New York Times Magazine*, she is the author of *They All Laughed at Christopher Columbus*, which chronicles Gary Hudson's quest to build the first civilian spacecraft, and coauthor of *Crib Notes*, a cradle-side companion of facts and charts for new parents. Weil's work has appeared in *Time* and *Rolling Stone* and on National Public Radio's "This American Life." She lives in San Francisco.

Adopting a New American Family

Adoption plays a key role in our nation's diversity, experts say, and merits more attention from psychology.

JAMIE CHAMBERLIN

Adoption is redefining the American family: International and transracial adoptions are speeding up the nation's diversity by creating more multicultural families and communities. And as more same-sex couples and single parents adopt, and more grandparents adopt their grandchildren following parental abuse or neglect, the 21st century American family has many looks and meanings, notes journalist Adam Pertman in his best seller *Adoption Nation: How The Adoption Revolution is Transforming America* (Basic Books, 2001).

In addition, adoption itself has changed over the last 20 years, experts say. Due to policy changes in many states, adoptions tend to be much more open than in years past, when adoption records were sealed and adopted children couldn't access their personal histories. Many adopted children have contact with their biological parents—or "birth-parents." In the case of many kinship or foster-care adoptions, they may also see members of their own extended family.

The increasingly diverse adoption population, and these changes in adoption policy and practice, are spurring the need for more research, say psychologists who study adoption. For starters, says longtime adoption researcher Harold Grotevant, PhD, of the department of family social science at the University of Minnesota (UM), researchers should be studying how to help children navigate their membership in multiple families and cultures. Research is also lacking on such issues as how adults adopted as children cope with issues of identity and loss, or with emotions that emerge when they start a family.

What's more, few practitioners specialize or receive graduate training in helping clients navigate these and related issues, such as the emotions that can accompany the decision to search out a biological mother. Those who do specialize in adoption or in disorders that may accompany international adoptions, such as attachment disorders, are likely to live in metropolitan areas and may be inaccessible to families in rural areas.

"More and more, people in small towns are adopting," says Cheryl Rampage, PhD, of the Family Institute at Northwestern University. "The factors that lead to adoption happen across the spectrum and geography of the country."

Research Strides

Among those striving to fill the adoption research gaps is UM associate professor of psychology Richard Lee, PhD, who participates in the university's multidisciplinary International Adoption Project, a large-scale survey of Minnesota parents who adopted internationally between 1990 and 1998. In the project, led by developmental psychologist Megan Gunnar, PhD, UM researchers surveyed more than 2,500 parents about their children's health, development and adjustment. They also asked participants whether their employers offered leave for the adoption, how their kids have fared academically and how they managed adoption costs, among other topics.

Lee, a second-generation Korean American, says his personal friendships with many in the Korean-American adoption community spurred his interest in this overlooked segment of the Asian American population. He's using the data to explore cultural socialization practices in families who have adopted internationally. Some adoptive parents expose their children to their birth culture by sending them to language classes and culture camps or setting up playdates with other internationally adopted children. They may also make a conscious effort to talk with their child about racism and discrimination. But what's not known, Lee maintains, is how these efforts affect their children's well-being or cultural or ethnic identity, or provide a buffer against racism or discrimination as they grow older.

"We presume that if parents socialize kids in a certain way, those outcomes will be protective factors," says Lee. "But there is actually very little research on that."

Grotevant, also of UM, heads a separate longitudinal study, the Minnesota Texas Adoption Research Project, on how openness in adoption affects the adopted child and members of the "adoptive kinship network," which includes the child, the extended adoptive family and the extended birth family. Among the salient findings of the first two waves of his study—conducted when the children were between 4 and 12 years old and 12 and 20 years old—is that, within the group of families having some birth-parent contact, higher degrees of collaboration and communication between the child's adoptive parents and birth-mothers were linked to better adjustment in the children during middle childhood. Grotevant is now gathering a third wave of data as the children—now in their 20s—become adults. He's looking at how they transition from school to work, how they have fared academically, their identity and interpersonal relationships, and if they are searching for or have contact with their birth-mother.

"We know from the research literature that many adopted children are in their 20s and 30s when they begin to seek information about their birth-relatives," says Grotevant. He's also asking the young adults what advice they have for people considering adoption, which he hopes—along with the rest of his findings—can be used to inform adoption practice and policy.

Like Grotevant, Rutgers University psychologist David Brodzinsky, PhD, is hoping his findings from a national survey of adoption agency opportunities for gay and lesbian adoptive parents can guide future policy on adoption. The study, conducted in 2003 through the Evan B. Donaldson Adoption Institute, showed that 60 percent of the agencies he surveyed were willing to accept applications from gay men and lesbians, but less then 39 percent had made such placements. Only 18 to 19 percent actively recruited adoptive parents in the gay and lesbian community, he notes.

"The trend has been for supporting gay and lesbian adoption—most states do, but a few ban it or have barriers that make it difficult," says Brodzinsky, a senior fellow at the institute.

Serving Families

The majority of adoptive parents turn to adoption agencies—or social work or adoption support groups—for postadoption counseling or services, but a handful of psychologists are also serving the adoption community. Take, for example, Martha Henry, PhD, of the Center for Adoption Research at the University of Massachusetts Medical School. As director of education and training there, Henry teaches an eight-week adoption course to medical students each semester that covers such topics as how to work with adoptive and foster-care families and to discuss adoption with couples facing infertility.

When she's not teaching medical students, Henry educates elementary school teachers on ways to keep their classrooms comfortable for children who were adopted or are in the foster-care system.

"Lots of classroom assignments are based on that perfect family model with two parents, a child, a dog and a picket fence," she says, such as asking children to bring in baby pictures to teach about change. That kind of activity is inappropriate if a class includes an adopted child, adds Henry.

"There are other ways to do the same lesson with something that doesn't put a child in a situation of having to say, 'I don't have a picture from when I was a baby,'" says Henry.

Likewise, psychologist Amanda Baden, PhD, a Chinese-American who was adopted from Hong Kong, teaches a course on adoption issues—which she believes is unique in any psychology training program—as part of a master's-level counseling program at Montclair State University in New Jersey. In it, she covers many of the issues she sees in her part-time practice working with families and individuals who are part of transracial adoptions. Many of her clients struggle with such issues as whether to search for their birth-mothers and how to manage conflicts between their birth culture and race and their adopted culture and race.

Cheryl Rampage sees many of these same issues in the Northwestern University Family Institute's Adoptive Families Program, which offers counseling and psychotherapy to adoptive families and school outreach programs that train teachers on adoption sensitivity. The program also hosts the Adoption Club, a biweekly support group for local adopted 7 to 11 year olds. The club is geared to preteens because in these years, "for the first time, loss becomes a real issue," she says. Preschool-age adopted children tend to talk about their being adopted matter-of-factly, but at 7 or 8 these same children start to feel scared and sad when they think of this other family they lost, says Rampage.

Through the club, children draw family pictures, play games and write stories or perform plays about adoption.

According to Baden, the adoption community could benefit if more psychologists specialized in adoption issues like Henry and Rampage do.

"Psychologists often think adoption is social work's domain," she says. "Psychologists have a tremendous amount to offer. . . . Adoption and the issues associated with it have moved beyond the domains of case management and adoption placements. It's time for psychologists to use their skills to develop treatment protocols and counseling process research."

UNIT 3
Family Relationships

Unit Selections

Key Points to Consider

- Is marriage necessary for a happy, fulfilling life? Why is or is not that so? When you think of a marriage, what do you picture? What are your expectations of your (future) spouse? What are your expectations of yourself?

- What are your views on spanking? Why is it seen as an ineffective parenting tool? What are other alternatives? What do you think of them? Why?

- What do you think is the appropriate adult-adult relationship between parents and children? At what point should parents back away to let their children "fly"?

- Who do you include in your family? Is everyone legally tied to you?

Student Web Site
www.mhcls.com/online

Internet References

Child Welfare League of America
   http://www.cwla.org
Coalition for Marriage, Family, and Couples Education
   http://www.smartmarriages.com
The National Academy for Child Development
   http://www.nacd.org
National Council on Family Relations
   http://www.ncfr.com
Positive Parenting
   http://www.positiveparenting.com
SocioSite
   http://www.pscw.uva.nl/sociosite/TOPICS/Women.html

*A*nd they lived happily ever after . . . The romantic image conjured up by this well-known final line from fairy tales is not reflective of the reality of family life and relationship maintenance. The belief that somehow love alone should carry us through is pervasive. In reality, maintaining a relationship takes dedication, hard work, and commitment.

We come into relationships, regardless of their nature, with fantasies about how things ought to be. Partners, spouses, parents, children, siblings, and others—all family members have at least some unrealistic expectations about each other. It is through the negotiation of their lives together that they come to work through these expectations and replace them with other, it is hoped, more realistic ones. By recognizing and acting on their own contribution to the family, members can set and attain realistic family goals. Tolerance and acceptance of differences can facilitate this process as can competent communication skills. Along the way, family members need to learn new skills and develop new habits of relating to each other. This will not be easy, and, try as they may, not everything will be controllable. Factors both inside and outside the family may impede their progress.

Even before one enters a marriage or other committed relationship, attitudes, standards and beliefs influence our choices. Increasingly, choices include whether or not we should commit to such a relationship. From the start of a committed relationship, the expectations both partners have of their relationship have an impact, and the need to negotiate differences is a constant factor. Adding a child to the family affects the lives of parents in ways that they could previously only imagine. Feeling under siege, many parents struggle to know the right way to rear their children. These factors can all combine to make child rearing more difficult than it might otherwise have been. Other family relationships also evolve, and in our nuclear family focused culture, it is possible to forget that family relationships extend beyond those between spouses and parents and children.

The initial subsection presents a number of aspects regarding marital and other committed relationships, decisions about whether or not one wants to enter such a relationship, and ways of balancing multiple and often competing roles played by today's couples, who hope to fulfill individual as well as relationship needs. It is a difficult balancing act to cope with the expectations and pressures of work, home, children, and relational intimacy. The first article, "Free As a Bird and Loving It" addresses the issue of remaining single in a culture that expects adults to pair up. Next, David Wagner discusses the introduction of same-sex marriage in New Jersey. What seemed like an easy task quickly became complex. "Two Mommies and a Daddy" discusses family forms that are common in some parts of the world, but illegal in the United States. The article presents positives and drawbacks of polygamous and polyamorous families, particularly with regard to the rearing of children. As various cultural groups come to the United States, unwilling to give up the cultural activities and beliefs of their home country, changes have begun to take place regarding marriage customs. "Marriage at First Sight," the story

Corbis/PictureQuest

of arranged marriages in the U.S. Indian community, may be a sample of what to expect in the broader culture. The various forms of therapy available to couples in the United States are discussed and critiqued in the final article in this section, "Couple Therapy."

The next subsection examines the parent/child relationship. In the first article, "Kaleidoscope of Parenting Cultures," author Vidya Thirumurthy provides a look at how culture influences children. She writes about different cultures, for example, collective versus individualistic ones, and how parenting styles differ so as to affect consequent child development in each. The next article, "Do We Need a Law to Prohibit Spanking?" addresses the fact that, although research strongly supports the drawbacks of corporal punishment, legislation may be necessary to end a practice that is commonly seen as relatively benign. The next reading, "Prickly Père," addresses concerns regarding one's responsibilities toward an abusive parent. 'Helicopter', parents are the focus of "When Parents Hover Over Kids' Job Search," and 'children' who return to live at home as late as middle adulthood are the focus of the final article in this subsection, "Last Hope in a Weak Ecnomy?."

The third and final subsection looks at other family relationships. Sibling relationships can be among the most important in one's life. They can also be one of the most challenging, especially if one's siblings have special needs. "Being a Sibling" addresses this relationship from the perspective of children. Families may be formed in nontraditional ways, with nontraditional connections. Friendships can grow in significance to become affiliative family connections that rival traditional family relationships in their meaning and significance. This expanded view of who we include as family members is presented by John Tyler Connolley in "Aunties and Uncles." The final two articles in this section address issues of concern among aged family members. "Roles of American Indian Grandparents in Times of Cultural Crises" depicts a significant enculturative role for grandparents, in which they teach about and reinforce their grandchildren's ties to their cultural past. "Aging Japanese Pen Message to Posterity" depicts elderly family members serving a similar role, but in a more intimate and relationship-centered way.

Free As a Bird and Loving It

More Americans are happy to marry later—or not at all.

SHARON JAYSON

Being single means bucking the pressure to join the married half of U.S. society.

Despite lavish celebrity weddings, a multitude of dating websites and stacks of self-help books about finding your soul mate, singles are a growing segment of the population—and increasingly say they are perfectly happy with their singlehood, thank you very much.

The Census Bureau reports about 97 million unmarried Americans age 18 and over in 2006, the most recent numbers available. That represents 44% of Americans 18 and over; a quarter have never been married; 10% are divorced, 6% widowed, and 2% separated.

"It's probably the best moment for singles in our history . . . because of the attitudes of popular support and the numbers," says Pat Palmieri, a social historian at Teachers College at Columbia University, who is writing a history of singles in America since 1870. She is 60 and has never been married.

Young adults are delaying marriage and have a longer life expectancy, experts say, so more Americans will spend more of their adult lives single. As their ranks multiply, singles aren't waiting for a partner to buy a home or even have a child. They've decided to embrace singlehood for however long it lasts.

"I don't have to be dating someone to be happy," says Jennifer MacDougall, 26, an office assistant in Wilmington, N.C. She says her friends share her outlook.

"When I was younger, I thought that was how it worked. You went to college and got married. When I got to college, I realized that was not how it worked and not how I even wanted it to work. I wouldn't mind being married someday, but I want to feel comfortable with myself and what I'm doing."

That attitude may arise from the frenetic quality dating takes on after college, says Barbara Dafoe Whitehead, co-director of the National Marriage Project, a research initiative at Rutgers University.

"It is not a bad trend that we are removing the stigma from being single and talking about alternative ways to lead a single life," she says.

Households in which no one is married now make up 47.3% of the USA's 114 million households, according to recently released Census data for 2006. (Numbers from 2005 released last year showed unmarried households at a 50.3% majority, but the percentage fluctuates year to year.)

> ## "I don't have to be dating someone to be happy."
> —Jennifer MacDougall, 26 of Wilmington, N.C.

"Unmarried here means not married right now," says Andrew Cherlin, a professor of sociology and public policy at Johns Hopkins University in Baltimore. The data reflect larger numbers of elderly singles, probably widowed or divorced, and twenty- and thirty somethings who haven't tied the knot, such as unmarried people who share living quarters or romantic partners who live together.

"Most people who are single seem to want to eventually be married," says Michael Rosenfeld, author of *The Age of Independence,* about young adults living on their own. "But they're putting it off. In the past, there just weren't that many single, young adults supporting themselves. It's a new phenomenon, post-1960, and getting stronger every day."

Singles do continue to face obstacles, from work policies and tax codes that favor married couples to extra fees lone travelers must pay. But society is beginning to recognize singles' needs: Individual servings of packaged grocery items are just one example.

Also, a Pew Research Center study released last year found that most singles aren't actively looking for a committed relationship: 55% of 3,200 adults 18 and older surveyed in 2005 reported no interest in a relationship. For ages 18–29, 38% said they weren't looking for a partner.

"When I graduated from college, I spent more time not in relationships than in relationships," says Len Sparks, 37, an engineer from Boston who says he's now in a relationship.

"Most of my 20s, I just didn't date. I had one relationship. Outside of that, I just worked. I worked really hard and was getting promotions and changing jobs and moving from city to city."

Bella DePaulo, 53, a social psychologist and author of *Singled Out: How Singles Are Stereotyped, Stigmatized, and Ignored and Still Live Happily Ever After,* says most books for singles try to teach "how to become un-single. What I love about my single life are the nearly limitless opportunities it offers," she says.

Other new books touting the solo-is-fine theme:

- *Better Single Than Sorry: A No-Regrets Guide to Loving Yourself and Never Settling* by Jen Schefft, who appeared on TV in *The Bachelor* and *The Bachelorette* and rebuffed two marriage proposals.
- *I'd Rather Be Single Than Settle: Satisfied Solitude and How to Achieve It* by Emily Dubberley, a relationship and sex writer from Brighton, England.
- *Naked on the Page: The Misadventures of My Unmarried Midlife* by Jane Ganahl, who previously wrote a newspaper column called "Single Minded."

- *On My Own: The Art of Being a Woman Alone* by Florence Falk, a "60-plus" psychotherapist in New York City.
- *Singular Existence: Because It's Better to be Alone Than Wish You Were!* by Leslie Talbot of Boston, founder of the website SingularExistence.com.

"We do have an unfortunate tendency to favor couples and perhaps disparage single people," Cherlin says. "These books are aimed at boosting the self-image of single people."

DePaulo agrees not everything is rosy. "I don't love everything about being single," she says. "I don't like the stigma or the stereotyping or the discrimination."

Talbot says she wrote her book to counter the belief that being single is "a deficiency or liability—a temporary condition that hopefully, if you're lucky, you'll get over."

She says there's a fine line between being alone and lonely. "There's nothing lonelier than being with somebody you don't want to be with."

Gay Marriage Lite

New Jersey's high court doesn't quite go all the way.

DAVID M. WAGNER

If not New Jersey, then (besides Massachusetts) where? A liberal state with no explicit prohibition on same-sex marriage in state law, and no law barring state officials from performing such marriages for out-of-staters—New Jersey would seem the perfect state in which to persuade the highest court to duplicate the Massachusetts holding. There the supreme judicial court declared that no rational basis exists for restricting marriage to opposite-sex couples, and that same-sex marriage must, then, be enacted posthaste.

Yet it didn't quite happen that way in Trenton. Instead, in *Lewis* v. *Harris,* handed down October 25, the Supreme Court of New Jersey went for what, in the present state of the marriage debate, passes for a Solomonic compromise: Hold that same-sex couples must be given all the legal benefits of marriage, but leave to the legislature the issue of whether the resulting legal relationship is to be called "marriage." This is similar to the path followed by the court in Vermont in creating those states' "civil unions." For the New Jersey court, no "substantial" basis exists for withholding from same-sex couples the benefits of marriage. Yet one may exist for reserving the name "marriage"—and the social symbolism that goes with it—to opposite-sex couples.

Remarkably, for an opinion that insists on equalizing the rights of same- and opposite-sex couples, *Lewis* v. *Harris* nonetheless recognizes that the U.S. Supreme Court's landmark 1967 decision *Loving* v. *Virginia,* striking down racial restrictions on marriage, does *not* create a "right to marry" independent of all traditional and societal understandings of what marriage is. "The heart of the [1967] case," the New Jersey court notes, "was invidious discrimination based on race, the very evil that motivated the passage of the Fourteenth Amendment."

"Despite the rich diversity of this State," the court continues (passing the hanky), "the tolerance and goodness of its people, and the many recent advances made by gays and lesbians toward achieving social acceptance and equality under the law, we cannot find that a right to same-sex marriage is so deeply rooted in the traditions, history, and conscience of the people of this State that it ranks as a fundamental right." New Jerseyans are good, it seems, but not *that* good.

After so holding, the court turns to the passage of the New Jersey Constitution that most closely tracks the U.S. Constitution's equal protection clause. For any suspect government classification (such as the one reserving marriage to male-female couples), New Jersey weighs "three factors: the nature of the right at stake, the extent to which the challenged statutory scheme restricts that right, and the public need for the statutory restriction."

The court then sums up the extensive rights that New Jersey has bestowed upon same-sex couples, and notes the "remaining" rights that are not included in the state's Domestic Partnership Act. Is there a reason, the court asks, for not sliding all the way down this slope?

"The State does not argue that limiting marriage to the union of a man and a woman is needed to encourage procreation or to create the optimal living environment for children." California did not press an affirmative case for traditional marriage either; that state's intermediate appeals court nonetheless deferred to legislative judgment. But New Jersey's legislature has *not* said that marriage is one man and one woman, and it *has* said that distinctions based on sexual orientation are to be removed. Given this legislative background, it takes perhaps only a smidgen of judicial activism to conclude: "It is difficult to understand how withholding the remaining 'rights and benefits' from committed same-sex couples is compatible with a 'reasonable conception of basic human dignity and autonomy.'" The court then ordered the legislature to correct its oversight in the next 180 days.

Despite the admittedly "extraordinary remedy," the four-judge majority nonetheless scolds its three dissenting colleagues, who wanted to order up same-sex marriage right now, Massachusetts-style. "We cannot escape," it says, "the political reality that the shared societal meaning of marriage—passed down through the common law into our statutory law—has always been the union of a man and a woman. To alter that meaning would render a profound change in the public consciousness of a social institution of ancient origin."

Speculation will swirl as to what drove this strange mixture of activism and restraint. It could be a set-up: If the legislature responds by enacting Vermont-style civil unions that are not called "marriage," the court can, in inevitable litigation to follow, hold that the legislature had not shown a "substantial" reason for a difference of nomenclature. The result would be a Massachusetts-style same-sex marriage mandate, only without an election-year backlash. Or it could be they blinked: Public resistance to same-sex marriage is being felt in the courts, and the New Jersey Supreme Court is, by its own admission—nay, proclamation—sensitive to changes in "times and attitudes."

DAVID M. WAGNER teaches constitutional law at Regent University, and blogs at ninomania.blogspot.com.

Two Mommies and a Daddy

ELIZABETH MARQUARDT

This spring HBO debuted a television series, *Big Love,* that features a likable polygamous family in Utah. An article in a March issue of *Newsweek,* headlined "Polygamists Unite!" quotes a polygamy activist saying, "Polygamy is the next civil rights battle." He argues, "If Heather can have two mommies, she should also be able to have two mommies and a daddy." That weekend on the *Today Show,* hosts Lester Holt and Campbell Brown gave a sympathetic interview to a polygamous family.

Western family law has so far not permitted children to have more than two legal (biological or adoptive) parents. This limitation could soon be a thing of the past. Trends in science, law and culture are threatening the two-person understanding of marriage and of parenthood. Though most advocates of same-sex marriage say they do not support group marriage, the partial success of the gay-marriage movement has emboldened others to borrow the language of civil rights to break open further our understanding of marriage.

If two parents are good for children, are three even better?

During the same month that *Big Love* debuted, the *New York Times* devoted much attention to the subject of polygamy. One article featured several polygamous women watching *Big Love's* first episode and sharing their view that polygamy "can be a viable alternative lifestyle among consenting adults." In an article in the paper's business section, an economist snickered that polygamy is illegal mainly because it threatens male lawmakers who fear they wouldn't get wives in such a system. In a separate piece, columnist John Tierney argued that "polygamy isn't necessarily worse than the current American alternative: serial monogamy." He concluded: "If the specter of legalized polygamy is the best argument against gay marriage, let the wedding bells ring."

It is not just *Big Love* that is putting polygamy in play in North America. In a development that shocked many Canadians this winter, two government studies released by the Justice Department in Ottawa recommended that polygamy be decriminalized. One report argued that the move is justified by the need to attract skilled Muslim immigrants.

Besides this movement for polygamy ("many marriages"), there is a movement on behalf of polyamory ("many loves"). Polyamory involves relationships of three or more people, any two of whom might or might not be married to one another. Whereas polygamists are generally heterosexual, polyamorous people variously consider themselves straight, gay, bisexual or just plain "poly." Polyamorists distinguish themselves from the "swingers" of the 1970s, saying that their relationships emphasize healthy communication and what they call "ethical nonmonogamy."

Polyamorous unions have been around for a while, but now they and their supporters are seeking increased visibility and acceptance. A recent *Chicago Sun-Times* article mentioned the "Heartland Polyamory Conference" to be held this summer in Indiana. (A similar Midwestern polyamory conference was held two years ago in Wisconsin.) A *Chicago Tribune* article in February featured Fred, Peggy, Bill, John and Sue, the latter two a married couple, who share their beds in various ways. The reporter termed them an "energetic bunch" of polyamorists. And articles about polyamory routinely appear in alternative periodicals such as the *Village Voice* and *Southern Voice* and, increasingly, in campus newspapers.

Support for polyamory and polygamy is found not only on the fringes. The topic is also emerging at the cutting edge of family law. Dan Cere of McGill University cites some examples, including: a substantial legal defense of polyamory published by University of Chicago law professor Elizabeth Emens in the *New York University Law Review;* a major report, "Beyond Conjugality," issued by the influential Law Commission of Canada, which queried whether legally recognized relationships should be "limited to two people"; and *An Introduction to Family Law* (Oxford University Press), in which a British law professor observes that "the abhorrence of bigamy appears to stem . . . from the traditional view of marriage as the exclusive locus for a sexual relationship and from a reluctance to contemplate such a relationship involving multiple partners."

Columnist Stanley Kurtz recently noted that a number of legal scholars are calling for the decriminalization of polygamy, including Jonathon Turley of George Washington University, who wrote a widely noticed opinion piece in *USA Today* in October 2004. According to Kurtz, a significant number of legal scholars argue that "the abuses of polygamy flourish amidst the isolation, stigma, and secrecy spawned by criminalization." In other words, the problem is not polygamy but the stigmatizing of it.

Meanwhile, the Alternatives to Marriage Project, whose leaders are often featured by mainstream news organizations in stories on cohabitation and same-sex marriage, includes polyamory among its "hot topics" for advocacy. Among religious organizations the Unitarian Universalists for Polyamorous Awareness hope to make theirs the first to recognize and bless polyamorous relationships (see www.uupa.org).

Advocates for polyamory often explicitly mimic the language used by gays, lesbians and bisexuals and their supporters. They say they must keep their many loves in the closet; that they cannot risk revealing their personal lives for fear of losing their jobs or custody of their children; that being poly is just who they are.

Web sites for practitioners of polyamory devote considerable space to the challenges of being a poly parent. On a blog at LiveJournal.com, one mom says, "Polyamory is what my kids know. They know some people have two parents, some one, some three and some more. They happen to have four. Honestly? Kids and polyamory? Very little of it affects them unless you're so caught up in your new loves you're letting it interfere with your parenting."

An older mom advises a young poly mother-to-be who isn't sure how to manage a new baby and her poly lifestyle: "Having a child . . . and being poly isn't exactly a cakewalk, but . . . it is possible. Sometimes it means that you take the baby with you to go see your OSO [other significant other], or your OSO spends more time at the house with you, your husband, and the baby. . . . There is a lot of patience that is needed from all parties involved, but it can be done. The first six months are extremely hard."

A pro-poly Web site despairs: "One challenge that faces poly families is the lack of examples of poly relationships in literature and media." A sister site offers the "PolyKids Zine." This publication for kids "supports the principles and mission of the Polyamory Society." It contains "fun, games, uplifting Poly-Family stories and lessons about PolyFamily ethical living." Its book series includes *The Magical Power of Mark's Many Parents* and *Heather Has Two Moms and Three Dads*.

A different set of challenges to the two-person understanding of marriage and parenthood is emerging from medical labs.

Scientists are experimenting with creating artificial sperm and eggs and fusing them in unexpected ways to create human embryos for implantation in the womb. Last year, British scientists at Newcastle University were granted permission to create a human embryo with three genetic parents. A team in Edinburgh announced that it had tricked an egg into dividing and created the first human embryo without a genetic father. But evidence from experiments with animals suggests that the physical—not to mention psychological—risks for such embryos and children are enormous. In Japan in 2004, scientists created a mouse with two genetic mothers and no genetic father. To achieve this result, they created over 450 embryos, of which 370 were implanted. Only ten were born alive, and only one survived to adulthood.

In the current explosion of reproductive technology the law is gasping to stay in last place. For example, only now are some nations beginning to recognize the moral and health risks of sperm donation, a relatively low-tech reproductive technology that has been in use for at least 40 years. Responding to donor-conceived adults who say they desperately wish to know and have a relationship with their sperm-donor fathers, expert commissions last year in New Zealand and Australia recommended allowing sperm and egg donors to opt in as third legal parents for children.

Such a move promises to create as many problems as it solves. Just one likely result: as soon as children are assigned three or more legal parents, the argument for legalizing group marriage will almost certainly go something like this, "Why should children with three legal parents be denied the same legal and social protections as children with only two parents have?"

Pity the children. We frequently see the havoc wreaked on children's lives when two parents break up and fight over their best interests. Imagine when three or more adults break up and disagree over the children to whom each has an equal claim. How many homes will we require children to grow up traveling between to satisfy the parenting needs of all these adults?

If two parents are good for children, are three even better? Should scientists try to make babies from three people, or babies with no genetic father (or mother)? Is the two-parent, mother-father model important for children, or does it just reflect a passing fixation of our culture? The debate is upon us.

ELIZABETH MARQUARDT is director of the Center for Marriage and Families at the Institute for American Values. This article is based on a report to be released in August by the Commission on Parenthood's Future.

Marriage at First Sight

They date, go to U2 concerts, hit bars with pals. But for the sake of tradition and family, even some highly Americanized Indian immigrants agree to wed strangers.

PAULA SPAN

On the evening before her engagement, Vibha Jasani found herself on the rooftop terrace of her uncle's house in India, feeling a breeze begin as the sun lowered, gazing out at the city of Rajkot and the mountains beyond, trying to be calm, and failing. She was about to cry, and not with joy.

When her father asked what was wrong, she just shrugged; she could hardly manage a reply. But he knew anyway.

Marrying a pleasant young man she'd just met was not the romance Vibha envisioned when she was a teenager playing volleyball at Annandale High; it was not the kind of courtship she yakked about with her friends at Virginia Tech or her co-workers in Arlington. This felt like—and was—a custom held over from a previous century. But because she was 25 and not-getting-any-younger, her parents had prevailed on her to do something she'd repeatedly vowed she wouldn't: fly to India to find a husband.

She'd spent the past three weeks meeting men—at least one each day—carefully prescreened by her uncle for their suitability. She'd poured them tea and passed platters of sweets and nuts, enduring awkward half-hour conversations that seemed more like interviews. She chose the one she could talk most comfortably with; they went out together three or four times; she met his family. All parties approved, and suddenly 300 people were about to stream into a rented hall the next day to celebrate their engagement, which everyone seemed delighted about, except the prospective bride.

"Everything's so out of control," Vibha worried. "Things just sort of happened." She'd gone along with the flurry of events, sometimes resentfully and sometimes obligingly, but she wasn't sure she could bring herself to take the next step. Her almost-fiancé, Haresh, appeared to be a nice guy—mature, considerate. But was he the man she wanted to spend the next 50 years with? How could she possibly know after such a brief time? What if, once she returned home to Northern Virginia, she was miserable with someone who'd grown up in such a different culture? Or he was? Divorce was not an acceptable option among Indians, in their home country or their new one.

"It's a shot in the dark," she thought, fearful of making a mistake. Maybe she should put a stop to it. Her eyes started to brim.

Her father, not a demonstrative man by nature, gave her a hug. "We only want you to do this if you're 100 percent sure," he told her in their native Gujarati. "If you're not, you don't have to . . . We just want you to be happy."

She looked at him—his eyes were reddening, too—and felt her opposition ebb away. "Screw it," she decided. "Okay. I can do it."

So the engagement proceeded last March, Vibha wearing a beautiful turquoise ensemble called a lengha and a blank expression. Guests were laughing and celebrating afterward, and she was thinking, with mingled panic and resignation, "Omigod, I'm engaged. I'm *done*." She packed up that night, flew home the following day and began planning a late-November wedding to a man she barely knew.

Now, with the big event just weeks away, Vibha (pronounced VEE-bah) flits around the Beltway, booking a deejay, making last-minute menu decisions, choosing the elaborate henna designs that will be applied to her hands and feet for the ceremony.

Yet even as she checks off the chores in a notebook she's labeled "wedding journal," uncertainty continues to eat at her. Should she really go through with this? Is she doing the right thing?

Arranged Happiness

Vinay Sandhir used to voice a lot of the same doubts about getting married the traditional way. He'd find his own spouse, he insisted. He didn't want a lot of familial meddling. He wanted to fall in love; in fact, "I wanted to be blown off my feet." But he was still single at 33, so one evening, his parents sat him down at their dining room table and had that same you're-not-getting-any-younger talk. So here he is in his home office in Annandale—he's an MBA and a management consultant in health care—printing out the latest batch of e-mailed responses to a matrimonial ad his parents placed in the weekly newspaper *India Abroad.* It read:

Punjabi parents desire beautiful, professional, never married, US raised girl for handsome son, 34, 5'10''/150, fair, slim, athletic, engineer/MBA, consultant in DC area. Enjoys travel, sports, music. Please reply . . .

Some of these criteria come from his parents. Vinay (pronounced Vin-NEIGH) thinks it's pointless to talk about appearances—though he himself actually *is* good-looking, rangy and dark-eyed, with an easy grin—since "everyone thinks their kids are beautiful." Nor does he particularly care which Indian state someone's forebears come from. But on this issue, he's yielded to the elder Sandhirs, who will be visiting this evening and will review the new candidates. They think someone from their home region would prove more "compatible."

Education is something they all agree on. The Sandhir family tree is heavy with doctors, including Vinay's father and two elder brothers and their wives. Vinay's intended need not be a physician, but he wants her to be ambitious and successful, "talented at what she does."

The "US raised" stipulation, on the other hand, comes from Vinay, who was 4 when his family settled in Western Maryland. He plays basketball a couple of times a week, lives to scale mountains (that's Mount Rainier—he's climbed it three times—on his screen saver) and ski and raft, caught five U2 concerts during last year's tour. He can't see himself with a woman raised in India, regardless of her graduate degrees. He wants a partner as Americanized as he is, "someone who's shared my experiences, someone I can laugh about things with, someone I don't have to explain everything to."

If such a prospect should surface in this batch, his parents will e-mail her parents, attaching his photo and "biodata," a document providing particulars and describing him as "intelligent, independent, dynamic . . . also deeply family-oriented and compassionate." If he passes muster, her parents will provide a phone number or e-mail address. Meanwhile, each family will conduct discreet background checks, making inquiries through friends and acquaintances to ensure the other is cultured, respectable, acceptable.

This week's possibilities, Vinay notices, include a health analyst in Toronto; an MBA from NYU; a Maryland social worker. "She'll probably get nixed just because she's older than me," he predicts. Oops, here's a woman he went out with a few times last year, until she stopped answering his e-mails. Chuck that one.

Which leaves 18 new responses to add to the 30 or so they've already received. "I didn't see anything totally, totally great," Vinay says. But he's loosened his requirements, having learned over the past months that this whole arranged marriage thing is more complicated than he'd foreseen.

The Lure of a Love Marriage

Love and marriage, in that order. The ethos so dominates mainstream Western culture, from Billboard charts to Hallmark racks, that other matrimonial approaches barely register. But in much of the Muslim world, in many Asian societies, among Hasidic Jews, and certainly in India—which has sent roughly three-quarters of a million immigrants to the United States since 1980—it's still common for people to pair up the other way around: marriage first, set up by one's elders and wisers, and then, with time, love. It's the historic norm, anthropologists say, not only the way kings and queens cemented strategic alliances, but the way ordinary folks—colonial Americans included—got hitched until comparatively recently.

It's how Vinay's parents married in 1959. Though his mother had never seen his father (he'd glimpsed her), she agreed to the engagement because she trusted her eldest sister, who'd set up the match. Vibha's parents had actually met—she silently served him tea—but hadn't exchanged a word. The album they keep to remember their 1975 wedding looks wonderfully romantic, with black-and-white photos of the groom arriving on horseback and the bride garlanded with marigolds, but they were strangers.

The process is so different now that young Indian Americans, who tend to shudder at the term "arranged marriage," cast about for more palatable phrases. "Semi-arranged marriage," for instance, or "arranged introduction." The updated version is no longer coercive (both the bride and groom have veto power), and traditional dowry transactions have largely been replaced, at least among the urban elite, by mutual exchanges of jewelry and clothing.

Some see these matches as a last resort, but since a single person who's reached the mid-twenties (for a woman) or late twenties (for a man) is probably causing an Indian family some anxiety, the need for a last resort can crop up fairly early in life. So if people haven't met spouses through school or work, or at networking events intended to bring marriageable Indians together, or via Web sites like *Indianmatchmaker.com*, or through newer permutations like the speed-dating sessions staged by a District firm called Mera Pyar ("My Love"), their parents may take up the traditional role.

They run ads, canvass Web sites, put the word out on the community grapevine: Dad's aunt knows a nice Bengali family in Atlanta whose nephew is an electrical engineer. Mom's medical school classmate in Detroit has a cousin with a single daughter working with computers in Bangalore.

After their parents perform due diligence—Hindu marriages are considered a union of two families, not merely two individuals, so bloodlines and reputations matter—the children meet and spend time together and decide whether their relationship has a future. A voluntary process, no different from having your friends fix you up, the fixed-up like to say.

But it *is* different. Families—many of whom disapprove of or forbid dating—don't want to introduce their kids to someone to hang out with or move in with; they want a wedding, and soon. Vinay's relatives think that after he's spent three or four evenings with a woman, he ought to know: She's his future bride or she's history. ("Not how it's going to work," he tells them.) And while both generations talk about having choices, most parents hope kids will choose to marry people of the same religious and ethnic background, the proper socioeconomic and educational level, acceptable lineage. Those are the factors that determine compatibility, not whether both parties treasure walking in the rain.

"It's a little like a debutante ball—'You can select freely, from among this preselected group of people,'" says anthropologist Johanna Lessinger, author of *From the Ganges to the Hudson.*

The so-called Second Generation of Indian immigrants (born here) and the 1.5 Generation (born there, raised here) are growing increasingly restive at these restrictions. They go off to college, where many date and have sex while their parents maintain a don't ask/don't tell policy. After that, though there are no reliable statistics, a growing number appear to opt for the do-it-yourself model known as a "love marriage." It's what Vibha and Vinay expected for themselves.

A preliminary analysis of Indian intermarriage rates in the United States by sociologist Maitrayee Bhattacharyya, a Princeton doctoral candidate, documents this trend. The 1990 Census showed that more than 13 percent of Indian men in this country, and 6 percent of women, were married to non-Indians—clearly love marriages, since Indian families might accept but wouldn't actively arrange such matches. But the rates for those born in the United States were dramatically higher, and among U.S.-born Indians under 35, about half had "married out." Those numbers may decline in the 2000 Census (that data is not yet available) because continuing immigration has broadened the pool, making it easier to meet an Indian spouse. Even so, for many immigrant families the love marriage remains a worrisome phenomenon.

So for all the change, the consensus is that most Indian American parents continue to exert significant influence over their children's courtships, and arranged marriages are common in Fairfax County as well as in Gujarat, the northwest Indian state Vibha's family started emigrating from more than 30 years ago.

Elders are better at this, the theory goes. "At least you know a bit about the boy, who he is and what he does, rather than just being emotional, being attracted to physical appearances, 'Oh, he's so cute,'" explains Vibha's aunt Induben Jasani. "Does he come from a good family? Does he have good morals and values? Character is something we can see a little better than youngsters do."

Besides, arranged marriages help keep traditions alive, stem the tendency toward out-marriage. "There's a sense of ethnic identity tied up in it," Lessinger says. "This is a way of holding on to their Indian-ness."

But a bubbly culture-straddler like Vibha—who's lived here since she was 5 and grew up watching *Xena: Warrior Princess,* who speaks Gujarati at home but elsewhere uses 80-mph unaccented English punctuated with *like* and *y'know* and *kinda deal,* who loves Bollywood movies but relaxes from pre-wedding stress by seeing the Eminem flick *8 Mile*—isn't always sure how much Indianness to keep and how much Americanness to embrace. She calls herself "pretty much a mix," and in trying to negotiate the milestone of marriage, she sometimes finds herself pretty much mixed up.

Giving It a Shot

"Very hard work, a wedding," says Vibha's father, Ramesh Patel, on a Saturday afternoon with the event bearing down on them. On the living room rug, relatives are helping with the task of the day: dozens of small silver cows, favors for wedding guests, must be enfolded in red or gold foil, then inserted into matching silk bags. Vibha, padding around in bare feet and rumpled clothes, hair in a ponytail, is steeling herself for an afternoon of errands. "Work-run-work-run"—that's her life these days.

This Colonial-style home is what families have in mind when they call themselves, in matrimonial ads, "well settled in U.S.," with a deck overlooking the yard and a Mercedes in the driveway. It looks like any of the other houses along the winding street, except for the rack near the front door where people place their shoes when they enter, and the carved wooden shrine in the dining room where her mother, Shanta, prays daily to Hindu deities. The Patels (Vibha's parents have taken the name of their caste as a surname; Vibha uses the family name Jasani) bought this place in North Springfield 15 years ago, when Ramesh was working 90 hours a week in two different restaurants, saving obsessively to buy a Dunkin' Donuts franchise. He now owns three, in Maryland, while Shanta works at the Postal Service facility at Dulles.

Vibha, who moved home after graduating from Virginia Tech in psychology and management, is in human resources at NCS Pearson, a half-hour drive away in Arlington. She's the eldest of the Patels' three daughters, and by the time she'd been out of school for two years, well, "you have no idea how much the pressure is on for an Indian woman."

"We were worrying," her mother concurs, keeping one eye on the cow-wrapping. "Time was passing." They would have accepted a son-in-law Vibha found on her own, she says. "She had freedom. We didn't tell her no." But "she didn't like anybody. She couldn't find anybody."

To Vibha, this constitutes considerable revisionism. Her own account—mostly related in a series of cell-phone conversations as she drives home from work in her slightly scuffed Honda—reflects the tensions between Indian customs and American expectations.

She had a couple of fairly serious relationships with men in high school and college, for instance, but never dared to tell her parents about them. "It's a no-no; you don't date," she explains one night, steering past the multicultural neon strip malls of Columbia Pike and then along Braddock Road—practically the only time in the day she's alone and free to talk. Anyway, those guys were a "didn't-work-out kinda deal." After graduation, she and her friends went to bars and clubs in the District, drinking and dancing, playing pool with friends, flirting. A smiley extrovert with vast dark eyes, she had no trouble meeting men. It was fun, but "the person you want to marry, you're probably not going to meet in a club," she decided.

Which was starting to matter. Apart from the pointed questions about marriage from family and friends (the Jasani/Patel clan in Northern Virginia, expanding as more relatives immigrate, now numbers about 80), Vibha herself felt increasingly ready to settle down, as virtually all her South Asian friends already had. "I was tired of all these casual relationships," she says. "I wanted something serious."

Her family's first matchmaking effort, an ad in *India Abroad,* led to a few desultory dates with men who met their ethnic, religious, linguistic, dietetic (the family is vegetarian) and socioeconomic standards. "Didn't click," Vibha found. So her parents returned to a favorite theme. "They'd bring it up, then drop it, then bring it up a month later: 'What do you think of going to India to look for a guy?'"

She resisted for months; she'd spent time in India and feared a "culture gap" with Indian men. "I'm being stereotypical when I say this, but I thought they'd want a wife at home, cooking and cleaning and taking care of them." Vibha had seen her mother play this role daily. "I'm traditional, but I'm not *that* traditional. I wanted someone who'd be fifty-fifty with everything, someone to share the responsibilities." She didn't think she'd find him in Gujarat.

But the Patels didn't drop the idea, and Indian daughters hesitate to defy their parents. Many times her mother had prepared vegetarian meals for Vibha while she was away at college, and her father had driven nearly five hours to Blacksburg to deliver them, then turned around and headed home—how could she now dismiss their wishes? Her father's eldest brother, dying in a nearby hospice with the whole family gathered around, yearned to see her engaged—shouldn't she give him this final pleasure?

"I was just like, okay, I'll give it a shot." She'd get her parents off her case, she told girlfriends from work, assuring them that she expected to return unattached. She and her mother left on their mission a year ago Valentine's Day, with a return flight booked in three weeks.

Thirty Men in Three Weeks

At her uncle's stucco house in Rajkot, Vibha donned a salwar kameez, a tunic over pants with a long scarf. Her uncle had culled 30 suitors from the hundred who'd responded to local newspaper ads, and day after day, as each came to call, the encounters unfolded the same way. First, her mother and uncle chatted briefly with the potential bridegroom as Vibha served refreshments ("I hate that!"). Then the young people could retreat to another room for a brief stab at getting to know each other.

The first man to call was a physician, "fairly intelligent, attractive kinda guy," accompanied by his parents. Their dialogue consisted of a series of standard questions: Hi, how are you? When did you arrive? How was your trip? Tell me about your family: Do you have brothers and sisters? What are your interests? She ran through the responses—fine, thanks; yesterday; uneventful; two sisters; movies and music and computers—that would soon come to feel routine. Meanwhile, she was muttering to herself, "I don't want to do this. Why do I have to do this?" This guy, she concluded, "wasn't that interested, and I wasn't that interested." Next.

There were engineers and pharmacists and dentists. Some, she could tell in the first two minutes, were ruling her out because her complexion was coppery (there's a cultural preference for light skin) or because she was "normal-sized," not super-slim. That was fine, because anyone who couldn't see beyond looks, who didn't notice that she had a brain and a personality, "I'm like, forget you."

Some seemed a bit intimidated; she wasn't deferential, she was fluent in both Gujarati and English. A few seemed more attracted to her U.S. citizenship, marriage being a legal and comparatively quick route to a green card, than to her. After each session, her family wanted to know how she liked the latest candidate, whether she wanted to get engaged, "like I was going to decide on the spot."

Take the "doctor guy," for whom her family had high hopes. He prattled on about how prestigious his university was and how well he was doing there; he had the self-awareness of a coconut. Her family was disappointed by Vibha's blase response. A doctor! From one of the best schools! "But I didn't believe anything my parents said. They just wanted me to get married." Next.

Though the encounters got easier as the days passed, and she tried to keep an open mind as her uncle had advised, she couldn't really embrace the process. "I'm like, 'No.' 'No.' 'No.'"

The exception was Haresh Umaretiya, slotted in at the last minute when someone canceled. He came by before Vibha had time to dress up or tense up—a tallish engineer her own age, friendly eyes, high cheekbones, "the first one I had a decent conversation with." He was interested in what she had to say. When she asked what he enjoyed doing, "He said, 'I like observing people.' I'm in psychology; we had things in common . . . He was honest, which was nice . . . I thought, 'Okay, this could work.'"

He also enjoyed their meeting, it turned out. He thought Vibha was beautiful, but more important, "if you meet local Indian girls, they are shy, they can't reply," he'd found. "She is educated. And she is forward, she can talk." Though frankly, when he called a few days later to see if she'd like to go out, it was her fever to flee the house and the marriage marathon, as much as a desire to see him again, that prompted her to agree.

They went to a local park, bought ice cream cones, sat on the grass and talked. "Totally general, nothing serious. I loved that," Vibha says. "It was like meeting a friend. I felt at ease with him. I had a nice time." A few days later they went to a movie and had dinner together. Three meetings—two more than most local women would've had, an allowance made for Vibha's Western ways—and then it was time to meet his family. "Omigod, a good 20 people came, his father, his brother, his brother's wife, his mom, his aunt, his other aunt . . . They're all staring at me. Normally, you're supposed to bow your head, not look people in the eye; I'm just sitting there smiling. They're shocked, but they think, 'Well, she's American, she doesn't know.'" They approved anyway.

In Western conceptions of romance, lovers supposedly get carried away by passion. In Indian culture, the wedding process itself sweeps people along, a dizzying round of planning and shopping and crowds and gifts and excitement. Yet even as she agreed to proceed and preparations were underway, Vibha agonized.

From her earlier relationships, she'd learned to be a bit wary of American casualness, people's willingness to dump a girlfriend or boyfriend and then start dating someone new two weeks later. But she had also discovered what it was to fall in love. "This wasn't the same feeling, and I knew the difference so well. I was like, 'Do I really want to be with someone I don't know, and don't know if I'll ever love? Whoa.'"

She swallowed her doubts after her father flew over for the engagement, and they had that teary last-minute talk on the rooftop. After the engagement party, though, when she and Haresh were finally alone in a room, he wanted to kiss her. "And I'm just like, no."

The Sandhir Scale

Vinay Sandhir managed to stave off such dilemmas for years. He had a grand time in a coed dorm at West Virginia University and still skis, hikes and tailgates with his friends from the honors program there. Afterward, he had an "American" girlfriend for six years, a fact he never shared with his parents and they seemed not to notice, even though she was virtually living with him, retreating to her own apartment when they came to visit.

His family is "really conservative" and wouldn't have accepted it, Vinay believes, "unless I was sure I wanted to marry her and fight for her." But he wasn't sure.

When that relationship ended, he dated a business school classmate and a military administrator. Then came the dining room table confrontation. Like most traditional Indians, his parents don't consider their parental duty done until all their children have married. Vinay protested. "I'd say, 'It *is* done! I'm educated! I'm successful!'" He usually turned their inquiries aside with a vague, "We'll see."

But this time he said, "Okay, try it your way." Since childhood, he had felt more American than Indian, but "some soul-searching" after his breakup had led to a realization: "I don't want to be the person who ends the relationship with India and the culture of Indian-ness."

That meant marrying an Indian American, though on his own terms and timetable. So he's been good-naturedly working with his parents to write his 35-word ad and pass along the responses; he's had long phone conversations with prospects he hasn't met; he's launched the series of dinners and brunches that will reveal if any of them "knock my socks off."

If only he could use that decision software a grad school professor gave him. "It would be absolutely perfect! It takes qualitative criteria and gives them a quantitative score." As it happens, though, Vinay has a nondigital means to the same end—his father has developed numeric rankings for the women whose parents respond to their ad. Call it the Sandhir Scale.

"We're not prejudiced against anybody," says Sikander Lal Sandhir, after he and his wife, Prabhat, an elegant couple, have arrived at their son's townhouse and greeted him with affectionate banter. "We're trying to find common factors, language, ancestral background, ethnicity, education. . . We might be able to guide Vinay."

Everyone settles in Vinay's living room, the stack of new printouts on the coffee table; his father takes out a pen. Some applicants don't even merit a score. The social worker, as Vinay predicted, gets an inked N for Not Rated. "This girl, unfortunately, is almost two years older than Vinay," his father murmurs in his formal English. "We'd prefer a girl who is younger; that's the norm in our culture. And it makes more sense. To start a family at 36—as a physician, I know there could be problems." On to the MBA from NYU.

His scale awards points for education and professional accomplishment: three for an MD or MBA, two for a CPA, one for a bachelor's degree. A woman gets a point if she's a Punjabi Hindu (half a point if she's northern Indian from another state), a point if she's born or raised in this country (deduct half a point if she's been here less than 10 years), a point for a desirable family background. Various physical attributes—slimness, height, fair skin, general attractiveness—can add up to four points. No one's ever received a perfect 10, but anyone with a 6.5 or higher is worth pursuing.

The MBA from NYU, for instance, "has been here for a while, and her family background is similar to ours; the father is a physician," Vinay's father muses, jotting notes. With an Ivy League undergraduate degree, "she gets good marks for her education." He's unimpressed with her photo ("I think she is so-so"), but overall she gets a 6.5. He passes the pages to his wife, who approves, and to Vinay, who shrugs but will forward his standard biodata package.

Sadly, the Sandhir Scale has proved more useful in theory than in reality. Take the dentist from Upstate New York whom his father had rated a 9. After several promising phone chats, Vinay flew up to visit and discovered "a very proper girl" who hadn't left India until she was 18. They seemed culturally out of synch. "No sparks or anything," he decided. Not wanting to make snap judgments, he invited her to Virginia and planned a lively weekend: an Orioles game, hiking in the Shenandoah Valley, brunch on Capitol Hill. Still no sparks. Trying to be gentlemanly, he called afterward to say he'd enjoyed meeting her but didn't think the relationship would "progress."

Sometimes an intriguing woman never replies to *his* e-mail. He's learned, too, that his initial disinclination to juggle several prospects simultaneously, which struck him as callous, was unwise: By the time he'd decided against Candidate A and was ready to move down his list, Candidate B might already be off the market.

At the moment, he's talking with a gynecologist from Alabama and a Houston computer trainer. The Alabaman was in Washington visiting her brother recently, so he took her to Jaleo for tapas and to a Georgetown piano bar.

"A very smart, talented girl," he reports. "Was a connection made, one way or the other?. . . I didn't feel like I got any closer to making a decision." The Houston woman will be in town in a few weeks; they've made dinner plans. Tonight's review adds two more possibilities to his roster.

He's getting frustrated with the ups and downs and delays. "It's a lot more give and take than people make it out to be," he's discovered. Maybe all those parental warnings were on target, maybe he's waited too long. Certainly, the long-distance process of phoning and meeting all these people is growing unwieldy.

In fact, he's mislaid the number of that pediatrician in New Jersey who got a ringing 8.0 on the Sandhir Scale. But he'll dig it out and call her, he promises his dad. She grew up on Long Island; she likes music and travel, Vinay's own passions. She sounds interesting.

A Tradition in Transition

It has worked this way for thousands of years, immigrant parents tell their acculturated and uneasy offspring. It works better than Americans' impulsive love marriages, which so often split apart. "We have less divorce," Vibha's mother points out. "That's what results tell us."

In fact, the advantages and drawbacks of arranged marriages can't be so easily appraised. The incidence of divorce among Indian-born Americans *is* dramatically lower than among Americans generally, but that partly reflects the continuing stigma of divorce. Even as the divorce rate among Indian Americans appears to be increasing, the topic is rarely discussed. Vibha knows people, including several in her own family, who have divorced, but she doesn't want to talk about them. Divorce reflects poorly on an Indian family, and some proportion of arranged marriages endure not because they are successful or rewarding, but because leaving them would bring such shame.

And many endure because the definition of success differs from Western ideas. Traditional Indians don't expect a partner to be that improbable combination of soul mate/confidante/red-hot lover/best friend. "The husband-wife bond is one of reliability and dependability and complementary family roles—raising children, caring for elders," explains Karen Leonard, author of *The South Asian Americans* and a University of California-Irvine anthropologist. "They may communicate very little in intimate ways, and it's still a good marriage."

When marriages do go seriously awry, people like Anuradha Sharma see the fallout. Dozens of support groups have formed across the country for South Asian women victimized by domestic violence. Sharma until recently was executive director of Washington's ASHA (which means "hope" and stands for Asian Women's Self-Help Association). Operating from a secret downtown address, its volunteers accompany clients (primarily Indian, Pakistani and Bangladeshi) to area hospitals and courts and immigration offices, help them find shelter and, sometimes, obtain restraining orders. "I've seen the system of arranged marriage work really well," says Sharma, whose own parents' marriage was arranged. "But the system has a lot of trust built into it, and, in my work, I've also seen men very purposely take advantage of that."

Her vantage point—she's spent a decade with organizations concerned with violence against women—acquaints her particularly well with the most painful stories. Men who live in the United States sometimes visit remote villages in their ancestral countries, accept large dowries and consummate arranged marriages, then leave and don't return. They bring brides here from abroad, exploit and isolate and batter them, then threaten them with deportation or loss of their children if they report the abuse.

"I've had teenagers call, or social workers on behalf of teenagers, to see what we could do for women under 18 who were being whisked off to India or Pakistan and forced into marriage," Sharma says. "I met a couple who tried to have a love marriage, and family members from abroad were stalking and threatening them."

Even without such coercion, some members of the Second Generation find their elders' matchmaking efforts oppressive. "People on the outside think arranged marriage is exotic, it's romantic, it's cute—like that show 'Meet My Folks,'" says Devika Koppikar, a congressional aide weary of fending off attempts to get her married. "It's not."

For years, she laments, her parents have told her she's not accomplished or beautiful enough to land a husband herself, circulated her photo and e-mail address without her permission, enlisted friends and relatives to badger her into accepting men she has no interest in. There is no model, in Indian tradition, of a satisfying life as a single person. Feeling angry and estranged from her family at 31, she's "kind of tempted to just meet someone and head for Vegas."

Koppikar has formed "a two-woman support group" with a friend, a 30-year-old optometrist who broke off one arranged engagement, then nearly cracked under her parents' relentless pressure—"shouts, arguments, tears"—to enter another. She found a South Asian therapist who urged her to move out of her volatile family home, and after one particularly ugly altercation, she did. "I didn't even pack a bag," she says. "I felt I wasn't safe, emotionally."

Even Vibha—whose parents treated her much more respectfully, whose decision to marry Haresh, however difficult, was her own—hopes her youngest sister, just 13, takes a different route. She'd be pleased if Shetal, born here and less tradition-bound than Vibha, could skip "the big ordeal": parental pressures and cross-cultural tensions, a compressed courtship, language difficulties and hassles at the INS office. "I want her to find someone here, on her own, fall in love, get married, be happy," Vibha says.

If young Indian Americans raise their children differently—and people like Vibha and Vinay vow that their kids will be free to date, to be open about their romances, to marry whom they please—then the arranged marriage may not survive more than another generation or two in this country. In India, too, love marriages have grown more common among urban sophisticates.

In matters of courtship and marriage, in fact, young, well-educated Indians often have more social freedom than their American cousins, whose parents' values were fixed when they emigrated decades ago. "They still think of the norms they grew up with as the only acceptable ones. They haven't been able to change, seeing that as a betrayal of Indian-ness," says Padma Rangaswamy, author of *Namaste America* and a Chicago historian. "But Indians in India are happy to change and don't have those hangups. My friends' children in India are all finding their own spouses."

That Vibha didn't shocked her "American" girlfriends. A couple of them met for lunch a few weeks after her Indian sojourn, and she stunned them with her news and her engagement photos. "I looked at her like, 'You're kidding me,'" says Tiffany Obenhein. "Serve somebody tea, have a conversation—and bang, you're getting married? It seemed awfully fast for Vibha, who's so American." It took her friends a moment to recover and offer hugs and congratulations.

But then, the whole venture felt pretty fast to Vibha, too. Back home and back at work, arranging for a priest and a florist and a hall at Martin's Crosswinds in Greenbelt, "everything was so rushed," she says. "I didn't have time to think, and nothing was stopping it."

Can This Be Love?

Haresh arrived in September, after six months of exchanging e-mail and instant messages with his intended, and moved in with her and her family. They got to kiss, finally, slipping off to the basement rec room for privacy, and Vibha was reassured: "He was a great kisser."

And yet. . . In mid-October, they'd planned to get their license at the county courthouse and be legally married, in order to speed up the immigration paperwork. Vibha canceled the appointment. "I'm like, no, I'm not going to do it. I wasn't sure. Plus, I was sick."

A week later, however, they went ahead and were married in a quick civil ceremony in a lawyer's office, and afterward Haresh made her a promise: He'd never lie to her. She thought that was sweet, she was "definitely moved," yet she didn't feel married. Or even, she acknowledged, in love. Haresh, the more amorous of this pair, sent her doting e-mail messages and a mushy birthday card, and she kept them all and waited for reciprocal feelings to smite her after the big Hindu wedding still to come. "I can't say I love him, but I'm pretty close," was her assessment. "And I know it's going to happen."

Because the thing was, he'd been growing on her week by week, with his quiet thoughtfulness, his steady support. "He puts up with my dad, who's hard to put up with," she reported from her car one night. "I run around doing all this wedding stuff, and he runs around with me. There's always family around—we haven't really spent much time together—but he hasn't complained once."

To Vibha's amazement, he pitched in with dish-washing and vacuuming and garbage-toting; it turned out he'd lived for a time with his grandparents, and helped with household chores when his grandmother was ill. This was major.

"Indian men don't tend to value the role women play, but he understands what they go through and respects it. He's like, why shouldn't women do what they want to do?" He didn't even care if she changed her last name or not, and since he didn't care, she decided she would.

On the Hindu New Year, Haresh was out doing errands with her dad instead of celebrating with the rest of the family at her aunt's house, and Vibha was ticked. "And then I went home and I was in my room and I'm waiting for him to come tell me 'Happy New Year,' and I'm *fuming*!" she recounts. "And I'm still mad about it the next day—and it hits me. Whoa. I missed him."

So the wedding, a four-day extravaganza for nearly 400 guests, is on.

'Body, Mind and Soul'

On Thursday night, a mehndiwalli from Gaithersburg came to the house and painstakingly applied paisley henna patterns to Vibha's hands and feet while her female relatives warbled traditional songs. The darker the mehndi, the more your husband will love you, goes the old saying, by which standard Vibha will have a deeply devoted mate.

Friday night, a few hundred people gathered at the Durga Temple in Lorton for garbas and dandia raas, the traditional Gujarati dances Vibha has loved since childhood, and she and her sisters and Haresh went flying across the floor until they were sweaty and exhausted, and her hair was coming unpinned.

Saturday, the family gathered for prenuptial ceremonies at the house ("Omigod, that was looong").

On Sunday, her wedding day, Vibha surprises even herself with her serenity. The photographer is urging her to smile; the decorator is setting up a glorious gold-embroidered white canopy (called a mandap); there's nothing left to prepare or decide. She might as well relax.

Wearing a ravishing embroidered lengha and extravagant amounts of gold jewelry, her face flecked with traditional bindya dots and her neck encircled by orchids, she's ready to be escorted to the ceremony on her uncle's arm. "Have you seen the mandap?" says Chetan Desai, one of her closest Virginia Tech buddies. "It kicks ass."

Under the canopy, with the bride and groom seated on silvery thrones, the songs and prayers continue for several hours in a mix of Sanskrit and Gujarati with a touch of English. The priest lights the sacred fire in a ziggurat-shaped brazier and Vibha and Haresh slowly circle it four times, symbolizing the stages of life and religious duty. They ask for prosperity and redemption from sin and future calamities. "Let us be like the earth and the sky," which are never separated, the priest intones on behalf of the groom. "Let us join our forces, let us have offspring, let us live a life of 200 years."

"I accept you as my husband and I offer my body, mind and soul to you," is the bride's response.

Vibha's Tech friends, most of whom have love marriages, are keeping a watchful eye on her. They've been a little worried, knowing Vibha's "adventurous spirit," about an arranged marriage to a guy from India. "How's this going to work?" Desai had wondered. "What if he's expecting some old-fashioned, stand-behind-your-man Indian woman?"

But seeing her calm gaze during the ceremony, noticing how glowy she looks at the reception afterward, they feel reassured. "We know her fake smile, her 'everything's all right' mode, but this was real," Desai says afterward, when Vibha and Haresh have left for a week's honeymoon—by a wide margin, the longest time they will ever have spent alone—in Hawaii. "He was happy, she was happy, she was at peace with herself. She was a *bride*."

The Date from Hell

That pediatrician from New Jersey? "We had a really good conversation" on the phone, Vinay says. "We had the same perspective on this whole India Abroad/meeting people stuff. . . She's very smart, she has passion for her work." She would shortly head overseas, and he wanted to meet her before she left, so they agreed to rendezvous in Philadelphia on a Friday night. Vinay bought tickets to a Sixers game, feeling upbeat.

Alas. "It was raining. It was miserable," he reports. "She was in a bad mood from the get-go." Arriving 45 minutes late, she stepped into a puddle en route to his car, complained about the long walk across the parking lot to the arena, barely initiated a conversation the entire evening. "I don't know if it was me, I don't know if it was the weather, I don't know if it was her day," Vinay says, nursing his disappointment and a glass of pink guava juice while relating the sorry saga to his visiting parents. Her pager went off, he adds, but she didn't have to leave, although he began to wish she did: "How bad is it that you're hoping some kid is sick enough that she has to go in to the hospital?"

En route to a restaurant in a neighborhood neither knew well, "she proceeds to bitch for 15 minutes in the car about how she couldn't read the map." An awkward dinner, a quick drop-off at the train station, "and I don't anticipate ever having to talk to or hear from her again. Because it was the worst, most miserable date of my life. Number one."

He's starting to wonder about this whole arrangement business. "Deep down, I don't think assessing someone from pictures and biodata tells you anything," he says. "There's probably lots of decent people we overlooked. There really isn't a foolproof way of doing it."

But he's still in touch with the Alabama doctor. He sees the Houston woman when she's in town visiting her brother. And there was an interesting ad in *India Abroad* his parents recently responded to:

> *Invitation for handsome, caring, outgoing, broad-minded, well-settled professionals, 31-plus; for beautiful, v. fair, slim, educated U.S. raised daughter. . .*

'My Man'

Back from her honeymoon, Vibha Umaretiya seems liberated from frenzy and pressure—and from doubt. When she's with Haresh, she's giggly and charmed; she finds reasons to touch his shoulder, and he squeezes her hand. When she's not with him, when she's finally able to put away her cell phone and actually talk over lunch at the pizza place across from her office, she's expansive, buoyant.

"Now that we're married, I'm okay," she announces. "No more ifs or ands or buts."

Perhaps it's wise that Indian wedding rituals have expanded to incorporate such Western ideas as honeymoons. On Maui there was time to just lie on a beach and listen to the waves, time to get to know the man she'd wed.

"He's really very romantic, more than I am," she confides. On the plane, he kept his arm around her practically the whole flight. At their hotel, he catered to her, fed her morsels from his plate. "So much care, it was just incredible. I'm like, 'Stop the madness.'"

Not that she really wanted him to stop. "He made coffee for me in the morning! I'm like, omigod. . . He was so sweet; he makes it really easy for me to like him." But what about—that annoying Western question—love? A pause.

"How do you know if you love someone? Does a light come on over your head?" Haresh wants to get his master's degree in engineering; he thinks he could finish in a year and a half. Vibha may decide to start a business one day. They want to buy a condo or a townhouse as soon as they can, have some time as a twosome before the children arrive—at least five years away—and possibly his family arrives, too, if they choose. And because Haresh is soft-spoken and understanding and fair-minded about women's roles, and because she also wants him to do what fulfills him, they will have a good life together.

"He's my man, and he will be my man up until the day I die, or whatever," she muses, launching into a monologue. "The way you feel about a person is constantly changing, y'know?. . . Maybe there are days when you don't want to deal with him, maybe there'll be days when you don't want to miss a second with him. Do I look forward to spending time with him? Yes. Do I look forward to getting to know him? Yes. Do I like him for what he is? Do I have a deeper understanding of him? Yes."

So how their meeting and their future were arranged, with all the attendant anxieties, is starting to seem beside the point. "For me, it was the right thing," Vibha says. And she laughs. "I never thought I'd do it this way. It's really weird how life works, y'know? But I'm happy with the way it ended up. Seriously happy."

PAULA SPAN (pspan@bellatlantic.net) is a *Post* staff writer.

Couple Therapy

Psychotherapy for Two and Two for Psychotherapy

The problems that confront the clients and patients of mental health professionals arise mostly in marriages and other intimate relationships. Marriage and family difficulties account for about half of all visits to psychotherapists, family therapy is increasingly popular as a mental health specialty, and most family therapists work chiefly with couples. The term "couple therapy" (or "couples therapy") is gradually replacing the older "marital therapy" in order to include unmarried and gay couples.

Licensed couple therapists include psychiatrists, psychologists, clinical social workers, psychiatric nurses, pastoral counselors, and marriage and family therapists who have taken specialized courses and undergone supervised training in the field. The therapist assumes that the unhappiness of a couple amounts to more than the sum of their individual problems and symptoms. They may be concerned about emotional distancing, power struggles, poor communication, jealousy, infidelity, sexual dissatisfaction, and violence. The therapist helps them examine their lives together and decide what changes are needed. They work on eliminating mutual misunderstandings, unreasonable expectations, and unstated assumptions that perpetuate conflict.

Couple therapists make little use of psychiatric diagnosis, but they do use many of the same methods employed by individual therapists: interpreting emotional conflicts and the influence of the past; assigning exercises for behavior change; challenging beliefs; offering advice, reassurance, and support; teaching social skills and problem solving. If the relationship is moribund, some couple therapists believe that they can help the couple make a break with a minimum of recrimination, bitterness, and suffering.

Family Systems and Patterns

Family systems theory was once dominant and is still influential as a blueprint for couple therapists. It emphasizes the patterns of communication, action, and reaction that create and reinforce a family environment. In an unhappy couple, the system resists change because it has reached a maladaptive equilibrium, just as individual symptoms may resist change because they preserve individual emotional balance. The couple may have unknowingly set rules for themselves that are working poorly. The therapist helps them become aware of these rules and patterns as a prerequisite to changing them.

Sometimes each partner demands too much of the same thing from the other—service, protection, care. Sometimes they adopt complementary roles. One member of the couple takes charge and the other becomes incompetent. An overbearing and emotionally distant husband responds to his dependent or melodramatic wife by becoming still more overbearing. A strong wife is constantly angry at her passive husband, whose passivity only increases. The husband or wife of a depressed and hypochondriacal person may act as a healer and savior.

Couple therapists try to help both individuals understand the function of their contributions to the system. The passive partner might learn about his need to suppress rather than productively express anger. "Saviors" may see how that role helps them deny their own sense of helplessness. An emotionally distant husband could learn about the fear of strong emotion. A dependent wife might confront her wish to avoid managing her own anxieties. By acknowledging their own contributions to the conflict, members of a couple can begin to weigh the benefits and costs of the bargain they've made with a partner.

When the two are not communicating well, verbally or nonverbally, each one may behave as though certain principles are accepted when they are not. For example, one partner believes the other has agreed that he or she can stay at work as long as he or she thinks is necessary, but the other thinks he or she has implicitly agreed to be home for dinner. Other misunderstood implicit promises include: I need a certain amount of sex, a certain degree of financial security, or a certain number of friends.

Family systems therapists often employ the concept of the double bind, a situation that results when members of a couple send mutually contradictory messages—often one in words and the other through the silent communication of emotion. The partner must not acknowledge the contradiction or respond to the underlying intentions if he or she wants to maintain the relationship. For example, one partner asks the other to come to him or her and stiffens at the other's approach. The second partner withdraws, and the first one says, "Why are you so cold?" The second person has no response: To point out what is going on would only alienate the first partner further. Eventually people who are communicating—or failing to communicate—in this way find it difficult to say what they mean, understand what the other person means, or even distinguish real from simulated feelings. Family systems therapy is designed to uncover and solve problems of this kind.

Behavioral Couple Therapy

Behavioral treatment of couples provides three kinds of help: behavioral exchange, communication training, and problem-solving training.

In behavioral exchange, each partner is helped to identify a desired change in the other partner's behavior, and they agree to reciprocate. The therapist encourages them to follow through and show gratitude. Communication training shows the couple how to listen sensitively and express their needs without accusations. From exercises in problem solving, they learn how to define the issues that generate conflict, find specific solutions, negotiate, and compromise.

Either during therapeutic sessions or as homework, behavior therapists may prescribe tasks that reveal maladaptive patterns. A woman might be told to exaggerate her criticism of her partner until he challenges her. If a couple is drifting apart, the therapist might arrange for the man (or woman) to be sure to come home for dinner four or five nights a week.

Today many behavior therapists also try to change the way each member of the couple responds to undesired behavior. They may also employ cognitive restructuring—changing the way the partners interpret one another's behavior. They learn to avoid using words like "always" and "never," to examine evidence before blaming the other, and to consider the consequences of living by doubtful implicit assumptions (such as the belief that you should never be angry at your partner).

Emotionally Focused Couple Therapy

Another kind of treatment, drawing on ideas from the client-centered therapy of Carl Rogers (see *Mental Health Letter*, January 2006) as well as family systems theory, concentrates on emotion rather than behavior. The therapist helps the couple recognize the emotions that drive their conflict as a precursor to stopping the resulting troublesome behavior patterns. They expose their vulnerability and express unacknowledged feelings, then reconsider their situation in the light of these feelings to work out new solutions.

Often the problem is stated as a matter of interrupting or escaping from rigid response patterns or cycles. In one pattern that arises repeatedly, an angry, critical, complaining partner confronts one who is defensive and withdrawn. The therapist helps the angry partner to feel his or her desperation about not getting through and the consequent fear of abandonment, while urging the withdrawn partner to temporarily disregard the feeling of being attacked and—instead of acting defensively—to listen to the concerns and respond with support.

Emotionally focused couple therapy may encourage the couple to reframe their problems in terms of attachment needs. The premise of attachment theory is that a safe emotional bond with another person is a basic survival need, providing a home base in the world. From infancy on, we all need contact with others who care for us and respond sensitively to our needs. Attachment patterns usually appear first in the relationship between parent and child and are often repeated throughout life.

A secure attachment provides both comfort and room for independent exploration. When attachment is insecure, people may become angry, and—if there is no response—depressed and despairing. They may also develop a distorted attachment that takes the form of anxious clinging, or a combination of the two, exemplified by the double bind: "Come here to me, I need you" and "You are dangerous, go away."

Couples often seek help when they have sustained an "attachment injury"—a crisis involving infidelity, financial deception, violence, deeply insulting words, or another apparent betrayal. One of the partners may feel emotionally abandoned at a critical moment such as job loss or serious illness. Divorce or separation may be threatening.

In therapy, at first the injured partner may angrily or sadly recount the incident while the offending partner minimizes the damage or becomes defensive. The injured partner is encouraged to show grief and fear instead of anger, and the offending partner is encouraged to acknowledge responsibility and show remorse. Then the injured partner may ask for comfort and care that was unavailable at the time of the incident, and the offending partner may come through, helping heal the attachment injury.

An example: Mary has discovered that her husband John had an affair three years ago. They've never discussed it, but John complains that she repeatedly reminds him of it. It is a typical pattern of anger and defensiveness. She worries about what he does when he goes out alone, and when he is at home he feels under siege and retreats to a room alone. Over a period of several months, the therapist helps him talk about his feelings of shame, and he tearfully expresses his sorrow and his love for her. As the complete range of their feelings becomes more apparent to both of them, she begins to move past her injury and expresses genuine forgiveness.

Psychodynamic Couple Therapy

Psychodynamic therapists believe that the way adult couples treat each other is strongly influenced by patterns established in childhood—lessons learned, mostly unconsciously, in their birth families. The therapist emphasizes unconscious wishes and the defenses, also mostly unconscious, that divert or prevent the full expression of those wishes.

Psychodynamic couple therapists sometimes pay special attention to projective identification, a defense that involves disavowing your own impulses or wishes, attributing them to another person, and behaving in a way that elicits responses that convince you that your attributions are right. A husband can't bear his own dependency or weakness and overcompensates by being controlling and rigid as an expression of strength. This evokes dependent behavior in his wife—which he can both identify with *and* resent. Projective identification can perpetuate a painful attachment when, as often happens, the partner uses the defense in a complementary way. In this example, the wife may need to disavow her own aggression, so her dependency also evokes even more rigidity and hostility in her husband. Such complementary patterns, psychodynamic therapists believe, often originate in childhood relationships with parents.

Psychodynamic therapists explore the influence of the past partly by pointing out how feelings originally directed at members of the birth family have been transferred to the partner, and sometimes to the therapist, too. They also show how emotionally charged fantasies blend with present reality. If all goes well, the members of the couple succeed in separating their feelings about one another from their feelings about their own parents and past experiences.

The Individual and the Couple

Individual psychiatric symptoms and the problems of couples are related in complicated ways. Often there is a vicious cycle in which a relationship is endangered by the withdrawal and irritability of a depressed person, the aggressive and impulsive behavior associated with mania, the need for constant reassurance resulting from anxiety, or the multifarious ravages of alcoholism and drug addiction. Conflict between the members of the couple exacerbates these symptoms until it is difficult to tell where the cycle began. According to some versions of family systems theory, individual symptoms serve to maintain arrangements that prevent change both partners need but fear.

Couple therapists may concentrate on specific actions that exacerbate individual symptoms, or they can enlist one partner as a surrogate therapist or coach. Partners can help with treatments such as relaxation training, exposure and response prevention, or cognitive restructuring, while monitoring changes as the therapy progresses and providing the therapist with information.

Alcoholism has been treated successfully with forms of behavioral couple therapy called community reinforcement and Project CALM (Counseling for Alcoholic Marriages). Emotionally focused couple therapy may be helpful for depressed people when the depression is associated with an insecure attachment. It has also been used for survivors of child abuse and Vietnam veterans suffering from traumatic stress reactions. Dialectical behavior therapy (see *Mental Health Letter,* August 2002) for couples can relieve depression and reduce emotional volatility in people with borderline personality disorder.

Individual and couple therapy are often combined. For example, a woman marries a divorced man with two young sons from a previous marriage, gives birth to a girl, and develops a postpartum depression. Her stepsons, already feeling displaced by the new baby, become angry and defiant. She is reminded of her own unhappy relationship with her stepmother and feels as though she is turning into an evil stepmother herself. The marriage is affected, and the couple seeks therapy. Her depression is part of the problem and might best be treated additionally with medications and her own psychotherapy.

In cases of serious domestic violence, the trend today is to separate the partners instead of treating them jointly. Some professionals reject the idea of couple therapy for batterers because it may suggest that someone or something other than the instigator of violence is to blame. But others believe that a combination of individual and couple therapy may be workable as long as the violence has stopped, the victim does not fear retaliation, and the perpetrator admits responsibility. The therapist must always make it clear that no alleged provocation justifies violence.

How Effective Is Couple Therapy?

Most studies find that couple therapy can be helpful, at least for a while, but not all studies meet the highest standards. It's also unclear whether the treatment can transform unhappy relationships into satisfactory ones, and whether the effects last. Behavioral couple therapy and emotionally focused couple therapy have been found more effective than a waiting list in controlled studies. The American Psychological Association approves behavioral couple therapy as "well established" and emotionally focused couple therapy as "probably efficacious." Other reviews support the value of cognitive behavioral couple therapy and family systems therapy.

Some of the research has raised doubt about whether all the components of behavioral or emotionally focused couple therapy are necessary, and whether these techniques work in the way that the underlying theory proposes.

Improvement is usually maintained for six months, but often there is a relapse after a year or two. In a four-year follow-up, the longest so far, researchers found that 38% of couples treated with behavioral couple therapy were divorced. But in some cases, a divorce—especially if it is amicable—may represent a good outcome. A recent two-year follow-up indicated that a year of therapy for a couple in which one partner was depressed gave better results—and produced fewer dropouts—than antidepressant drug treatment.

There is only a little evidence on who couple therapy works best for. Younger couples seem to improve more in some studies. One study found that couples did better when they had been together longer; another, that couples with the most serious problems were least likely to benefit; and still another, that in heterosexual couples, therapy worked out better when the woman was the main problem solver in the family.

Like individual therapists, couple therapists are becoming more eclectic in their approach. A method called integrative couple therapy combines emotional acceptance with behavioral strategies. Therapists are also trying different approaches with different couples, or emphasizing features that all treatments have in common, such as the therapeutic alliance.

According to the United States Department of Health and Human Services, the number of specialists in marriage and family therapy has increased from about 2,000 in 1966 to almost 50,000 today. The American Association for Marriage and Family Therapy estimates that more than 3% of the nation's 57 million married couples see a psychotherapist for marital difficulties each year. The line between enhancement and therapy is becoming blurred with the development of programs aimed at preventing marital conflict and improving relationships. Because it is increasingly understood that emotional disturbances and behavior problems originate *between* people as well as within them, psychotherapy for two will continue to thrive.

References

Cournos F. "Psychodynamic Couples Therapy," in Hersen M, et al., eds, *Encyclopedia of Psychotherapy.* Academic Press, 2002.

Gurman AS, et al. "The History of Couple Therapy: A Millennial Review," *Family Process* (June 2002): Vol. 41, No. 2, pp. 199–260.

Makinen JA, et al. "Resolving Attachment Injuries in Couples Using Emotionally Focused Therapy: Steps toward Forgiveness and Reconciliation," *Journal of Consulting and Clinical Psychology* (December 2006): Vol. 74, No. 6, pp. 1055–64.

O'Farrell TJ, et al., eds. *Behavioral Couples Therapy for Alcoholism and Drug Abuse,* Haworth Press, 2006.

Snyder DK, et al. "Current Status and Future Directions in Couple Therapy," *Annual Review of Psychology* (2006): Vol.57, pp. 317–44.

Kaleidoscope of Parenting Cultures

Vidya Thirumurthy

Educator: Immigrant parents from Asia in my class have a dogmatic parenting style and I don't know how to make them change their parenting style. They show little interest in the class when we discuss parenting issues. Should they not be expected to adapt to this culture? After all, it was their choice to move here.

Vidya: Should we expect them to change?

An uneasy silence pervaded the room full of experienced educators, who are grappling with similar situations. They are clueless as to how to approach it.

I will share here some observations I made of parents and children from over 27 countries who participated in a university preschool program. The emotionally enmeshed relationship between a Jewish parent and child, the teacher-taught behavior of an Indian father, the nonverbal relationship of a Brazilian couple with their child, the filial piety approach of a Chinese father, the friendly and playful demeanor of an African American mother, and the negotiation-oriented and self-explaining conduct of an Euro-American mother are descriptors of only a few characteristics observed among the preschool parents. I rely on a few examples to illustrate some cultural variations in parenting.

What is proper or improper behavior is based on cultural expectations and contexts (Brooks, 1999). Western cultures focus on the empowerment of individualism and autonomy in the child (Rudy, Grusec, & Wolfe, 1999). Freedom and individuality are the core values and parents do not view a child's defiance when asked to comply with a request as a threat. They may disagree with their child; nonetheless, they may still perceive the child's behavior as his/her way of asserting him/herself.

As a contrast, parents in most non-Western cultures believe in imposing absolute standards on their children. They value obedience and expect their children to respect authority. Their goal is to promote interdependency and cooperation. "Interdependence is promoted by fostering intense emotional bonds with children at an early age . . . children are motivated to cooperate and meet the needs of others, since [their activities] promote a sense of self-worth and emotional security" (Rudy et al., p. 302).

Defiance is the opposite of cooperation and a non-cooperative behavior is perceived as a threat to maintaining their family unity. Asian and Hispanic cultures typically value individualism less and collaboration and cooperation more. They exercise more control over the child to achieve these goals. But most Westerners perceive this approach as being demanding. They fear such parenting styles would result in "poor school achievement among Euro-Americans" (Chao, 1994, p. 1111). Yet, obedience is a virtue for the non-Western parents and they have implicit faith in punishment.

Similarly, Chinese and Asian parents equate parenting to teaching (Rudy et al., 1999). For example, an Indian father expected forceful cooperation rather than cooperation through negotiation when he instructed his son several times each morning to greet his teachers. "Beta (Son), say good morning to all your teachers and friends," was a mantra he chanted. As a contrast to this, the Brazilian couple would enter very quietly and slip out of the classroom as though they would disturb the serenity of the class. They rarely exchanged greetings with the teacher or with other parents. Smith (1997) explains that Brazilians often use silence as a way to greet others. They seldom greeted or interacted with other parents when they entered the classroom in the morning.

When a child controls the behaviors of his parents, Baumrind (1991) calls it a permissive parenting style. The daily routine of a Jewish couple and their son lasted for about an hour. This little boy had a difficult time letting go of his parents. The observer noticed the emotional entanglement in their relationship—yet another characteristic of the permissive style. "Parents promote the child's assertion of his or her will: Israeli mothers, for example, are more likely than those in Japan to value disobedience when it is a reflection of the child's assertion of individuality" (Osterweil & Nagano, 1991, as cited by Rudy, Grusec, & Wolfe, 1999, p. 302). But what we must realize is that emotionally enmeshed behaviors are considered healthy in many cultures and it is believed to strengthen the bond between parents and children. It cannot be labeled as inappropriate parenting.

The communication patterns of most Euro-American parents were different from the rest. They got down to the eye-level of the children when talking with them. They spoke softly to their children and were non-intrusive. A few of them held their children on their laps or hugged them while they talked. Western culture promotes looking the speaker straight in the eye to show "interest and attention" (Smith, 1997, p. 349). Therefore, making eye contact is considered very important when communicating with others. This is in stark contrast to many other cultures that teach their children not to establish such eye contact with elders and persons of authority because it is considered disrespectful.

The patterns of parental attitudes and behaviors exhibited in the preschool differed greatly across cultures. The cultural contexts in which parents grew up, the experiences they have had with their own parents, and the experiences they have with their own children affect parent cognition and behavior. Parents hold a mental representation of relationships, which they develop based on their own childhood experiences (Grusec, Hastings, & Mammone, 1994). It does not mean that parents passively accept and mirror the parenting styles of their parents. They filter through the behaviors and absorb only those that are in accordance with their individual beliefs. Thus, variations in approaches illustrate both cultural and individual differences in parenting styles.

Immigrants leave their lands, families, and cultural settings behind. Even though it was their choice to move here, they face an overwhelming challenge in adapting to new situations, land, and culture. Educators can state their expectations clearly and let the parents do it in their own way. As long as there is no abuse, we must strive to help parents maintain their cultural identities and be successful. As one of my students put it, our goal should be to support them in their parenting and help them gain a deeper understanding of our parenting styles.

References

Baumrind, D. (1991). Parenting styles and adolescent development. In R. M. Lerner, A. C. Petersen, & J. Brooks-Gunn (Ed.), Encyclopedia of adolescence (pp. 746–758). New York: Garland.

Brooks, J. (1999). The process of parenting (5th ed). Mountain View, CA: Mayfield.

Chao, R. K. (2004). Beyond parental control and authoritarian parenting style: Understanding Chinese parenting through the cultural notion of training. Child Development, 65, 1111–1119.

Grusec, J., Hastings, P., & Mammone, N. (1994). Parenting cognitions and relationships schemas. In J. Smetana (Ed.), Beliefs about parenting: Origins and developmental implications (pp. 5–19). San Francisco: Jossey-Bass.

Rudy, D., Grusec, J., & Wolfe, J. (1999). Implication of cross-cultural findings for family socialization. Journal of Moral Education, 28, 299–310.

Smith, T. J. (1997). Early childhood development. Upper Saddle River, NJ: Merrill.

Do We Need a Law to Prohibit Spanking?

MURRAY STRAUS, PHD

The proposal by a member of the California legislature to prohibit spanking and other corporal punishment of children age three and younger has attracted nationwide interest—and outrage. Newspapers around the country published editorials about it. I read many of them, and all opposed the proposal. The two main objections are that spanking children is sometimes necessary and that it is an unprecedented and horrible example of government interference in the lives of families. The editorials usually also say or imply that "moderate" spanking does not harm children. These objections accurately represent the beliefs of most Americans, but they are not accurate representations of the scientific evidence on the effectiveness and side effects of spanking. They are also historically inaccurate about government interference in the family.

The research on the effectiveness of spanking shows that it does work to correct misbehavior. But the research also shows that spanking does not work better than other modes of correction and control, such as time out, explaining, and depriving a child of privileges. Moreover, the research clearly shows that the gains from spanking come at a big cost. These include weakening the tie between children and parents, and increasing the probability that the child will hit other children, hit their parents, and as adults hit a dating or marital partner. Spanking also slows down mental development and lowers the probability of a child doing well in school and in college. There have been more than a hundred studies of these side effects of spanking, and there is over 90% agreement between them. There is probably no other aspect of parenting and child behavior where the results are so consistent.

Despite this overwhelming evidence, few believe that "moderate" spanking harms children, including few psychologists. It seems to contradict their own experience and that of their children. They say "I was spanked and I was not a violent kid and I did well in school." That is correct, but the implication that spanking is harmless is not correct. Like smoking, spanking is a "risk factor"—not a one-to-one cause of problems. About a third of heavy smokers die of a smoking related disease. That is gruesome, but it also means that two thirds can say "I smoked all my life and I am OK." Does that mean smoking is OK? No, it just means that they are one of the lucky two thirds. Similarly, when someone says "I was spanked and I am OK," that is

correct. However, the implication that spanking is harmless is not correct. The correct implication is that they are one of the lucky majority, rather than one of those harmed by spanking.

The large and consistent body of evidence on the harmful side effects of spanking is also not believed because because so few get to know about it.

Another reason the evidence is not believed is because the harm from spanking occurs down the road. Parents can see that the spanked child stopped what they were doing wrong. They cannot see the harmful effects that occur months or years later.

The large and consistent body of evidence on the harmful side effects of spanking is also not believed because so few get to know about it. I analyzed the content of ten child psychology textbooks published in the 1980's, ten in the 1990's, and ten published since 2000. These giant textbooks averaged only half a page on spanking, despite the fact that almost all American toddlers are spanked. None reported the fact that over 90% of the studies found harmful side-effects. Or putting it the other way around, none let their readers know that children who are not spanked, rather than being out of control brats, are more likely than spanked children to be well behaved and to have fewer psychological problems. This may be the best kept secret of American child psychology.

What about no-spanking legislation being an unprecedented interference in the family? Until the 1870's husbands had the right to use corporal punishment to correct an "errant wife." When the courts started to rule that this aspect of the common law was no longer valid, it was regarded by many as an outrageous interference in what should be a private family matter. Government now prohibits "physically chastisting an errant wife" and prohibits many other things to protect family members and to enhance the stability of the family, starting with prohibiting marriage at an early age.

The proposed California law, however, has two major problems. First, it applies only to children age three and younger. Therefore it has the ironic implication of endorsing the hitting of older children. A second irony is that this law would be doing the very thing it wants parents not to do—use harsh punishment to correct misbehavior. A better model is the 1979 Swedish no-spanking law. It has no criminal penalty. The purpose of that type of law is to set a standard for how children should be treated, and to make money available to educate the public about these standards and to provide services to help parents who are having enough difficulty with their children that they spank. The Swedish law has proven to be very effective. Spanking children has declined tremendously. Opponents of the law feared that Swedish children would be "running wild." The opposite has happened. Youth crime rates, drug use, and suicide have all decreased.

Fifteen nations now prohibit spanking by parents. There is an emerging consensus that this is a fundamental human right for children. The United Nations committee charged with implementing the Charter of Children's Rights is asking all nations to prohibit spanking. Never spanking will not only reduce the risk of delinquency and mental health problems, it will also bring to children the right to be free of physical attacks in the name of discipline, just as wives gained that human right a century and a quarter ago.

MURRAY A. STRAUS PHD has studied spanking by large and representative samples of American parents for thirty years. He is the author of *Beating The Devil Out Of Them: Corporal Punishment In American Families And Its Effects On Children* (Transaction Press, 2001). He has been president of three scientific societies including the National Council On Family Relations, and an advisor to the National Institutes of Health and the National Science Foundation. He can be reached at 603 862-2594 or by email at murray.straus@unh.edu. Much of his research on spanking can be downloaded from http://pubpages.unh.edu/~mas2.

Prickly Père

What are your obligations to a parent who's smothering or abusive?

ELIZABETH SVOBODA

As a child, Michael Levine yearned to please his mother, but her drinking gave rise to mood swings so extreme that living at home felt like performing a high-wire act. "You didn't know what was going to happen from one day to the next," says Levine, now a Los Angeles public relations executive. "Monday you might be told you were God Almighty, and Tuesday you might have things thrown at you."

We each owe our existence to our parents, and in many cases, we'll never fully appreciate their sacrifices on our behalf. But prospective parents don't have to pass mental-health tests to procreate, and parents with difficult personalities come in as many flavors as emotionally challenged suitors. Some are "helicopter parents," always hovering, anxious and overprotective; some neglect their children's needs out of selfishness or mild depression; others seethe with anger, unhappiness, or jealousy, lashing out at their offspring—physically or verbally—on a regular basis. But such parents can nevertheless come across to outsiders as involved and loving, so children receive little independent confirmation that something is wrong with the way they're being treated.

Many people born into difficult families spend their childhoods looking forward to leaving their parents' orbit. But when they do, the parameters that define the relationship must be redrawn: How can adult children strike a balance between maintaining a healthy measure of personal freedom and keeping difficult parents satisfied? Are they obligated to keep communication lines open as a gesture of filial loyalty? Can anything positive be salvaged from the relationship? Regardless of parents' past wrongs, the duty to "honor thy father and mother" exerts a strong pull.

Parents with toxic personalities can feel threatened by their grown children's independence, making this balancing act treacherous. Other parents make drastic impositions on their adult children's lives in an effort to reassert closeness.

We want so badly to believe that our parents are perfect, and we resist the idea that they need to change. We tend to hope that with enough love from us, they'll smooth out the rough edges of their personalities. But ironically, their confidence in our unconditional support can make them feel like changing is unnecessary. "Most parents continue the behavior that has always 'worked' for them, since it gets them what they want," says syndicated advice columnist Amy Alkon. The best way to sustain a relationship with a troubled parent is to set clear boundaries for your interactions with them. Allowing parents unlimited access to your time and resources might seem like the most selfless option, but it can backfire: You'll rack up so much resentment that you lose sight of your parents' positive qualities, and what's left of the relationship shrivels.

If problem parents are confident of their kids' unconditional support, they will feel little pressure to improve.

The best way to negotiate these boundaries varies depending on the type and severity of a parent's problems, says Barbara Kane, a psychologist who specializes in family issues. One basic rule of thumb, though, is to take a calm but uncompromising stand against unreasonable demands, vicious put-downs, and other bad behaviors. If your mother insists that you drive an hour and a half just to fix her thermostat and fires off a volley like "You're a horrible daughter for not wanting to help me," or even "I'll kill myself if you don't come," stand your ground while still acknowledging your parent's feelings—which communicates a message of caring. "Try saying something like 'I understand you're disappointed I can't do this right now,'" says Kane.

"You can't change a parent," emphasizes Karen Shore, a Santa Monica, California, clinical psychologist. "What you can do is change how you react to them. Anger will push you back into the old, unbalanced parent-child dynamic."

To cultivate empathy for your parents, it helps to view them objectively, says psychologist Cheryl Dellasega, author of *Forced to Be Family*. If Dad is verbally abusive, or Mom seems forever in need of affirmation, think about what might have made them that way. As children, were they neglected? Mistreated? Bullied? Did they grow up in households where

ming the Toxic Parent

Problem parents can dominate your life. Here's how to manage them without sacrificing happiness or autonomy.

- **Set firm boundaries** for approaching a difficult parent. If your parent is smothering or narcissistic, opt for shorter or less frequent visits.
- **If your parent is verbally abusive,** walk away when insults start to fly.
- **Stop trying to "fix" your troubled parent.** Recognize that you're not to blame for his or her shortcomings.
- **Don't let past infractions poison your relations now.** Forgiving doesn't mean forgetting, but be open to healthy new developments in the relationship.
- **Avoid situations that trigger underlying conflict.** If your parents act toxic at large family gatherings, try suggesting a park outing or a play.
- **Think about what the relationship means to you** and whether it's worth saving *even if he or she never changes.* Your parents aren't total monsters: They influence your life in positive ways as well as negative ones—so think hard before deciding to cut them off.

screaming fits were the primary mode of communication? Life experiences don't excuse rotten behavior, but understanding what's shaped someone can help you come up with more compassionate and appropriate responses to inappropriate behavior. When your investment-banker dad ridicules your job as a day-care instructor, try "I realize your priorities in life are different from mine." When your mother begs you to stay overnight with her at the assisted-living center, try "You know I'm never going to abandon you, Mom."

Interacting with an unpleasant parent on a day-to-day basis is only half the battle; adult children must also tackle the broader question of what exactly they "owe" the person who gave them life—but now makes them miserable. Some children opt to love and stand by their difficult parents no matter what, treasuring the sense of self-worth that comes from honoring the relationship.

Other offspring embrace the possibility—however disconcerting—that filial closeness is best found outside the family they were born into. "Some parents think, Ha, ha, you're stuck with me, I can do anything I want," says Alkon. "But to me, family are people who really treat you like family. People shouldn't focus so much on DNA." Shore agrees: "We should not judge children who decide to distance themselves from their parents. To the outside world, it looks callous, but if a parent has really destroyed a child's life, it can be the healthiest thing."

For children who resolve to stick it out with problem parents, the struggle is not without reward. Levine worked hard at maintaining regular contact with his mother in the years before she died. The decision to stay in touch wasn't easy—each time he visited her, the pain and bad memories came flooding back—but he doesn't regret it. "You need to be able to put the past in some kind of bracketed perspective," he says. "Opportunities to truly resolve all your issues with a parent are few and far between, but I feel a little bit more peaceful knowing that I made the effort."

ELIZABETH SVOBODA is a freelance writer based in San Jose, California.

When Parents Hover Over Kids' Job Search

Boomers just keep coddling; says one HR specialist 'It's unbelievable'.

Some parents are writing their college-age kids' resumes. Others are acting as their children's "representatives," hounding college career counselors, showing up at job fairs and sometimes going as far as calling employers to ask why their son or daughter didn't get a job.

It's the next phase in helicopter parenting, a term coined for those who have hovered over their children's lives from kindergarten to college. Now they are inserting themselves into their kids' job search—and school officials and employers say it's a problem that may be hampering some young people's careers.

"It has now reached epidemic proportions," says Michael Ellis, director of career and life education at Delaware Valley College, a small, private school in Doylestown, Pa.

At the school's annual job fair last year, he says, one father accompanied his daughter, handed out her resume and answered most of the questions the recruiters were asking the young woman. Even more often, he receives calls from parents, only to find out later that their soon-to-be college grad was sitting next to the parent, quietly listening.

Jobs counselors at universities across the country say experiences like those are now commonplace.

"My main concern is the obvious need of the students to develop their independence and confidence," says Kate Brooks, director of the Liberal Arts Career Center at the University of Texas. "I think it's great that parents want to share their advice—and even better that students of this age are willing to listen—but I think the boundaries get crossed sometimes."

Donnell Turner, assistant director of the career center at Loyola University in Chicago, is just starting to notice the trend. He couldn't believe it when he saw the first of a few parents walk into a recent job fair for students.

"What is she doing here?" he thought to himself. Some students had the same thought.

"My parents are very supportive, but they're certainly not telling me what to do," said Ferris Wilson, a senior majoring in accounting and finance at Loyola who navigated the job fair by herself.

That said, she has seen many examples of parents who "dictate every move—even what their kids major in."

Often parents don't even know they're overdoing it. And it's not just at college.

Barbara Dwyer, a career coach in Sacramento, Calif., says she spoke at a Future Farmers of America meeting and met a mother whose son wanted to raise sheep for a living. The mom excitedly told Dwyer how she had done extensive research to find out what it would take for her son to get started in the business.

"I asked, 'Why did YOU do it?' And she looked shocked," Dwyer says.

Indeed, while many people have heard about the helicopter parent phenomenon, it's tough to find moms or dads who consider themselves one.

"You know, somebody called me that," says Diane Krier-Morrow, whose son recently graduated from Saint Louis University and is now teaching English in Taiwan. She came to the Loyola job fair to get information from employers for her son and brought copies of his resume to hand out.

"But believe me, I'm just going to hand him the bag," she said of the stack of jobs brochures and business cards she had gathered. "The rest is up to him."

She says parents sometimes worry that today's young people aren't as motivated to work as previous generations, so they feel inclined to do some nudging.

Marisa Wetzel, who graduated from New York University in May, knows what that's like. During her job search, her parents called her frequently to track her progress and to suggest friends who might have connections.

"Obviously, it can get a little annoying at times—but it's done with my best interest at heart," says Wetzel, 22. A month after she graduated, she landed a job as a publicity assistant in New York City.

She and other students say they use their parents as sounding boards because they trust their opinions—and don't want to repeat their mistakes.

But Ellis, at Delaware Valley College, says some students are too dependent.

He puts some of the blame on baby boomer parents, who have a reputation for coddling their children, but even more on the students.

"They've become so accustomed to having their parents take care of every aspect of their lives—and not assuming any responsibility or taking any initiative for themselves—that they expect their parents to continue to take care of things for them," Ellis says.

Eileen Tarjan, a human resources specialist at NCH Marketing Services in Deerfield, Ill., says she gets tired of making offers to students, only to hear them say, "Can I have the weekend to talk about it with my parents?"

"Why can't they just say, 'Let me think about it,'" she asks.

And it doesn't stop there. A few colleagues have told Tarjan that parents are now calling to discuss their kids' first performance reviews.

She shakes her head: "It's unbelievable."

Last Hope in a Weak Economy?
Mom and Dad

Emily Fredrix

After being laid off from her job as an events planner at an upscale resort, Jo Ann Bauer struggled financially. She worked at several lower-paying jobs, relocated to a new city and even declared bankruptcy.

Then in December, she finally accepted her parents' invitation to move into their home—at age 52. "I'm back living in the bedroom that I grew up in," she said.

Taking shelter with parents isn't uncommon for young people in their 20s, especially when the job market is poor. But now the slumping economy and the credit crunch are forcing some children to do so later in life—even in middle age.

Financial planners report receiving many calls from parents seeking advice about taking in their grown children following divorces and layoffs.

Kim Foss Erickson, a financial planner in Roseville, Calif., north of Sacramento, said she has never seen older children, even those in their 50s, depending so much on their parents as in the last six months.

"This is not like, 'OK, my son just graduated from college and needs to move back in' type of thing," she said. "These are 40- and 50-year-old children of my clients that they're helping out."

Parents "jeopardize their financial freedom by continuing to subsidize their children," said Karin Maloney Stifler, a financial planner in Hudson, Ohio, and a board member of the Financial Planning Association. "We have a hard time saying no as a culture to our children, and they keep asking for more."

Bauer's parents won't take rent money or let her help much with groceries. She's trying to save several hundred dollars a month for a house while working as a meetings coordinator.

Bauer would prefer to live on her own, but without her parents' help would "probably be renting again and trying to stick minimal money in the bank," she said.

Shirley Smith, 80, said she and her husband didn't hesitate when they invited Bauer to return to their home in Eden, Wis. Buying groceries for another person isn't stretching her budget too much, she said.

"I've got three kids and any of them can come home if they want," she said.

But plenty of well-meaning parents must delay retirement or scale back their dreams because they have to help their children, Stifler said.

Some of Erickson's clients are giving as much as $50,000 at a time to their kids, many of whom have overextended themselves with big houses or lavish lifestyles. And the sliding economy might threaten their jobs.

Parents feel guilty if they don't offer help, but she warns them to be careful with their savings.

"I almost have to act like a financial therapist if you will," she said. "'Here is the line I'm drawing for you. That's fine. You can do up to this point, but at this point, now you're starting to erode your own wealth.'"

Anna Maggiore, 27, lost her job as a publicist in Los Angeles about three years ago and moved into her parents' house in Los Alamos, N.M.

She tried to find jobs, but nothing stuck, so she enrolled full-time at the College of Santa Fe to finish her bachelor's degree in business.

She figures her parents spend about $1,000 a month on her, including a car payment, car and health insurance, school and other costs. Her father is a retired nuclear physicist and her mother, a guidance counselor, will retire this spring. Now Maggiore is looking for work so she can supplement their income.

"It's kind of hitting me finally that I need to get out there and find a job," she said. "Even if it's just part-time just to help out however I can."

A new survey by the retiree-advocacy group AARP found that one-fourth of Generation Xers, those 28 to 39 years old, receive financial help from family and friends.

The online survey of nearly 1,800 people ages 19 to 39 also found 57 percent believed they were "financially independent." But in a separate question, 33 percent said they received financial support from family and friends.

Bauer was caught by surprise when her job at a resort in Kohler, Wis., was cut four years ago, one year after she got divorced. The single mother bounced around to several lesser-paying jobs, declared bankruptcy and even moved 60 miles south to Milwaukee.

Her daughter, now 12, moved in with Bauer's ex-husband near her hometown.

Bauer decided to move to be closer to her and in December she found a job with the Experimental Aircraft Association in nearby Oshkosh. She tried to buy a house but needed 5 percent down. She only had 2 percent. She's now saving for a down payment and hopes to have it as early as June.

Bauer said she gets along well with her parents and knows she'll never get to spend so much time with them again. But it hurts her ego to live at home.

"I've had people say to me, 'Oh God, I could never do that,'" she said. "But you take humble steps in order to move forward."

Being a Sibling

The purpose of this descriptive exploratory study was to explore the meaning of being a sibling using Parse's human becoming perspective. Twelve children between 5 and 15 years of age with a younger sibling with a cleft lip and palate or Down Syndrome participated. Through semi-structured interviews and the use of art children talked about their experiences. Major themes portrayed the complex and paradoxical nature of being a sibling. The themes also revealed that having a sibling with special circumstances includes some unique opportunities and challenges. The finding of this study is the descriptive statement, being a sibling is an arduous charge to champion close others amid restricting-enhancing commitments while new endeavors give rise to new possibilities. Implications for nursing are discussed in the context of understanding being a sibling.

STEVEN L. BAUMANN, RN; PhD
Associate Professor, Hunter College, The City University of New York, New York

TINA TAYLOR DYCHES, EdD
Associate Professor, Brigham Young University, Provo, Utah

MARYBETH BRADDICK, MS
Ingram Visiting Nurses, Lansing, Michigan

The sibling relationship can be one of the longest and most important relationships in a person's life. Having a sibling can be very formative for children and instrumental in life. In an age when many people choose not to marry, marry later in life, and many marriages end in divorce, a sibling tie can provide stability and consistency. A sibling can provide fulfilling child-rearing experiences for people who do not have their own children. Yet for many, having a sibling fails to fulfill this potential. Despite years of research on the sibling relationship it is still not well understood (Dunn, 2000). Like being a parent, being a sibling includes much that is not in our control (Baumann & Braddick, 1999). This is particularly evident when a family has a child with special circumstances, or what most of the current literature describes as a child with *special needs*. The phrase *special needs* is avoided here because it imposes meaning, and labels, on the person. In the words of one participant from this study, siblings with special circumstances are *just different*. The authors of this study do assume that siblings of children with a cleft lip and palate (CL&P) or Down Syndrome (DS) in particular, can teach us not only about their personal experiences of being a sibling, but also about being a sibling in general.

Some researchers have said that having a sibling with special circumstances is stressful and problematic for the other children in the family (Murray, 1998, 1999, 2000; Senel & Akkok, 1995; Terzo, 1999). Others have reported that there is not much difference between having a sibling with special circumstances and having a sibling in general (Benson, Gross, & Kellum, 1999; Stawski, Auerbach, Barasch, Lerner, & Zimin, 1997). Still others have identified some benefits for siblings of children with special circumstances (Derouin & Jessee, 1996). It remains unclear what it means to children to have a sibling, with or without special circumstances. Therefore, the purpose of this descriptive exploratory study was to explore what it means to be a sibling. The primary aim of this inquiry was to add to the current understanding about being a brother or sister from the perspective of Parse's (1998) theory of human becoming. Parse holds that children, like adults, live situated freedom as full participants in the cocreation of their lives.

Relevant Literature

The word *sib* is thought to be derived from an Old English word *sib,* meaning relative, and from the Germanic word *sibja,* which means both blood relation and "one's own" (American Heritage Talking Dictionary, 1994). In everyday use, the word *sibling* refers to having one or both parents in common, or having a common ancestry. The terms *sister* and *brother* have numerous meanings, mostly related to close association or shared background (American Heritage Talking Dictionary, 1994).

Family psychoanalytic theory, on the other hand, focuses primarily on parent-child family processes and attributes both the closeness and tensions among family members to conscious and unconscious dynamics (Nichols & Schwartz, 1998). Families and social groups tend to impose expectations on siblings.

Sociologists, such as Mendelson, de Villa, Fitch, and Goodman (1997), have said that adult role expectations for siblings differ with age and gender of the sibling.

A family systems theory (Nichols & Schwartz, 1998) which views the family as an interactive system where what happens to one member affects all members, posits that the siblings represent a subsystem. Some family systems theorists hold that sibling position is very important to both the family and the child development. From this perspective, sibling experiences are shaped by birth order and gender (Silver & Frohlinger-Graham, 2000), and sibling relationships cannot be understood apart from other family relationships and events.

Most social scientists now view being a sibling as both a relationship and a family role (Dunn, 2000). It is likely that this dual nature of being a sibling contributes to the conflict that is common among many siblings. Pollack (2002) suggested that expecting older children to be the primary caregivers of their younger siblings contributes to intersibling tension and can lead to long-term resentment. Family size and the age differences of siblings may also influence sibling relationships, but this effect varies with the age of the siblings, proximity of one to another in the sibling constellation, and gender (Newman, 1996). Larger families may demonstrate both more affection and conflict, whereas wider age spacing between siblings has been observed to be related to less closeness and conflict (Newman, 1996).

Parents and researchers are generally impressed with how different siblings are from one another (Dunn, 2000). These differences are particularly evident in families with a child with special circumstances. As mentioned above, some authors have reported that siblings of children with special circumstances have more stressful lives, exhibit fewer competencies, have more psychopathologies, and may have more unrealistic housework and caregiving demands than siblings in general (Fisman et al., 1996; Fisman, Wolf, Ellison, & Freeman, 2000; Murray, 1999; Williams, 1997). These children are also described as having more limited playtime and opportunities to be with their friends (Seligman & Darling, 1997). Age is considered to be an important factor in understanding how children experience the circumstances of their siblings; older siblings of children with special circumstances have been reported to have more behavioral problems than younger siblings of children in the same situation (Morrison, 1997; Skidmore, 1996; Stawski et al., 1997).

Siblings of children with special circumstances have also been described as harboring intense emotions, such as anger and guilt (Meyer, Vadasy, & Vance, 1996). In addition, unequal parental attention, insufficient information, and ineffective communication between parents and children have been associated with misunderstandings, resentment, and conflict (Brody & Stoneman, 1996; Kowal & Kramer, 1997). Dunn (2000) reported that this pattern is also common in families stressed by separation or illness.

Siblings of children with special circumstances may also face comments by others who equate differences with moral inferiority (Goffman, 1963). These siblings must then make sense of incorrect assumptions, over generalizations, and insults, and

have to respond in awkward social situations. Some siblings have been observed altering their thinking or frame of reference in relation to these family members to mitigate their emotional involvement and negative feelings (Andersson, 1997). This shift in frame of reference could be seen as a defense, which minimizes the differences among the siblings, or it could be that they appreciate underlying likeness and the gifts that their siblings possess. Some health professionals judge the quality of life of persons with special circumstances as more negative than the individuals report themselves (Albrecht & Devlieger, 1999). This *disability paradox* can be explained by the pathological orientation of many biomedical-oriented health professionals, and their failure to appreciate factors which account for health and well being, such as how all individuals cocreate meaning with their values and choices (Parse, 1998).

Cuskelly, Chant, and Hayes (1998) found no significant differences between siblings of children with DS and a comparison group of siblings from the general population in relation to parent-reported behavioral problems. In addition, siblings of children with special circumstances have been found to demonstrate greater sensitivity and nurturing behaviors (Seligman & Darling, 1997), closer family relationships, more independence, and greater satisfaction in seeing improvement in their ill sibling than children without siblings with special circumstances (Derouin & Jessee, 1996).

The contributions of children with special circumstances to the family and community have also been described. Teachers have reported that siblings of children with special circumstances were more cooperative and had greater self-control than other children (Mandleco, Olsen, Robinson, Marshall, & McNeilly-Choque, 1998). Dunn (2000) suggested that sibling relationships offer children opportunities to learn about and better understand people and themselves. Vanier (1997) referred to the family as places where *lessons of the heart* can be learned, and children with special circumstances as particularly attentive to this dimension of human and family life. For Vanier, the heart is the affective core of the human being and its most fundamental reality (Downey, 1986). Being a sibling of a child with special circumstances can contribute to the sibling's identity and career direction (Seligman & Darling, 1997).

In summary, being a sibling is a significant experience for children and the literature is mixed regarding the experience of being a sibling of a child with special circumstances. Clearly unrealistic parenting roles assigned to siblings can contribute to sibling conflict and resentment. Further information is needed to explore the meaning of being a sibling, especially from the child's perspective. Therefore, through this study the authors sought to better understand the experience of being a brother or sister from the child's own perspective.

Conceptual Framework

The human becoming theory (Parse, 1998) views individuals and families as in mutual process with the universe. It represents a synthesis of selected existential phenomenological tenets and Rogers' science of unitary human beings (Parse, 1981). Three

Table 1 Demographics of Participants

Participant	Age	Gender	Number of Siblings	Birth Order	Special Circumstance
Mary	5	Girl	2	Oldest	Cleft Lip and Palate
Joe	6	Boy	1	Oldest	Cleft Lip and Palate
Marvin	8	Boy	7	3rd youngest	Cleft Lip and Palate
Marie	9	Girl	2	Middle	Cleft Lip and Palate
Jane	10	Girl	7	4th youngest	Cleft Lip and Palate
Peter	12	Boy	2	Oldest	Cleft Lip and Palate
Bob	13	Boy	2	Middle	Cleft Lip and Palate
Rebecca	14	Girl	7	Oldest	Cleft Lip and Palate
Mark	15	Boy	2	Oldest	Cleft Lip and Palate
Maura	9	Girl	1	Oldest	Down Syndrome
Sue	10	Girl	1	Oldest	Down Syndrome
Barbara	11	Girl	1	Oldest	Down Syndrome

major themes emerging from Parse's assumptions are meaning, rhythmicity, and cotranscendence. In Parse's (1998) terms, meaning is cocreating reality through the languaging of valuing and imaging. In other words, individuals, including young children, choose personal meaning in situations based upon their values. Rhythmicity is explained by Parse (1998) as patterns of relating which are paradoxical in nature, such that in the process of revealing something, one is also concealing, and likewise with enabling-limiting and connecting-separating. This view shows appreciation for the many levels and complexities that unfold in relationships of all kinds. It acknowledges that possibilities and limitations arise from choice-making. Cotranscending with the possibilities describes how one continually transforms one's view of the world based on life experiences (Parse, 1981). The theory holds that children, like adults, define what health and well-being is for them. Parse's theory guided the researchers in focusing on how siblings construct language to make sense of their experiences, how siblings live their patterns of relating, and how they participate in constructing their view of the future. The research question is, *What does it mean to be a sibling?*

Method

This descriptive exploratory study used the philosophical assumptions and the framework of the human becoming theory (Parse, 1998) to guide the researchers in viewing the participants, being with the participants, and designing objectives and questions to ask the participants. The objectives were: (a) to describe the meaning of being a sibling, (b) to describe changing relationship of living with a sibling, and (c) to describe views of the future in light of having a sibling.

Participants

Twelve biological siblings (ages 5–15), from eight families with a child with cleft lip and palate or DS participated in this descriptive exploratory study. Eight were the oldest children in their family, four were middle children, and all were older than

their sibling with special circumstances (see Table 1). Most participants were recruited after their parents responded to notices in newsletters of support groups in the northeast or midwestern United States; three were referred by others. All of the participants were Caucasian, but they represented several different cultures and religions. The human subjects institutional review board of a university approved the study; steps to safeguard minor-age participants' rights for self-determination and confidentiality were taken. The use of informed consent/assent and all other guidelines for protection of human subjects were followed, including the right to withdraw at any time. Each participant was given a pseudonym.

Procedure

Children were asked to describe (a) what it means to be a brother or sister, (b) how their relationships with others were different because they had a brother or sister, and (c) how their view of the future or what they wanted to be when they grew-up, had been altered by being a brother or sister. The special circumstances of their siblings were not mentioned in the questions used by the researchers, but it was in the consent. Specific questions included, What is it like for you to be a brother or sister? What is most important for you about being a brother or sister? How has being a brother or sister changed the way you relate to the people who are most important to you? How has it changed your relationships with others? Do you feel you relate differently to people because of your experiences as a brother or sister? What do you want to be when you are older, and has that changed because you are a brother or sister? Have your dreams changed? How has your view of life been changed by your experience of being a brother or sister? Tape-recorded interviews, guided by the open-ended questions, were conducted in a private area of the participants' homes. After being interviewed, participants were invited to draw or use a laptop with art software (Adobe Illustrator 7.0 or Microsoft Paint) and talk about their artwork. Children's art has been used with human becoming theory by the primary researcher in two previous studies (Baumann,

Table 2   The Findings Reflecting the Human Becoming Theory

Objectives of the Study	Theoretical Concepts	Participants' Language	Researchers' Language
To describe the meaning of being a sibling.	Structuring meaning multi-dimensionally	Being a brother or sister was a big responsibility, especially when they have something like Down's, "because you have to watch out for them," "you have to be there for them, defend them, protect them, or stand up for them."	An arduous charge to champion close others
To describe the changing relationship of living with a sibling.	Cocreating rhythmical patterns of relating	Having a sister or brother had "not changed their relationships with others much," they had less time to play with their friends, "learned how to treat others, to share, take care of people, and be nice to people who are different."	Restricting-enhancing commitments
To describe the views of the future in light of having a sibling.	Cotranscending with the possibilities	"Plans for the future had not changed," "interested in what their siblings like to do," "wanted to do things differently than their siblings had done," "careers where they would protect or care for others."	New endeavors give rise to new possibilities

1999a, 1999b). From this perspective, the interpretation of the art is left to the participant. The children were asked to talk about their drawings. The interviews and art sessions with each participant lasted 30–60 minutes.

Data Analysis

In a process Parse (2001) referred to as analyzing-synthesizing, major themes were identified according to the objectives of study. In this study, all interviews were transcribed and major themes of what being a brother or sister was like for the participants were determined by reading and contemplating participants' comments and artwork (Parse, 2001, 1987). These data contained answers to the specific questions asked by the researchers. Themes arose directly from the language of the participants, and were then synthesized to construct a descriptive statement in the language of the researcher, reflecting Parse's theory (Parse, 1998, 2001). All of the analysis-synthesis in this study was conducted by the primary researcher (SB). An earlier work by two of the authors on fathering used a similar methodology (Baumann & Braddick, 1999).

Findings

The finding of this study is the descriptive statement: *being a sibling is an arduous charge to champion close others amid restricting-enhancing commitments while new endeavors give rise to new possibilities.* The process of going from objectives to findings is outlined in Table 2. In Table 2, column 1 contains the objectives of the study and column 2 contains the themes of the human becoming theory. Column 3 presents participants' comments and column 4 presents the researchers' synthesis of being a sibling in the researcher's language.

Discussion
The Meaning of Being a Brother or Sister

Although the participants' comments clearly identified who is older, or *bigger* using their words, and the gender of each sibling, they were less likely to refer to the special circumstances of their brother or sister. One participant's comment regarding a sibling's special circumstances demonstrates this relative lack of attention to the special circumstance: In Barbara's (age 11) words, "I kind of forget that he has DS and I just see him as a boy." Some authors see this inattention to details as related to siblings' lack of information and awareness about the medical and other special circumstances of their sibling (McHale & Pawletko, 1992).

The participants' comments could also be seen as part of their way of "constructing reality through assigning significance to events" (Parse, 1998, p. 35). For example, when asked about being a sister, Mary (age 5) talked about her cousin, who was older than her, and about her brother who died without coming home from the hospital (at age 7 days), and not much about her two sisters with whom she lived. She also named one of her favorite stuffed animals after her brother who had died, which can also be seen as her defining of the membership of her family and how she is keeping her deceased brother present in her life.

For most of the participants in this study, being a sister or brother is a "big responsibility," which at times is fun. Participants said they have to "be there for their sibling, to stand up for them and protect them." Jane (age 10) said, "It's tough, you have to watch out for the others." Peter (age 12) said,

> If someone is pushing my brother I have to be there, or if my sister gets into trouble I have to be there, I have to

defend them. That's what being a brother or sister is all about. If I'm a big brother I have to defend littler kids than me, like the kid next door, I'll do that. One time I saw these kids go over to this kid and say, "Do you want to play Power Ranger?" The kid was little, he picked him up and threw him on the ground, so I went over there and stared at him and told him not to, he just stared right back at me. You kind of pester these kids or they don't listen.

Rebecca (age 14) said, "Well, it's hard sometimes because there are things to be taken care of, and you have to help them, but it's still fun, because they help you and they can be fun. So it's fun, but it's hard." Rebecca's comments reveal that being a sibling is both a duty and a source of enjoyment or amusement.

The participants in this study described the role of older sibling as being *fill-ins*. One participant said that when her mother was not around she had to tell her siblings what to do and what not to do. Mark (age 15) said, "for me as the oldest, I always felt that I had to look out for Dan, like when my mother has to go out." Bob (age 13), the middle brother in that same family, said, "I have to fill in for Mark, when he is not around, in looking out for Dan." Pollack (2002) referred to the caregiving role of older siblings as *auxiliary parents*. She said that in the United States since the 1970s older children spend less time in this role, than in earlier generations. She stated that this has reduced the resentment and conflict that can arise when older children's own needs and education were to some degree shortchanged because of their caregiving responsibilities.

Several participants discussed the moods and behaviors of their siblings, which they described as *difficult*. Sue (age 10) said, "Well, it gets kind of annoying sometimes, but if you don't have a really restless sister, it can be kind of fun. My sister, as she is younger than me, she's kind of restless and sometimes it bothers me, she bugs me so much. Sometimes I wish she was not even there." Maura (age 9) said, "Well, I think it is sort of a responsibility, because you have to look after your brother. I think it is a little harder with a kid having DS, but it's not that much harder. It's a big responsibility." She described him as "rough" and having a "tough build," and that used to bother her until she realized that this is "the way he is." Peter (age 12) created a computer image of an oval face and described it as his brother when he gets mad—he gave him concentric red circles in his eyes. He also drew himself offering his brother who fell while skating on the sidewalk a band aid from a first aid kit.

When asked what was the most important thing about being a brother or sister, several participants again mentioned having to be responsible. Others mentioned caring, listening, and "cheering each other up." Maura (age 9) said, "I think it's really important for me to listen to him and understand what he's saying, not to ignore him, to understand that he has feelings too." While none of the participants focused on the learning differences of their siblings, this comment by a very articulate sibling of a child with DS, hints at the effort she has to make to understand what her brother is saying and her choice to see it as important. Rebecca (age 14) said, "to be able to help them and care about them." Sue (age 10) said what was most important for her was when her sister was there for her, "Like when my

grandpa died . . . she pats you on your back. It's like when you cry, she cries." Peter (age 12) said,

> Being there for them when they are sad or depressed, or mad about something, I go there and talk to them, I sought out the problems that they are having, like when Jim got mad at something, I got mad at him, I gave him a piece of gum, and he was happy again, he came downstairs and we went outside. I help Marie (age 9) sometimes, when Mom yells at her, I comfort her.

The synthesis of the participants' comments related to the first objective, which was to describe the meaning of being a brother or sister, in the language of the researcher is: *an arduous charge to champion close others.* Being a sister or brother is a mix of feelings, including feeling dutiful, antagonism, and enjoyment, from which a mutually nurturing presence can arise. This synthesis also exemplifies the complexity of being a sibling. Longitudinal studies of sibling relationships have suggested that close relationships between siblings can become closer as siblings provide assistance and support for each other (Dunn, 2000). The participants' comments also suggest that courage and commitment is required when being a brother or sister, particularly when *being there* for a younger sibling with special circumstances. This finding is related in this study to the first principle of human becoming theory (Parse, 1998), structuring meaning multidimensionally is cocreating reality through the languaging of valuing and imaging (p. 35). Being a sibling is a paradoxical rhythm of confirming-not confirming that one is neither alone nor without obligations.

The Way Relationships Unfold

Several participants said they did not think having a brother or sister changed their relationships with others very much. However, others said their mothers spent more time with younger siblings than they did with them. Mary (age 5) said her youngest sister (who has a cleft lip and palate) slept in her mother's bed, "because she could suffocate." She also said, "My daddy used to be home more. He used to buy me rainbow cookies, but when my sister was born he had to work all the time." Some participants said being a brother or sister decreased the time they had to be with and play with their friends.

Several participants described how being a brother or sister had altered their relationships with other people. As mentioned above, some participants reported that there had been times when having to take care of their sibling reduced the time they could spend with their friends. A few reported incidents when their sibling's *difficult* behaviors were directed at their friends, or were embarrassing. What they said also suggested that having a sibling, especially one with special circumstances, can deepen relationships with others. Peter (age 12) said,

> Sometimes my friends tease my brother, so I say, "Don't do that;" but I am not too harsh on them. My friends have been there for Marie and my brother too, they like them and care for them too. When I baby sit my brother, and Linda comes over and she helps me, or Tracy, they come

over and help me with my brother and Marie. They help out, almost like they are part of the family.

In this way several participants came to value and appreciate their friends who had shown understanding and helpfulness to their siblings. Several said that they had looked out for the well-being of other young children as well, recalling how their own brother or sister had been treated by other people. Having a sibling at times interfered with their plans. Having a sibling also served to encourage children to try things, they might not have done alone, such as a pair of brothers in this study who chose to be in their school plays.

The way relationships unfold when being a sibling was stated in the language of the researcher as the paradox: *restricting-enhancing commitments*. At times participants had to forego their own plans because they had a sibling, but most times this was not without satisfaction and learning. While the conflict and tensions evident in some of the participants' comments could be related to their perception of having less time to be with their parents or friends, it can also reflect their annoyance that siblings wanted what they had. Marie's (age 9) drawing of being a sibling was very similar to her brother's (Peter, age 12) which she had seen, but she was happy to point out the differences. The annoyance of having younger siblings imitate them was evident in Sue's (age 10) comment that her sister "loves every single thing that I have." Girard (1996) saw rivalry for the same object as a basis of most social conflict, and he said such conflicts arise because a person wants to be like their model. He called this phenomenon *mimetic desire* and he saw this in most cultures and religions. Girard (1996) did not see this as a bad thing, because imitating ultimately involved "opening oneself out" (p. 64).

One participant (Sue, age 10) mentioned how unfair some children are to children with DS. She described children with DS as "just different." Her use of the word *just* suggested that to her they were essentially like other children, despite their obvious differences. She was also referring to the importance of including all children, and this reveals her growing awareness of the importance of being sensitive to the feelings of others. Some participants also found ways to cheer up their siblings when they were feeling down, and learned how to accept their anger without needing to retaliate. The second principle of human becoming theory (Parse, 1998) is: Cocreating rhythmical patterns of relating is living the paradoxical unity of revealing-concealing and enabling-limiting while connecting-separating (p. 42). For example, Peter's computer graphic of one of his brother's anger, could be seen as his revealing, while concealing, his own differences and difficult feelings. The second part of the finding of this study, restricting-enhancing, can be described as reflecting the enabling-limiting of connecting-separating of being a sibling. Being a sibling involves decisions which alter one's view of the past, and living out of one's present and future possibilities.

How One's View of Life Has Changed When Being a Sibling?

Several participants said being a brother or sister had not changed their view of their future or the world, but some children said they had learned from their sibling's mistakes. Others identified their own interests by trying and liking things their siblings liked. For example Bob (age 13) got involved in school plays like this older brother Mark (age 15), and both wanted to continue to be in plays in high school and maybe go into acting.

Several participants were able to connect their thoughts about their future with their current family situation. Peter (age 12) said he wanted to be a police officer so that he could "be responsible to take care of other people." Another said she wanted to be a pediatrician to take care of children. One participant planned to go into business with her siblings. Dunn (1999) observed that in sibling interactions, play, and conversations, there is evidence that children read each other's feelings and intentions and explore their abilities and differences. Most participants' comments suggested that they accepted their situation as siblings of children with special circumstances, and accept these children for who they were. This appeared to be a transformative process for them.

The concept of psychosocial adjustment as applied to the situation of siblings of children with special circumstances (Murray, 2000), fails to appreciate the transformative possibilities in the experience. In the present study, the researchers, led by the assumptions of human becoming theory, synthesized these comments as the theme: *new endeavors give rise to new possibilities*. Children participate in cocreating their world by their choices in given circumstances. Often children are particularly imaginative in their envisioning of new possibilities.

The possibilities that arise for young children reflect their exposure to various experiences and to close others, including parents, siblings, and teachers. The personal meanings and imaginations of children also reflect this cocreating process. For example, they and their siblings are from time to time transformed into various characters from their favorite stories. The special circumstances of siblings in this study did not hamper these participants' abilities to make choices, to play, or to use their imagination; however, it did give them some different options to consider. The third principle of the human becoming theory is cotranscending with the possibles is powering unique ways of originating in the process of transforming (Parse, 1998, p. 46). The tasks and challenges of being a sibling faced by the participants of this study were different from most of their friends and it gave rise to personal uniqueness, if not distinction.

Conclusions and Implications

Like all qualitative research, the findings of this study are not meant to be generalized to other groups or suggest causal relationships. This study is also limited because it did not include children of color. It also did not include enough varied participants to explore the differences between the experiences of siblings of children with CL&P and DS and those without siblings with special circumstances. The reader is also encouraged to keep in mind that most of the participants were the oldest child in these families.

For the most part, the participants of this descriptive exploratory study talked about being a brother or sister in general, but some of their comments related to having siblings with special circumstances. The participants' comments suggest that the *special circumstances* of their siblings were generally accepted and relatively unimportant to them. Only one participant said there were times she wished her sibling "wasn't even there." All participants found both challenges and opportunities in having a sibling, for example, they generally understood that younger children need more attention from their mothers, and they realized that some children require special arrangements. The participants generally took their responsibilities very seriously, and for the most part, felt it gave them a sense of purpose and direction. Many admitted their experiences contributed to how they were with other people. There were three sets of participants from the same family in this study. These sibling pairs seemed to share much in common and be cohesive, perhaps in part because of their relationship and duties with their sibling with special circumstances.

The findings related to Parse's (1998) theory suggest being a sister or brother is *an arduous charge to champion close others amid restricting-enhancing commitments while new endeavors gives rise to new possibilities.* Being a sibling is a complex, paradoxical and ever-changing experience. It includes making choices and being responsible. This investigation also uncovered a definition of being a sibling that reflects shifting rhythms and changing perspectives of what is possible.

Parents and nurses should provide opportunities for children to talk about their feelings and thoughts regarding being a sibling in general and in particular about being a sibling of a child with special circumstances. The use of art can be a particularly helpful means of communicating with such children. It may also be helpful if nurses can get to know children's favorite stories and toys, to explore new meaning in difficult situations, such as discovering that a child's favorite stuffed animal was named after a family member who had died. The tendency of many children, especially older children of siblings with special circumstances, to feel overly responsible can interfere with their ability to enjoy the pleasure of being a child (Pollack, 2002). Childhood is the secret place where imagination, uniqueness, and hope are most alive. This place is a vital resource not only for them but also for their families and close others. Some families with unexpected birth events and children with special circumstances have a difficult time finding new meaning. For them there is incongruence between what they had previously hoped and dreamed for and their present lives. This is a particularly good opportunity for nurses who practice nursing in a way which is "illuminating meaning, synchronizing rhythms and mobilizing transcendence" (Parse, 1998, pp. 69–70).

This study also suggests that nurses can help families find ways to understand the difficult behaviors of children, especially those with special circumstances. These behaviors can be difficult for siblings to understand and live with. While providing siblings with more information may be needed at times, each child's view of his or her family and sibling's circumstances should be respected. Longitudinal studies of being a sibling, and a sibling of children with special circumstances would provide valuable understanding of this important and common life experience.

References

Albrecht, G. L., & Devlieger, P. J. (1999). The disability paradox: High quality of life against all odds. *Social Science & Medicine, 48,* 977–988.

The American heritage talking dictionary of the English language (3rd ed.). (1994). New York: Houghton Mifflin.

Andersson, E. (1997). Relations in families with a mentally retarded child from the perspective of the siblings. *Scandinavian Journal of Caring Sciences, 11,* 131–138.

Baumann, S. (l999a). Art as a path of inquiry. *Nursing Science Quarterly, 12,* 106–110.

Baumann, S. (1999b). The lived experience of hope: Children in families struggling to make a home. In R. R. Parse, *Hope: An international human becoming perspective* (pp. 191–210). Boston: Jones & Bartlett.

Baumann, S., & Braddick, M. (1999). Out of their element: Fathers of children who are not the same. *Journal of Pediatric Nursing, 14,* 369–377.

Benson, B. A., Gross, A. M., & Kellum, G. (1999). The siblings of children with craniofacial anomalies. *Children's Health Care, 28,* 51–68.

Brody, G. H., & Stoneman, Z. (1996). A risk-amelioration model for sibling relationships: Conceptual underpinning and preliminary findings. In G. H. Brody (Ed.), *Sibling relationships: Their cause and consequences* (pp. 231–247). Norwood, NJ: Ablex.

Cuskelly, M., Chant, D., & Hayes, A. (1998). Behaviour problems in the siblings of children with Down Syndrome: Associations with family responsibilities and parental stress. *International Journal of Disability, Development & Education, 45,* 295–311.

Derouin, D., & Jessee, P. O. (1996). Impact of a chronic illness in childhood: Siblings' perceptions. *Issues in Comprehensive Pediatric Nursing, 19,* 135–147.

Downey, M. (1986). *A blessed weakness: The spirit of Jean Vanier and l'Arche.* New York: Harper & Row.

Dunn, J. (1999). Making sense of the social world: Mindreading, emotion and relationships. In P. D. Zelazo, J. W. Astington, & D. R. Olson (Eds.), *Developing theories of intention: Social understanding and self control* (pp. 229–242). Mahwah, NJ: Lawrence Erlbaum.

Dunn, J. (2000). State of the art: Siblings. *The Psychologist, 13,* 244–248.

Fisman, S., Wolf, L., Ellison, D., & Freeman, T. (2000). A longitudinal study of siblings of children with chronic disabilities. *Canadian Journal of Psychiatry, 45,* 369–375.

Fisman, S., Wolf, L., Ellison, D., Gillis, B., Freeman, T., & Szatmari, P. (1996). Risk and protective factors affecting the adjustment of siblings of children with chronic disabilities. *Journal of the American Academy of Child & Adolescent Psychiatry, 35,* 1532–1541.

Girard, R. (1996). *The Girard reader* (J. G. Williams, Ed.). New York: Crossroad.

Goffman, E. (1963). *Stigma: Notes on the management of spoiled identity.* Englewood Cliffs, NJ: Prentice-Hall.

Kowal, A., & Kramer, L. (1997). Children's understanding of parental differential treatment. *Child Development, 68,* 113–126.

Mandleco, B., Olsen, S., Robinson, C., Marshall, E., & McNeilly-Choque, M. (1998). Social skills and peer relationships of siblings of children with disabilities: Parental and family linkages. In P. Slee & K. Rigby (Eds.), *Children's peer relations: Current issues and future directions* (pp. 106–120). London: Routledge.

McHale, S. M., & Pawletko, T. (1992). Different treatment of siblings in two family contexts: Implications for children's adjustment and relationship evaluations. *Child Development, 63,* 68–81.

Mendelson, M. J., de Villa, E. P., Fitch, T. A., & Goodman, F. G. (1997). Adult expectations for children's sibling roles. *International Journal of Behavioral Development, 20,* 549–572.

Meyer, D. J., Vadasy, P., & Vance, R. S. (1996). *Living with a brother or sister with special needs: A book for sibs* (Rev. ed.). Seattle, WA: University of Washington Press.

Morrison, L. (1997). Stress and siblings. *Pediatric Nursing, 9,* 26–27.

Murray, J. S. (1998). The lived experience of childhood cancer: One sibling's perspective. *Issues in Comprehensive Pediatric Nursing, 21,* 217–227.

Murray, J. S. (1999). Siblings of children with cancer: A review of the literature. *Journal of Pediatric Oncology Nursing, 16.* 225–234.

Murray, J. S. (2000). Attachment theory and adjustment difficulties in siblings of children with cancer. *Issues in Mental Health Nursing, 2,* 149–169.

Newman, J. (1996). The more the merrier? Effects of family size and sibling spacing on sibling relationships. *Child Care, Health and Development, 22,* 285–302.

Nichols, M. P., & Schwartz, R. C. (1998). *Family therapy: Concepts and methods* (4th ed.). Boston: Allyn & Bacon.

Parse, R. R. (1981). *Man-living-health: A theory of nursing.* New York: Wiley.

Parse, R. R. (1987) Parse's man-living health theory of nursing. In R. R. Parse, *Nursing science: Major paradigms, theories, and critiques* (pp. 181–204). Philadelphia: Saunders.

Parse, R. R. (1998). *The human becoming school of thought: A perspective for nurses and other health professionals.* Thousand Oaks, CA: Sage.

Parse, R. R. (2001). *Qualitative inquiry: The path of sciencing.* Sudbury, MA: Jones and Bartlett.

Pollack, E. G. (2002). The children we have lost: When siblings were caregivers, 1900–1970. *Journal of Social History, 36,* 31–61.

Seligman, M., & Darling, R. B. (1997). *Ordinary families, special children: A systems approach to childhood disability* (2nd ed.). New York: Guilford Press.

Senel, H. G., & Akkok, F. (1995). Stress levels and attitudes of normal siblings of children with disabilities. *International Journal for the Advancement of Counseling, 18,* 61–68.

Silver, E. J., & Frohlinger-Graham, M. J. (2000). Brief report: Psychological symptoms in healthy female siblings of adolescents with and without chronic conditions. *Journal of Pediatric Psychology, 25,* 279–284.

Skidmore, K. L. (1996). Childhood cancer, families and siblings. (Doctoral dissertation, Loyola University, 1996), *Dissertation Abstracts International, 56*(12B), 7056.

Stawski, M., Auerbach, J. G., Barasch, M., Lerner, Y., & Zimin, R. (1997). Behavioral problems of children with chronic physical illness and their siblings. *European Child and Adolescent Psychiatry, 6,* 20–25.

Terzo, H. (1999). Evidence-based practice: The effects of childhood cancer on siblings. *Pediatric Nursing, 25,* 309–311.

Vanier, J. (1997). *Our journey home: Rediscovering a common humanity beyond our differences* (M. Parham, Trans.). Maryknoll, NY: Novalis.

Williams, P. D. (1997). Siblings and pediatric chronic illness: A review of the literature. *International Journal of Nursing Studies, 34,* 312–323.

Aunties and Uncles

JOHN TYLER CONNOLEY

When Mom was a kid, her nuclear family consisted of her mom and dad, one sister, two brothers, one cousin and his wife, and Grandpa and Grandma. They all lived together in an Indiana farmhouse, where 40 relatives (the extended family) would arrive each Sunday afternoon for chicken and dumplings. Family holidays, like Thanksgiving and Christmas, included even more people, many of whom were not strictly relatives but were "church family." Like a quilt, Mom's childhood family was constructed from many pieces sewn together with love.

When Mom grew up and left home, she became a missionary and moved to Africa with her husband and two kids, but she took her family values with her. Family in our house meant all the people we cared about. Of course, we had relatives in the United States, but we also had our missionary family.

My sister and I called all the missionaries Auntie and Uncle, which I suppose made their children our "cousins." When I think of my earliest memories, I think of eating Auntie Eleanor's cheesecake, being scared by Auntie Rosemary's funny faces, and visiting Uncle Ora and Auntie Linda in South Africa.

The first time we came back to the United States, the terms grandma and grandpa confused my sister and me: We kept calling them Auntie Grandma and Uncle Grandpa because that's how one referred to relatives.

These aunties and uncles who made up my familial world are the people I learned to depend on. They're the ones who taught me what it meant to be a grown-up. Their children were the kids I wrestled with and fought with and played Star Wars with. Later they would become the people I'd pick up the phone and call for help if I needed it. It never occurred to me that family should be related by blood or marriage, or that familial responsibility might extend only to the people to whom you are legally bound.

I've grown up and moved away, but I've taken my mom's inclusive definition of family with me. Like my grandparents in their Hoosier farmhouse and my parents on their mission sta-tion, my partner, Rob, and I have a door that's always open. We intentionally moved to a small town here in New Mexico so we could afford to buy a big house with lots of space for guests and where we would have a close community of people we cared about. We don't have kids yet, but we know when we do they'll be raised in an extended family that includes lots of relatives and lots of friends.

We believe children should be raised by a community—of aunties and uncles, of friends and relatives, of all the people we love. And we trust that if our child's immediate household doesn't include a mother and a father, well, that's OK, because the quilt is bigger than our little corner. And there will always be adult role models around.

Rob and I have embraced a traditional meaning of family that is expansive enough to include the whole world. And this family tradition of inclusiveness has made us wary of "traditional family" rhetoric. Why would anyone want to limit the definition of family to a mother, father, and two kids? It's like substituting a quilted place mat for a warm bedspread.

The way we understand it, family is just another word for the people we love, and the nuclear family is everyone we can fit under our roof. If one of our friends loses his job and needs a place to stay, he might become part of the nucleus. If Rob's mom decides to move to New Mexico, she might join the nucleus too. It doesn't matter how or if we're legally related; what matters is that family takes care of each other.

Instead of limiting the legal definition of family, we would like to expand it. Let the patchwork connections we make with one another be reflected in the way the government treats us. Let people choose their families, and then write the laws to support those choices. To do anything else seems contrary to my family's values.

JOHN TYLER CONNOLEY cowrote *The Children Are Free: Reexamining the Biblical Evidence on Same-Sex Relationships.* He lives in Silver City, N.M.

Roles of American Indian Grandparents in Times of Cultural Crisis

This study examined the roles of contemporary American Indian grandparents in the lives of their grandchildren. Structured interviews were conducted with 20 American Indian grandparents. Analysis of interviews followed a sequence of strategies traditionally identified with the process of data reduction and analysis using qualitative methodologies. Participants reported enculturative responsibilities for their grandchildren in regard to traditional tribal values and knowledges such as tribal spirituality and protocol, cooperative interaction, tribal language and appreciation of nature. Methods of enculturation took the form of stories, modeling, direct teaching and playful interaction.

ROCKEY ROBBINS, PHD, ET AL.

Given the dearth of articles about American Indian grandparents in psychological journals, it is necessary to briefly review relevant articles in order to provide an enriched context for this study. In many cultures, grandparents are seen as "fun relatives," offering treats and activities that parents were unable or unwilling to provide, such as social games, companionship, community events and domestic help (Kennedy, 1992). Grandparents are also seen as the designated repository of family histories, culture and memories (Williams, 1995). In some cultures, grandparents are viewed as community leaders, mediators and to some extent, lawgivers (Bahr, 1994). Grandparents are also seen as transmitters of family values, such as morality, altruism, social identity, a sense of accomplishment, competency and affiliation (Timberlake & Chipungu, 1992).

Grandparents are frequently mentioned as providers of emotional and tangible support for their grandchildren (Scherman, Goodrich, Kelly Russell, & Javidi, 1988; Scherman, Beesley, & Turner, 2003). However, this varies, due in part to the grandparents' health, geographical proximity and financial ability. Grandparents often provide support for their children who have young children of their own. The support can be monetary, advice giving, baby sitting or emotional support. This role changes depending on the perceived needs of the family, and the grandparents situation. The grandparents may become the ones needing care and support due to health problems (Creasey & Kahiler, 1994, Sander & Trygstad, 1993). The frequency and quality of contact between grandparents and grandchildren also affect the roles adopted by the grandparents, as well as the level of perceived support (Creasey & Kahiler, 1994).

Few articles have been written specifically about American Indian grand parenting. Those have focused primarily on grandmothers, changing status, and social culture (Barr, 1994; Nahemow, 1987; Schweitzer, 1987; Williams, 1995) and their place in the American Indian extended family (Coleman, Unau, & Manyfingers, 2001). They have also been described as storytellers (Barnett, 1955) and mentors (Elmendorf & Kroeber, 1960). Weibel-Orlando (1990) conducted interviews with 28 American Indian grandparents to determine grand-parenting styles. She found five basic styles: ceremonial, which entails grandparents acting as models of appropriate ceremonial behavior; fictive, which entails older persons nurturing children as an alternative to the lack or absence of biological grandchildren; custodial, which entails grandparents taking on full child care responsibilities for their grandchildren; distanced, which entails almost complete lack of contact with grandchildren; and cultural conservator, which entails grandparents and ways of life.

Williams (1995) differentiated the roles American Indian grandfathers and grandmothers played. Grandfathers are more likely than grandmothers to view grand-parenting as an opportunity to share information with grandchildren and to take pride in grandchildren's accomplishments. Noor Al-Deen (1997) lists American Indian women's traditional roles as life-givers, healers, caregivers, mothers, guardians, nurturers, family counselors, providers, and sources of wisdom and knowledge to their nations, including council decisions and participation in battle. She noted that female American Indian elders experience conflict that may result from divergent tribal and dominant culture's pressures and expectations regarding their grand-parenting roles. Noor Al-Deen proposes three factors which contribute to these conflicts: 1) cultural deprivation caused by prejudice from Euro-American mainstream populations; 2) restricted traditionalism from governmental and societal pressures coupled with the loss of tribal lands; and 3) federal bureaucratic health care from Indian Health Services.

According to Coleman, Unau, and Manyfingers (2001), the extended family plays a central role in raising Indian children. Grandparents and community elders are considered potent sources of influence for children, families, and communities as a whole. It is common for grandparents to willingly assume childcare responsibilities for their grandchildren and for parents to seek advice from community elders. This study attempts to explore and explicate the specific contents of the roles of American Indian grandparent's roles in the enculturation process of passing down values, stories and songs, as well as the cultural costumes, and their function as a nurturer and protector.

Methodology

Three American Indian and one Euro-American interviewers met with 20 American Indian grandparents. Interviews were conducted in American Indian mental health centers and in the homes of participants. A structured interview schedule was used to conduct the interviews (a copy of the structured interview is available from the first author). Information was collected on contents of grandparents roles play in lives of their grandchildren, the relationships between grandparents.[sic] Each interview was summarized and transmitted electronically to the person analyzing the data.

Eighteen of the twenty participants in this study were from Oklahoma. The tribes represented were: Cherokee, Creek, Chickasaw, Commanche, Lakota, Pawnee, Pottawatomi, Seminole, and Shawnee. Participants included seven grandfathers and thirteen grandmothers, ranging in age from 42 to 79, averaging 59. Eight participants reported that they spoke their tribal language fluently and two participants reported they could understand their tribal language, but could not speak it fluently. Two other participants reported being able to speak their tribal language as young children but could not speak it now. Ages of participants ranged from 42 to 79, averaging 59. The grandchildren participants described ranged in age from 2 to 18 years and averaged 11. Seven participants reported that the grandchild they described lived with them. Six participants reported that the grandchild they described lived over 30 minutes away from them. Six grandparents reported that they and their families participated in the Relocation Program for American Indians during the 1960's. Three grandparents had attended Indian Boarding Schools and none of the grandchildren described attended Indian Boarding Schools.

Participants were asked to describe the roles they played in the lives of one of their grandchildren. The questions were open-ended, and throughout the interview each grandparent was provided as much time and autonomy to answer the questions as she needed. The interviewer was allowed to rephrase or probe as a way to elicit clarification, additional information, detail, or elaboration (Bodgan & Biklen, 1992; Survey Research Center, 1982). When supplemental questioning occurred, non-directive probing techniques (Survey Research Center, 1982), whereby the interviewer's response is only a simple acknowledgement using a neutral follow-up question or comment (such as "could you tell me more," or "what do you mean by that"), were used

to insure that the interviewer did not influence the grandparents' responses.

Analysis of the interviews followed a sequence of strategies traditionally identified with the process of data reduction and analysis using qualitative methodologies (Bogdan & Biklin, 1992; Creswell, 1998; Huberman & Miles, 1994; Lincoln & Guba, 1985). The analysis began by independently reviewing the transcripts through multiple readings, taking a micro analytic perspective, and using grounded theory methodology to identify concepts and generate potential categories to represent participant responses (Strauss & Corbin, 1994, 1998). Categories and themes that existed across all interviews, as well as those within the context of specific questions, were identified. A series of meetings were then held where identification and discussion of potential concepts, their properties and constructions, and metaphors to realistically represent grandparents' responses were shared. Over the course of these meetings, initial themes and coding conventions were established, resulting in a process often referred to as "open coding" (Strauss & Corbin, 1998). It was also determined that in most cases the level of coding would anchor on phrases or sentences (Strauss & Corbin, 1998), and that frequency counts (Huberman & Miles, 1994) would be collected to aide in the representation of themes and concepts.

Having identified the coding conventions, two raters independently returned to the transcripts and coded the responses to each question. The process of coding and data analysis in qualitative research is one that is fluid and dynamic, and can often result in intuitive modifications regarding the labeling and meaning of themes and categories (Criswell, 1998; Straus & Corbin, 1998). Therefore during this phase of the coding process, the raters continued to document new or alternative constructions of themes and concepts. Huberman and Miles (1994) view data analysis as an interactive process where data reduction, data display, and conclusion drawing interact with one another. These components do not occur in a single linear sequence, rather they revolve around each other, indicating that the process of data analysis can go through a number of iterations. Subsequent to independent analysis, the raters held a second set of meetings, and applied procedures consistent with the principle of multiple investigator corroboration (Lincoln & Guba, 1985) and the value of employing multiple perspectives during analytic interpretations (Strauss & Corbin, 1998). They reviewed and compared their analyses, held additional discussion, and combined their interpretations, finally reaching a consensus regarding how each participant's responses were coded for each question.

Results

In many ways contemporary American Indian grand-parenting roles are similar to grand-parenting roles in general. For instance, participants in this study frequently reported partaking in general custodial and care taking responsibilities such as babysitting, transporting, disciplining, coordinating extended family gatherings and cooking for their grandchildren (Sherman, 2003). They also emphasized their role of cultural conservator through telling traditional and family stories (Sherman, 1988). The styles with which they performed these roles were also often commensurate to the styles described in previous studies. For instance, participants spoke of "spoiling," "giving more space," and offering unconditional love to their grandchildren (Sherman, 2003). Nonetheless, contemporary American Indian grand-parenting roles and styles emerge from unique socio-economic and cultural conditions that dress them in unique costumes.

All of the participants expressed feelings of enculturative responsibilities, in greater and lesser degrees. Only one person was tentative, stating that he would not take an assertive role in this area, but would wait to respond to his granddaughter's own interest to discuss tribal history and beliefs. All other participants reported that they engaged in active efforts to pass on American Indian traditional knowledge. Nineteen of the twenty grandparents interviewed expressed grave fears about the possibility of tribal culture being lost. One grandfather said, "Our ways are dying out with the death of every elder."

The most commonly mentioned strategy of cultural preservation took story form. Sixteen participants mentioned that they told stories to their grandchildren. The stories that were retold during the interviews might be categorized as nature, prudence, historical and ghost stories. In one story a duck rescues a man from drowning and in another a reed offers life saving air to a girl who is hiding from a fight at home. Stories such as these seem to imply that if nature is respected it will provide human beings with survival. Several participants told stories suggesting a prudence theme, recommending that children should think before acting. For instance, one interviewee related a story about Indian boys thoughtlessly playing a game of shooting arrows straight up into the air. One day an arrow came down onto the head of one of the boys, injuring him. Another person told a story of how "White people" came onto their land wanting to set up a trading post, which many feared would disrupt their way of life, and were directed to locate on a hill away from the Indian community. Some told stories of spirits. One warned of not telling ghost stories to grandchildren until they "grew older" and another warned not to tell ghost stories after dark. The stories suggest that many Indian grandparents are intent on their grandchildren knowing that the world consists of more than its material surface and that traditional rules function as forms of protection.

American Indian grandparent participants almost unanimously provided active support in their grandchildren's' participation in both tribal and pan-Indian activities, ceremonies, and ways of interacting. The list of these activities include facilitating grandchildren's participation in pow-wows, gourd dances, sweats, Indian church, dressing out in appropriate traditional regalia, Indian games, naming ceremonies, adoption ceremonies, stomp dances, bread dances, making tribal foods, crafts, and drumming. Several grandparents expressed great concern that their grandchildren know the differences and protocol regarding tribal dress at pow-wows, understanding different perspectives regarding "stomp dancers" and "pow-wow people," and distinguishing between stomp dance beliefs and Indian church beliefs. Another grandmother claimed to be so concerned that her son learn to drum and sing his tribal songs that she had taken the lead to teach him rather than leaving it to

males in her tribe. Also, the majority of the participants mentioned that it was important to teach at least some words of their tribal language to their grandchildren. Their language teaching ranged from teaching their grandchildren to be fluent to teaching them basic introductions, words for relatives, and songs. Almost all participants spoke of tribal language being an important element or their tribal culture.

Every American Indian grandparent interviewed stressed a concern for passing down values, which she believed to be colored by their ethnicity. Thirteen participants discussed their desire to teach their children a love and respect for nature. For some an ecological mindedness for clean water and respect for plants and animals was expressed, while for some it was an appreciation for nature's beauty. Just under half the participants said that "respect" was a value they wished to pass on. When asked to define this word it was usually defined as "honoring your elders." Other values mentioned at from three to six times were: showing appreciation, courage, unselfishness, hard work, giving, quietness, kindness, pride in being Indian, balance, and regular prayer. Participants said they taught these values by role modeling and through direct verbal communication. Several participants complained that their children were not teaching the above values to their grandchildren.

Acting as a facilitator in "bringing the family together" was another role participants believed that they regularly performed to help grandchildren. This idea was expressed in the following ways: "I feel a responsibility to bring the family together for meals. My grandchild can get to know his family this way." "I bring him to Indian church and show him off." "I look forward to the day I can bring her to my tribal pow-wow. When she gets old enough, her white father won't be able to stop me. My tribal people know she is alive and they will be so happy to meet her." "It is important for me to have her mix with her cousins and aunts. She will need them for support." "It is great to get the nephews and nieces together to fish and play softball." "Our land has been in our family for 150 years. We clean it up and I get everybody together there. My grandchild fishes there with his cousins." "My grand daughter sits right there next to me and her family at the pow-wows." The preceding remarks reflect the grandparents' values of regular interaction and closeness across generations and among extended family members. While one does not detect a law like regularity that governs interactions, there appears to be an expectation of continuous exchanges. Grandparents also appear to view this role as a source of self-worth.

All participants expressed the belief that as grandparents they had unique offerings for their grandchildren. Several mentioned the love, support and interaction that they had with their grandchildren as more egalitarian and less structured, characterizing it as "less directive," "more imaginative" and "more flexible" than parent/child interactions. One grandmother described her role with her granddaughter as being a "playmate." Others spoke again of their responsibilities to transmit "old ways" and "family history" and to gather the extended family together. One person reflected comments several others made when she described herself as a "safety net" when problems arose with her grandchild's parents. One grandparent said his unique contribution to his grandson's life was starting a drum group for his grandson to participate in.

When asked about what they would prefer to do as a grandparent, comments reflected desires to be useful and attached, yet not overused and inextricably bound to their grandchildren everyday. Several wished for greater proximity in order to interact more frequently with their grandchildren. One grandfather wished his granddaughter lived with him, while three, who had custodial care of their grandchildren, expressed a desire to live separately and to have fewer obligations, including financial responsibility. Two participants suggested that their interactions contrasted with mainstream grandparents because they lacked financial resources. They were proud to offer their grandchildren "stories," "histories" and "good cooking" rather than "finances." Two said that they "just wanted to be there to soothe" their grandchildren emotionally when they needed it, contrasting this relationship with parents' interactions which one described as "picky or critical." Another's comment reflected many of the comments when she said, "I just want to be useful, you know, to be needed, like to be asked for something. I can give good advice because I have lived a lot."

Discussion

The status of American Indian grandparents has until recently been of an exalted nature. Today there are traces or this past reverence in speeches made about grandparents at pow-wows and other ceremonies, but as indicated in the above fragments of interviews the deferential attitude shown is often a matter of form and devoid of power. Many elders feel the wisdom they believe they possess is too often unappreciated. The grandparents in this study often expressed low levels of antagonism toward their children for not working to preserve tribal culture. Still they reported that they continue to transfer tribal values and knowledge to their grandchildren through telling stories, modeling, direct communicative teaching, and playful interaction.

Almost all of the American Indian grandparents interviewed in this project felt great responsibility for mediating American Indian religion and culture. They felt they were at a crossroads at which they could let the old ways go forever or try to pass some of the ways down to their grandchildren. For some the possibility of preserving heritage was seen as remote. In spite of the cultural bombs dropped to annihilate beliefs and tribal unity by the American government, almost all participants in this study took active roles to pass down at least a few of the old ways. Nonetheless, there appeared to be an anxious awareness among participants that their present predicament was not purely a matter of personal choice but it arose from a historical situation. They were all too aware that economic, political, cultural, psychological and military pressures have quite a strangle-hold on tribal culture.

Such responses indicate that American Indian grandparents want the cultural needs of their grandchildren met despite the fact that they themselves were taught by educators who were probably emphatic assimilationists. American Indian elders have lived through periods when tribal customs and ways were either disregarded or vehemently opposed as uncivilized and

anti-Christian (Szasz, 1984). Nonetheless, the grandparents in this study expressed the desire to teach aspects of American Indian culture to their grandchildren. But because of past and present, covert and overt discrimination and assimilation policies they are limited. It is no accident that grandparents in this study frequently mentioned language and love of the land, values often used to define American Indian peoples (Sue & Sue, 2003), as two of the most important gifts they might impart to their grandchildren.

The interviewers in this study could not help but be cognizant of the contradiction of having American Indian grandparents define their roles in terms of a language (English) of imperialist imposition. Possibly the most meaningful information offered regarding the grandparent's relationship to their grandchildren came when they used the Indian names of their grandchildren. One musically breathed, "My grandson's Indian name is Onsehoma . . . Red Eagle." From such tribal words, phrases, and names one can glean norms, attitudes and values of tribal grandparents in regard to their grandchildren. Some researchers contend that language is the primary factor of cultural identity because it connects persons to their cultures' traditions, customs, unique styles of humor, history, and understandings of ceremonies (Eastman, 1985; Dividoff, 2001). Unfortunately, while many American Indian grandparents wish to pass on their tribal language, many are limited by their own lack of fluency that comes as a consequence of having had it forbidden for generations. Some grandparents expressed despair about having lost their tribal language. Stealing language from a people is the bullet of spiritual subjugation. Many of the participants in this study are attempting to pass down tribal language with all its cultural attachments to their grandchildren.

For American Indians love of the land and nature in general (Highwater, 1982), is one of the most essential values because, unlike many values, it is concrete and bound up with history and contemporary politics. The valuing of land and the protection of natural sites is a passionate concern for many American Indians. In fact, many claim that the Great Spirit has given American Indians a special vocation to model respect and love Mother Earth for other races (Highwater, 1982). But tribal lands were taken away by conquest, unequal treaties, or by genocide. American Indian grandparent participants in this study wished to teach their children about the importance of the unique historical character of American Indians' connections to their land and nature. Tragically, for many of the participants, tribal land has been wrested from their families, which has had devastating consequences. For example, American Indians are now the most poverty stricken of all races in the United States (Sue & Sue, 2003), which undermines cohesiveness among tribal members who find themselves fighting against each other for limited resources. In Oklahoma, where all the land was taken from tribes and redistributed according to checkerboard plans (farms given to Whites to separate American Indian families) in the early twentieth century, American Indians find themselves separated from other tribal members, as well as from their historical and spiritual connections to their land (Sue & Sue, 2003), Nonetheless, though the American government robbed American Indians of their land, they were not successful in stealing their dignity. In heroic fashion, the participants in this research project expressed a profound love of the land and a passionate desire to pass this love of land on to their grandchildren.

Grandparents also asserted that telling stories to their grandchildren was important. Stories act as mechanisms through which grandparents can teach succeeding generations how to live life consistent with tribal values (Robbins, 2002). Both traditional and personal stories were told by participants to add meaning and coherence to their grandchildren's lives and to offer structures with which to frame their experiences. They were told to grandchildren to help clarify their cultural and personal self-concepts and to unravel confusing rules, ceremonial expectations and relationships. Many of the traditional stories had animals as main characters. While sometimes small and weak, they were full of wit and cunning when claiming victory over stronger enemies or saving someone from hostile nature. The stories appeared to reflect past and present real life psychological and political struggles. Dances, songs, and ceremonies taught and promoted by grandparents served similar purposes. But for participants in this study, storytelling roles no longer could be assumed in the same fashion as they were historically. For instance, many grandparents in this study were separated geographically not only from their grandchildren, but also from tribal gatherings where they might have told their grandchildren seasonally appropriate stories. The grandparents in this study told their stories in situations when the opportunity presented itself.

In addition to the values often taught indirectly through stories, there were many taught directly and others were demonstrated through modeling. Spiritual and community values appeared to be the most cherished. Grandparents taught grandchildren to pray and continue customs as well as to show appreciation, to be generous, and unselfishness) as the ultimate good their communities. Grandparents taught values that might provide the foundation for tribal renewal and cooperative communities. It is not easy for American Indians to maintain traditional values in the wake of years of gradual accumulation of Euro-American values, which easily over time become almost self-evident truths governing what is right and wrong, and good and bad. Still, the grandparents in this study expressed a commitment to preserve and renew traditional tribal values.

Lastly, the grandparents in this study repeatedly expressed the complex predicament of being somewhat marginal in their grandchildren's' lives, yet also in better positions to joke and laugh with their grandchildren. Their marginality was typically explained as being the result of living at a distance from grandchildren, lack of mobility, feelings of a decline in influence and loss of culture. Their "special" intimacy was often either directly or indirectly explained as being the result of being freed from the disciplinarian role. Those who had not been forced to become custodial described teasing, kind, close, playful and affectionate relationships with their grandchildren. Some grandparents' descriptions of their interactions contrasted with the severity of the parents' involvement with their children. While custodial grandparents complained of the tension associated with establishing rules and enforcing punishments on their grandchildren, non-custodial grandparents could indulge their grandchildren, being in positions where they were free from the taboos of parental discipline.

Recommendations, Limitations, and Further Directions

The recommendations of this study are for democratic initiatives and human liberation. They directly address the deepest fears of many of the grandparents' of this study who feel they are at a dramatic crossroads that requires nothing less than fundamental social and political transformation. It is a call for rediscovery and for regenerative reconnections. This begins with the resumption of tribal languages. Tribal governments should employ American Indian grandparents who speak their tribal languages to teach their grandchildren their tribal languages before those languages, with their unique cultural nuances, are irrevocably erased. To lose one's tribal language is to lose, to a large extent, a tribal sensibility and to be alienated from much of one's tribal culture. Language is an enormous carrier of culture, and many American Indian grandparents have this part of culture to share. Secondly, tribes could employ grandparents to teach tribal arts and crafts, tribal religions, and tribal history to their grandchildren. All this must be done soon, taking into account that many elders are taking traditional tribal culture with them and that children must be taught early in life before the values of Euro-American society become implanted and nearly impossible to eradicate. Thirdly, there must be a systematic effort to reclaim tribal lands. Many tribes are already attempting this. Grandparents might lobby for this sort of political directive. Without a doubt the reacquisition of tribal lands would provide renewed dignity and greater cohesiveness among tribal members. Support in these endeavors from culturally sensitive, non-American Indians is welcomed.

Due to the fact that almost all of the participants in this study live in Oklahoma and do not live on reservations, the generalizability of the study is limited. There was a profound commitment Researchers expected a lower level of commitment to the transference of tribal values among this non-reservation sample. One might expect an even greater commitment among American Indians living on reservations. A replication of this study might bear this hypothesis out.

Future research might also explore the impact of American Indian grandparents' efforts in the role of cultural conservator in specific areas such as story telling, participation in tribal activities and in the transference of tribal values on their grandchildren. Such a study may entail interviewing grandchildren as well as grandparents. Efforts to develop reliable and valid acculturation instruments might facilitate further research.

References

Bahr, K. S. (1994). The strength of Apache mothers: Observations on commitment, culture and caretaking. *Journal of Comparative Family Studies, 25,* 233–248.

Barnett, H. (1955). *The Coast Salish of British Columbia.* Eugene, Oregon: University of Oregon.

Bogdan, R. C., & Biklen, S. K. (1992). *Qualitative research for education.* Boston: Allyn & Bacon.

Coleman, H., Unau, Y.A, & B. Manyfingers, (2001). Revamping Family Preservation Services for Native Families. *Journal of Ethnic & Cultural Diversity in Social Work, 10* (1), 49–65.

Cooney, T., & Smith, L. (1993). Young adults relations with grandparents following parental divorce. *Journal of Gerontology Services B: Psychological Sciences and Social Sciences, 51B,* 591–595.

Creasey, G. L., & Kaliher, G. (1994). Age differences in grandchildren's perceptions of relationship quality with grandparents. *Journal of Adolescence, 17,* 411–426.

Creswell, J. W. (1998). *Qualitative inquiry and research design: Choosing among five traditions.* Thousand Oaks, CA: Sage Publications.

Elendorf, W. W., & Kroeber, A. (1960). *The structure of Twona with notes on Yurals culture.* Pullman, WA: Washington State University.

Gladstone, J. W. (1988). Perceived changes in grandmother-grandchild relations following a child's separation or divorce. *The Gerontologist, 28,* 66–72.

Highwater, J. (1982). *The primal mind.* Hammondsworth: Penguins Books.

Huberman, A. M., & Miles, M. B. (1994). *Data management and analysis methods.* In N. K. Denzin, & Y. S. Lincoln, Handbook of qualitative research (pp. 428–444). Thousand Oaks, CA: Sage Publications.

Jaskowski, S., & Dellasega, C. (1993). Effects of divorce on grandparent-grandchild relationship. *Issues in Comprehensive Pediatric Nursing, 16,*125–133.

Kennedy, G. E. (1992). Shared activities of grandparents and grandchildren. *Psychological Reports, 70,* 211–227.

Lincoln, Y. S., & Guba, E. G. (1985). *Naturalistic inquiry.* Newbury, CA: Sage Publications.

Nahemow, N. O. (1987). Grandparenthood among the Baganda: Role option in old age. In Sokolovski, J. (ed.). *Growing old in Societies.* Belmont, CA: Wadsworth.

Noor Al-Deen, Hana S. (Ed.) (1997). *Cross-cultural communication and aging in the United States.* Mahwah, NJ: Lawrence Erlbaum Associates.

Robbins, R. R. (2002). The role of traditional American Indian stories and symbols in counseling adolescents with behavior problems. *Beyond Behavior, 16,* 12–19.

Sander, G. F., & Trygstad, D. W. (1993) Strengths of grandparents and grandchildren relationships. *Activities, Adaptation and Aging, 17,* 43–53.

Scherman, A., Beesley, D., & Turner, B. (2003). Grandparents' involvement with grandchildren during times of crisis in the family. *Oklahoma Association of Teacher Educators, 7,* 47–61.

Scherman, A., Goodrich, C., Kelly, C., Russel, T., & Javidi, A. (1988). Grandparents as a support system for children. *Elementary School Guidance and Counseling Journal, 37,* 16–22.

Schweitzer, M. M. (1987). The elders: Cultural dimensions of aging in two American Indian communities. In Sokolovski, J. (ed.). *Growing old in Societies.* Belmont, CA: Wadsworth.

Strauss, A., & Corbin, J. (1998). *Basics of qualitative research: Techniques and procedures for developing grounded theory.* Thousand Oaks, CA: Sage Publications.

Sue, D. W., & Sue, D. (2003). *Counseling the culturally diverse.* New York: John Wiley & Sons.

Survey Research Center (1982). *General interviewing techniques.* Ann Arbor, MI: Institute for Social Research.

Szasz, M. C. (1984). *Education and the American Indian.* Albuquerque: University of New Mexico.

Timberlake, E., & Chipungu, S. S. (1992). Grand motherhood: Contemporary meaning among African American middle class grandmothers. *Social Work, 37,* 216–222.

Weibel-Orlando, J. (1990). Grand parenting styles: Native American Perspectives. In Sokolovski, J. (ed.). *The cultural context of aging* (pp 109–125). Westport, CT: Greenwood Press.

Williams, E. (1995). Father and grandfather involvement in childrearing and the school performance of Ojibwa children: An exploratory study. (Doctoral dissertation, University of Michigan, 1995). *Dissertation Abstracts International, 56* (4-A), 1530.

ROCKEY ROBBINS, PHD (Cherokee/Choctaw), is in the Counseling Psychology Department at the University of Oklahoma in Normal, OK 73019. **AAVRAHAM SCHERMAN, EDD,** is also in the Counseling Psychology Department at the University of Oklahoma. **HEIDI HOLEMAN, MS** and **JASON WILSON, MS** are doctoral students in the Counseling Psychology Department at the University of Oklahoma. Dr. Robbins may be reached at 405/325-8442 or E-mail: Rockey@ou.edu.

From *Journal of Cultural Diversity,* Summer 2005, pp. 62–68. Copyright © 2005 by Tucker Publications, Inc. Reprinted by permission.

Aging Japanese Pen Messages to Posterity

Heartfelt 'Ending Notes' Give Elderly a Voice in Traditionally Reticent Society

ANTHONY FAIOLA

Living alone in a tidy little house on the outskirts of Tokyo, 75-year-old Tomohiro Ishizuka spends hours dwelling on things unsaid. There are, he recalls, the stories he never told his two adult children—such as the horror of finding the charred remains of boyhood friends after the U.S. firebombing of Tokyo in 1945. And then there are stories half-told—such as the depth of his pain after the sudden death in 2002 of his wife of 45 years.

In a society where the expression of innermost thoughts is considered awkward or self-indulgent, Ishizuka was never able to find the right moments to share such personal things with his family. So last month he joined the growing ranks of elderly Japanese who are writing down what they cannot manage to say.

"Ending notes" is what the resulting works are called. An estimated 200,000 seniors have taken to composing these often candid autobiographical reflections, in the hopes that family members will read them after the authors' deaths. A few of the works have gone on to be published posthumously and sold in bookstores. Ranging from synopses a few pages long to book-length epitaphs, they all serve as records for posterity of things too important to be lost at death.

The advent of ending notes, experts here say, reflects changing notions of old age and death in Japan, which has the longest average life expectancy on Earth—now 81.9 years, more than four years longer than the average in the United States.

Seniors are living longer even as centuries-old family traditions are eroding. Many grandparents no longer live with their children or grandchildren, for instance, as housing becomes more affordable, due to a protracted recession in the 1990s, and society places greater emphasis on privacy. In 2003, almost half of Japanese over 65 lived alone or with a spouse, compared with only 37.7 percent in 1991.

"For years, senior citizens in Japan let their emotions and histories be known to younger generations through everyday gestures or simple words around the house," said Haruyo Inoue, who last year published an updated version of her best-selling book on how to write ending notes, now one of about a half-dozen available in Japan.

"But as many are no longer living with their families, it has reduced the ways in which they can share their feelings or pass on their personal histories to their children or grandchildren," she said. "That is one important reason they have turned to writing ending notes."

Ishizuka is composing his note in his straw-matted living room, writing in a lustrous purple notebook. "When my wife died, I realized that there was nothing tangible for me to remember her by. . . . I lost so much, all her stories, all her memories," he said. It would have been different had she left an ending note.

Indirectness is highly prized in Japanese conversation; to avoid embarrassment, husbands and wives or parents and children often use the word "like" instead of "love" to express their affection for one another.

"It is easier for me to write it down so they can read it when I am gone," Ishizuka said of his grown children. "That way they will know what their father and mother were really like . . . and understand why we made the choices in life that we made."

In his draft, he writes of his deep depression after his wife succumbed to a brain hemorrhage in 2002 and his hopes that his children will someday come to understand his eccentricities.

"You often tell me, 'Father is greedy,'" he says in the draft. "But the truth is I love you all dearly. I want to be with you forever and see my grandchildren grow, to feel your kindness, a kindness that has been handed down to you from your late mother.

"I want you to understand that, when I spend time alone, to draw, to go listen to music, to go watch a movie or go for a drive in the mountains, it is to confirm the bond I had with your mother. To reflect on my life, and understand what it means to be me."

Living so long—often while remaining in extraordinarily good health—can force older Japanese to confront death often. In the five-year period ending in 2003, for instance, Ishizuka lost his wife, his mother and his son-in-law.

For Ishizuka, writing his autobiography proved cathartic, a way to come to grips with such massive loss. "There was so much death around me that I felt I needed to write about life," he said.

The many changes in what it means to be old have led to a surge of so-called late-life crises in Japan. Analysts say more senior citizens are making pilgrimages, often mostly by foot, to the 88 holy sites on the island of Shikoku, for example, or engaging in metaphysical experiences such as standing under bitterly cold waterfalls in search of enlightenment.

Japan's record-low birthrate, a result of women choosing to stay single or couples deciding not to have children, has meant that many elderly people here do not have grandchildren, which in Japanese culture poses practical problems for the aged.

New generations—almost always eldest sons, but sometimes daughters—are expected to financially maintain hereditary tombs, mostly inside Buddhist temples. If, after the sons and daughters die, there is no grandchild to assume the responsibility, cremated remains are often removed and placed in common rooms, a fate that is now troubling many older Japanese.

One study conducted by Inoue showed a massive boom in so-called independent cemeteries, where people can make an advance payment ensuring that their bodies will be kept indefinitely in a marked burial compartment. In 1989, there were only four such cemeteries in Japan; last year there were more than 500.

"Japan is not like the United States, where the aged have a culture of self-dependency," said Sumire Nohara, who offers seminars on aging and wrote a how-to book on ending notes. "The Japanese have long depended on their children. But lifestyles are changing here, and that is no longer possible, or desired, in many cases. So the elderly, especially as they live longer and longer, are searching for new ways to leave their legacy."

Enter the ending note. The practice began, experts say, in the 1990s, part of a similar trend in the United States and Europe for people to write extended wills or leave detailed instructions regarding funerals or medical care in case they become mentally or physically incapacitated.

But in Japan, the concept took a broader form because of traditional inhibitions about sitting down and talking intimately. "There are some things that are just easier for me to write than to say," said Juniko Kuriyama, 62, who began writing her ending note last year. She is older than her husband, Junichi, who is 57, and admitted she was writing it as much for him as for her childless adult daughter. "There are so many things that he and I have never spoken about," she said—and, she added, probably never would.

Inside the cozy uniform store that the couple runs near Yokohama, their third attempt at a business after two previous enterprises failed, her husband shook his head as his wife spoke.

"We've made it this far precisely because we don't talk so much," he said. "There are things I don't want to know. It would only make me feel worse to know that I did or did not do something and I can't make up for it anymore."

"You say that now," she replied. "But there are still things I want you to know. . . . And this is also about what I want. I feel as if I need to leave behind evidence of my life."

Special correspondent Akiko Yamamoto contributed to this report.

UNIT 4
Challenges and Opportunities

Unit Selections

Key Points to Consider

- How does an abusive relationship develop? What, if anything, can be done to prevent it?

- What are the risk factors for child abduction? Why do we hold the belief that it is strangers who are more likely to abduct children? What can be done to protect children from family abduction?

- What are the particular risks for Children of Alcoholics? What contributes to resilience for them?

- If you felt your intimate relationship was troubled, how would you act? Would you discuss it with your partner? Would you hope that it would correct itself without your doing anything?

- What is the best way to work out the competing demands of work and family?

- How do you think you would respond if your partner was diagnosed with a life-threatening disease? What is the relationship among loss, grief, and care?

- How can you go about helping a child cope with trauma?

- Discuss how the breakup of a relationship or a divorce affects the people involved. Is it possible to have a "good" divorce? What would that good divorce look like? What are the particular issues related to remarriage and the family dynamics associated with it?

Student Web Site
www.mhcls.com/online

Internet References

Alzheimer's Association
http://www.alz.org
Caregiver's Handbook
http://www.acsu.buffalo.edu/~drstall/hndbk0.html

National Crime Prevention Council
http://www.ncpc.org
Widow Net
http://www.widownet.org

Stress is life and life is stress. Sometimes stress in families gives new meaning to this statement. When a stressful event occurs in families, many processes occur simultaneously as families and their members cope with the stressor and its effects. One thing that can result is a reduction of the family members' ability to act as resources for each other. Indeed, a stressor can overwhelm the family system, and family members may be among the least effective people in coping with each other's behavior.

In this unit, we consider a wide variety of crises. Family violence is the focus of the first article. "Recognizing Domestic Partner Abuse" presents warning signs and resources for those who experience or those who hope to help those experiencing domestic partner abuse. "The Myths and Truths of Family Abduction" confronts commonly held, but incorrect beliefs about child abduction. Stranger abduction is much rarer than abduction by family members. With this in mind, the article suggests several tips for anticipating and preparing children for the risk of family abduction.

Substance abuse is next addressed in "Children of Alcoholics." This article looks at ways in which children of alcoholics (COA) are put at risk by substance abuse in their families, while it also presents surprising resilience factors that may serve to protect these children from their family dysfunction.

Next, infidelity is addressed in "My Cheatin' Heart" and "Love but Don't Touch." The former concerns the choices people make that lead to infidelity. The latter addresses emotional infidelity, a form of unfaithfulness that many see as less serious than sexual infidelity, but others view as just a damaging to a couple's relationship. In this article, Mark Teich addresses a variety of ways of spotting emotional cheating as well as ways of strengthening a relationship after or in anticipation of its happening. A new phenomenon, "Is This Man Cheating on His Wife?," is explored in the final article in this subsection.

The subsection that follows, Economic Concerns, looks at the work/family connection with interesting results. In "Becoming Financial Grown-Ups," George Mannes addresses ways of managing an ongoing stressor in the lives of families—family financial management. He recommends a series of steps that move couples toward financial stability. The view that family and work life must arrive at some form of appropriate balance is the focus of "Making Time for Family Time."

The nature of stress resulting from a life-threatening illness as well as loss and grief are the subject of the next subsection. Life-threatening illnesses can place tremendous strain on couples' relationships. "Partners Face Cancer Together" documents the ways in which couples survive breast can-

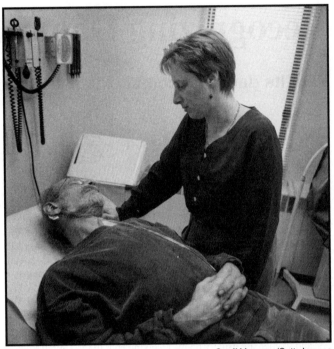

Geoff Manasse/Getty Images

cer together with a stronger relationship in the bargain. The remaining articles address issues of caregiving. In the first, "A Guide for Caregivers," the focus is on advising caregivers on how best to provide care. The second article, "Caring for the Caregiver," addresses an often invisible health risk—the stress experienced by caregivers. This stress puts them at risk and this article provides suggestions on how caregivers can care for themselves. The final article, "Bereavement after Caregiving," shows that the stress of caregiving does not end with death.

In the next section, the crises of war and terrorism are portrayed. Terrorism is addressed in "Terrorism, Trauma, and Children." Suggestions about how to address children's concerns are highly pragmatic and, focused on building a sense of safety and comfort for them. For some children, war and its effects are very close and very personal.

Divorce and remarriage are the subjects of the final subsection. The first articles in this subsection, "A Divided House" and "Civil Wars," both address ways in which the divorcing (and then divorced) couple may use their children as pawns in their battles with each other. The needs of the children must be paramount when a couple divorces—this is too often not the case. Finally, "Stepfamily Success Depends on Ingredients" details characteristics of successful stepfamilies, paying particular attention to ways of building resilience into the family system.

Recognizing Domestic Partner Abuse

With its daunting complexities, the path to change takes courage and support.

omestic abuse. Battering. Intimate partner violence. These are terms that make us wince. And they should: The phenomenon is widespread in the United States, and its effects can be long-lasting and life-threatening. Breaking the pattern of domestic violence can be extremely difficult and may take a long time. It requires courage, planning, and a support network.

The U.S. Department of Health and Human Services defines domestic violence as "a pattern of assaultive and/or coercive behaviors . . . that adults use against their intimate partners to gain power and control in that relationship." It includes not only physical and sexual abuse but also emotional abuse. All can have serious health consequences.

Domestic violence affects people of all ethnic backgrounds; it occurs among the poor and the rich and among the well educated and the poorly educated. Men are usually (though not always) the abusers, and women are usually on the receiving end. In the United States, a woman's lifetime risk of being a victim of such violence is 25%. Women who were abused as children are at an increased risk for being in an abusive relationship as an adult.

First Signs

Women don't consciously choose to have an abusive partner. In fact, the abuser may be charming and well liked by most of the people who know him, but at home he shows a different side. Friends, family, and colleagues are often shocked when his abusive behavior becomes known. In the beginning, it may also be a shock to the abused woman. She may have regarded her relationship with this man as the most

---

Selected Resources

National Domestic Violence Hotline
800-799-7233 (toll free)
800-787-3224 (for the hearing impaired; toll free)

National Sexual Assault Hotline
800-656-4673 (toll free)

National Women's Health Information Center, "Violence against Women"
womenshealth.gov/violence/domestic/
800-994-9662 (toll free)

United Way First Call for Help
800-231-4377 (toll free)

---

wonderful, romantic, fairy tale–like experience imaginable, says Susan Neis, executive director of Cornerstone, a shelter that serves five suburbs of Minneapolis.

Changes in the relationship can be difficult to see at first. The abuser's need for control often begins to show itself in little things he says and does. He may criticize the way his partner acts or looks. He may say deeply hurtful things, such as accusing her of being a bad mother. "When somebody says this to you, somebody you're in love with, it's devastating," says Neis, who is herself a survivor of domestic abuse.

Over time, the abuser's words can chip away at a woman's sense of herself. She starts to doubt her perceptions and may even come to believe the horrible things he says about her. She feels isolated, ashamed, and helpless, but at the same time may feel an obligation to keep herself convinced of the fairy tale because "there's nothing else to hold onto," says one 35-year-old woman who received help from Cornerstone.

Control and Power

At the center of domestic violence is the issue of control. The abuser is intent on gaining and maintaining power over his partner through fear and intimidation. Abuse doesn't necessarily involve physical harm. Threats can also be highly effective and should not be minimized, suggests Dr. Judith Herman, clinical professor of psychiatry at Harvard Medical School and training director of the Victims of Violence Program at Cambridge Health Alliance in Cambridge, Mass. A man who says "If you leave me, I'll track you down and kill you and anyone who helps you" can instill as much (or more) fear as one who strikes his partner.

The abusive partner uses various tactics to achieve control. He may intimidate and demean his partner by constantly criticizing her, monopolizing household finances, or telling her what she can wear, where she can go, and whom she can see. He may play "mind games," such as suggesting that she's hypersensitive, hysterical, or mentally unbalanced. Often he isolates the woman from family, friends, and colleagues, either by removing her from them physically or by limiting her employment options and social contacts. Abuse may also take the form of pathological jealousy, such as false accusations of adultery. Soon, the woman may find that she's cut off from all outside connections, no longer in touch with the people and services that could help her.

Isolation may also disconnect her from a sense of what's normal. She may not even think of herself as a victim of domestic violence, says Dr. Megan Gerber, an internist at Cambridge Health Alliance who specializes in women's health and an instructor of medicine at Harvard Medical School. After an incident, the abuser often apologizes and tries to placate his victim. There may be periods of relative calm. It may take a victim a long time to recognize that her partner's behaviors aren't random but form a pattern of abuse.

Intimate Partner Abuse Is a Health Issue

Intimate partner abuse can have profound effects on a woman's health, both physical and mental. Physical harm, including fractures, lacerations, and soft tissue trauma, is one obvious effect. Intimate partner abuse is also linked to chronic health problems and even death—from either suicide because of depression or murder (or manslaughter) by the partner.

The intense, ongoing stress may result in chronic pain or gastrointestinal symptoms. Victims of domestic abuse are more likely to have arthritis, neck pain, pelvic pain, and migraine headaches. They also have an increased risk of menstrual problems and difficulties during pregnancy, including bleeding, low birth weight, and anemia.

Domestic abuse is closely linked with mental illness and substance abuse. A recent study found that 47.6% of battered women were depressed and 63.8% had post-traumatic stress disorder; 18.5% used alcohol excessively; 8.9% used drugs; and 7.9% committed suicide.

Because women in abusive relationships often need emergency room and primary care services, physicians, nurses, and other clinicians are often the first outsiders to learn about the emotional or physical abuse. Women are often reluctant to mention the subject on a patient history form, but if asked by a clinician, they may be relieved to acknowledge it.

Getting Out

Walking away from an abusive relationship is a process more than a single action. Women usually make several attempts—five, on average—before they leave the partner for good. Isolation and fear may prevent a woman from leaving, even when she knows it is probably for the best. She may still love her partner or worry about what will happen to her children if she leaves. She may be unsure how to escape or how to survive financially and care for her children.

Community support can be crucial (see "Selected Resources"), although a woman in an abusive relationship often has difficulty taking advantage of that support. The abuser may track her computer use, looking for visits to Web sites and evidence of keyword searches. If that's a concern, says Rita Smith, executive director of the National Coalition Against Domestic Violence in Boulder, Colo., she should use a computer outside the home—for example at a library or a friend's home or work place. As a safeguard, the coalition's own site (www.ncadv.org) features a red "Escape" button that immediately switches the user to an Internet search engine.

Care for the Children

Each year, up to 10 million children witness the abuse of a parent or caregiver. Many women stay in an abusive relationship because they think it's best not to disrupt the children's lives so long as they're not being abused themselves. But children who live with domestic violence are at serious risk for behavioral and cognitive problems. In later life, they may suffer depression and trauma symptoms, and they may tolerate or use violence in their own relationships.

Experts say that women leaving an abusive relationship should take their children with them. Otherwise, it can be difficult to get the children later, because police may not want to remove them from the home if the abusive partner is their biological father. Also, the abuser may later try to get custody by arguing that the woman abandoned her children.

What Can I Do to Help?

You suspect that your friend is in an abusive relationship. For example, she seems anxious and fearful when she recounts arguments with her husband. Or she may mention having to ask him each time she needs money. (While by itself not a sign of abuse, controlling finances can be part of a pattern of abuse.)

Part of you wants to rescue her and take her to a safe place where her husband can't find her. Yet you worry that any action you take could make things worse, increasing the danger she's already in. You know the decision is hers to make, not yours. But you can do a lot to help. Here are some things to consider:

- Think about your relationship with your friend. When and where might you talk with her safely, and what could you say? Does she trust you? Does she feel that she can confide in you without fearing that you'd judge her harshly or dismiss her concerns?
- Ask questions that let her know of your suspicions and concern. One question might be: Are you afraid of your husband? Understand that she might be hesitant to talk about this directly—or might deny or minimize what's happening. Assure her that you'll keep what she says strictly confidential.
- When she talks about the situation, believe what she says and validate her concerns. Let her know you don't think she's crazy or it's all in her head. And let her know that she's not to blame, despite what her partner may have told her.
- Help your friend make use of local resources—public health services, a hospital or clinic, a women's shelter, or a legal assistance program. If she thinks the abuser is monitoring her phone calls, offer her the use of your home phone or cell phone to make these contacts.
- Work with your friend to develop a personal safety plan. One resource for this step is the National Coalition Against Domestic Violence, www.ncadv.org/protectyourself/MyPersonalSafetyPlan_131.html.
- Help her prepare to leave if the danger and abuse escalate. Your friend should have coins with her at all times for phone calls, or a phone card. She should prepare a small bag with clothes, cash, and copies of important documents (birth certificate and passport, for example) and keep it in a safe place. Would you be willing to keep the bag for her in case of need?
- Knowing that someone believes her and is ready to help can be crucial to your friend's safety and eventual escape from the abusive relationship. Be patient, listen, and offer her hope. Recognize that it may take a long time, and often several attempts at leaving, for the relationship to end.

The Myths and Truths of Family Abduction

Nancy B. Hammer

The very idea of child abduction is met by parents in equal measures of fear and disbelief—it can't happen to us. The series of high-profile abductions of children in 2002 raised the country's awareness. The kids spanned the ages of two to 15 and came from all types of families and environments, both urban and rural, across the U.S. In the more horrific cases, the abductor was someone the child did not know. Yet, a recently published study by the U.S. Department of Justice confirms that, compared to the frightening, but relatively rare, kidnappings by strangers, family abductions are commonplace.

In 1988, the Federal government first attempted to count the number of children who become missing each year. In 2002, the Second National Incidence Studies of Missing, Abducted, Runaway, and Thrownaway Children (NISMART-2) was published. The study confirms, once again, that offspring taken by a family member without the knowledge or consent of the custodial parent continues to represent the second-largest category of missing children, with a total of 203,900 youngsters abducted by a family member, as opposed to 115 stereotypical kidnappings by a stranger. Indeed, in your lifetime, you are likely either to experience within your own family or know someone who has gone through some type of family abduction.

Despite the fact that so many kids are abducted by a family member, many people do not fully understand this issue. The public generally views these incidents as infrequent, minor occurrences best handled privately. "After all," people believe, "the child is with a parent; it can't be that bad." Or can it?

On a clear autumn day, John Cramer (name changed) did not return his daughter, age 11, or son, age nine, from his scheduled weekend visitation. John and his wife Sandy (name changed) had separated several months earlier and had begun divorce proceedings. After Sandy contacted police, John's car was found inside a storage locker with a hose running from the tailpipe to the driver's side window. Inside, police found the lifeless bodies of John and the two children. Although it was known that he was unhappy about his failing marriage, no one suspected the level of John's despondency or that he was capable of taking his children's lives as well as his own. While the typical incident of family abduction does not end in death, every time it occurs there is the potential for horrible consequences.

Though the public believes the incidences of these kidnappings are infrequent, they rank as the second-largest category of missing children in the U.S.

In family abduction cases, kids typically are taken by a parent, although in a few cases, a grandparent or other relative may be the abductor. Parents who abduct often do so when they feel their relationship with the child somehow is threatened. Research indicates that fathers, who are slightly more likely to abduct than mothers, often flee before a custody order is issued, perhaps spurred on by the fear that they are about to lose meaningful contact with their offspring. Mothers, however, typically kidnap after a custody order has been issued, perhaps reacting when the terms of the custody and visitation don't meet their expectations. Regardless of who the abductor is, the overriding motivation is a desire to control the child's relationships and hurt the other parent. The abducting parent often is unable to consider the effects on the youngster and thinks only of his or her immediate situation. One father, after the eight-year abduction of his children, reflected that his actions were motivated by his own inadequacies and need to control, not for the love of his kids.

The public has a tendency to minimize the risk to offspring involved in a family abduction in the mistaken belief that a child is safe in the hands of a parent. A simple scan of the headlines of any major newspaper reveals stories of child abuse, neglect, and even death of kids at the hands of their own parents. In this way, abduction is no different from any other crime committed against a child—kids often are at risk from those they know. Official statistics may not fully reflect the danger inherent in family abduction situations. Some cases resulting in death may be counted as murder or suicide, without reference to the family abduction incident that started it all.

This oversight may leave family abduction out of the crime statistics, yet abduction of a child, even if perpetrated by a parent, is a felony in every state. The state laws often are referred to as "custodial interference" statutes and, if charged as felonies, carry a jail sentence of one year or more and allow the abducting parent, when caught in another state, to be extradited for prosecution in the state from which he or she fled. A conviction of child abduction can have a serious effect on subsequent custody decisions in family court. The FBI can become involved under Federal law if the abducting parent flees with the child across state lines. Further, if the abducting parent takes the child outside the U.S., he or she has violated the Federal international parental kidnapping law, thus involving the FBI and other Federal resources to locate and prosecute the abducting parent.

Research conducted on the consequences of family abduction confirms the seriousness of these cases. In the best-known study of this issue, researchers Geoffrey Greif and Rebecca Hegar interviewed 371 parents whose kids were abducted by a noncustodial parent and found a seven percent incidence of sexual abuse, 23% incidence of physical abuse, and five percent incidence of both physical and sexual abuse.

In addition to statistical information, adults who were parentally abducted as children have begun to raise their collective voices through a new organization called Take Root. This group formed after an initial meeting hosted by the National Center for Missing & Exploited Children (NCMEC) and provides an online venue (www.takeroot.org) for the sharing of stories—in addition to hosting a newsletter called "The Link." One of the members of the organization chronicles her own struggle for identity and self-awareness after having lived on the run and under many aliases during the period of her abduction. She writes, "I have had many [names] in my life. The first, my birth name, the name lovingly bestowed upon me as a newborn child, was Cecilie . . . until my abduction at age four I was called Sissi or Sisselina, in the sweet custom of nicknaming a young child. After my abduction my father changed my name to Sarah Zissel, the first of many aliases, and for all intents and purposes my birth name was no more."

It can be very difficult to locate the abducting parent and captive child. An abductor can find many hiding places. While some abductors simply adopt new names, others seek to alter their identities illegally. Information on forging birth certificates and creating assumed identities is only a click away on the Internet. Other abductors get assistance from relatives willing to hide a child in violation of the law, or from more formal groups, sometimes known as underground networks, which help abductors violate the law by providing funds and housing. Many abducting parents seek refuge in a foreign country. Not all international abduction cases involve parents of two nationalities. Often, American parents choose to flee to a foreign destination in order to better hide their crime or to be with a new partner.

Parents as Abductors

Regardless of the method or the destination, parents considering abduction must realize that, one day, they could be found. NCMEC's nationwide poster distribution program leads to the recovery of one in six children featured. A growing awareness of missing children and an increasingly vigilant public shed light into the dark corners where abducting parents once hid their children from the other parent, extended family, friends, and law enforcement. In the past year, the U.S. has seen several recoveries of children who had been missing for more than five years. Abducting parents find, upon their return, that the problems they tried to run away from still exist. In addition, their actions have created new ones. Facing the issues now, however, requires being honest with the child about the left-behind parent, often for the first time since the abduction, and may result in a sense of betrayal in the child who does not know whom to trust. Moreover, the child frequently suffers emotional confusion and depression, as he or she is left to wonder what will subsequently happen. The irony for some parents is that the same child they fought so hard to keep for themselves can become estranged once he or she learns the full truth of the abduction.

If you are concerned about the potential of family abduction, there are steps that can be taken to lessen the risk. Every parent should strive to reduce the tension with the other parent throughout the separation, divorce, or custody process. As difficult as it may be to go through divorce and resolve the custody issues, children need both parents in order to become the individuals they were meant to be. For some families, seeking help from a mediator to define custody and visitation helps both parties to feel as though their concerns have been addressed. A resolution reached together may help prevent one side from feeling like he or she "lost," and therefore, prevent a potential "lashing out" through abduction. In addition, a mediator can talk openly about how parents should strive to remember that their child's need for access to both parents must come first.

Parents should take any threats of abduction seriously and evaluate the risk. Additionally, lawyers should encourage the court handling custody issues to do the same. Recently, California enacted legislation requiring courts to consider whether such a risk exists. The law is modeled on a Department of Justice report, "Early Identification of Risk Factors for Parental Abduction," and can be obtained at www.ojjdp.ncjrs.org. If the court finds a risk of flight, it is required to consider certain measures designed to prevent the abduction from occurring. They include:

Child custody bond. The court may require parents to post a financial bond or give some other guarantee that they will comply with its order. Such a bond may be obtained from an insurance carrier or bail bonding company. The Professional Bail Agents of the U.S. maintains information on how to find a company able to write this type of bond and may be reached at 1-800-883-7287.

Supervised visitation. The terms may allow visits only at certain places, such as the custodial parent's home or a visitation center to be supervised by a professional or other intermediary. This may be appropriate in cases in which an abduction has occurred previously; where there is violence in the relationship; or when threats of abduction have been made.

Restrict child's removal from state or country. The court may require either parent to obtain legal permission prior to removing the child from the state. If there is a risk of international abduction, the court will issue a bulletin with the U.S.

Department of State's "Children's Passport Issuance Alert Program." It requires a written request to enter the child's name and enables the Department of State to notify a parent before issuing a U.S. passport for the child. Information can be obtained at www.travel.state.gov.

Parents also should take certain practical steps to reduce the risk of family abduction and ensure swift action to locate the child:

- Keep a current photograph of your offspring.
- Maintain a complete description of your child, including height, weight, birthmarks, and other unique physical characteristics. Fingerprints also are provided by most law enforcement agencies. All copies of the fingerprints should be turned over to the parent for safe keeping.
- Teach kids to use the telephone. Make sure they know their home phone number, including area code, as well as emergency numbers such as "911" and "0."
- Notify schools, babysitters, and day care centers of the terms of your custody order and who is permitted to pick up the child.
- Maintain identifying data about your former spouse, including description, date of birth, social security number, and contact information for friends and relatives.

Once it is determined that the child is missing, a parent immediately should take the following steps: Contact the local law enforcement agency to make a missing child report; ask that the child be entered into the National Crime Information Center computer as missing (NCIC is the national law enforcement database, operated by the FBI, that allows law enforcement in other states access to information about the child's disappearance); call NCMEC at 1-800-843-5678 and report the child as missing; ask local missing child organizations for assistance; aid law enforcement's search by providing all information available to help locate the child and the abductor; and obtain temporary or sole custody if it was not already court-ordered.

Family abductions are real crimes with real child victims and no winners. If you are considering abducting your child or are concerned that your child might be abducted, help is available. Besides maintaining a 24-hour hotline, NCMEC provides information on family abduction and other child protection issues on its website, www.missingkids.com.

Despite the frequency of these cases and the trauma caused to the families involved, there is hope in every child recovery. The public's understanding of this issue and awareness in looking at the pictures of missing children and reporting suspicious circumstances involving children will yield even more happy endings.

NANCY B. HAMMER is the director of the International Division of the National Center for Missing & Exploited Children, Alexandria, Va.

Children of Alcoholics
Risk and Resilience

CARA E. RICE, MPH, ET AL.

In 2002, over 17 million people in the United States were estimated to suffer from alcohol abuse or alcohol dependence (NIAAA, 2006). These alcohol disorders have devastating effects on the individuals, their families, and society. It has been reported that one in four children in the United States has been exposed to alcohol abuse or dependence in the family (Grant, 2000). A 1992 survey revealed that over 28 million children in the United States lived in households with one or more adults who had an alcohol disorder at some time in their lives, while nearly 10 million children lived with adults who reported alcohol disorders in the past year (Grant, 2000). Children of alcoholics (COAs) are at increased risk for a variety of negative outcomes, including fetal alcohol syndrome, substance use disorders, conduct problems, restlessness and inattention, poor academic performance, anxiety, and depression (West & Prinz, 1987). Furthermore, children of alcoholics are more likely to be exposed to family stressors such as divorce, family conflict, parental psychopathology, and poverty, which, in turn, may contribute to their negative outcomes.

In particular, COAs show increased risk of alcoholism and other substance use disorders. Genetic factors have been identified as increasing the risk of developing substance use problems among COAs (Schuckit, 2000). However, the risk faced by COAs is best understood as resulting from the interplay of both genetic and environmental factors (McGue, Elkins, & Iacano, 2000). We will discuss the factors that influence the development of substance abuse and other negative outcomes in COAs. We will also review three models in the development of substance disorders for COAs. These models are not mutually exclusive, and all three may influence a child. We will also discuss protective factors that may decrease COAs' risk for the development of future negative outcomes.

Prenatal Risk

One pathway for increased risk among COAs is through prenatal exposure to alcohol. Fetal alcohol syndrome (FAS), which can occur if a woman drinks alcohol during pregnancy, is a condition characterized by abnormal facial features, growth retardation, and central nervous system problems. Children with FAS may have physical disabilities and problems with learning, memory, attention, problem solving, and social/behavioral problems (Bertrand et al., 2004).

Pathways of Risk for the Development of Substance Disorders

Multiple pathways have been studied in the development of substance use disorders. Three important ones are the deviance proneness model, the stress/negative affect model, and the substance use effects model (Sher, 1991). Although these models were originally proposed to explain the development of alcohol disorders among COAs, they can also be extended to a consideration of other negative outcomes.

Deviance Proneness Pathway

The deviance proneness pathway theorizes that parental substance abuse produces poor parenting, family conflict, difficult child temperament and cognitive dysfunction. Poor parenting along with conflicted family environment are thought to interact with a child's difficult temperament and cognitive dysfunctions, which raises the child's risk for school failure and for associating with peers who themselves have high levels of conduct problems. Affiliation with these antisocial peers then increases the likelihood of antisocial behavior by COAs, including substance use (Dishion, Capaldi, Spracklen, & Li, 1995). Conduct problems in childhood and later adolescence predict the development of substance use disorders in young adulthood (Chassin et al., 1999; Molina, Bukstein, & Lynch, 2002).

One component of the deviance proneness model is difficult temperament or personality. The temperament and personality traits that are associated with adolescent substance use include sensation seeking, aggression, impulsivity, and an inability to delay gratification (Gerra et al., 2004; Wills,

Windle, & Cleary, 1998). For example, 3-year-old boys observed to be distractible, restless, and impulsive were more likely to be diagnosed with alcohol dependence at the age of 21 (Caspi, Moffitt, Newman, & Silva, 1996). Importantly, these characteristics, which are associated with adolescent substance use, have also been shown to be more common among COAs and children of drug users. (e.g., Carbonneau et al., 1998). This suggests that COAs may be at risk for substance use, in part, because of their personality traits.

One in four children in the United States has been exposed to alcohol abuse or dependence in the family.

Another component of the deviance proneness model is a deficit in cognitive function. Children of alcoholics may also be at risk for substance abuse because of deficits in cognitive functioning that have been called "executive" functions. Executive functioning refers to the ability to adjust behavior to fit the demands of individual situations and executive functioning includes planning, working memory and the ability to inhibit responses (Nigg et al., 2004). COAs have demonstrated poor response inhibition (Nigg et al., 2004), and impairments in executive functioning have found to predict drinking among young adult COAs (Atyaclar, Tarter, Kirisci, & Lu, 1999).

The deviance proneness pathway also suggests that COAs may be at risk because of the poor parenting that they receive. Decreased parental monitoring of the child's behavior, inconsistent discipline, and low levels of social support from parents are associated with increased levels of adolescent substance use and conduct problems (Brody, Ge, Conger, Gibbons, Murry, Gerrard, & Simons, 2001; Wills, McNamara, Vaccaro, & Hirky, 1996). These negative parenting behaviors have been found in substance-abusing families (Chassin, Curran, Hussong, & Colder, 1996; Curran & Chassin, 1996), suggesting that alcoholic parents may engage in poor parenting practices, which may in turn place their children at risk for substance use and/or conduct problems.

Most researchers have assumed that poor parenting leads to behavior problems in children, making it the basis for many prevention and intervention programs. However, developmental researchers have suggested that child behavior also affects parenting (Bell & Chapman, 1986). For example, Stice and Barrera (1995) found that low levels of parental control and support predicted adolescent substance use. However, adolescent substance use, in turn, predicted decreases in parental control and support. Therefore, the link between parenting and adolescent conduct problems and substance use may best be thought of as a system in which parents affect children, and children affect parents.

Stress and Negative Affect Pathway

The stress and negative affect pathway suggests that parental substance abuse increases children's exposure to stressful life events such as parental job instability, familial financial difficulty, parental legal problems, etc. (Chassin et al., 1993; Sher, 1991). These potentially chronic stressors may lead to emotional distress in COAs such as depression and/or anxiety. Substance use may then be used to control this distress.

Research has shown a link between negative affect and substance use in adolescence (see Zucker, 2006, for a review). For example, depression has been found to co-occur with adolescent substance abuse (Deykin, Buka, & Zeena, 1992) and heavy alcohol use (Rohde, Lewinson, & Seely, 1996). Moreover, negative life events have been associated with adolescent substance use (Wills, Vaccaro, & McNamara, 1992). However, not all findings support a negative affect pathway to adolescent substance use problems.

One explanation for the conflicting findings is that not all adolescents with negative affect will be at risk for substance use. Rather, adolescents who suffer from negative affect may only use alcohol and drugs if they also lack good strategies to cope with their negative moods and/or if they believe that alcohol or drugs will help them cope. Therefore, helping COAs to develop coping strategies can potentially serve as an intervention. There may also be gender differences in the extent to which COAs use substance use to cope with stress and negative mood (Chassin et al., 1999).

Substance Use Effects Model

The substance use effects model focuses on individual differences in the pharmacological effects of substances. It is hypothesized that some individuals are more sensitive to the pleasurable effects of alcohol and substance use and/or less sensitive to the adverse effects. For example, Schuckit and Smith (1996) found that male COAs with extremely low levels of negative responses to alcohol were more likely be to diagnosed with alcohol abuse/dependence almost a decade later. It is possible that individuals who do not experience negative effects from drinking may lack the "natural brakes" that limit drinking behavior. Some researchers have also suggested that COAs receive greater stress reduction effects from drinking alcohol (Finn, Zeitouni, & Pihl, 1990). Thus, COAs would be expected to engage in more stress-induced drinking than non-COAs because they derive greater physiological benefit from it. It is important to note, however, that not all studies have supported this finding and more research is needed to draw concrete conclusions concerning COAs' physiological response to alcohol (see Sher, 1991, for a review).

Resilience/Protective Factors

Despite the risks presented by genetic, social, and psychological variables, not all COAs experience negative outcomes. These individuals who, despite high-risk status, manage to defeat the odds, are labeled resilient (Garmezy & Neuchterlein, 1972). Resilience has been extensively studied in a variety of populations, but resilience among COAs remains an area that needs further research (Carle & Chassin, 2004). Sher (1991) hypothesized that factors that can help protect COAs from developing alcoholism include social class, preservation of family rituals, amount of attention received from primary caregivers, family harmony during infancy, parental support, personality, self-awareness, cognitive-intellectual functioning, and coping skills.

COAs show increased risk of alcoholism and other substance use disorders.

Carle and Chassin (2004) examined competence and resilience of COAs and found a significant difference between COAs and non-COAs in competence with regards to rule-abiding and academic behaviors, but no differences in social competence. A small subset of resilient COAs demonstrated at or above average levels of academic and rule-abiding competence. These resilient COAs also had fewer internalizing symptoms and reported increased levels of positive affect than did the general COA population (Carle & Chassin, 2004). This suggests that COAs with average or above average academic and rule-abiding competence as well as low levels of internalizing symptoms and high positive affect may be resilient to the risk associated with having an alcoholic parent.

Another potential source of resilience for COAs may be the recovery of the alcoholic parent. Hussong and colleagues (2005) found support for this idea in a study of social competence in COAs. Results from this study indicated that children of recovered alcoholics demonstrated comparable levels of social competence when compared to children of nonalcoholic parents, suggesting again that not all COAs are at equivalent levels of risk.

Along with recovery of parental alcohol symptoms, previous research has also demonstrated the importance of a number of familial factors in buffering the risk associated with parental alcoholism. For example, parental social support, consistency of parental discipline, family harmony, and stability of family rituals have all been shown to protect COAs from the development of alcohol and drug use and abuse (King & Chassin, 2004; Marshal & Chassin, 2000; Stice, Barrera, & Chassin, 1993).

Although there is evidence to suggest that family factors play a protective role in children's risk for substance use and substance use disorders, there is evidence to suggest that this protection may not be equal for all children (Luthar, Cicchetti, & Becker, 2000). In other words, the protective family factor may reduce the negative effect of parental alcoholism for some children, but may lose its effectiveness at the highest levels of risk. For example, King and Chassin (2004) found that parental support reduced the negative effect of family alcoholism for children with low and average levels of impulsivity and sensation seeking, but not for children with high levels of impulsivity and sensation seeking. In other words, parental support was protective for most children, but not for those with the highest levels of risk. Similarly, Zhou, King, and Chassin (2006) found that the protective effect of family harmony was lost for those children with high levels of family alcoholism. Together these studies provide evidence that consistent and supportive parenting and family harmony are protective for many children of alcoholics, but those children at especially high risk may not benefit from these familial protective factors.

Family relationships, though clearly an important aspect of resilience in COAs, are not the only relationships that appear to contribute to positive outcomes in children of alcoholics. There is also evidence to suggest that, for older children, peer relationships may be as influential as family relationships on adolescents' decision to use substances (Mayes & Suchman, 2006). Therefore, peer relationships may also provide protection against the risk associated with having an alcoholic parent. For example, Ohannessian and Hesselbrock (1993) found that COAs with high levels of social support from friends drank at levels similar to non-COAs, indicating that friendships may also work to reduce the negative effects of parent alcoholism.

Conclusion

Although much work remains to be done in understanding both risk and resilience among COAs, the work that has been done provides important implications for preventive interventions. For example, family factors appear to protect many COAs from negative outcomes. This knowledge supports the need for family-based preventive interventions, which seek to improve both parenting practices and family relationships among families of alcoholics. As research in this area continues to uncover the complex interplay of both the genetic and environmental factors that contribute to COA risk and resilience, prevention researchers will be afforded the opportunity to design and implement interventions to assist this prevalent and heterogeneous population of children.

References

Atyaclar, S., Tarter, R.E., Kirisci, L., & Lu, S. (1999). Association between hyperactivity and executive cognitive functioning in childhood and substance use in childhood and substance use in early adolescence. *Journal of the American Academy of Child and Adolescent Psychiatry, 38,* 172–178.

Bell, R.Q., & Chapman, M. (1986). Child effects in studies using experimental or brief longitudinal approaches to socialization. *Developmental Psychology, 22,* 595–603.

Bertrand, J., Floyd, R.L., Weber, M.K., O'Connor, M., Riley, E.P., Johnson, K.A., Cohen, D.E., National Task Force on FAS/FAE.

(2004). *Fetal Alcohol Syndrome: Guidelines for Referral and Diagnosis.* Atlanta, GA: Centers for Disease Control and Prevention. Available online at http://www.cdc.gov/ncbddd/fas/documents/FAS_guidelines_accessible.pdf

Brody, G.H., Ge, X., Conger, R., Gibbons, F.X., Murry, V.M., Gerrard, M., & Simons, R.L. (2001). The influence of neighborhood disadvantage, collective socialization, and parenting on African American children's affiliation with deviant peers. *Child Development, 72*(4), 1,231–1,246.

Carbonneau, R., Tremblay, R.E., Vitaro, F., Dobkin, P.L., Saucier, J.F., & Pihl, R.O. (1998). Paternal alcoholism, paternal absence, and the development of problem behaviors in boys from age 6 to 12 years. *Journal of Studies on Alcohol, 59,* 387–398.

Carle, A.C., & Chassin, L. (2004) Resilience in a community sample of children of alcoholics: Its prevalence and relation to internalizing symptomatology and positive affect. *Applied Developmental Psychology, 25,* 577–595.

Caspi, A., Moffitt, T., Newman, D., & Silva, P. (1996). Behavioral observations at age 3 years predict adult psychiatric disorders. *Archives of General Psychiatry, 53,* 1,033–1,039.

Chassin, L., Curran, P., Hussong, A., & Colder, C. (1996). The relation of parent alcoholism to adolescent substance use: A longitudinal follow-up study. *Journal of Abnormal Psychology, 105,* 70–80.

Chassin, L., Pillow, D., Curran, P., Molina, B., & Barrera, M. (1993). The relation between parent alcoholism and adolescent substance use: A test of three mediating mechanisms. *Journal of Abnormal Psychology, 102,* 1–17.

Chassin, L., Pitts, S.C., DeLucia, C., & Todd, M. (1999). A longitudinal study of children of alcoholics: Predicting young adult substance use disorders, anxiety, and depression. *Journal of Abnormal Psychology, 108,* 106–118.

Curran, P.J., & Chassin, L. (1996). Longitudinal study of parenting as a protective factor for children of alcoholics. *Journal of Studies on Alcohol, 57,* 305–313.

Deykin, E.Y., Buka, S.L., & Zeena, T.H. (1992). Depressive illness among chemically dependent adolescents. *American Journal of Psychiatry, 149,* 1,341–1,347.

Dishion, T.J., Capaldi, D., Spracklen, K.M., & Li, F. (1995). Peer ecology of male adolescent drug use. *Development and Psychopathology. Special Issue: Developmental Processes in Peer Relations and Psychopathology, 7*(4), 803–824.

Finn, P., Zeitouni, N., & Pihl, R.O. (1990). Effects of alcohol on psychophysiological hyperreactivity to nonaversive and aversive stimuli in men at high risk for alcoholism. *Journal of Abnormal Psychology, 99,* 79–85.

Garmezy, N., & Neuchterlein, K. (1972). Invulnerable children: The fact and fiction of competence and disadvantage. *American Journal of Orthopsychiatry, 42,* 328–329.

Gerra, G., Angioni, L., Zaimovic, A., Moi, G., Bussandri, M., Bertacca, S., Santoro, G., Gardini, S., Caccavari, R., & Nicoli, M.A. (2004). Substance use among high-school students: Relationships with temperament, personality traits, and personal care perception. *Substance Use & Misuse, 39,* 345–367.

Grant, B.F. (2000). Estimates of U.S. children exposed to alcohol use and dependence in the family. *American Journal of Public Health, 90,* 112–115.

Hussong, A.M., Zucker, R.A., Wong, M.M., Fitzgerald, H.E., & Puttler, L.I. (2005). Social competence in children on alcoholic parents over time. *Developmental Psychology, 41,* 747–759.

King, K.M., & Chassin, L. (2004). Mediating and moderated effects of adolescent behavioral under control and parenting in the prediction of drug use disorders in emerging adulthood. *Psychology of Addictive Behaviors, 18,* 239–249.

Luthar, S.S., Cicchetti D., & Becker, B. (2000). The construct of resilience: A critical evaluation and guidelines for future work. *Child Development, 71*(3), 543–562.

Marshal, M.P., & Chassin, L. (2000). Peer influence on adolescent alcohol use: The moderating role of parental support and discipline. *Applied Developmental Science, 4,* 80–88.

Mayes, L.C., & Suchman, N.E. (2006). Developmental pathways to substance use. In D. Cicchetti & D.J. Cohen (Eds.), *Developmental Psychopathology: Vol. 3. Risk, Disorder, and Adaptation* (2nd ed., pp. 599–619). New Jersey: John Wiley & Sons.

McGue, M., Elkins, I., Iacono, W.G. (2000). Genetic and environmental influences on adolescent substance use and abuse. *American Journal of Medical Genetics, 96,* 671–677.

Molina, B.S.G., Bukstein, O.G., & Lynch, K.G. (2002). Attention-deficit/hyperactivity disorder and conduct disorder symptomatology in adolescents with alcohol use disorder. *Psychology of Addictive Behaviors, 16,* 161–164.

National Institute on Alcohol Abuse and Alcoholism. (2006). NIAAA 2001–2002 NESARC [Data File]. Accessed August 1, 2006. from http://niaaa.census. gov/index.html.

Nigg, J.T., Glass, J.M., Wong, M.M., Poon, E., Jester, J.M., Fitzgerald, H.E., Puttler, L.I., Adams, K.A., & Zucker, R.A., (2004). Neuropsychological executive functioning in children at elevated risk for alcoholism: Findings in early adolescence. *Journal of Abnormal Psychology, 113,* 302–314.

Ohannessian, C.M., & Hesselbrock, V.M. (1993). The influence of perceived social support on the relationship between family history of alcoholism and drinking behaviors. *Addiction, 88,* 1,651–1,658.

Rohde, P., Lewinson, P.M., & Seeley, J.R. (1996). Psychiatric comorbidity with problematic alcohol use in high school students. *Journal of the American Academy of Child and Adolescent Psychiatry, 35,* 101–109.

Schuckit, M.A. (2000). Genetics of the risk for alcoholism. *The American Journal on Addictions 9,* 103–112.

Schuckit, M.A., & Smith, T.L. (1996). An 8-year follow-up of 450 sons of alcoholic and control subjects. *Archives of General Psychiatry, 53*(3), 202–210.

Sher, K.J. (1991). *Children of Alcoholics: A Critical Appraisal of Theory and Research.* Chicago: University of Chicago Press.

Stice, E., & Barrera, M. (1995). A longitudinal examination of the reciprocal relations between perceived parenting and adolescents' substance use and externalizing behaviors. *Developmental Psychology, 31*(2), 322–334.

Stice, E., Barrera, M., & Chassin, L. (1993). Relation of parental support and control to adolescents' externalizing symptomatology and substance use: A longitudinal examination of curvilinear effects. *Journal of Abnormal Child Psychology, 21,* 609–629.

West, M.O., & Prinz, R.J. (1987). Parental alcoholism and childhood psychopathology. *Psychological Bulletin, 102*(2), 204–218.

Wills, T.A., McNamara, G., Vaccaro, D., & Hirky, A.E. (1996). Escalated substance use: A longitudinal grouping analysis from early to middle adolescence. *Journal of Abnormal Psychology, 105,* 166–180.

Wills, T.A., Vaccaro, D., & McNamara, G. (1992). The role of life events, family support, and competence in adolescent substance use: A test of vulnerability and protective factors. *American Journal of Community Psychology, 20,* 349–374.

Wills, T.A., Windle, M., & Cleary, S.D. (1998). Temperament and novelty seeking in adolescent substance use: Convergence of dimensions of temperament with constructs from Cloninger's theory. *Journal of Personality and Social Psychology, 74*(2), 387–406.

Zhou, Q., King, K.M., & Chassin, L. (2006). The roles of familial alcoholism and adolescent family harmony in young adults' substance dependence disorders: mediated and moderated relations. *Journal of Abnormal Psychology, 115,* 320–331.

Zucker, R.A. (2006). Alcohol use and the alcohol use disorders: A developmental-biopsychosocial systems formulation covering the life course. In D. Cicchetti & D.J. Cohen (Eds.), *Developmental Psychopathology: Vol 3. Risk, Disorder, and Adaptation* (2nd ed., pp. 620–656). New Jersey: John Wiley & Sons.

Cara E. Rice, MPH, is Project Director of the Adult and Family Development Project at Arizona State University. **Danielle Dandreaux,** MS, is a doctoral student in applied developmental psychology at the University of New Orleans and is currently employed by the Department of Psychology at Arizona State University. **Elizabeth D. Handley,** MA, is a doctoral student in clinical psychology at Arizona State University. Her research and clinical training are focused on at-risk children and families. **Laurie Chassin,** PhD, is Professor of Psychology at Arizona State University. Her research focuses on longitudinal, multigenerational studies of risk for substance use disorders and intergenerational transmission of that risk.

Preparation of this article was supported by grant AA16213 from the National Institute of Alcohol Abuse and Alcoholism to Laurie Chassin.

My Cheatin' Heart

When love comes knocking, do you answer the door?

DAPHNE GOTTLIEB

Let's just get this out in the open.

I was 14 and madly in love for the first time. He was 21. He made me suddenly, unaccustomedly beautiful with his kisses and mix tapes. During the year of elation and longing, he never mentioned that he had a girlfriend who lived across the street. A serious girl. A girl his age. A girl he loved. Unlike inappropriate, high school, secret me.

The next time, I was 15 and visiting a friend at college. It was a friend's friend's boyfriend who looked like Jim Morrison and wore leather pants and burned candles and incense. She was at work and I wanted him to touch me. She found out. I don't know what happened after that.

I was 19 and he was my boyfriend's archrival. I was 20 and it was my lover's girlfriend and we had to lie because otherwise he always wanted to watch. I was 24 and her girlfriend knew about it but then changed her mind about the open relationship. We saw each other anyway. I was 30 when we met—we wanted each other but were committed to other people; the way we look at each other still scorches the walls. I turned thirtysomething and pointedly wasn't invited to a funeral/a wedding/a baby shower because of a rumor.

I am a few years older now and I know this: That there are tastes of mouths I could not have lived without; that there are times I've pretended it was just about the sex because I couldn't stand the way my heart was about to burst with happiness and awe and I couldn't be that vulnerable, not again, not with this one. Waiting to have someone's stolen seconds can burn you alive, and there is nothing more frightening than being willing to take this free fall. It is not as simple as we were always promised. Love—at least the pair-bonded, prescribed love—does not conquer all. It does not conquer desire.

Arrow, meet heart. Apple, meet Eve.

Call me Saint Sebastian.

Out there in self-help books, on daytime television shows, I see people told that they're wrong to lust outside their relationships. That they must heal what's wrong at home and then they won't feel desire "inappropriately." I've got news. There's nothing wrong. Desire is not an illness. We who are its witnesses are not infected. We're not at fault. Not all of us are running away from our relationships at home, or just looking for some side action. The plain fact about desire is that sometimes it's love.

If it were anything else, maybe it would be easier. But things are not as simple as we were always promised: Let's say you're a normal, upstanding, ethical man (or woman) who has decided to share your life with someone beloved to you. This goes well for a number of years. You have a lot of sex and love each other very much and have a seriously deep, strong bond. Behind door number two, the tiger: a true love. Another one. (Let's assume for the moment that the culture and Hollywood are wrong—we have more than one true love after all.)

The shittiest thing you can do is lie to someone you love, yet there are certain times you can choose either to do so or to lie to yourself. Not honoring this fascination, this car crash of desire, is also a lie. So what do you do? Pursue it? Deny it? It doesn't matter: The consequences began when you opened the door and saw the tiger, called it by its—name: love. Pursue it or don't, you're already stuck between two truths, two opportunities to lie.

The question is not, as we've always been asked, the lady—beautiful, virtuous, and almost everything we want—or the tiger—passionate, wild, and almost everything we want. The question is, what do we do with our feelings for the lady *and* the tiger? The lady is fair, is home, is delight. The tiger is not bloodthirsty, as we always believed, but, say, romantic. Impetuous. Sharing almost nothing in common with the lady. They even have a different number of feet. But the lady would not see it this way. You already know that.

You can tell the second love that you can't do this—banish the tiger from your life. You can go home to the first, confess your desire, sob on her shoulder, tell her how awful you feel, and she (or he) will soothe you. Until later, when she wonders if you look at all the other zoo animals that way, and every day for a while, if not longer, she will sniff at you to see if you've been near the large cat cages. Things will not be the same for a long time. And you've lost the tiger. Every time the housecat sits on your lap, you tear up thinking of what might have been, the love that has been lost. Your first love asks you what's wrong and you say "nothing." You say nothing a lot, because there's nothing left, nothing inside.

So instead, let's say you go home and tell your first love, *This new love is a love I can't live without. What can we do?* She will say, *All right, I want to meet her right away. I get all holidays and weekends with you, and there will be no sleepovers with the new love, and I expect the same for myself, and you are never to call her any of the nicknames you have ever used for me,* and the whole thing starts to remind you of a high school necking session—under the sweater; over the bra, but not under it.

You feel like an inmate all the time, and, moreover, where is your first love tonight? She's out with someone you've never met while you're out with your second love, who once had been amenable to an affair. She looks at you sadly and says, "So you think I'm only a half-time tiger?" Her fangs are yellowed and sharp and she finds herself unable to stop staring at the clock, which shows when you will have to leave her to return to the lady.

Maybe there is no "happily ever after" here, but I think there's an "after." I have been the first love; I have been the second; and I have tried to decide between my own firsts and seconds. I have walked through each ring of fire, and I've found no easy answers. It could be that hearts are dumb creatures, especially mine. It could be that there are no good answers. Whether we're admitting desire, lying about it, denying it, or fulfilling it, the consequences are staggering, sometimes ruinous.

So, heart firmly sewn onto sleeve, assured that there is an "after," what can we do but stride forth? It seems clear that no system—polyamory, monogamy, or stand-on-your-head-for-me—will sanitize the astonishing highs and the bereft lows of desire and betrayal. And even if they did, who wants a sanitized heart? So it's up to us: to work together, to love what's so human about us, to understand that the risk of love is loss, and to try to grant desire without eviscerating ourselves. I'm not sure how to do this, but I'm still trying. Because above all, I know this: It's grace to try, and fail, and try again.

A version of this essay appeared as the introduction to *Homewrecker: An Adultery Reader* (Soft Skull Press, 2005), edited by Daphne Gottlieb.

Love but Don't Touch

Emotional infidelity is intense but invisible, erotic but unconsummated. Such delicious paradoxes make it every bit as dangerous as adultery.

Mark Teich

She was the first girl Brendan ever kissed, the first he made love with, the first he truly loved. They'd lost their virginity together on a magical trip to Amsterdam. He felt they were soul mates and believed that their bond would never be severed. But she had suddenly broken up with him after eight months, and they lost touch until 2000, when he paid her a visit. Their exchange was unremarkable, but they traded e-mail addresses. At first, they merely sent an occasional message, chatting superficially. But the correspondence became more frequent and personal. It was easy—she was sunnier and more passionate than Brendan's wife, Lauren, who was bleary-eyed from caring for their sick son while working full-time to pay the bills. Without the burden of these responsibilities, his old love divided her days between visits to the gym and e-mails to him. Yes, she had a husband: but while Brendan was "witty and creative," she said in her lustful notes, her husband was a drone. What a high it was for Brendan to see himself through this complimentary lens after Lauren's withering view of him: hypercritical, angry, money-obsessed.

At the same time, Lauren found herself drawn to a love interest with roots in *her* past: a man she met through a Web site devoted to the neighborhood she grew up in. In short order, Lauren was deeply involved in an Internet relationship that kept her mood aloft throughout the day. In every way, her new companion was superior: While Brendan had set out to be a novelist, he now worked for a little health newsletter. It was Lauren's online friend, a research biologist, who spent his free hours writing a novel, and what a gifted writer he was! While Brendan talked about bills past due and criticized everything from her clothes to her weight, her online partner was fascinated by her thoughts and the minutiae of her day. He abounded in the type of wit and imagination Brendan had lacked for years. Sure, her online partner was married, too; he described his wife as remote and inaccessible—a scientist like himself, but so involved with her work that she left the child-rearing to him and almost never came home.

The New Anatomy of Infidelity

Brendan and Lauren never slept with or even touched their affair partners. Yet their emotional involvements were so all-consuming, so blinding, that they almost blew off their marriage for the disembodied fantasies of online love. Infidelity, of course, is older than the Bible. And garden-variety cheating has been on the rise for 25 years, ever since women swelled the workforce. But now, infidelity has taken a dangerous—and often profoundly stirring—new turn that psychologists call the biggest threat marriage has ever faced. Characterized by deep emotional closeness, the secret, sexually charged (but unconsummated) friendships at issue build almost imperceptibly until they surpass in importance the relationship with a spouse. Emotional involvement outside of marriage has always been intoxicating, as fictional heroines such as Anna Karenina and Emma Bovary attest. But in the age of the Internet and the egalitarian office, these relationships have become far more accessible than ever before.

The late psychologist Shirley Glass identified the trend in her 2003 book, *Not Just Friends.* "The new infidelity is between people who unwittingly form deep, passionate connections before realizing they've crossed the line from platonic friendship into romantic love," Glass wrote. Eighty-two percent of the unfaithful partners she'd counseled, she said, had had an affair with someone who was at first "just a friend." What's more, she found 55 to 65 percent of men and women alike had participated in relationships she considered *emotional*ly unfaithful—secret, sexually energized and more emotionally open than the relationship with the spouse.

Glass cited the workplace as the new minefield for marriage; 50 percent of unfaithful women and 62 percent of unfaithful men she treated were involved with someone from work. And the office has only grown more tantalizing, with women now having affairs at virtually the same rate as men. Factor in the explosive power of the Internet, and it's clear that infidelity has become an omnipresent threat. No research exists on how many affairs are happening online, but experts say they're rampant—more common than work affairs and multiplying fast.

> "You go on the Internet and ask, 'Whatever happened to so and so?' Then you find him. As soon as you do, all of those raw emotions flood back."

The Slippery Slope

An emotional affair can threaten any marriage—not just those already struggling or in disrepair.

"No one's immune," says Peggy Vaughan, author of *The Monogamy Myth* and creator of the Web site, DearPeggy.com, where surveys and discussion reflect the zeitgeist. Although those with troubled marriages are especially susceptible, a surprising number of people with solid relationships respond to the novelty and are swept away as well.

Because it is so insidious, its boundaries so fuzzy, the emotional affair's challenge to marriage is initially hard to detect. It might seem natural to discuss personal concerns with an Internet buddy or respond to an office mate having trouble with a spouse. But slowly, imperceptibly, there's an "emotional switch." The friends have built a bubble of secrecy around their relationship and shifted allegiance from their marriage partners to the affair.

Web of Deceit

The perfect petri dish for secret, sexually charged relationships is, of course, the Internet. The new American affair can take place right in the family room; within feet of children and an unsuspecting spouse, the unfaithful can swap sex talk and let emotions run amok.

Often, it's the anonymity of online encounters that invites emotional disclosure, says Israeli philosopher Aaron Ben-Ze'ev, president of the University of Haifa and author of *Love Online*. "Like strangers on a train who confess everything to an anonymous seatmate, people meeting online reveal what they might never tell a real-world partner. When people reveal so much, there is great intimacy." But the revelations are selective: Without chores to do or children to tend, the friends relate with less interference from practical constraints, allowing fantasy to take hold. Over the Internet, adds Ben-Ze'ev, the power of imagination is especially profound.

In fact, says MIT psychologist Sherry Turkle, author of *Life on the Screen: Identity in the Age of the Internet,* it's particularly what's *withheld*—the "low bandwidth" of the information online partners share—that makes these relationships so fantasy-rich and intense. She compares the phenomenon to that of transference in psychotherapy—where patients, knowing little about their therapists, invest them with the qualities they want and need. Similarly, the illicit partner is always partly a fantasy, inevitably seen as wittier, warmer and sexier than the spouse.

So is online love real? "It has all the elements of real love," says Ben-Ze'ev: obsessive thoughts of the lover, an urgent need to be together and the feeling that the new partner is the most

---

Are You an Emotional Cheat? 7 Telltale Signs

Ever since Scarlett O'Hara flirted in front of Rhett Butler, the jury has been out on extramarital friendships that are sensual, even intimate, yet don't cross the line to actual sex. With emotional affairs so prevalent, psychologists studying the issue have finally drawn some lines in the sand. You may be emotionally unfaithful, they say, if you:

- Have a special confidante at the office, someone receptive to feelings and fears you can't discuss with your partner or spouse.
- Share personal information and negative feelings about your primary relationship with a "special friend."
- Meet a friend of the opposite sex for dinner and go back to his or her place to discuss your primary relationship over a drink, never calling your partner and finally arriving home at 3 A.M.
- Humiliate your partner in front of others, suggesting he or she is a loser or inadequate sexually.
- Have the energy to tell your stories only once, and decide to save the juiciest for an office or Internet friend of the opposite sex.
- Hook up with an old boyfriend or girlfriend at a high school reunion and, feeling the old spark, decide to keep in contact by e-mail.
- Keep secret, password-protected Internet accounts, "just in case," or become incensed if your partner inadvertently glances at your "private things."

---

wonderful person on earth. You experience the same chemical rush that people get when they fall in love.

"But the chemicals don't last, and then we learn how difficult it is to remain attached to a partner in a meaningful way," points out Connecticut psychologist Janis Abrahams Spring, author of *After the Affair.*

Blasts from the Past

People may be exceptionally vulnerable to affairs when they reconnect with someone from their past, for whom they may have long harbored feelings. "It's very common online," says Vaughan. "You go on the Internet, and the first thing you say to yourself is, 'What happened to so and so?' Then you go find them."

Lorraine and Sam had been high school friends during the Sixties, and even camped out together at Woodstock in 1969. In love with Sam but "awed by his brilliance," Lorraine remained too shy to confess. Then he went off to the University of Chicago while she stayed in New Jersey. She married and had a family, but the idea of Sam still smoldered: If only she had admitted her love!

One day she Googled him and located him in Chicago—and they began to correspond by e-mail. He was a partner in a law firm, had a physician wife and coached his daughter's

Inoculating Your Relationship

The biggest mistake couples make is taking monogamy for granted. Instead, they should take affairs for granted and protect themselves by heading infidelity off at the pass.

As part of a proactive approach, psychologist Barry McCarthy suggests couples discuss the importance of fidelity from the outset, identifying the type of situation that would put each at greatest risk. Is drinking on a business trip your downfall, or the novelty of an exotic individual from a far-off locale? Whatever your weakness, work together to make sure you help each other walk past it.

As for Internet relationships, Peggy Vaughan says the safest way to protect the primary relationship is to "make sure that no online interactions are secret. This means having your partner agree that neither of you will say anything to someone online that you aren't willing for the other one to read. If they resist and invoke privacy rights," she adds, "it is probably because they already have something to hide."

Miami Beach psychologist M. Gary Neuman recommends that in addition to setting limits, you actively build the bond with your partner every day. Among the protective strategies he suggests are exchanging "five daily touch points," or emotional strokes, ranging from bringing your partner a cup of tea to a kiss and hug. He also suggests that partners talk for 40 minutes, uninterrupted, four times a week and go on a weekly date. "It's so easy," Neuman says, "to forget why we fell in love."

—MT

Little League team. "Originally I e-mailed just to say, 'hi,'" she explains. But after a few friendly notes, Sam sent a confession. He'd always been in love with her. But her beauty had daunted him, so he'd settled for a plain, practical woman—his wife—instead. E-mails and then phone calls between Lorraine and Sam soon became constant, whipping both of them into a frenzy of heat and remorse. "I can't stop thinking about you. I'm obsessed," one of Sam's e-mails said. But Sam could never get away, never meet face-to-face. "I feel so guilty," he confessed.

That's when Lorraine stopped sending e-mails or taking his calls. "He was a coward," she says, adding that he disappointed her even more by "begging to continue the affair over the phone."

What kind of person chooses to remain immersed in fantasy? It could be someone who "compartmentalizes the two relationships," psychologist Janis Abrahms Spring suggests. "The person may not want to replace the marriage partner, but may want that extra high."

A woman may languish for years in the throes of her "special friendship," while her male counterpart considers it a nice addition to his life.

Women in Love

Frank Pittman, author of *Private Lies,* says that Lorraine lucked out. If she's like most of those involved in Internet affairs, "the face-to-face meeting would have killed it." And if she'd run off with Sam, it probably would have been far worse. "In the history of these crazy romantic affairs, when people throw everything away for a fantasy, the success rate of the new relationship is very low," he explains.

But Lorraine was just acting true to her gender. It is the woman who typically pushes the relationship from friendship to love, from virtual to actual, says Pittman. It's the woman who gets so emotionally involved she sees the affair as a possible replacement for her marriage—even if her marriage is good—and wants to test that out.

American University professor of psychology and affair expert Barry McCarthy explains that for men, "most affairs are high opportunity and low involvement. For women, an affair is more emotional. President Clinton and Monica Lewinsky are the prototypes," he says.

How does this translate to emotional infidelity, where opportunity may be thwarted but emotion reigns supreme? Some men have begun following female patterns, placing more emphasis on emotion than in the past, while women are increasingly open to sex, especially as they achieve more financial independence and have less to fear from divorce.

Even so, says Peggy Vaughan, women are usually far more involved in these relationships than men. A woman may languish for years in the throes of her "special friendship," while her male counterpart considers it a nice addition to the life he already has. As a result, men and women involved in emotional dalliances often see the same affair in different ways. The woman will see her soul mate, and the man will be having fun. Sometimes, says Ben-Ze'ev, a woman will feel totally invested in an affair, but her partner will be conducting two or even four such affairs at once. (The pattern holds for consummated affairs, too.)

For women, the dangers are great. When an emotional affair results in sex, the man's interest usually cools instantly, says Pittman. Meanwhile, husbands are less forgiving than wives, making it more likely for a woman caught up in such an entanglement to be slammed with divorce.

Total Transparency?

With easy access to emotional relationships so powerful they pass for love, how can we keep our primary relationships intact? Psychotherapist M. Gary Neuman of Miami Beach, author of *Emotional Infidelity,* draws a hard line, advocating a rigorous affair-avoidance strategy that includes such strictures as refusing to dance or even eat lunch with a member of the opposite sex. Vaughan suggests we put transparency in our Web dealings—no secret e-mail accounts or correspondence a partner wouldn't be welcome to see.

Others say such prescriptives may be extreme. "Some Internet relationships are playful," Turkle comments. "People may take on different identities or express different aspects

After Infidelity: The Road Back

An emotional affair can deliver a body blow to a marriage, but it rarely results in divorce. Instead, couples can navigate recovery to make their union stronger than before.

The first step in recovery, says psychologist Barry McCarthy, is honesty. "It is secrecy that enables affairs to thrive. The cover-up, for most people, is worse than the actual infidelity," he says. "So it's only by putting everything on the table that you'll be able to move on."

"The involved partner must be honest about all aspects of the affair," says author Peggy Vaughan. Moving on too fast usually backfires, leaving the injured party reeling and the problem unresolved. "Many people believe that too much discussion just reopens the wound; but, in fact, the wound needs to be exposed to the light of day so that it can heal." The involved partner must answer questions and soothe the injured partner for as long as that person needs.

Psychologist Janis Abrahms Spring says the ultimate goal is restoring trust and suggests couples make a list of the trust-enhancing behaviors that will help them heal. Both partners may need compassion for their feelings, she says, but "the hurt partner shoulders a disproportionate share of the burden of recovery and may require some sacrificial gifts to redress the injury caused." These may range from a request that the unfaithful partner change jobs to avoid contact with the "special friend" to access to that partner's e-mail account.

McCarthy, meanwhile, emphasizes that sexual intimacy should resume as soon as possible, as part of the effort to restore closeness and trust.

"In the course of an emotional affair, you open the window to your affair partner and wall off your spouse," McCarthy says. "To repair the marriage, you must open your windows to your partner and wall off the affair."

—MT

"Someone may want just a chess partner, and the technology allows for that."

But if you're going to permit some leeway in the context of your marriage, where do you draw the line? "It's a slippery slope," says Ben-Ze'ev. "You may set limits with your spouse—no phone contact, don't take it off the screen. But people can break the deal. It is a profound human characteristic that sometimes we cross the line."

At best, notes Turkle, a serious emotional affair can alert you to problems in the primary relationship. The injured partner can view it as "a wake-up call" that needs are not being met.

It was perhaps no more than the glimmer of that alarm that enabled Brendan and Lauren to navigate back home. For both, that happened when fantasy clashed with reality—especially when they needed to pull together and care for their sick son. Brendan told Lauren he wanted to take some time to "visit his dad," when his intent was to see his old girlfriend. "I'm so exhausted. Please don't go," Lauren had said, finally asking for help. Using the excuse of a book deadline, she soon began answering e-mails from her online partner only sporadically, then hardly at all.

The illicit partner is always partly a fantasy, she or he is inevitably seen as wittier, warmer and sexier than the spouse.

What had caused them to pull back? On one level it was the need to care for their child, but on another, it was the realization that their online affairs had been a diversion from intimacy, not intimacy itself.

"The idea of actually meeting made me feel ill. I was relieved when Lauren asked me to help at home," Brendan confesses.

"There was so much about my life I never discussed in those e-mails," says Lauren. "In the end, all that witty, arch banter was just a persona, and another job."

MARK TEICH is publications manager of the Skin Cancer Foundation.

of self; an introvert can play at extroversion, a man at being a woman." The experience may be transformative or casual.

Is This Man Cheating on His Wife?

ALEXANDRA ALTER

On a scorching July afternoon, as the temperature creeps toward 118 degrees in a quiet suburb east of Phoenix, Ric Hoogestraat sits at his computer with the blinds drawn, smoking a cigarette. While his wife, Sue, watches television in the living room, Ric chats online with what appears on the screen to be a tall, slim redhead.

He's never met the woman outside of the computer world of *Second Life,* a well-chronicled digital fantasyland with more than 8 million registered "residents" who get jobs, attend concerts, and date other users. He's never so much as spoken to her on the telephone. But their relationship has taken on curiously real dimensions. They own two dogs, pay a mortgage together, and spend hours shopping at the mall and taking long motorcycle rides. This May, when Ric, 53, needed real-life surgery, the redhead cheered him up with a private island that cost her $120,000 in the virtual world's currency, or about $480 in real-world dollars. Their bond is so strong that three months ago, Ric asked Janet Spielman, the 38-year-old Canadian woman who controls the redhead, to become his virtual wife.

The woman to whom he's legally wed is not amused. "It's really devastating," says Sue Hoogestraat, a 58-year-old export agent who married Ric just seven months ago. "You try to talk to someone or bring them a drink, and they'll be having sex with a cartoon."

While many busy people can't fathom the idea of taking on another set of commitments, especially imaginary ones, *Second Life* and other multiplayer games are complicating many lives besides the Hoogestraats.' With some 30 million people now involved worldwide, there is mounting concern that some are squandering, even damaging their real lives by obsessing over their "second" ones. According to a recent survey of 30,000 gamers, nearly 40 percent of men and 53 percent of women who play online games said their virtual friends were equal to or better than their real-life friends. More than a quarter of gamers said the emotional highlight of the past week occurred in a computer world.

A burly man with a long gray ponytail and a handlebar mustache, Ric Hoogestraat looks like the cross between a techie and the Grateful Dead fan that he is. He drives a motorcycle and wears faded black Harley-Davidson T-shirts around the house. A former college computer graphics teacher, Ric was never much of a game enthusiast before he discovered *Second Life.* But since February, he's been spending six hours a night as Dutch Hoorenbeek, his 6-foot-9, muscular, motorcycle-riding cyberself.

In the virtual world, he's a successful entrepreneur with a net worth of about $1.5 million in the site's currency, the linden, which can be purchased through the site at a rate of about 250 lindens per U.S. dollar. He owns a mall, a private beach club, a dance club, and a strip club. He has 25 employees, online persons known as avatars who are operated by other players, including a security guard, a mall concierge, and the "exotic" dancers at his club. He designs bikinis and lingerie, and sells them through his chain store, Red Headed Lovers. "Here, you're in total control," he says, moving his avatar through the mall using the arrow keys on his keyboard.

Virtual worlds like *Second Life* have fast become a testing ground for the limits of relationships, both online and off. The site's audience of more than 8 million is up from 100,000 in January 2006, though the number of active users is closer to 450,000, according to the site's parent company, Linden Lab. A typical "gamer" spends 20 to 40 hours a week in a virtual world.

Though academics have only recently begun to intensively study the social dynamics of virtual worlds, some are saying that they are astonished by how closely virtual relationships mirror real life. On a neurological level, says Byron Reeves, a Stanford University professor, players may not be distinguishing between virtual and real-life relationships. "Our brains are not specialized for 21st-century media," he says. "There's no switch that says, 'Process this differently because it's on a screen.'"

On a Saturday afternoon in July, Ric Hoogestraat decides to go to the beach. So he lights a cigarette and enters *Second Life,* becoming one of 42,752 people logged on at the time. Immediately, he gets an instant message from Tenaj Jackalope, his *Second Life* wife, saying she'll be right there.

They meet at their home, a modern-looking building that overlooks the ocean, then head to his beach club. A full-blown dance party is under way. A dozen avatars, digital representations of other live players, gyrate on the sand, twisting their hips and waving their arms. Several dance topless and some are fully nude. Dutch gets pelted with instant messages.

"What took you so long, Dutch?" a dancer asks.

"Howdy, Boss Man," an avatar named Whiskey Girl says.

Before discovering *Second Life,* Hoogestraat had bounced between places and jobs, working as an elementary schoolteacher and a ski instructor, teaching computer graphics, and spending two years on the road selling herbs and essential oils at Renaissance fairs. Along the way, he picked up a bachelor's degree and took graduate courses at both the University of Wyoming and the University of Arizona. He currently works as a call-center operator for Vangent Inc., a corporation that outsources calls for the government and private companies. He makes $14 an hour.

Hoogestraat learned about *Second Life* in February, while watching a morning news segment. His mother had just been hospitalized with pancreatic cancer—she died two weeks later—and he wanted a distraction. He was fascinated by the virtual world's freewheeling atmosphere. With his computer graphics background, he quickly learned how to build furniture and design clothing. He upgraded his avatar, buying stomach muscles and special hair that sways when he walks. Before long, Hoogestraat was spending most nights and weekends acting out his avatar's life.

When Hoogestraat was diagnosed with diabetes and a failing gallbladder a few months ago, he was homebound for five weeks. Some days, he played from a quarter to 6 in the morning until 2 in the morning, eating in front of the computer and pausing only for bathroom breaks.

During one marathon session, Hoogestraat met Tenaj (Janet spelled backward) while shopping. They became fast friends, then partners. A week later, he asked her to move into his apartment. In May, they married in a small ceremony in a garden over-looking a pond. Thirty of their avatar friends attended. "There's a huge trust between us," says Spielman, who is a divorced mother of two living in Calgary, Alberta. "We'll tell each other everything."

That intimacy hasn't spilled into real life. They never speak and have no plans to meet.

Still, Hoogestraat's real-life wife is losing patience with her husband's second life. "Everybody has their hobbies," says Sue Hoogestraat, who is dark-haired and heavy-set. "But when it's from 6 in the morning until 2 in the morning, that's not a hobby, that's your life."

The real Mrs. Hoogestraat is no stranger to online communities—she met her husband in a computer chat room three years ago. Both were divorced and had adult children from previous marriages, and Sue says she was relieved to find someone educated and adventurous after years of failed relationships. Now, as she cooks, does laundry, takes care of

three dogs, and empties ash-trays around the house while her husband spends hours designing outfits for virtual strippers and creating labels for virtual coffee cups, she wonders what happened to the person she married.

One Saturday night in early June, she discovered his cyber wife. He called her over to the computer to show her an outfit he had designed. There, above the image of the redheaded model, it said "Mrs. Hoorenbeek." When she confronted him, he huffily replied that it was just a game.

Two weeks later, Sue joined an online support group for spouses of obsessive online gamers called EverQuest Widows, named after another popular online fantasy game that players call Evercrack.

"It's avalanched beyond repair," says Sharra Goddard, 30, Sue Hoogestraat's daughter. Goddard says she and her two brothers have offered to help their mother move out of the house.

Sue says she's not ready to separate though. "I'm not a monster; I can see how it fulfills parts of his life that he can no longer do because of physical limitations, because of his age. His avatar, it's him at 25," she says. "He's a good person. He's just fallen down this rabbit hole."

Ric, for his part, doesn't feel he's being unfaithful. "I tried to get her involved so we could play together," he says. "But she wasn't interested."

Early in the morning on the day after Dutch and Tanej's virtual beach party, Ric Hoogestraat is back at his computer, wearing the same Harley-Davidson T-shirt he had on the day before. Four hours after logging on, he manipulates his avatar, who is wearing cut-off denim shorts and renovating the lower level of his mall. "Sunday is my heavy-duty work day," he explains.

From the kitchen, Sue asks if he wants breakfast. Ric doesn't answer. She sets a plate of breakfast pockets on the computer console and goes into the living room to watch a dog competition on television. For two hours, he focuses intently on building a coffee shop for the mall. Two other avatars gather to watch as he builds a counter, using his cursor to resize wooden planks.

At 12:05, he's ready for a break. He changes his avatar into jeans and motorcycle chaps, and "teleports" to a place with a curvy mountain road. It's one of his favorite places for riding his Harley look-alike. The road is empty. He weaves his motorcycle across the lanes. Sunlight glints off the ocean in the distance.

Sue pauses on her way to the kitchen and glances at the screen.

"You didn't eat your breakfast," she says.

"I'm sorry, I didn't see it there," Ric responds.

Over the next five hours, he is barely aware of his physical surroundings. He adds potted palms to his cafe, goes swimming through a sunken castle off his water-front property, chats with friends at a biker clubhouse, meets a new store owner at the mall, counsels an avatar friend who had recently split up with her avatar boyfriend, and shows his wife, Tenaj, the coffee shop he's built.

By 4 P.M., he's been in *Second Life* for 10 hours, pausing only to go to the bathroom. His wrists and fingers ache from manipulating the mouse. His back hurts. Yet he feels it's worth the effort. "If I work a little harder and make it a little nicer, it's more rewarding," he says.

Sitting alone in the living room in front of the television, Sue says she worries it will be years before her husband realizes that he's traded his real life for a pixilated fantasy existence, one in which she's been replaced.

"This other life is so wonderful; it's better than real life," she says. "Nobody gets fat, nobody gets gray. The person that's left can't compete with that."

Becoming Financial Grown-Ups

First comes love, then comes marriage, and then the house, the emergency fund, the 401(k)s . . .

GEORGE MANNES

Until recently, Ari and Jennifer Donowitz had no problem deciding what to do with their money. It was easy. They didn't have any.

The couple married young—they were just 21—while both were still in school. That first year, they scraped by on $20,000 in income, mostly from Jennifer's work as a student aide while she wrapped up a master's in special ed (she financed her degree with money they'd gotten as wedding gifts). Ari, a scholarship student, did odd jobs while finishing his senior year of college. They paid rock-bottom rent for a little one-bedroom in Far Rockaway, Queens, on the fringes of New York City, and they skipped the honeymoon entirely.

Three years later, their finances have taken a decided turn for the better. Jennifer is now a special-education instructor, Ari is a director of finance for a nursing-home operator, and together they're on track to earn $130,000 this year. Their expenses have grown along with their income: They have a son, Eli, almost two, and they've moved into a bigger rental to accommodate their growing family. Still, they're saving in earnest for the first time in their lives—just six months after Ari landed his job, they've already socked away $10,000 in their checking account.

The only problem is that the Donowitzes have no clue what to do with the money. They know what they want: Jennifer wants a house, Ari wants an M.B.A.; they know they need life insurance and that they should be saving for retirement too. But they don't know where to start. "I'm not confident about the concrete stuff we have to do to reach our goals," says Ari. "And we have so many goals—I'm not sure what to do first."

In other words, they face the same problems as other couples in their twenties and thirties. They're finally earning decent money and are ready to behave like financial adults, but need some guidance on how to get there. These tips should help.

- **Set Priorities**—When you're just starting a career and a family, and all of your goals seem urgent and wildly expensive, you can feel so overwhelmed, you end up doing nothing. The key to overcoming paralysis is to zero in on the two or three goals that are most important, and to reassure yourself that you'll tackle the others

eventually. The Donowitzes, for example, have decided to make saving for retirement and Ari's M.B.A. their top priorities now. Buying a house can wait a few years, and they're not even thinking yet about a college fund for Eli.

42% of employees ages 25 to 34 don't invest in their 401(k)s.

Once you have your short list, make the goals more tangible by assigning each one a number and a time frame for achieving it. You'll erase your credit-card debt in two years by paying double the minimum each month, or you'll put $25 a month aside for emergencies until you reach $3,000. If the amounts seem laughably small, don't worry. You'll kick it up over time. The important thing now is to get started. "Saving is a skill," says Ruth Hayden, author of *For Richer, Not Poorer: The Money Book for Couples.* "You need to practice it even when you don't have a lot of money."

- **Work with a Net**—Part of growing up means planning for the worst—or at least the unexpected. That's why one of those first goals should be to build that emergency fund—a stash of cash equal to three to six months of your living expenses that can tide you over if you lose your job or your car breaks down. Getting to that target may take a while; in the meantime, a low-rate credit card with a zero balance can substitute for cash in the bank. Just make sure you save the card for real emergencies, and that your idea of an emergency isn't a family vacation at the beach.

Fortunately, with 10 grand in the bank, the Donowitzes have the emergency fund covered. What they don't have is life insurance that will provide financial security for Eli if one of them dies unexpectedly. The good news about life insurance when you're young: It's cheap. Ari

3 Fast Fixes
A Smart Start on Building Wealth

Now that Ari and Jennifer Donowitz are earning more money, they're eager to tackle bigger financial goals. New York City planner James Kibler offers this advice:

1. **Borrow for the M.B.A.**—Unlike many young people, Ari and Jennifer hate to borrow. Kibler says they're right to avoid credit cards but shouldn't be so quick to shun student loans to help Ari earn a degree that will help him qualify for a better job. "There is such a thing as good debt, which helps you acquire an asset that will outlive the loan," he notes. "The benefit from the M.B.A. lasts forever."
2. **Wait on the House—for Now**—It pains the Donowitzes to pay rent when they could be building equity in their own home. But the couple needs more time to save for an adequate down payment, says Kibler, who suggests they aim to put down at least 10% of a home's price and confine their search to houses that cost no more than 3½ times their pretax income (or 2½ times pretax income if they lived in a less costly housing market).
3. **Save Now for Retirement**—Kibler urges Ari to enroll in his 401(k) plan right away, and he advises Jennifer to open a Roth IRA since her employer doesn't offer a retirement plan. Don't put off signing up until you figure out investing, he says—just get that tax-advantaged growth working for you. "You can always switch investments later," says Kibler. "The important thing is to get the plan going."

much about investing, you're loath to take a risk, so you put your money in the bank where at least you know it will be safe and always accessible. Safe and accessible are good for your emergency fund and savings for other short-term goals, such as a down payment on a house. But there are better places to find those qualities than in a checking account. A savings account at an online bank, with recent rates as high as 4.5%, would provide much higher returns and, since it'd also be insured by the FDIC, just as much safety.

- **Make It Automatic**—You'll greatly improve your odds of success if you organize your finances so that you don't have to discipline yourself to make progress every month, but can instead let things just kind of happen on their own. Most major banks, brokerages and fund companies will allow you to set up automatic monthly cash transfers from your bank or paycheck into a designated savings or investment account. You can also automate your credit-card and other bill payments, which has the added benefit of ensuring that your payments will arrive on time. That, in turn, helps improve your credit score.

Keep It Simple
Worried that you don't know how to pick the right investments for your 401(k)? Go with a life-cycle fund. The manager does the work for you, with a mix of stocks and bonds that's right for your stage in life.

can likely get a $500,000, 20-year term policy for about $265 a year; the same coverage for Jennifer will probably run $230. (To calculate how much you'll need, go to life-line.org; get price quotes at accuquote.com.)

- **Put Your Money to Work**—Now, about that $10,000 that the Donowitzes have saved. The couple get major points for socking away so much cash in so little time, but they've chosen just about the worst place to park the money: a checking account, which typically pays less than 1% in interest or, in their case, no interest at all. It's a classic beginner's mistake—when you don't know

- **Don't Forget the Future**—As hard as it is to plan for life at 65 when you're only 25, you'll end up with tons more money if you start saving for retirement when you're young. Contributing 10% of your income is ideal. But realistically, cash-strapped young adults may need to start with 3%, then raise it a percentage point every six months. "One percent of your salary—you'll hardly feel it," Hayden says.

The payoff is emotional as well as financial. Once you take those first halting steps toward your goals, you'll feel more confident and less stressed. Just ask the Donowitzes. "Having a clear idea of what we need to do is a great relief," says Ari. "We feel like we're on our way."

Making Time for Family Time

Advice from early-career psychologists on how they juggle family and career.

Tori DeAngelis

Starting your psychology career is one of the most exciting—and stressful—times of your life. It's also a period when many early-career psychologists take on new personal responsibilities, such as marrying, starting families and caring for aging parents.

Pulling this off is a lot like spinning plates, and the field's expectations don't make it any easier, says Carol Williams-Nickelson, PsyD, associate executive director of the American Psychological Association of Graduate Students (APAGS), herself working at APA and raising a family.

"There's still a pretty strong undercurrent, especially for women, that career needs to come first if you want to advance," she says.

Other factors make this scenario even more complex, other early-career experts say. For some women, it's the ticking biological clock; for many men, it's changing roles in relation to family and work.

Capt. Jason Prinster, PhD, whose internship led into his current job heading the mental health clinic at the Nellis Air Force Base in North Las Vegas, reflects this attitude.

"Three years from now, my wife could be the one making more money, and I could be the one taking the kids to work and working part time," Prinster says. "I don't think my dad ever had that thought 30 years ago."

Yet to some extent, work places still stigmatize men who openly say they value family as much as work, which puts such men in a bind, Williams-Nickelson adds.

Given these complexities, it helps to get advice from people on the front lines. Early-career experts recommend that you:

- **Communicate.** It's Psych 101, but it's true: Good communication greases the wheels of family sanity, other early-career experts say. A case in point is Jay Robertson-Howell, PsyD, a psychologist at Seattle University's counseling and psychological services center who is raising two young children with his partner, veterinarian Travis Robertson-Howell, DVM. He and Travis make sure to talk not only about each other's needs, but also the needs of the family and their professional concerns, Robertson-Howell says. As time

pressures mount, it's easier to avoid hard topics: "We constantly have to remind ourselves to keep at it," he says.

- **Negotiate.** A central tenet of good communication is agreeing on the particulars of duties and schedules, other early-career psychologists say. While couples arrange these basics in different ways, it's important for both people to discuss and agree on the arrangements and be willing to tweak them as necessary, Prinster says.

Balancing work and family is a lot like spinning plates, and psychology's expectations don't make it any easier.

For instance, Prinster and his wife, Colleen, had many discussions before deciding to split their duties along fairly traditional gender lines, with Colleen staying home with their two children and Prinster bringing home the paycheck. "We talked a lot about our respective roles and made peace with that, at least while the kids are young," Prinster says. "That's really helped. I don't feel guilty working all day, because I know we've already talked about what she expects and what I expect."

- **Schedule time for your family and yourself.** Make sure to ink in family time as an explicit part of your schedules, adds Kristi Sands Van Sickle, PsyD, who is starting her career as an assistant professor at the Florida Institute of Technology and is raising a young daughter with her husband, retired business executive Paul Van Sickle.

"We carve out family time so that even if I'm really busy, we have one day on the weekend when we're all together," says Van Sickle. The two also plan regular visits with Paul's two children from a previous marriage, who live about an hour away. "It's important to put in extra effort to make sure they feel included," she says.

Schedule time for yourself, too, for exercise, hobbies or just to regroup, advises Robertson-Howell. "Sometimes we get going so fast in this society that we forget about that."

- **Trim the excess.** Just as important as good communication is a strategy many of our parents advised us to use: Boil things down to the basics, Prinster says. He and Colleen went from being a couple that pursued many individual interests before they had children, to a team that pursued their family's interests, he says.

"I work to make money to support my family, and I spend time with my wife and kids," Prinster says. "Beyond that, only the things that are really, really important get the resources." That applies to money, too: Colleen works at their children's cooperative preschool in exchange for reduced tuition, and they cut out cable TV—a sensible move, because "we don't have time for TV!" Prinster says.

- **Pick a job that makes sense.** Some early-career psychologists consciously choose jobs that may lack outward razzle-dazzle but offer reasonable hours, decent pay and good boundaries. To spend more time with his partner, David, and their young twins, Seth Williams, PsyD, left a job that expected him to be on "24/7, 365" to one with more reasonable hours and expectations.

"If the kids are sick, I can leave any time if there's nothing life-or-death hanging on it," says Williams, associate director of clinical training at the online graduate school Capella University. He got lucky with his supervisor, too: She has a family and "walks the talk" of work-family balance, he notes.

- **Get more creative.** While there's nothing wrong with traditional job trajectories, other early-career experts say it's worth thinking outside the typical career box to accommodate family needs.

Although her graduate program emphasized academic careers, Eileen Kennedy-Moore, PhD, chose to write books and have a small clinical practice instead. The combination allowed her to work and meet the needs of her four children.

"It gave me flexibility," Kennedy-Moore explains. "If a kid was sick one day, I could handle that and just work harder the next day." It also proved a smart career move: Her books have been published by major publishing houses, and she's garnered many therapy clients and speaking engagements as a result.

- **Find support.** Relying on trusted others is vital, whether it's fellow moms or dads to vent with, or relatives or babysitters who can give you breaks, Van Sickle says.

But your most important support may be your spouse, so nurture that relationship, she recommends. "Paul is my anxiety barometer," she says. "He's better at reading when I'm feeling anxious and overwhelmed than I am."

- **Put family first.** You only have one chance to raise your children, says Williams-Nickelson, who has two young daughters with her husband, psychologist and attorney David Nickelson, PsyD, JD. An avid careerist before she had children, she was overwhelmed by the strength of her feelings toward her girls and now knows they will be her top priority for a long time.

"I feel like I've given a lot to my career and to the profession, and now it's time to give to my kids," she says.

Williams-Nickelson adds that she now understands what mentors advised her in the years before she had children.

"You can have it all," they told her. "Just not all at once."

Partners Face Cancer Together

Couples identify with struggle of Elizabeth and John Edwards.

LIZ SZABO

When Al Shockney's wife was diagnosed with breast cancer, he was gripped by fear. For about half an hour.

But her diagnosis, which could have paralyzed him, instead gave Shockney a mission.

"It did cross my mind, 'What would I do if she wasn't around?'" says Shockney, 66, of Reisterstown, Md.

"But then I thought, 'What can I do now? I know I can't stop this from happening, but I've got to make her realize that whatever she is going to go through, I'm going to be there with her.'"

With a woman as special as his wife, Lillie, "you do what you have to do," he says, "because you want that girl with you for the rest of your life."

"There is not always an answer to 'Why me?' At some point, you have to mobilize around what you're going to do instead of why it happened."

—Laurel Northouse

The Shockneys are among a growing number of couples living with breast cancer. Nearly 2.3 million women in the USA have had breast tumors, making them the largest group of cancer survivors, according to a report in 2005 from the Institute of Medicine, which advises Congress on health.

Couples such as the Shockneys say they've been inspired by presidential candidate John Edwards and his wife, Elizabeth, who announced last month that her breast cancer has spread to her bones, an incurable condition.

Experts praise John Edwards for supporting his wife and commend Elizabeth Edwards for speaking openly about a disease that women once commonly hid. Yet experts say Elizabeth Edwards' fighting spirit, along with her desire for normalcy and her reluctance to let cancer define her, is not uncommon, even among women who have advanced cancer.

Laurel Northouse, a professor at the University of Michigan School of Nursing who studies the needs of families with cancer, says a diagnosis of advanced cancer forces couples to find ways to live fully—often for several years—under the shadow of a fatal disease.

"While the 'temporarily well' look at someone who is ill as beyond the pale and in the land of the dying, the patient just wants whatever time they have to be as rich as possible," says Diane Meier, director of the Center to Advance Palliative Care.

"They are thinking about how to live and how to live better."

Although all diseases are difficult, breast cancer poses special challenges for couples, Northouse says. According to the American Cancer Society, the average age at diagnosis for breast cancer is 61—six years younger than for cancer in general. One-quarter of patients are under 50. Like Elizabeth Edwards, 57, many patients are still raising children.

The partners of cancer patients face tremendous stress, Northouse says.

"Having to watch someone die in slow motion is about the hardest thing you can do," says John Noss, 55, of Round Hill, Va., whose wife, Karin, has advanced cancer. "There is not a day that goes by that I don't think about the fact that I'm going to be on my own.

"I try to steel myself against it. I don't know if it helps."

A Sense of Isolation

Male caregivers grapple with unique burdens, says Marc Silver, who wrote *Breast Cancer Husband* after his wife developed the disease. Many fear saying something that might make their wives more upset, he says.

Husbands often feel isolated when their wives fall ill, he says. Unlike women, who may find emotional sustenance from a wide network of friends, men often confide only in their wives. And friends who shower attention on patients may forget their husbands also feel terrified and overwhelmed.

Spouses of cancer survivors are as likely to be depressed as patients, yet are less likely to receive help, according to a study of nearly 500 people published online Tuesday in the *Journal of Clinical Oncology*. Spouses were lonelier than patients, with worse spiritual well-being and marital satisfaction.

Spouses also were less likely to report personal growth because of the experience. In the study, 27% of husbands reported marital distress, compared with 11% of wives.

John Noss says spouses often experience a mixture of grief and guilt. Many careen between such thoughts as "Why is this happening to me?" and "Oops, it's not happening to me. Get over it."

"Men assume that if they're not the ones with cancer, then they're not suffering as much," Northouse says. "But the depth of their suffering is pretty extensive, whether they recognize it or not."

Though spouses don't need to "beat themselves up" for feeling vulnerable or tired, Northouse says, couples eventually need to move past their initial shock.

"There is not always an answer to 'Why me?'" Northouse says. "At some point, you have to mobilize around what you're going to do instead of why it happened."

'The Breast Cancer Husband's Motto Should Be: Shut Up and Listen'

Experts and cancer veterans say husbands can help their wives cope with breast cancer in many ways:

- Couples often feel hopeless and helpless when facing cancer, says Laurel Northouse of the University of Michigan School of Nursing. They can regain some sense of control by focusing on short-term achievable goals, such as finishing chemotherapy or staying healthy enough to attend a wedding.

  Tom Foley of Somerset, Mass., says he has learned to savor "small victories," such as finding his wife a drink she likes while she's in the hospital.

- Couples should try to stay positive, Northouse says. Though a good attitude has no effect on the cancer itself, it can improve a patient's quality of life. She also suggests avoiding people who are critical or negative.

  "As long as you can find one thing to be happy about each day, you're OK," says John Noss, 55, of Round Hill, Va., whose wife has advanced breast cancer.

- Marc Silver, author of *Breast Cancer Husband,* says many men want to "fix" a woman's cancer. Others act as cheerleaders, trying to convince their wives that things aren't so bad.

  "Not only does that not help, but it makes your wife feel like she doesn't have a right to her feelings," Silver says. "The breast cancer husband's motto should be: Shut up and listen. Sometimes you just need to listen and learn to say, 'Yup, that sucks.'"

- Husbands should take positive action, such as attending as many medical visits as possible, Silver says. Even better, men should take notes or record the conversation. That can reduce stress later, because couples won't worry about whether they misunderstood critical details.

- Although certain treatments can wreak havoc on a couple's love life, such as wiping out a woman's libido and making intercourse painful, Silver says couples can continue to show affection. Men shouldn't withdraw just because the couple has put their sex life on hold.

  "Sometimes a back rub or foot rub can mean a lot, just to help you stay physically connected."

Even the most devoted husbands can become exhausted, Northouse says. Men are often a family's sole financial provider, working full time while ferrying their wives to medical appointments, providing complex nursing care and assuming additional household duties, such as child care, cleaning and errands.

"I used to feel like I was walking around with a big plate on my hand, and people kept piling on it and worrying, 'When am I going to drop it?'" Silver says.

Yet husbands can give their wives great strength.

Shockney says he tried to be prepared to see his wife's mastectomy scar for the first time. He remembers how she scrutinized his reaction. "She could have stared a hole through me. I knew I couldn't let her see that I was shocked or disappointed. I said that everything looks fine and tried to look as normal as I could. I guess I pulled it off."

Making a Woman Feel Beautiful

Experts say women may need extra nurturing during therapy, which can strip them of their hair, sexual organs and libido. Some medications can make intercourse difficult or even painful, says Lillie Shockney, 53.

She says her husband helped her make peace with her scars. Al Shockney, a former truck driver, says she wasn't losing her breast, she was gaining a chance at life.

"I never looked down in the shower and said 'My breast is gone,'" recalls Lillie, whose cancer has not spread to other organs. "I said, 'My cancer is gone.'"

Al also found ways to make his wife feel beautiful after she underwent a second mastectomy, two years later. During a drive in the country, he surprised her by announcing that they were actually heading to a honeymoon suite in the Pocono Mountains. When she protested that she hadn't packed a bag, he informed her that they wouldn't need a change of clothes.

"He said, 'I don't plan on us leaving the hotel room. I heard when you lose one of your senses, the others become more intense. So maybe when you lose your breast, your other erotic zones become more significant, too. I plan to test out this hypothesis over the next 48 hours.'"

Planning a Legacy

And though cancer can be grueling, Northouse says, it also can prompt couples to change their lives for the better. When faced with a life-threatening illness, many look to leave a legacy.

Many cancer patients say they long to spare others from the pain or loneliness they endured. Silver says he wrote his book to provide other husbands with the kind of guidance he wished he had had.

Karin Noss, 49, says anger made her want to change the system. A doctor in 1994 initially dismissed her breast lump, which allowed the tumor to grow for more than a year before it was correctly diagnosed. In 2000, cancer returned in her spine and hip. Now, as a member of the board of the National Breast Cancer Coalition, she campaigns to improve quality and access to care.

Breast cancer also gave Lillie Shockney a new direction. She says it forced her to ask, "How do I want to leave my mark on this world?"

Today, she organizes college "breastivals" to teach young women about cancer, using humor to make the topic more approachable. Participants can even earn "booby" prizes.

Lillie, an oncology nurse, began volunteering at the Johns Hopkins Avon Foundation Breast Center in Baltimore shortly after her cancer returned. Although she initially planned to volunteer six hours a week, she soon was working 20.

She is now the breast center's administrative director. "My husband said this is what I was destined to do," she says. "And I feel energized by every woman that I have the privilege of healing."

A Guide for Caregivers

It's a big, complicated job, and somebody's got to do it. What you need to know to provide for your loved one.

JOAN RAYMOND

Some 20 million boomers are caring for their families while trying to provide care for aging parents. Few know what they are getting into, says Donna Schempp, program director of the Family Caregiver Alliance, a San Francisco advocacy group. "Caregiving simply happens," says Schempp. "No one really chooses their caregiver. It's almost always a default decision based on who is available." Taking care of a parent can be tough. But there are some extraordinary resources available. The smartest approach is to plan ahead, recognizing that someday you will be a caregiver or someone will be caring for you. Here are some tips to help lighten the load.

Medical Issues

There will come a time when an adult child must make decisions regarding a parent's health care. To ease the way, there are two legal documents that experts say are vital. The first is a health-care proxy. This document, also called a health-care power of attorney, appoints a specific person to make all decisions regarding health care and end-of-life care, including refusal of treatment. The health-care proxy goes into effect when the attending physician determines that an individual is no longer able to make decisions on his or her own.

The second critical document is an advance directive, also known as a living will, which allows the person to state what kind of medical care he wants and which life-support procedures he doesn't want. "One of the greatest gifts an adult child can give to parents is to speak for them when they can't speak for themselves," says Kathy Brandt, vice president of the National Hospice and Palliative Care Organization. According to Brandt, advance directives can be powerful tools alone, but generally carry the most weight when combined with a health-care proxy. "It's kind of an insurance policy that your wishes will be carried out," she says.

It's very important for parents to talk about their spiritual beliefs and values, which may shape their decisions about the procedures they may or may not want at the end of life, says Brandt. One caveat: the laws governing advance directives vary from state to state, so it is important that they make sure their advance directives are state-specific.

Another type of advance directive is the Do Not Resuscitate order, or the DNR. Unlike the living will or health-care proxy documents, the patient does not prepare this document. The DNR is a request not to have cardiopulmonary resuscitation if the heart or breathing stops. Though it may be requested by a patient or by a health-care proxy, it is valid only if it is signed by a doctor. A DNR order will then be put into your medical chart. DNRs are accepted in all states.

Finances

Talking to parents about their finances can be extraordinarily difficult, but not talking about finances can be worse, especially if a parent's health starts to decline rapidly. In the past, estate planning involved little more than a will. Now, due to better medical care, people are living longer. That's why estate planning must cover long-term incapacity, including out-of-pocket expenses for assisted living, nursing homes (which, contrary to popular belief, Medicare does not cover long term), in-home care and other expenses related to aging. Long-term-care insurance is an option for some, but it is not a panacea, especially if people cannot keep up with rising premiums. Even if you are already a caregiver and your parents don't have an estate or financial plan in place, it is not too late. There are many strategies, such as reverse mortgages, living trusts and other options that may offer a solution to their long-term needs. A number of professionals can help form a plan, including attorneys, accountants, estate specialists and others.

Legal Issues

At a minimum, a caregiver should have a document called durable power of attorney, which gives you authority to make legal decisions when your parent becomes incapacitated or incompetent. These legal decisions can involve bank accounts, real estate and other personal matters. The durable power of attorney is extremely important for both the parent and adult child, explains Mark Shalloway, president of the National Academy of Elder Law Attorneys. "Financial, legal and other everyday routine decisions need to be made even if a parent suffers a catastrophic event or becomes impaired," says Shalloway. "This is a simple document that reduces hassles with banks, doctors, anyone the parent did business with." Though there are no hearings necessary to set up the durable power of attorney, the person granted the power has a fiduciary duty not to take advantage of the situation. "By law, people must act in good faith," says Shalloway. "There can be some very real legal consequences if someone sells off assets for their own use." If you don't have a durable power of attorney, and if your parent becomes incompetent, you'll need to be appointed guardian by the court, which is "expensive and time-consuming," and removes all legal rights of an older person, says Shalloway.

Also, make sure your parents have wills. This simple document names a person who will manage the estate upon your parents' deaths and the beneficiaries of the estate. If a person dies without a will in place, state "intestacy" statutes will determine who gets the property. Keep all legal documents, including the deed to the house, life-insurance policies and other important papers, in one place, such as a safe-deposit box. If your parents have a safe-deposit box, make sure that you are a signer.

Housing

Ask any older person where he or she wants to live and chances are good they'll say they want to stay in their own homes. But where Mom and Dad eventually live will more than likely be determined by their health, available resources and caregiver's needs. If a parent is healthy and mobile, one option is to make an existing home safer by reducing fall risks. Simple improvements can include adding grab bars in the shower and getting rid of throw rugs. Adult children can also help their parents by arranging for someone to prepare meals and do light housekeeping or to assist with more-personal tasks, such as dressing and bathing. Your local Area Agency on Aging, a governmental program that provides a network of elder services throughout the United States, can help you find a qualified home health-care outfit or individual, as well as provide tips and services on making homes more senior-friendly. But no matter what you do, it's important that your parent be comfortable with the person or persons providing care. So a meet-and-greet between your parents and their aides is essential. And, of course, get references.

When a parent wants to leave a home and is still healthy, there are many options available, including independent senior communities, continuing-care retirement communities and assisted-living facilities. Independent senior communities usually feature private apartments with senior-friendly designs. Some may offer 24-hour emergency-call services, group outings, social activities and other amenities.

Assisted-living facilities cost on average $32,000 per year, while a semiprivate room in a nursing home runs about $65,000 annually.

The continuing-care retirement model offers numerous services that allows people to stay in place, even if their needs change. Generally, these facilities provide services that include housekeeping, emergency help, personal care and social activities. According to the American Association of Homes and Services for the Aging (AAHSA), these continuing-care communities differ from other senior-housing options in that they agree under contract to provide residents with housing and services for life. They do require a one-time entrance fee and monthly payments that vary by region and by the type of housing and services needed. And some groups do operate on a rental basis.

For folks who need daily help with bathing or dressing, assisted-living residences are another option. These facilities can be part of a retirement community or nursing home. Most offer single rooms, but some offer suites or apartments, according to the AAHSA.

When someone is too sick to live on his own and requires round-the-clock care or is recovering from an illness or operation, a nursing home is generally the best choice. These facilities are state licensed, providing nursing and personal care and needed medical services. Like other facilities, nursing homes do offer social activities to residents.

Assisted-living facilities cost on average about $32,000 per year; a semiprivate room in a nursing home runs about $65,000 per year. While Medicare will pay for nursing-home services for a specified period of time for people recovering from surgery or in need of rehabilitation, it does not cover long-term-care expenses. Nor does Medicare pay for assisted living or any of the other senior housing options. "People will say to me, 'What do you mean, Medicare doesn't pay for assisted living or nursing homes?' " says Larry Minnix, AAHSA president. "People are in a world of hurt when they do the math." Your best bet, again, is to plan ahead.

Sometimes a move to an assisted-living facility can help elders socialize. "The decision to move from an existing home is really tough," says Minnix. "Within reason, the wishes of the parent should come first. If a parent wants to stay in the home, do all you can to help them stay there." Internet resources provide a wealth of information on how to choose the best facility or how to help parents make a decision to stay or leave their homes. To help assess your parents' needs, your first stop should be your local Area Agency on Aging.

Family Dynamics

Providing care for an aging parent can create friction among family members. Some siblings may be in denial about a parent's condition; others may not want to be involved in caregiving. "There is no easy way to straighten out years of problems among siblings," says the Family Caregiver Alliance's Schempp.

"Sometimes when a parent requires care it can bring out the best in people. Sometimes it can bring out the worst." If you're having trouble in the sibling-rivalry department, try a family meeting with an outside facilitator, such as a close family friend, attorney, social worker or clergy member. This mediator can make sure that all siblings get their say.

One of the most undervalued roles that siblings can play is providing respite care to the primary caregiver, helping with shopping, transportation, doctor's visits and other tasks. According to the Family Caregiver Alliance, baby boomers caring for aging parents while juggling work and their own family responsibilities are at increased risk for depression and chronic illness and an overall decline in quality of life. Ask for help from siblings or local resources, such as senior centers and the local Area Agency on Aging. Support groups can help, too.

Resources

There is a wealth of resources to help caregivers with information on legal, medical, financial and support issues. Here are a few good places to start:

Administration on Aging (aoa.gov): Provides caregivers and their parents information on various services including elder rights.

Area Agency on Aging: This government program provides a national network of social services. See n4a.org (National Association of Area Agencies on Aging) or call 800-677-1116 for your local agency.

Family Caregiver Alliance (caregiver.org): Offers programs at national, state and local levels to support caregivers.

AARP (aarp.org): Membership organization for people age 50 and older; provides numerous benefits to members.

Eldercare Locator (eldercare.gov): A service of the U.S. Administration on Aging; links caregivers with senior services.

National Academy of Elder Law Attorneys (naela.org): Provides searchable database to assist in finding an elder-law attorney.

Medicare Rights (medicare rights.org): Independent source of health-care information and assistance for people with Medicare.

National Hospice and Palliative Care Organization (nhpco.org): Offers information on end-of-life issues and state-specific advance directives.

Nursing Homes (medicare.gov/nhcompare): Provides detailed information on the past performance of every Medicare- and Medicaid-certified nursing home in the country.

Caring for the Caregiver

They're often the last to ask for help, but the millions of people who manage the care of ailing family members and friends are themselves among the neediest.

SHEREE CRUTE

Four years ago Susan Jordan was dutifully making the three-mile drive from her suburban Nashville home to her elderly mom's house. It was a daily routine she cherished. "I'd check on her and help with her meals and her medication," Susan says. The two would chat, share a laugh, make plans.

Then one day, a desperate call: "My mom had lost her car," Susan, 55, recalls. "She just couldn't remember where it was; then she got lost trying to go home. A friend found her." Susan instinctively knew this was "more than just a memory problem," but before she could even make the doctor rounds, her mother, Virginia Vanleer, then 88, fell and broke her hip.

Fiercely independent and determined to take care of the woman who'd given her the "perfect" childhood, Susan sprang into action. With the blessings of her husband, Ross, she brought her mom to the family house to live. "I was so happy, I cried," she says. But in short order, reality hit: her mom began wandering, moving furniture—and each time Susan left the house, her mom would let out a disturbing wail. Meantime, Ross, a cancer patient, was dealing with his own recovery from chemotherapy. And Susan herself was juggling a full-time career evaluating child-care agencies.

"The entire family was in shock," she says. "I felt trapped, depressed. I found myself thinking, 'What have I *done?*'"

Not one to sit on her hands, Susan set about finding help—all the while trying by herself to manage the bulk of her mother's care. But things went from bad to worse: Susan severely injured her knee after regularly trying to lift her mom, who had taken another fall. "I was so tired," she said.

Finally, after nearly a year of searching, Susan discovered a support group organized by the local Alzheimer's Association, and for the first time, she says, "I knew I wasn't so alone."

The leader of the group gave her a book on caregiving "that became my bible," she says, and members guided her to resources that led to the in-home care her mother needed.

It was, Susan says, the gift that saved her life. Not only did her new friends help stave off depression and a host of stress-related health problems; they showed her how to put some breathing room in her life and live again.

Caregivers stand at particular risk for a host of mental and physical illnesses, many of which have roots in stress, exhaustion, and self-neglect.

Among the 45 million caregivers of family and friends in this country, most don't get thrown that kind of life raft—and the toll, experts say, is enormous. A cascade of studies in recent years has shown that caregivers stand at particular risk for a host of mental and physical illnesses, many of which have roots in stress, exhaustion, and self-neglect—symptoms some medical professionals have begun calling caregiver syndrome. Caregivers appear more likely than noncaregivers to get infectious diseases, plus they are slower to heal from wounds, says Janice Kiecolt-Glaser, Ph.D., director of the Division of Health Psychology at Ohio State University in Columbus. Kiecolt-Glaser has conducted several caregiver research studies with her husband, immunologist Ronald Glaser, Ph.D.

Caregivers also have greatly elevated blood levels of a chemical that is linked to chronic inflammation. And that puts them at increased risk for heart disease, arthritis, diabetes, cancer, and other diseases. Notably, says Kiecolt-Glaser, those levels are still high three years after caregiving duties end, especially among caregivers over 65. What's more, the studies found a greatly increased risk for anxiety and depression.

The implications are far-reaching, given the millions of Americans who report devoting 12 to 40 hours each week or more to the most basic needs of loved ones. "Eighty percent of the long-term care in the country is done by friends and family; we are the care system," says Suzanne Mintz, president and cofounder of the National Family Caregivers Association.

According to a 2004 national survey by AARP and the National Alliance for Caregiving, nearly 23 million households are currently home to a caregiver, most often a woman who is taking care of someone 50 or older. Some 43 percent of these caregivers are over 50 themselves—13 percent are over 65—and they spend good chunks of their weeks on a heady range of chores, from medication management and bathing to feeding, clothing, and arranging health care services.

They cross all ethnic, economic, and religious lines, too, with African Americans and Hispanics more likely to report having to struggle to get patient needs met. Medicaid, Medicare, and the majority of private medical-insurance plans offer little or nothing in the way of payments for home-care assistance—the most commonly needed care in later life. So, many caregiver families find themselves reaching into their own pockets, often straining the family coffers and boosting stress levels even more. Many also pass up job transfers and promotions, abandon hobbies, forgo vacations, and—most dangerous of all—give up the very relationships Kiecolt-Glaser says are "perhaps the single most important factor" in keeping health problems at bay. Exhausted, anxious, and pressed for time, caregivers, she says, "tend to lose their networks and separate from their friends."

For those peering in from the outside, the solution for the caregiver might seem obvious: speak up. Get help. In fact, experts say, that's often the hardest step to take. "You know what they say: anything that doesn't kill you will make you stronger," says Barbara Phenneger, 56, a full-time hospital accounts-payable clerk who for eight years looked after Bill Warren, her 87-year-old neighbor in West Chester, Pennsylvania. Though she never complained, Barbara became so exhausted that she finally sought out a home aide to give her a little relief. "I started imagining Bill; my husband, Bud; and the dog—all looking down on me laid out on the floor and saying, 'Boy, she really did take good care of us!'"

For many caregivers, though, the thought of reaching out for help never occurs.

"I really believed I could do it on my own," recalls Ann Barry, 70, a Brunswick, Maine, mother who has been a 20-year caregiver to her husband, Bill, 82. As his illnesses—heart disease, hydrocephalus (fluid on the brain), and dementia—advanced and he eventually needed a wheelchair, "I just kept trying to adjust my life," says Ann, her girlhood southern accent still in evidence. But it didn't work. "I lost my sense of myself. After a while I had to start taking antidepressants." Finally, a friend who develops community resources for the elderly recognized her pain. "She said to me, 'You can't do this alone,' and led me to many resources," says Ann, who joined a church caregiver group and ultimately became a caregiver supporter herself.

Unfortunately for many friends and family members of caregivers, it is difficult to know when to step in—or what to do, Mintz says. Some caregivers actually rebuff offers of help because they see acceptance as a sign of weakness or a "shirking of their duty," says Barry J. Jacobs, Psy.D., a clinical psychologist in Springfield, Pennsylvania, and author of *The Emotional Survival Guide for Caregivers: Looking After Yourself and Your Family While Helping an Aging Parent* (Guilford, 2006).

A Champ's Champ

"When you're with Muhammad Ali, your day is never normal or predictable," says Lonnie Ali, with a broad grin and a glint of mischief in her eye. The Champ, 65, may be challenged by his struggle with Parkinson's disease, says Lonnie—his wife of 21 years and mother of their son, Asaad—but he's still fighting to get the most out of life. And so is she.

These days Lonnie has been on the stump for a national initiative called Fight for MORE (www.fightformore.com), created to give caregivers of people living with Parkinson's a new venue to find resources and tap into a supportive online community.

It's exciting, says Lonnie, a longtime advocate for Parkinson's research. But while her advocacy largely has centered around this one disease and its impact on 1.5 million patients, much of her caregiving advice is universal. She says her many years as a caregiver have given her unusual clarity about what it takes to live a healthy life.

"Perhaps the most important thing I've learned is to try to stay positive," Lonnie says. Also, "never, ever try to go it alone or stop taking care of yourself."

Lonnie notes that life partners like herself may have special challenges, but she says she's learned that couples can continue to enjoy their relationships. "Do things together, even small things," she advises. For example, she says, Muhammad loves to tag along on grocery runs, chatting up fans and tossing his favorite treats into the cart. The two also pack up the van and take day trips. "Those normal activities help keep him engaged—and we're together.

"Muhammad taught me never to let an illness define you or your mission in life," Lonnie says. For caregivers, that means "focusing on what you can do with the person, not what they can no longer do."

—S.C.

For others, something even more profound may be at play: an attempt to quash emotions simmering just beneath the surface.

Many caregivers "experience profound sadness and rage," says Jed Levine, director of programs and services for the New York City chapter of the Alzheimer's Association. While their caregiving may be driven by empathy and love, they're also dealing with guilt over the anger and frustration they feel. The very touchstones that define their lives—careers, love relationships, friendships, even their dreams—are often being sacrificed. Letting others in, says Levine, invites the risk that those nearly overwhelming emotions will be on display.

Mintz, who has been taking care of a husband with multiple sclerosis since the 1970s, says she knows from experience about that desire to protect pride and emotions. Her "breakthrough moment" didn't come, she says, until the day her husband, Steven, lost his balance and fell in the family bathroom. "All I could do was drag him, slowly, across the floor to our bedroom.

9 Ways to Make It Better

Here's advice about relieving the burdens of caregivers, from veteran caregivers and the experts who have dedicated their careers to the issue.

1. Compromise

Work hard to avoid family fights and resentments if you're a sibling or a relative of the primary caregiver. Don't let old issues pull you apart. This is a time to stick together.

2. Coordinate

Offer your services if you have skill with insurance forms, Medicare, or legal documents. Try to help prepare a game plan for when an illness becomes more severe or fatal. Adult kids often avoid that conversation.

3. Encourage

Help the caregiver find some type of professional support. If he or she is not comfortable with in-person support groups, suggest online chatrooms. Many organizations have them.

4. Facilitate

Ask somebody who can be objective—a cleric, a social worker—to act as a negotiator in stressful situations where the caregiver may be struggling with the patient, other family members, or even health care providers.

5. Investigate

Find books, go to websites, or get in touch with organizations that can help caregivers learn about the illness of the person they're caring for; it will save them time.

6. Organize

Work with the caregiver to make a list of people who can be called upon for different duties, if needed. If time is what is needed, help the caregiver schedule friends to work shifts.

7. Discuss

Ask the caregiver to tell his or her story or keep a journal. Writing things down can be a release and might help others better understand the caregiver's needs.

8. Plan

Think about the services that you can offer, and be specific with the caregiver. Making yourself clear makes it easier for the caregiver to ask for your help.

9. Socialize

Create events for the caregiver and, if possible, the person for whom he or she is caring. Include them in community and family activities.

—S.C.

I'm five feet one; he's five feet eight. It took 45 minutes—it was awful. That's when I knew it was not a one-person job." And her husband agreed.

But Mintz is the first to admit it's not easy getting people to let others into their lives. This is especially true of people in their 70s and 80s, who may be taking care of spouses or other close relatives. "They weren't raised to talk about their problems," Mintz says.

Research suggests it's difficult for African Americans and Hispanics to open up, too, says geriatric psychiatrist Rita Hargrave, M.D., a clinician and researcher at the University of California at Davis. These groups "are less likely to admit being stressed, burdened, or depressed by caring for loved ones, when asked," she says. "But if you evaluate their physical symptoms of depression and stress, you'll find high levels of both conditions."

Mintz says such cultural and age barriers are all worth considering when attempting to give family caregivers a hand. But no matter who's needing the help, she advises a gentle start. She suggests first encouraging the caregiver to find a "caregiving buddy"—a person who's facing similar caregiving challenges and could be a trustworthy confidante. Often, she says, the road to asking for broader support is shorter after that initial step.

If the caregiver resists, friends and family members should be patient, Jacobs says, because getting pushy or controlling will just make things worse. Praise the work the caregiver is already doing. If necessary, ask an empathetic health care provider to recommend your help. And, if possible, enlist the person receiving care. "Permission to get help will have more force coming from the patient than anyone else," says Jacobs.

Once the caregiver begins to share some of the stresses, don't feel you have to move mountains, but do pitch in. "It almost doesn't matter what you do for a caregiver, as long as you do *something*," Jacobs says. Levine says simple gestures—offering to stay with the patient while the caregiver catches a Saturday matinee or runs errands, taking the caregiver and the patient to lunch, bringing over a casserole—can have a tremendous impact. If you're great with paperwork, helping out with the piles of insurance forms can be a thoughtful and much appreciated gift.

Denise Gilardone says she can attest to that. Until last June, when George Engdahl, her fiancé of 18 months, died of brain cancer at 58, the 50-year-old marketing manager had been his primary caregiver for a year. "People would say, 'Let me know if I can do anything,' and as goodhearted as that gesture was," she says, "it was not helpful." Often what she needed was specific offers, particularly offers of time. "It sometimes became stressful in and of itself to make a lot of calls for relief when I needed to go somewhere," she says. "Then people would feel bad or guilty if they couldn't come."

Nudged by a hospice-care worker, Denise, who lives in Hingham, Massachusetts, eventually hired an aide to come two to three hours every Thursday—and that spared her the discomfort of having to explain to others that she wanted to "go to the

Getting Help

These organizations offer a wide variety of classes, support groups, online chats, and other services for caregivers.

Alzheimer's Association
800-272-3900; www.alz.org

Family Caregiver Alliance,
National Center on Caregiving
800-445-8106; www.caregiver.org

The Leeza Gibbons Memory Foundation
888-655-3392; www.leezasplace.org

Lotsa Helping Hands
www.lotsahelpinghands.com

The National Alliance for Caregiving
301-718-8444; www.caregiving.org

National Family Caregivers Association
800-896-3650; thefamilycaregiver.org

ShareTheCaregiving
To learn how to set up your own caregiving network: 646-467-8097; www.sharethecare.org; or Share the Care: How to Organize a Group to Care for Someone Who is Seriously Ill by Sheila Warnock (Fireside, 2004)

The Relaxation Response
To learn the nine steps: www.mbmi.org/basics/whatis_rresponse_elicitation.asp

Visit www.aarpmagazine.org/caregiving for related articles, resources, and message-board discussions. **See also** *Caring for Your Parents: The Complete AARP Guide* by Hugh Delehanty and Elinor Ginzler (AARP Books/Sterling, 2005).

The Power of (More Than) One

Interested in going several steps beyond helping out a caregiver now and then? One innovative idea is shared-care networks—groups of people who get together to share the work that otherwise would fall on one caregiver.

"I think of it as barn building," says Sheila Warnock, founder of Share The Caregiving (see "Getting Help," left). "Everyone has to lend a hand."

A care network can be two people or many more, Warnock says. "It works as a way of recreating the nuclear families that we had years ago."

That's precisely what happened five years ago in Honolulu, where volunteers formed a network to help 80-year-old Elroy Chun and his son and daughter-in-law care for Elroy's wife, Peg, 61, who has ALS, a progressive neurological disease.

There are now 25 volunteers, and they call themselves Peg's Legs. They work in four-hour shifts alongside paid health care workers. That allows Elroy to report to work each day as a building-industry consultant and to do manageable tasks such as laundry. "Thank God they are here," Elroy says. "They help keep me alive and Peg at home."

—S.C.

health club, as opposed to the grocery store, which somehow seemed more acceptable." George's "very supportive" son, Eric, started coming Tuesday nights, and good friends came when she called. But it wasn't until the very end, she says, that it occurred to her to put eager helpers on a schedule.

Careful listening, Levine says, can often tip off family and friends to those kinds of practical needs, or signal when a caregiver may be "truly lost in an emotionally wrenching situation" and should be guided to professional help. Keeping a close watch can also clue friends to health problems caregivers may be developing, or existing problems that are getting worse.

That's what happened for Susan Jordan, when her daughter, Stacy, began noticing Susan's energy just wasn't what it used to be, even after she'd gotten in-home help. Susan concedes that after she injured her knee, "I stopped my daily walking routine for three years." But it was Stacy, a former high-school athlete, who saw what her mother could not. "She said, 'Come on, Mom, you can do this! You're walking and going to the gym with me,' " Susan says. "Now, I'm going to the water-aerobics

class at the local Y, too! People say I look a lot better—and I feel a lot better."

Giving attention to health can save a life, experts say, so think broadly—even beyond walks or yoga classes. Take the caregiver in your life along when you have your next cholesterol or blood pressure check. Or help schedule mammogram or colonoscopy tests for the caregiver and then arrange for transportation. This can be of particular help to people in their 70s and 80s, who "are at especially high risk for health problems if they are handling caregiving alone," says Richard Schulz, Ph.D., director of the University Center for Social and Urban Research at the University of Pittsburgh and lead scientist on the nation's largest study of Alzheimer's caregivers, Resources for Enhancing Alzheimer's Caregiver Health (REACH I and II).

Because many of these 70-plus caregivers are caring for spouses, though, Schulz advises being especially sensitive to relationship issues. The couple may need counseling for long-simmering marital stresses, or they may be embroiled in battles with adult children, he says. They may also be dealing with a basic, and profoundly sad, inability to communicate the way they once did—what caregiving experts refer to as relational deprivation, explains Rose A. Beeson, D.N.Sc., R.N., a researcher and the director of the Center for Gerontological Health Nursing and Advocacy at the University of Akron in Ohio.

"Caregivers of spouses with dementia or Alzheimer's lose the element of reciprocity that is the basis of a marital relationship," Beeson says. "When this is gone, the sense of loss is tremendous."

Beeson says she's found in her research that wife caregivers often are hardest hit by the phenomenon, as they tend to give up social activities or other vital parts of their lives more readily. "Women in this position need to keep going out with friends," Beeson advises. So encourage that. Take them places—"play cards; go to church." Men, she says, tend to be relatively less depressed or isolated, in part because "people are much more likely to rush to help." Also, men tend to be more circumspect and see taking care of their elderly wives "as an opportunity to give back to the woman who reared their children and took care of them and their home," Beeson says.

Still, because all caregivers struggle in some way, experts say that reaching out to help them ease stress, while finding a bit of spiritual peace, might be one of the most positive moves of all. In the groundbreaking Alzheimer's-caregivers study, deep breathing and other relaxation methods emerged as among the most effective tools for doing this, and these techniques have been highly encouraged since, says Schulz.

That's not surprising, notes Herbert Benson, M.D., director emeritus of the Benson-Henry Institute for Mind Body Medicine at Massachusetts General Hospital and author of *The Relaxation Response* (Harper Paperbacks, 1975, 2000), which introduced millions to the concept of mind-body healing and a simple form of meditation. A friend to a caregiver, Benson says, does not have to be a spiritual master to learn a few techniques and then teach. And the payoff can be big.

"You can give a caregiver the ability to be less frightened and to relieve themselves of stress-related problems, such as headaches, irritability, and illness," he says. "The key is to open yourself to the caregiver's belief system and work within that." The relaxation process itself is easy and can be done anywhere and anytime, says Benson. (See "Getting Help.") "All that's required is the choice of a favorite phrase—a prayer or a word will do—and the willingness to clear your mind."

However you choose to help the caregiver in your life, experts say you should connect in the ways you think will be most meaningful and life-enhancing. And recognize that for all the caregiver's stress—and the rebuffs of help—that person's priority is to be of service to loved ones. As Susan Jordan puts it, "I look in the mirror and I can see that I am really tired some days." But, she adds, "I had a wonderful childhood, thanks to my mom. I'm happy to do this for her. I feel that I'm the one receiving the blessings."

SHEREE CRUTE is a freelance writer based in New York City.

Bereavement after Caregiving

Richard Schulz, PhD, Randy Hebert, MD, MPH, and Kathrin Boerner, PhD

O f the approximately 2.4 million deaths that occur in the United States each year, nearly 70% are the result of chronic conditions such as heart disease, cancer, stroke, and respiratory diseases. The large majority of decedents are older persons suffering from one or more disabling conditions which compromised their ability to function independently prior to death. As a result, a typical death is preceded by an extended period of time during which one or more family members provide unpaid care in the form of health and support services to their disabled relative.[1] A recent survey estimates the out-of-pocket cost of caring for an aging parent or spouse averages about $5500 a year.[2]

Our understanding of bereavement is undergoing fundamental changes as a result of recent prospective studies of bereavement that focus on circumstances surrounding the death of a loved one. One important finding to emerge in recent years concerns the impact of family caregiving on caregiver response to death of a loved one.[3,4] Family members involved in care provision before death show remarkable resilience in adapting to the death of their relatives. Symptoms of depression and grief decline rapidly after the death and return to near normal levels within a year of the death.[5] This may be due to multiple reasons, including having time to prepare for the impending death and life afterward, relief from the burdens of caregiving, an end to the suffering of their loved one, and the absence of guilt over having done the "work of caregiving."

Despite the generally positive prognosis for most bereaved caregivers, a sizable minority continues to experience high levels of stress and psychiatric problems after death. Approximately 10% to 15% of people experience chronic depression.[6] In our own work with caregivers of patients with dementia, we found that 30% of caregivers were at risk for clinical depression 1 year post-death, and 20% experience complicated grief.[4,5] As described below, complicated grief is distinct from both depression and normal grief reactions.

Understanding the variability in response to death and the role of caregiving factors as predictors of bereavement outcomes is critical to developing effective interventions for this group. To address this issue, we distinguish among 2 types of predictors of pathologic depression and grief outcomes among caregivers: Factors associated with the caregiving experience prior to death, and factors associated with depression and grief assessed postbereavement. The rationale for making this

Approximately 20% of bereaved caregivers will experience a variety of psychiatric symptoms including depression and/or complicated grief, a disorder characterized by persistently high levels of distress that impair functioning in important life domains. We identify prebereavement risk factors for poor adjustment after the death of a loved one along with preventive strategies that can be implemented prior to death as well as diagnostic procedures and therapeutic strategies that can be used to identify and treat individuals who develop complicated grief disorder after death.

Schulz R, Hebert R, Boerner K. Bereavement after caregiving, *Geriatrics,* 2008:63(1):20–22.

distinction is that each factor provides a different opportunity for intervention. Identifying which caregiving factors contribute to poor bereavement outcomes provides us with important leads about interventions that could be delivered during caregiving. Likewise, postbereavement factors linked to poor bereavement response may help identify intervention options that can be delivered after death.

Caregivers at Risk for Poor Bereavement Outcomes

The most common finding across multiple studies is that prebereavement levels of mental distress such as depression and anxiety are predictive of postbereavement adjustment. A related finding is that high levels of burden, feeling exhausted and overloaded, lack of support, and having competing responsibilities such as work or caring for younger children are all associated with negative postbereavement outcomes.[3,7,8] The fact that increased burden is a risk factor for poor bereavement outcomes may explain in part the higher mortality rate observed among caregivers of terminal patients who do not use hospice services when compared to those who do.[9] Demographic factors also play a role. Individuals with lower income, lower education, and those who are African Americans are also more likely to exhibit greater depression and complicated grief after the death.

Table 1 Questions to Identify Caregivers at Risk for Negative Postbereavement Outcomes

Do you feel overwhelmed by the responsibilities of providing care to your relative?

Do you feel isolated from family and friends?

Do you feel prepared for the death of your loved one?

In the past month have you felt depressed, sad, or anxious much of the time?

Table 2 Symptoms of Complicated Grief

Trouble accepting the death

Inability to trust others since the death

Excessive bitterness related to the death

Feeling uneasy about moving on

Detachment from formerly close others

Feeling life is meaningless without the deceased

Feeling that the future holds no prospect for fulfillment without the deceased

Feeling agitated since the death

A recent randomized trial of dementia in caregivers showed that psychosocial-behavioral interventions designed to decrease caregiver burden and distress had the added benefit of preventing complicated grief after the death of their loved one.[4] This suggests that adverse effects of bereavement can be addressed through preventive treatments delivered to family caregivers prior to the death of their loved one. Individuals at risk for negative postbereavement outcomes can be identified by asking a few questions to determine how stressful caregiving is, the availability of support from family and friends, how depressed and anxious they feel, and whether or not they feel prepared for the death of their loved one (see Table 1). Treatment options for caregivers thus identified include interventions to reduce caregiver burden, such as hospice care, behavioral and pharmacologic treatment of depression and anxiety, and referral to religious counselors.

Diagnosis and Treatment of Complicated Grief

One of the hallmarks of poor response to death is persistent (ie, 6 months or longer) complicated grief. This disorder is distinct from normal grief reactions or depression. It is characterized by an intense longing and yearning for the person who died and by recurrent intrusive and distressing thoughts about the absence of the deceased, making it difficult to concentrate, move beyond an acute state of mourning, form other interpersonal relationships, and engage in potentially rewarding activities. Complicated grief is a source of significant distress and impairment and is associated with a range of negative psychiatric and physical health consequences.[10]

Formal diagnostic criteria for complicated grief disorder have been proposed for inclusion in the *Diagnostic and Statistical Manual of Mental Disorders, Fifth Edition (DSM-V).*[11] A diagnosis of complicated grief disorder requires that the bereaved person must have persistent and disruptive yearning, pining, and longing for the deceased. The individual must experience 4 of the 8 symptoms at least several times a day and/or to a severely distressing disruptive degree (see Table 2). Symptoms of distress must endure for at least 6 months and significantly impair functioning in important life domains.

Complicated grief often occurs along with other disorders such as major depression and post-traumatic stress disorder (PTSD) and is associated with suicidality and self-destructive behaviors,[12] but it is a distinct disorder requiring treatment strategies different from those used with major depression and PTSD. A recent randomized trial found higher and faster rates of improvement among persons with complicated grief using loss-focused, cognitive behavioral therapy techniques when compared to rates obtained with a standard interpersonal therapy approach used to treat depression.[13] Components of effective treatment included repeated retelling of the story of the death, having an imaginary conversation with the deceased, and working on confronting avoided situations. In general, although traditional treatments for depression after bereavement such as referral to a psychiatrist or psychologist for medications and/ or psychotherapy can be effective in treating depression and to some extent, complicated grief, there is added benefit to treatments that are specifically tailored to address symptoms of complicated grief.[6]

Hundreds of studies carried out in the past 2 decades have documented the negative health effects of caregiving, showing that caregivers are at increased risk of psychiatric and physical morbidity.[14] The challenges of caregiving become even more extreme as the care-recipient nears death. When the death does occur, the caregiver enters bereavement already compromised with high levels of depression and anxiety and sometimes physical exhaustion brought about by the caregiving experience. Even with these vulnerabilities, caregivers, for the most part, adapt well to the death of their loved one. Psychiatric symptomatology typically improves and caregivers are able to effectively reengage in activities that may have lapsed while caregiving.

Opportunities for Intervention

Despite this generally positive picture of caregiver adaptation to bereavement, a minority of caregivers exhibit adverse bereavement outcomes in the form of high levels of depression and/or complicated grief. High levels of burden, physical exhaustion, lack of social support, along with traditional predictors, such as prebereavement anxiety and depression, are all associated with negative postbereavement outcomes. Although empirical support for the efficacy of bereavement interventions to enhance adaptation to bereavement is mixed at best,[13,15] researchers have generally not tested preventive approaches in which interventions are delivered prior to death. In addition, new treatment strategies described above specifically designed to treat complicated grief hold promise for helping individuals who are not able to effectively cope with the death of a loved one.

References

1. Emanuel EJ, Fairclough DL, Slutsman J, et al. Assistance from family members, friends, paid care givers, and volunteers in the care of terminally ill patients. *N Engl J Med,* 1999; 341(13):956–63.

2. Gross J. Study finds higher outlays for caregivers of older relatives. *New York Times,* November 19, 2007:A18.

3. Schulz R, Boerner K, Hebert RS, Caregiving and bereavement. In Stroebe MS, Hansson RO, et al, eds. *Handbook of Bereavement Research and Practice: 21st Century Perspectives.* Washington, DC: American Psychological Association Press; in press.

4. Schulz R, Boerner K, Shear K, et al. Predictors of complicated grief among dementia caregivers: a prospective study of bereavement. *Am J Geriatr Psychiatry,* 2006;14(8):650–658.

5. Schulz R, Mendelsohn AB, Haley WE, et al. End of life care and the effects of bereavement on family caregivers of persons with dementia. *N Engl J Med.* 2003;349(20): 1936–1942.

6. Hensley PL, Treatment of bereavement related depression and traumatic grief. *J Affect Disord.* 2006;92(1):117–124.

7. Hebert RS, Dang Q, Schulz R. Preparedness for the death of a loved one and mental health in bereaved caregivers of patients with dementia: findings from the REACH study. *J Palliat Med.* 2006;9(3):683–693.

8. Boerner K, Schulz R, Horowitz A. Positive aspects of caregiving and adaptation to bereavement, *Psychol Aging.* 2004;19(4):668–675.

9. Christakis NA, Iwashyna TJ. The health impact of health care on families: a matched cohort study of hospice use by decedents and mortality outcomes in surviving, widowed spouses, *Soc Sci Med.* 2003;57(3):465–475.

10. Prigerson HG, Bierhals AJ, Kasi SV, et al. Traumatic grief as a risk factor for mental and physical morbidity, *Amer J Psychiatry.* 1997;154(5):616–623.

11. Zhang B, El-Jawahri A, Prigerson HG, Update on bereavement research: evidence-based guidelines for the diagnosis and treatment of complicated bereavement. *J Palliat Med.* 2006;9(5):1188–1203.

12. Latham AE, Prigerson HG. Suicidality and bereavement: complicated grief as psychiatric disorder presenting greatest risk for suicidality. *Suicide Life Threat Behav.* 2004;34(4): 350–362.

13. Shear K, Frank E, Houck PR, et al. Treatment of complicated grief: a randomized controlled trial. *JAMA.* 2005;293(21):2601–2608.

14. Schulz R, Beach S. Caregiving as a risk factor for mortality: the caregiver health effects study. *JAMA.* 1999;282: 2215–2219.

15. Schut H, Stroebe MS. Interventions to enhance adaptation to bereavement. *J Palliat Med.* 2005;8(suppl 1):S140–147.

Dr Schulz is Professor of Psychiatry, Director, University Center for Social and Urban Research, University of Pittsburgh, Pittsburgh, Pa. **Dr Hebert** is Assistant Professor of Medicine, Division of General Internal Medicine, University of Pittsburgh. **Dr Boerner** is Senior Research Scientist, Jewish Home Lifecare, Research Institute on Aging, New York, NY.

Disclosures: Drs Schulz, Hebert, and Boerner disclose that they have no financial relationship with any manufacturer in this area of medicine.

Terrorism, Trauma, and Children

LINDA GOLDMAN

"I never knew grief could feel so much like fear."
—C. S. LEWIS

On September 11, 2001, our children, either directly or vicariously, witnessed the terrorist assault upon our nation, watching over and over again as fanatics crashed American planes into the World Trade Center, the Pentagon, and the fields of Pennsylvania. Our young people witnessed adults running frantically out of control, jumping blindly out of windows, screaming, crying, and appearing bewildered—through black smoke-filled skies and burning buildings—as an insidious and non-locatable enemy emerged to wreak pandemonium and panic upon their lives. The media acted as a surrogate parent and extended family *before* this horrific event, and shared with our children *during* this event visually, aurally, and viscerally. These were sounds and images so graphic that they will forever be imprinted upon their psyche and ours. This unprecedented horror is now a traumatic overlay, potentially triggering all of the pre-existing grief-related issues that our children were carrying before September 11.

Death-related tragedies involving suicide, homicide, and AIDS, and non-death-related traumas such as bullying and victimization, divorce and separation, foster care and abandonment, violence and abuse, drugs and alcohol, and sexuality and gender identification had left many youth living their lives with overwhelmed feelings and distracted thoughts. After September 11, these issues still prevail, infused with the paradigm of terrorism, war, biological destruction, and nuclear annihilation—ideas that are entirely new for our children, for whom "war" is part of a history lesson. In the adult world our children look to for security and comfort, they now see or sense a world of terror, panic, and anxiety, with too many questions and too few answers about their future.

Children processing their grief and trauma may not necessarily progress in a linear way through typical grief phases. The four phases of grief are shock and disbelief, searching and yearning, disorganization and despair, and rebuilding and healing (*Life and Loss,* 2002). These phases may surface and resurface in varying order, intensity, and duration. Grief and trauma work can be messy, with waves of feelings and thoughts flowing through children when they least expect them to come. Kids can be unsuspectingly hit with "grief and trauma bullets" in the car listening to a song or the news, seeing or hearing an airplane overhead, or watching the video of the New York devastation or the Pentagon crash. A fireman's siren, a jet fighter, a soldier in military uniform, a letter in the mailbox, or a balloon bursting can trigger sudden intense feelings without any warning.

Children's Voices

Children's reactions to terrorism, war, anthrax, and the perceived loss of safety and protection provide a window into their psyches and help suggest ways the adults around them can help. Our ability to listen to questions, thoughts, and feelings is paramount in creating a safe zone for our children to process these life-changing times.

Children normally assume they live in a friendly, safe, and caring world. The terrorist attacks of September 11 amplified the pre-existing signs that their world is unprotected, scary, and contains an uncertain future. This deepened loss of the assumptive world of safety for our children creates a new set of voices that all parents, educators, and health professionals must heed.

Five-year-old Tommy, after sitting and listening to his Mom's careful explanation about the terrorist attack, explained why he was really upset about the terrorism: "This is a real tragedy, because I kept searching and searching all day and couldn't find any of my cartoons on TV."

Talking to Children about Terrorism, Trauma, and War

One question weighing heavily on the minds of parents, educators, and mental health professionals is "How do we talk to our children about war, terrorism, prejudice, biochemical attack, and nuclear destruction?"

Sometimes it may help to ask children if they have been "thinking about world events" and if they are, open a dialogue. Some children don't want to talk about it. Some live in fear they will be killed, others say there is nothing to worry about. Some may want to know the facts; therefore we need to choose words that will help them understand what is happening around them. Because so many of us feel "it's just too big," we need to be able to discuss each piece of this huge experience a little

Darian, age 6, illustrates his fear for his own safety after September 11.

"If the terrorists can crash into the World Trade Centers and the Pentagon, they can crash into a regular house like mine!"

at a time. The following are examples of definitions helpful to initiate dialogue with children.

Terrorism is an act or acts of violence, abuse, murder, or devastation against unsuspecting people and countries by a person or group of people that believe their cause is more important than human life or property. Their feeling of "being right" is sometimes more important to them than their own lives. Terrorists can be big or small, black or white, or any color, American or foreign. Their goal is to create terror, disruption, and vulnerability.

Trauma is an experience that can be scary and difficult. It may create feelings of fear, anger, rage, and revenge. A trauma can be a death of someone close to use, caused by a car accident or a terrorist bombing. It can also be from knowing something scary that happened on TV, or to someone we know, or even to a stranger we see on a news video.

Creating Dialogues

When creating dialogues with children, use accurate, real, and age-appropriate language, avoiding clichés or denial of their experience. Concentrate on giving the facts, and keep responses to questions simple and age-appropriate. This helps adults follow the lead of children as to how much information they choose to take in. Especially with young children, minimize the scope of the tragedy, without contemplating with them what did or may happen.

Keeping explanations developmentally appropriate allows children to process this experience at their own level. Young elementary school children need simple information balanced with reassurance that trustworthy adults are bringing stability to their day-to-day life. Middle school children may seek out more facts and want to know more about what is being done to keep them safe and healthy at home, school, and in the community. High school students may outspokenly voice opinions about what happened and why, and may need to develop ways to combat terrorism, rationalize war, and prevent world annihilation. (Adapted from National Association of School Psychologists, NASP, www.nasponline.org.)

Telling children the truth in an age-appropriate way is very important. They often have a conscious or unconscious knowledge of events happening around them and can sense the impact of the terrorist trauma on the adult world. One mom shared just such an experience in the car with her four-year-old son, Andy. She was "sneaking" a listen to the news on the day of the attack. As the reporter began talking about the destruction of the World Trade Center, she quickly turned it off so Andy couldn't hear. Andy immediately explained his level of awareness: "Mommy, they are talking about the plane crash that blew up buildings today."

He just knew about it. If Andy had then been told his experience wasn't real, he may have begun to doubt himself and/or the adult world and question his mother's truthfulness. If Andy felt his mom was hiding the truth about what happened, he might worry more, thinking his mom was too afraid to tell him what really happened. Either way, Andy may have another loss—the loss of the trust in the adult world. Teachable moments for all children can evolve with teachers and parents on subjects such as bullying, violence, prejudice, sexual discrimination, and conflict resolution.

It's OK to let children know you are upset and worried too. Using mature modeling of this upset and worry can create examples for children to follow. It's often hard for them to reconcile a message of "Don't worry; everything is fine" with the enormity of anxiety they may feel coming from the adult world. Find out what they may know about the traumatic event, remembering that they may process what they see and hear inaccurately. Search for faulty perceptions and replace these with simple truths. Young children usually worry about their immediate environment, their family and friends and pets, and their ongoing day-to-day routine. Kids may worry something will happen to their dog, their home, or their friend.

Prepare Children for Dialogue

Reassure children that what they are feeling is very common. Emphasize to them that adults are feeling the same things that they are. Remind them that everyone has different ways of showing their feelings and that is OK. Restore confidence by reassuring them that problems are being handled, people who were hurt are being cared for, buildings are being cleared, and that things are getting a little better each day.

Helping our children grieve can only help the grieving child in each one of us.

Mature modeling guides children to create responsible ways to be helpful during the crisis. Emphasize ways that adults can help. Parents can volunteer to give blood, food, time, and money. Relief agencies such as the Red Cross issued appeals for help. Contributions of needed goods and family money can be taken to needy areas. Children can be included in planning ways families can help and joining in delivering food and clothing. Families and schools may want to join together in saying a prayer for the victims that were attacked, for their families, and for world leaders to bring about peace.

Accept Children's Reactions

While there are several commonly seen reactions to trauma in children, these reactions range widely. Some children will listen to your explanation and then go out to play. Others will want to stay near you and talk about it for a length of time, or maybe ask you to drive them to school instead of taking the bus. Still others may be angry that adults can't immediately fix the problem.

Children can use many activities to safely tell their story. Props like firefighter and police hats, doctor kits, toy soldiers, and hand puppets can be used to reenact the tragedy and war. Toys, puppets, art, clay modeling, collage, letter writing, journaling, and other projective play can be used for role-play and expression of emotions. Positive visualizations and breathing exercises can help kids to relax.

Activities to Help Children Participate in World Events

Children can create rituals that allow commemoration and avenues to voice feelings. Lighting candles, planting flowers, writing letters, raising money for victims, or saying prayers for survivors or world peace allow children to be recognized mourners. Thirteen-year-old Helen lived in a New Jersey community where many families, especially those of firefighters and police, had been deeply affected by the World Trade Center disaster. "Let's make brownies," she told her younger brother and sister, "and sell them to raise money for the firefighters. Everybody likes brownies."

Communities can involve children in participating in fundraisers for the survivors of terrorist attacks. Making patriotic pins and selling them to raise money to help victims and survivors, creating Web sites for world peace, or having a poster contest at school on "What We Can Do to Feel Safe" are ways to give children back a sense of control and participation in their own lives.

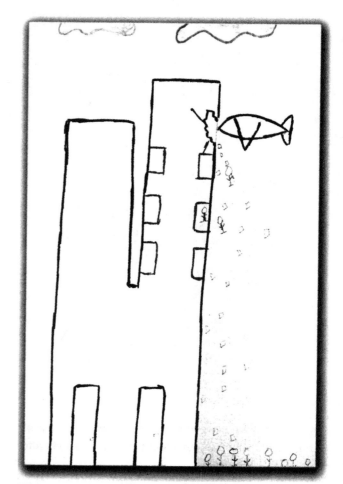

With this recreation of the World Trade Center destruction, 13-year-old Tiara illustrates her grief over the horrific footage she viewed on TV.

What Kids Can Do about Terrorism

1. Talk about their feelings. Allow children ways to tell their story as much as they need to. Draw pictures, create poems, write letters, or offer suggestions about ways to help.
2. Make a fear box. Cut out pictures from newspapers and magazines about what frightens them and paste these around the box. Write down their fears and put them inside.
3. Create a worry list. Make a list of worries from 1 to 5; number 1 is the biggest. Suggest that children talk about this list with someone they trust, like their mom or dad, their sister or brother, their guidance counselor, or a good friend.
4. Put together a "peaceful box." Ask kids to find toys, stuffed animals, and pictures that make them feel safe and peaceful, and keep these items in the box.

5. Help others. Help boys and girls give food or clothing to people who need it. Suggest that the family donate money to a good cause, like the Red Cross, the fund for victims and survivors of terrorist action, or the children in Afghanistan.

6. Display an American flag and create an original global flag. Children can place these flags together outside their house to remind everyone of their support for their country and their hope for world peace.

7. As a family, say a nightly prayer and light a candle for world peace.

Helping Our Children Grieve

We are now a nation and a world of grieving, traumatized children, and the terror of bullying lives inside most of us on this planet and threateningly looms over our everyday life. Our children fear terrorism from foreign strangers and bullying from well-known classmates, siblings, and adult figures. If we can help our kids to see the relationship between terrorist attacks, bullying behaviors, and issues of power and control, we can begin rooting out the behaviors that create oppression, prejudice, misguided rage, and destruction of people and property as a justification for a cause or self-serving purpose.

Responsible adults need to help children cope with trauma and loss and grief from the terrorists outside their country and the bullying within their homes, schools, and community. Providing information, understanding, and skills on these essential issues may well aid them in becoming more compassionate, caring human beings and thereby increase their chances of living in a future world of inner and outer peace.

When the crisis interventions have passed, we will need extensive training in schools and universities to prepare to work with kids in the context of a new paradigm of trauma and grief. Educators, parents, health professionals, and all caring adults must become advocates in creating understanding and procedures to work with our children facing a present and future so different from their past. Our task is to help our children stay connected to their feelings during the continuing trauma of terrorism and war.

The terrorist attack has transformed us all into a global community joining together to re-instill protection and a sense of safety for America and for the world. Helping our children grieve can only help the grieving child in each one of us.

Read more about children and complicated grief issues in Linda Goldman's book *Breaking the Silence: A Guide to Help Children With Complicated Grief/Suicide, Homicide, AIDS, Violence, and Abuse* (Taylor and Francis, 2002). To contact Linda Goldman, e-mail her at lgold@erols.com or visit her Web site at www.erols.com/lgold.

A Divided House

In an era of bitter divorce battles, parents often use children as hammers to bash each other, manipulating not only the legal system but also their children's affections. Can a broken parent-child bond be restored?

MARK TEICH

In 1978, after Cathy Mannis and her future husband moved into the same cooperative at U.C. Berkeley, they ran into each other often. She was not immediately smitten. "I detested him at first, and I should have stayed with that feeling," recalls Cathy Mannis of her now ex-husband. "He was overweight and always very critical. Then he lost weight, became cuter, and started paying attention to me. He was going to be a doctor and he seemed so trustworthy; he said he would never desert his family as his own father had done to him." They started dating, and she ultimately cared for him enough to marry him. "I thought he'd be a good father, and I was dying to be a mother. I thought we'd have a good life."

She worked full-time as a legal secretary to put him through medical school. She also bought the two of them a town house with money she'd saved before marriage. When she gave birth to a boy, Matt (not his real name), she was as happy as she'd ever been. Over time, she saw signs that her husband was cheating on her, but she always forgave him.

Their second son, Robby, was born autistic, and things went downhill fast. The boy had speech and learning problems and was frequently out of control. Her husband was appalled. "He's dumber than a fish," he said.

Still, they had one more child, Harry (the name has been changed), hoping to give Matt a sibling without Robby's problems. Harry turned out normal, but he bonded most closely with Robby; they became inseparable.

When Cathy once again became convinced her husband was cheating—he inexplicably never came home one night—she finally threw him out. He filed for divorce before she could forgive him again.

Cathy was granted primary custody of the kids, and her ex soon married the woman he'd been seeing on the side. Because of all she had to do to help Robby as well as her other two kids, Cathy could no longer hold a full-time job. Meanwhile, her ex declared two bankruptcies and, at one point, even mental disability, all of which kept alimony payments to a trickle.

Eventually Cathy was so broke that her electricity was turned off; she and the boys ate dinner by candlelight. Then she became

so ill she had to be hospitalized for life-threatening surgery. She had no choice but to leave the kids with her ex. "He promised to return them when my health and finances improved," she says.

That was almost seven years ago. Her health has long since returned and she has a good job she can do from home, but the only child ever restored to her, despite nonstop court battles, was Robby. In fact, her ex got the courts to rule that the children should be permanently separated, leaving the other two children with him, since Robby was a "threat" to his younger brother's well-being.

Through all those years, Cathy says she faced a campaign of systematic alienation from Matt and Harry. "When I called to speak to them, I was usually greeted with coldness or anger, and often the boys weren't brought to the phone. Then my ex sent letters warning me not to call them at home at all. Whenever the kids came to stay with me, they'd report, 'Dad says you're evil. He says you wrecked the marriage.'" Then he moved thousands of miles away, making it vastly more difficult for her to see her children.

As time has passed, the boys have increasingly pulled away. Matt, now grown and serving in the military, never speaks to Cathy. Thirteen-year-old Harry used to say, "Mommy, why can't I stay with you? All the other kids I know live with their moms," before leaving visits with her. Now he often appears detached from her and uninterested in Robby, whom he once adored. His friends at his new home think his stepmother is his mom, because that's how she introduces herself. "She told me she would take my kids, and she did. The alienation is complete," rues Cathy. "All I ever wanted was to be a mom."

Divorcing parents have long bashed each other in hopes of winning points with kids. But today, the strategy of blame encompasses a psychological concept of parental alienation that is increasingly used—and misused—in the courts.

On the one hand, with so many contentious divorces, parents like Cathy Mannis have been tragically alienated from the children they love. On the other hand, parental alienation has been seized as a strategic tool in custody fights, its effects exploited in the courtroom, often to the detriment of loving parents protecting children from true neglect or abuse. With the impact of alienation so devastating—and false accusations so prevalent—it may take a judge with the wisdom of Solomon to differentiate between the two faces of alienation: a truly toxic parent and his or her victimized children versus manipulation of the legal system to claim damage where none exists.

The maligning of an ex need not be conscious—or even particularly extreme—to inflict lasting damage on a parent-child relationship.

A Symptom of Our Time?

Disturbed by the potential for alienation, many divorce courts have today instituted aggressive steps to intervene where they once just stood by. And with good reason: Alienation is ruinous to all involved. "In pathological or irrational alienation, the parent has done nothing to deserve that level of hatred or rejection from the child," explains University of Texas psychologist Richard Warshak, author of *Divorce Poison: Protecting the Parent-Child Bond from a Vindictive Ex*. "It often seems to happen almost overnight, and neither the rejected parent nor even the rejecting child understands why."

Often, in fact, it's the emotionally healthier parent who gets rejected, Warshak adds. That parent tends to understand that it's not in the child's best interests to lose the other parent. In contrast, the alienating parent craves revenge against the ex—then uses the child to exact that punishment. "It's a form of abuse," Warshak says. "Both parent and child are victims."

The alienating parent could vilify the ex to rationalize the dissolution of the relationship, explains Atlanta family therapist Frank Pittman, M.D. "Even though they managed to stay married to that person for 10 or 15 years, they now see him or her as the devil's spawn. It's the only way they can justify the breakup of their marriage, because otherwise, it would be their own fault." Once they've convinced themselves of that, it's easy enough to see why their children should be kept away from the other parent.

The maligning of an ex need not be conscious—or even particularly extreme—to inflict lasting damage on a parent-child relationship. "The child can hear negative comments inadvertently," notes Diane McSweeney, a marriage, family, and child counselor for the San Diego Unified School District. "Mom is on the phone with a friend, or Dad is talking to his girlfriend and the child happens to hear negative things. I don't think most people mean to insult the other parent to the child, but they're caught up in their grief for their failed marriage and don't appreciate that the kid can hear everything."

Alienation is especially damaging when one parent can't contain the anger—Mom cheated, or Dad hasn't visited or paid child support—and the wounded parent starts venting to the child. "They're just so desperate to talk to someone, and there's no one else they trust left to talk to. They would never do that to

---

Divorce without Devastating the Kids

Clearly, some parents—those who are physically or emotionally abusive—should be separated from their children. But these are the rarity, and in virtually all other cases, children would do better if their divorced parents stayed amicable partners in raising them. To keep a divorce as healthy as possible for children, follow these rules:

- **Never put** the other parent down. Divorce uproots children's feelings of stability badly enough—trashing or eliminating one of the parents magnifies the instability exponentially.
- **Rather than using** kids as a sounding board, divorced parents who are struggling with each other should seek outside emotional help.
- **Hold any charged** or volatile discussions far out of earshot of the children.
- **Do everything in** your power to accept your ex's next mate, since this person will also play an important role in your child's future stability and happiness.

Parents Who Alienate May Use the Following Tactics

- **Limiting the time** a child can spend with the other parent, and even violating court-ordered visitation schedules.
- **Making false** or unfounded accusations of neglect or abuse, especially in a legal forum. The most damaging expression of this is the false accusation of sexual abuse.
- **Creating fear** of rejection and threatening to withhold affection should the child express positive feelings about the absent parent.
- **Saying negative things** about the other parent in front of or within earshot of the child.
- **Blaming the other** parent for the collapse of the marriage.
- **Moving far away,** making it difficult for the other parent to have a regular relationship with a child.

---

their child in any other situation, but now they are in no shape or form ready to parent," says McSweeney. "The child is then thrown into confusion, feeling the need to take sides. 'I love Mom, but Mom hates Dad, so how can I love them both?' Or, 'I'll make Dad mad if I keep loving Mom, so I have to choose him over her.' "

"I was an adolescent when my parents were divorced," recalls Michelle Martin. "You were either on my mother's side or against her, and if you were on her side, you had to be against my father. She was so angry at him for walking out on her, felt so much shame and betrayal, that you couldn't possibly have a relationship with him if you wanted one with her."

Decades later, Michelle recalls her father (who has since died) as a gentle, caring man. But from the moment he left, her mother systematically worked to convince her that he had been abusive. "She really could not have portrayed him more negatively. 'How can you love him?' she'd say. 'You can't count on him.' He'd call, and she'd tell him my siblings and I didn't want to talk to him, then she'd tell me he didn't want to talk with us."

Afraid to lose her mother's love on top of having had her father walk out, Michelle ended up buying the brainwashing. Eventually, her father married another woman and moved away. At first he came into town regularly to visit, but the ever-renewing hostility gradually became too much for him, and the visits became few and far between.

Her father's reluctance to criticize her mother allowed Michelle's misconceptions to continue unabated, keeping up the walls her mother had created between them. It wasn't until she was 17 that her father finally said to her, " 'You know, a lot of the things you've been told about me were untrue.' It was instantly eye-opening." By her early twenties she'd reconnected with her father, but they only had about 15 years together; he died when she was 38. "I'd lost all those years with a wonderful man, as well as with the members of his family that I loved."

Strategies of War

There's another side to the alienation phenomenon: the hard-edged legal one. Although it is a psychological issue, parental alienation can be truly addressed only in the legal system. Remedy for alienation, say experts, requires an order from a court to allow a manipulated child time to bond with the alienated parent. It is critical, therefore, that there be proof that alienation has in fact occurred. If a parent seeking custody can document the phenomenon, the system—if it is working—will adjust a custody arrangement to promote relationship repair.

The courts worked fairly for Larry Felton, an orthodontist in Detroit (identifying details changed). His wife, an architect who had put her career on hold to raise their daughter, Emily, left Larry and later divorced him. Immersed in his practice, he settled for the once a week plus every other weekend visits the court imposed. "I was devoted and determined to make it work. I wasn't going to let anything keep me from having a relationship with my daughter," he says.

But when Emily grew older and he asked for a little more time with her, things turned ugly. By unilateral decree of his ex, he stopped getting even the limited time that was his due. By the time the court got involved, Emily had grown distant and withdrawn, blaming him for all that had happened. She resisted seeing him at all.

He might have lost his bid for more time with his daughter if not for a key piece of evidence. His ex called to tell him she was canceling yet another weekend with Emily. Then, thinking she'd disconnected the phone when she had not, she said to the daughter and Felton's answering machine, "Your father is evil, a bad man, but we need him for his money. At least he's good for that."

After hearing the tape, the judge awarded primary custody to Larry in hopes of reversing the alienation that had been ongoing for years. Seven years later, 17-year-old Emily has reaped the benefits. Though it took time to earn her trust back, her father now has a solid relationship with her, and her time with her mother is more positive. "I think it saved her," Felton says.

Things are hardly ever so clear-cut in court. Often, judges don't have access to proof like Felton's incriminating voice mail. In the end, after listening to expert witnesses from both sides, decisions are often based on impressions and even the testimony of the children, the very ones who are brainwashed and may be least reliable of all.

"Even when a judge acknowledges that alienation occurred, the court can end up siding with the alienating parent because of the child's wishes," Warshak says. "Otherwise, they fear, the child in his anger might hurt himself or someone else."

In fact, it takes a sophisticated judge to realize what psychologists might see as obvious: Deep down, the child has never really stopped loving the other parent. He or she has just been brainwashed like a prisoner of war or a cult victim, programmed to accept destructive beliefs until critical thinking can be restored.

"Even if they say they don't want to see the parent, underneath they might be longing to reconnect," says Warshak. "These kids need more time with that parent rather than less. Only then will they have a chance to see that the poisoned thoughts are wrong." In the most extreme cases, children are permitted to see the alienating parent only during therapy sessions until the alienation has been resolved.

Other times judges listen mostly to the parent who says he or she has been wronged—and that too can be misleading. According to John E. B. Myers, a professor of law at the University of the Pacific McGeorge School of Law in Sacramento, California, false accusations of parental alienation do "tremendous harm to many children and their parents, particularly mothers seeking custody in family court."

According to Myers, fathers accused of sexual or other abuse by mothers often hide under the protective mantle of "parental alienation" in court, pitting accusation against accusation. The alleged alienator may be dismissed as manipulative, an assumption not always representing truth. The charge could paint a protective parent as a liar trying to poison a child instead of keeping him from harm.

University of California at Davis law professor Carol Bruch adds that the theory of parental alienation fails to account for the anger often felt by children of divorce, especially the kind of contentious divorce that results in custody fights in the first place. "Sometimes the child's feelings are prompted by the behavior of the noncustodial parent. That parent may not be abusive, but just deficient in some way. A parent can become estranged from a child without any provocation whatsoever from the other parent."

The estranged parent could accuse the custodial parent of alienating behavior through blindness to his or her own role.

It takes a sophisticated judge to realize what psychologists might see as obvious: that deep down, the child has never stopped loving the other parent.

Loss and Repair

With knowledgeable experts and astute judges, real alienation can be discerned from false accusations. When alienation is accurately recognized, appropriate intervention on the part of the court can certainly help families heal the damage.

Without the right intervention, however, the result is a scenario of loss and unresolved grief like that of Cathy Mannis. Ironically it is Robby, Cathy's autistic son, who is most acutely in touch with his pain.

"What his father did, first trying to institutionalize him as dangerous, then separating him from his brothers, gave him a devastating signal that he was not worthy, that he deserved punishment rather than help and love," explains Stephen Stahl, MD, PhD, Robby's psychiatrist and a professor of psychiatry at the University of California at San Diego.

Now 18, Robby feels rejected by both his father and his younger brother, both of whom have very little to do with him anymore. "My father never cared about me, so I don't care about him anymore," he says. "But I loved being with Harry every day and every night. I try to call him a lot, but my stepmom is often mean to me or hangs up on me. I almost never get to see him, and he doesn't call. It all makes me so sad."

Parents' grief is also profound. "The child is alive but still lost to you, so close but yet so far, there but not seeing you, and you're uncertain if you'll ever have the relationship back again," Warshak says. "You can't grieve the final loss, because you can never accept that it's final."

As for Cathy Mannis, she recently had Harry with her in San Diego for a one-week court-ordered visit. She and Robby were both thrilled to have the chance to reconnect with him. But as wonderful as that week was, it only set Mannis up for further heartbreak. "He left on Sunday," she says, "and I won't see him again for four months."

MARK TEICH is a writer in Stamford, CT.

Civil Wars

Psychologists who work as parenting coordinators help moms and dads keep the peace.

CHRISTOPHER MUNSEY

Research suggest that it's not divorce in itself that most harms children, but the tension between divorcing parents, some of whom repeatedly appear before judges to battle over drop-off times or visitation rights.

One review of studies in *Children and Divorce,* for example (Vol. 4, No. 1, pages 165–182), found that children whose parents bitterly fight over divorces scored as significantly more disturbed on standardized measures of maladjustment.

"In a lot of these cases, the individual parents 'parent' fine. It's when they interface that all hell breaks loose," says Matt Sullivan, PhD, a Santa Clara, Calif., psychologist, who works with many divorcing clients.

But help is at hand: Through the growing practice area of parenting coordination, psychologists are helping feuding parents call a truce, communicate and work out their disagreements with the goal of better-adjusted children and less-burdened courts.

"It can be helpful for parents to have someone who can help them work out how they're going to keep conflict away from the kids, and help them focus on what the kids need, as opposed to what's going on between the two of them," says Judge Judith Bartnoff of the District of Columbia Superior Court, who has seen the benefits of parenting coordination in several custody disputes.

With their communication skills, psychologists are uniquely qualified for parenting coordination, says Robin Deutsch, PhD, of Harvard Medical School who has served in the role and provided training as well. "Psychologists can help people stuck in ineffective communication patterns learn to communicate better," she says. "It's the bread and butter of what [we] know how to do."

A Growing Field

Parenting coordination typically starts with a court-ordered parenting agreement establishing a detailed custody schedule, with exact drop-off and pickup times listed, plus arrangements for vacations and holidays. When a dispute arises—such as which sport a child should play—the parenting coordinator can step in, halt the angry back-and-forth between the parents and gather feedback from all parties involved.

Besides hearing from the adults involved, a parenting coordinator pays close attention to the child's needs. After gathering the different perspectives, the coordinator—depending on the state where the parents live—either makes the decision, or recommends a solution.

Eight states have passed laws setting up parenting coordination procedures since 1989: Minnesota, Oklahoma, Idaho, Oregon, Colorado, Texas, Louisiana and North Carolina. Meanwhile, a number of other states rely on existing laws that give judges leeway to appoint parenting coordinators (see sidebar).

Demanding Work

Sullivan and co-author Karl Kirkland, PhD, recently completed a survey of 54 parenting coordinators. They found that 44 percent of the responding parenting coordinators were licensed psychologists. Other mental health professionals such as master's level social workers and licensed professional counselors also do the work, with attorneys forming the third-largest share.

For all the different ways parenting coordination is carried out, psychologists say common issues arise for practitioners who move into the area of practice: chiefly, the need for balance, and avoiding falling into dual roles, Deutsch says. Parenting coordinators can't become therapists to their clients, and they have to make decisions fairly, Deutsch says.

"Maintaining impartiality is very important," she says.

From a practitioner's perspective, parenting coordination can be lucrative, without the hassle of third-party payers. In most cases, parents pay the parenting coordinator on a fee-for-service basis, says Sullivan, adding that many coordination agreements spell out the hourly cost of the service, how

---

State by State

Here's a snapshot of how parenting coordination works and is developing in several states and the District of Columbia:

- **California:** If both parents agree, a judge can appoint a parenting coordinator, using a statute already on the books. Called "special masters," these coordinators make legally binding decisions when disputes arise between parents.

- **Maryland:** Although efforts are under way to draft legislation to define parenting coordination, judges in several Maryland counties began turning to parenting coordinators several years ago, says Paul Berman, PhD, a psychologist who also serves as the professional affairs officer for the Maryland Psychological Association. If both parties sign off, the judge can name a parenting coordinator once a child custody order has been signed.

   In his work, Berman is empowered to decide what's best, presenting his decision in writing to both parents.

- **Massachusetts:** Legislation establishing a parent coordination program hasn't moved out of committee in the state legislature in the past two years, but judges do appoint parenting coordinators, says parenting coordinator Robin Deutsch, PhD, relying on their traditional discretion to take action in the best interest of children. If both parents agree, the state allows judges to appoint a parenting coordinator at the time of divorce to help resolve disputes that the parties can't resolve on their own.

- **District of Columbia:** As part of a pilot project of APA, Argosy University, the D.C. Bar and the D.C. Superior Court, family law judges can appoint a licensed clinical psychologist as a special master, who works in a team format with advanced doctoral students from Argosy University in Washington, D.C., to provide parent coordinator services to caregivers who otherwise couldn't afford it, says Giselle Hass, PsyD, an associate professor at Argosy who serves as clinical director for the program.

   Besides helping caregivers learn to communicate effectively with each other, the students can help connect them with resources for themselves and their children, Hass says. Those resources might include helping arrange the evaluation of a child for a possible developmental disability, referring a caregiver for treatment of a mental health issue or helping connect with free legal help.

- **Texas:** Under a state statute, a judge can order a parenting coordinator to get involved if parents agree or if there is evidence of high conflict. However, Texas parenting coordinators do not have authority to make decisions, says Lynelle Yingling, a marriage and family therapist in Rockwall, Texas. Instead, parenting coordinators talk with both parents and help parents develop solutions, Yingling says.

—C. Munsey

---

the parents will split the costs, and what happens if fees go unpaid. Some programs offer pro[[check]] bono parenting coordination to low-income parents, such as one based in Washington, D.C.

The work is also attractive to many psychologists because of its flexible scheduling. And the field is growing, as more judges turn to the idea of using parenting coordinators to help defuse the most problematic cases, several observers say.

It can be very demanding though, judging from the comments of several psychologists experienced in parenting coordination. Getting in the middle of disputes where the parties are often very angry at each other requires a thick skin.

"It's just tough work," says Sullivan. "These are difficult people to work with." He adds that having a "directive, take-charge" personality helps a psychologist succeed as a parenting coordinator. "It takes a particular brand of psychologist to fit this role."

APA's Pilot Parenting Coordination Program

An APA-initiated program enables family law judges in Washington, D.C., to appoint licensed clinical psychologists as special masters who work with Argosy University doctoral students to smooth out disputes between caregivers. Since the program started in January 2005, parenting coordinators have handled 19 cases.

In June, APA's Practice Directorate honored several people who consulted on and helped develop the program including APA's Shirley Ann Higuchi, JD; Dr. Robert Barrett, of the American School of Professional Psychology at Argosy University—Washington, D.C., campus; Judge Judith Bartnoff of the District of Columbia Superior Court; and Dr. Bruce Copeland, formerly of Washington, D.C.

—C. Munsey

Stepfamily Success Depends on Ingredients

One in three Americans is part of a stepfamily, each with its own flavor. How can psychologists help them thrive?

Tori DeAngelis

If Tolstoy were alive today, he might have penned his famous line like this: Happy families are all alike—and every stepfamily is complex in its own way.

Take one example. If a stepparent is frequently battling his former spouse, research shows that his children suffer. But if he is *close* with his ex-partner, his new spouse may feel anxious and insecure. On top of this, say experts, many children don't view their stepparents as "real parents" for the first few years—if ever—and parents in second marriages may treat their biological children differently from their stepchildren.

"Stepparents once were viewed as 'replacing' biological parents, thus recreating a two-parent family," notes University of Virginia (UVA) psychology professor Robert E. Emery, PhD, author of *The Truth about Children and Divorce: Dealing with the Emotions So You and Your Children Can Thrive* (Viking/Penguin, 2004). "Economically, there may be some truth to this, but psychologically, that is not the reality. Remarriage and stepparenting are new, tricky transitions for children, the stepparent and the biological parents."

Fortunately, researchers and clinicians today better understand the common pitfalls of such "blended" families and how they can overcome them. That's important because one in three of us is a member of a stepfamily, according to the Stepfamily Association of America, and that number is likely to grow as traditional family bonds grow more fragile. The demographics of stepfamilies are as complex as the psychological ones: About a quarter are headed by unmarried parents, for example, and stepfamilies make up the full spectrum of our nation's citizens, according to the association.

The Role of Children

Given the complexity of the subject matter, researchers and clinicians are looking at stepfamilies through many lenses. A major one is via the children, who often suffer the most through divorce, remarriage and stepfamily situations. They are particularly at-risk if their biological parents are in conflict (see box, next page), the divorce situation is protracted, they receive less parenting after the divorce or they lose important relationships as a result of the divorce, according to a 2003 article in *Family Relations* (Vol. 52, No. 4, pages 352–362) by Emery of UVA and Joan B. Kelly, PhD, a psychologist and divorce expert in Corte Madeira, Calif.

"When the kids aren't happy, they'll say things like, 'I don't like your new husband—he's mean to me.' That creates conflict in the marriage. In a first-marriage family, if a kid says, 'I don't like my dad,' the mom says, 'So?'"

James H. Bray
Baylor College of Medicine

Indeed, children of divorce—and later, remarriage—are twice as likely to academically, behaviorally and socially struggle as children of first-marriage families: About 20 to 25 percent struggle, compared with 10 percent, a range of research finds. They're also more likely to get divorced themselves, reports University of Utah sociologist Nicholas H. Wolfinger, PhD, in his book, *Understanding the Divorce Cycle* (Cambridge University Press, 2005). Adults whose parents divorced but didn't remarry are 45 percent more likely to divorce than adults whose parents never divorced, he notes, and 91 percent more likely to divorce if their parents divorced and remarried.

Furthermore, children often "calls the shots" on the emotional trajectory of family life, says psychologist and stepfamily expert James H. Bray, PhD, of the Baylor College of Medicine.

"When people get married for a second time, the biological parent really feels they need to attend to the kids," explains Bray, author with writer John Kelly of *Stepfamilies* (Broadway, 1998). "And when the kids aren't happy, they'll say things like,

Containing Conflict in Divorce Battles

As a parent coordinator who helps to resolve custody disputes in divorce cases, Bruce Copeland, PhD, JD, has seen his share of high-drama conflict.

"I had one case involving the father's infidelity with a close relative of the mother's," the Bethesda, Md., psychologist and attorney recalls. "You can imagine the level of intensity around that issue."

Despite the high-octane feelings between the couple, Copeland acted as a conduit so they could exchange information about their two young children. The process went well enough that six months later, "They were able to have a conversation, to make some decisions and to coordinate their children's care," he says.

Parent coordination–a growing niche for qualified psychologists (see the September 2004 *Monitor*)—addresses an important research finding: The level of conflict between parents is one of the key predictors of children's long-term adjustment following a divorce.

"Children in these cases are often caught in a tug of war," says Michelle Parker, PhD, a clinical psychologist and parent coordinator in Washington, D.C. "Much of the energy of the family is being diverted toward the conflict, which doesn't leave an appropriate level of energy and space for the children to grow and develop."

Parent coordinators are meant to help create that space. Unlike mediators and custody evaluators, they have, in many instances, quasi-judicial clout allowing them to make binding recommendations to the courts about parenting arrangements, even if the parents can't agree. Often their work centers on helping parents create specific, developmentally appropriate schedules and plans for their children and teaching them communication skills so they can eventually co-parent without intervention.

Because of the complexity of the work, parent coordinators need special backgrounds, including expertise in child psychology, dispute resolution, marital conflict and legal issues, says Copeland. They also need a solid emotional foundation, since their task is to remain neutral vis á vis the parents, while ensuring—and enforcing if necessary—that children receive the best possible arrangements.

"You need all your clinical skills and more," he says.

The role is gaining in importance, Copeland adds: Courts are calling in coordinators at increasingly early stages of the process to help contain conflict before it gets too toxic for children. Such early intervention also can serve a reporting function, he notes, where coordinators are able to give courts useful psychological information if the case ends up litigating.

—T. DeAngelis

Parenting Plans with Kids in Mind

Many courts still order a one-size-fits-all custody arrangement in which fathers see their children every other weekend, and mothers assume parenting duty the rest of the time.

However, psychological research suggests families fare better with individualized custody plans tailored to fit children's developmental stage and individual circumstances, as well as the particular relationship between children and their parents.

That research shows that children experience cookie-cutter plans as confusing and arbitrary, notes clinical psychologist and divorce expert Joan B. Kelly, PhD. Especially affected are children who have good relationships with their fathers and those so young they "have no cognitive capacity to understand why this abrupt decrease in their contact with the object of their affection occurred," she notes.

Other research she cites in a paper in press at the *Journal of the American Academy of Matrimonial Lawyers* finds that:

- About half of children want more contact with their noncustodial fathers than they have.
- Children are rarely asked about living arrangements, but when they are and their input is used, they report high levels of satisfaction with postdivorce living arrangements.
- Children whose fathers are more involved with them postdivorce generally do better socially, behaviorally and academically than those whose fathers are less involved.
- Children in joint-custody arrangements have better emotional, behavioral and general adjustment than those living only with their mother, according to a 2002 meta-analysis of 33 studies.

University of Virginia psychology professor Robert E. Emery, PhD, co-author with Kelly of a 2003 paper in *Family Relations* (Vol. 52, No. 4, pages 352–362) on children's postdivorce adjustment, puts some of these findings into concrete and user-friendly terms on his Web site at http://emeryondivorce.com/parenting_plans.php. Using a review of the developmental literature, Emery spells out specific custody schedules for children in six developmental periods from birth to 18 years old. He further separates them into categories for angry, distant and cooperative divorce situations.

Meanwhile, APA has embarked on a number of projects to aid the work of psychologists working in the child-custody area. These include collaborative ventures with a range of children-and-law organizations, including the Family Law Section of the American Bar Association (ABA), says Donna Beavers of APA's General Counsel's Office. APA and the ABA section have joined on a number of projects, including a successful joint conference on children, divorce and custody in 1997. Now, the two groups are establishing an interdisciplinary committee aiming to develop projects to ease child-custody conflict.

—T. DeAngelis

'I don't like your new husband—he's mean to me.' That creates conflict in the marriage. In a first-marriage family, if a kid says, 'I don't like my dad,' the mom says, 'So?'"

That said, UVA psychologist and professor emeritus E. Mavis Hetherington, PhD, found in a much-publicized 20-year study that the vast majority of children of divorce do well. As adults, many still feel pain and sadness when they think about their parents' divorce, but they still build productive and satisfied lives, and they don't experience clinical levels of depression, anxiety or other mental health disorders, Hetheringon concludes in her and writer John Kelly's book, *For Better or For Worse: Divorce Reconsidered* (Norton, 2002).

Fostering Resilience

Indeed, many researchers are focusing on these young people's resilience and how to build on it. Psychology professor Allen Israel, PhD, of the University at Albany of the State University of New York, for example, has been developing and evaluating a model of family stability that he believes has special relevance to children in divorce and stepfamily situations.

Family stability, he and his team are finding, isn't contingent on whether you live in a first-marriage, stepfamily or single-parent family, but more particularly on the environment that parents create for their kids, such as the presence of regular bed- and meal-time hours.

That's heartening, Israel believes, because it suggests intervention potential: "You can't always prevent the big things that are causing stress in these kids, such as parents moving or parents who have periods of low contact," he says. "But you might be able to affect the little things that are happening in the home."

In a related 2002 study in the *Journal of Marriage and Family* (Vol. 64, No. 4, pages 1,024–1,037), Kathleen Boyce Rodgers, PhD, a child and family studies researcher at Washington State University, found that outside influences like friends and neighbors can help youngsters undergoing such transitions cope better.

Analyzing data on 2,011 children and adolescents in first-marriage families, stepfamilies and single-parent divorced families, she found that teens who lived with a single, divorced parent and who said they received little support from that parent were less likely to have internalizing symptoms like depression, suicidal ideation and low self-esteem if they had a friend to count on.

In addition, Hetherington has found that consistency in school settings helps predict positive adjustment in children, especially when their home lives are chaotic.

Successful Stepfamilies

Bray examined factors that may predict stepfamilies' success in a nine-year, National Institute of Child Health and Human Development-funded study of 200 Texan stepfamilies and first-marriage families.

Classifying stepfamilies into categories of neotraditional, matriarchal and romantic, he found that neotraditional families fared the best. These parents formed a solid, committed partnership so they could not only nurture their marriage, but effectively raise their children. They didn't get stuck in unrealistic expectations of what the family should be like.

A Sea Change in Family Values?

Researchers consistently find that children of divorce do as well as their nondivorced peers on academic, social and behavioral measures.

But what about their internal lives? And how will their experiences shape their future family choices?

In a March paper in the *Journal of Sociology* (Vol. 4, No. 1, pages 69–86), Katie Hughes, PhD, a senior lecturer in the department of communication, culture and languages at Victoria University in Melbourne, Australia, explores those questions via in-depth interviews with 31 gen Xers, ages 29 to 44–all children of divorced parents who grew up in single-parent or stepfamily homes. These young adults demonstrated:

- An emphasis on individual growth, as opposed to a family or couple focus. "They argue very strongly that personal and intimate relationships are about personal growth," Hughes notes. "They've almost completely replaced old-fashioned notions about gender roles, obligation and duty, and sticking to things, with notions of self-actualization."
- The willingness to abandon a relationship if it turns sour or is not promoting growth.
- The use of subliminal "exit strategies," such as deciding not to have children or declining to pool resources with one's partner.

When Hughes probed the interviewees on their transient views of relationships, many expressed a strong belief that all relationships would inevitably end.

"That's where the divorce patterns kick in," she notes, "because people from intact families don't have that belief."

Reasons they held this notion, interviewees told her, included their own bad memories about their parents' breakup, and their observations that if their parents did remarry, their second marriages often were happier than their first, Hughes says.

While Hughes' study lacks a control group, her subjects' demographics parallel the quantitative literature on children of divorce, she notes. In her sample, 36 percent lived alone, 18 percent cohabited only with a partner, 10 percent lived in stepfamilies and 15 percent lived in shared-house arrangements, she notes.

—T. DeAngelis

Relatively successful were matriarchal families, headed by strong, independent women who remarried not to gain a parenting partner, but a companion. While their husbands were devoted to these women, the men had fairly distant relationships with the children, Bray found.

Matriarchal families functioned well except in parenting matters, Bray found. Conflicts arose, he says, either when the men decided they wanted to play a greater role in parenting—in which case the women were loathe to relinquish their parenting power—or when the women decided they wanted their partners to get more involved. In one common scenario, the woman asked her husband for parenting help but he prevaricated. "She'd ask him to pick up the kids, for example, and he'd forget," Bray says. "That created a lot of conflict."

Romantic families were the most divorce-prone, Bray found. Couples in these families had unrealistic expectations, wanting to immediately create the perfect family atmosphere, and they took their stepchildren's ambivalent reactions to the family transition personally instead of seeing them as normal reactions to a stressful situation.

Tips for Clinicians

Bray and others also have put their heads to creating research-based clinical suggestions for those working with stepfamilies (Bray's suggestions, called "Making Stepfamilies Work," are summarized at www.apahelpcenter.org/articles/article.php?id=41).

These include encouraging second-marriage parents to:

- Discuss and decide on finances before getting married.
- Build a strong marital bond "because it will benefit everybody," says Bray.

- Develop a parenting plan, which likely will involve having the stepparent play a secondary, nondisciplinary role for the first year or two. "Otherwise, even if you're doing a good job, the children will rebuff you," he says.

Family psychologist Anne C. Bernstein, PhD, author of *Yours, Mine and Ours: How Families Change When Remarried Parents Have a Child Together* (W.W. Norton, 1990), additionally advises parents to:

- Take time to process each transition.
- Make sure that big changes are communicated adult-to-adult, not via the children.
- Work with therapists who are specially trained in stepfamily dynamics.

Finally, parents in these families need to "take the long view," Emery advises. "You're going to be a parent forever," he says. "For the sake of the kids, you want to at least make that a working relationship."

TORI DEANGELIS is a writer in Syracuse, N.Y.

UNIT 5

Families, Now and into the Future

Unit Selections

Key Points to Consider

- After having charted your family's lifestyle and relationship history, what type of future do you see for yourself? What changes do you see yourself making in your life? How would you go about gathering the information you need to make these decisions?

- What role does spirituality play in the life of your family?

- What is the state of rituals in your family? What rituals might you build in your family? Why? How might you use family gatherings and other traditions to build family integration?

Student Web Site

www.mhcls.com/online

Internet References

National Institute on Aging
  http://www.nih.gov/nia/

Ryan McVay/Getty Images

*W*hat is the future of the family? Does the family even have a future? These questions and others like them are being asked. Many people fear for the future of the family. As previous units of this volume have shown, the family is a continually evolving institution that will continue to change throughout time. Still, certain elements of family appear to be constant. The family is and will remain a powerful influence in the lives of its members. This is because we all begin life in some type of family, and this early exposure carries a great deal of weight in forming our social selves—who we are and how we relate to others. From our families, we take our basic genetic makeup, while we also learn and are reinforced in health behaviors. In families, we are given our first exposure to values and it is through families that we most actively influence others. Our sense of commitment and obligation begins within the family as well as our sense of what we can expect of others.

Much that has been written about families has been less than hopeful and has focused on ways of avoiding or correcting errors. The five articles in this unit take a positive view of family

and how it influences its members. The emphasis is on health rather than dysfunction.

Knowledge is the basic building block of intelligent decisions regarding family relationships. "The 3rd National Family History Initiative" details the importance of knowing your own family's history. In this, Susan Reece describes ways of using a genogram to map out your family history so that you can anticipate, plan, and possibly change the choices you make in relationships and lifestyle. Information is important in planning for our family's future. One way to gather this information is through interviews and "Get a Closer Look" explains just how this can be done. Next, "Spirituality and Family Nursing" explores the meaning of faith and spirituality for families. Although directed toward nurses, this article provides an in-depth exploration of the relationship between spirituality and various components of health for both individuals in the family and the family as a whole. Concluding this volume, family rituals are examined as being a powerful force for family cohesion and change, and the nature of family rituals is described in "The Joy of Rituals" and "Sustaining Resilient Families for Children in Primary Grades."

The 3rd National Family History Initiative

SUSAN MCCLENNAN REECE, DNSc, APRN, BC

Thanksgiving Day 2006 marks the 3rd annual National Family History Day. Whenever families gather, the surgeon general wants to encourage them to talk about and write down health problems that seem to run in their family. Learning about their family's health history may help ensure a longer future together.[1]

Knowledge about inherited genetic susceptibility, family behaviors, and the shared environments of family members helps to identify major risk factors for subsequent development of disease. Attending to these factors allows an individualized approach to prevention and sets the stage for genomics as the future of health assessment.[2]

Family history plays a critical role in determining patients who may benefit from predictive genetic testing and can facilitate individualized approaches to health promotion, early detection of disease, laboratory investigation, and genetic and health promotion and lifestyle behavior counseling.[3]

Family History and Prevention

The family history guides prevention. In a study of family practice clinicians, those who focused on family history tended to be up-to-date in screening and have a preventive counseling approach.[4] Another study described the family history pedigree as a tool for developing rapport, educating the patient in addition to diagnoses and risks, reproductive options, and a method for distinguishing genetic risk factors from other risk factors.[5]

A wide variety of conditions and illnesses have genetic ties including suicide, abdominal aortic aneurysm, dementia and Alzheimer's disease, autism, and cerebral anerurysms.[5–9]

Research points to the value of family history from the patient/family point of view as well. Using a mailed survey of 4,305 households in the United States, researchers examined perceptions of the importance of family history. Family history was considered to be important in relation to their own health in 96% of those who responded to the survey. Yet, only about 30% of those respondents were involved with actively collecting family health data. Those who reported that the family history was very important tended to be female, better educated, and under 55 years of age.[2]

Content of the Family History

The number of conditions with possible hereditary links is exhaustive; there are well over 1,000 heredity conditions.[5] Questions may need to reflect the type of practice; and in family practice may include cancers, cardiovascular diseases, mental illness, and lifestyle or social issues.

Ideally, family history information is gathered at the first encounter with the patient and is obtained with one or more family members present in a face-to-face interview. The patient should be dressed and the interview conducted in a comfortable, private setting.[5,10] By the time the provider begins to elicit family history data, the patient has developed some trust and may be more willing to share sensitive family information. Allowing patients to verbalize family stories enhances rapport and provides the opportunity to observe the patient's reactions to diagnoses and family life events that are described.[5] These reactions provide an early glimpse of health and psychosocial issues to be further probed later in the interview. The purpose for gathering family data should be explained up front to ease concerns about why the provider is asking about other people. In the traditional organization of eliciting and documenting patient health history, family history follows past medical history and precedes social history.

Knowledge about inherited genetic susceptibility helps identify major risk factors for disease.

The provider may begin the interview by saying, "Certain conditions and illnesses tend to run in families. For that reason, I'd like to learn more about the health of the members in your family." Sensitive circumstances such as divorce or death can be pursued and addressed.

Recording the Family History

A genogram, or diagram of the family, is one of the most effective ways of displaying and communicating the family history. The genogram contains relational, biologic, and legal relationships, yet transcends the pedigree chart by including social, structural, and environmental information about the family such as communication patterns, divorce or separation, and ethnicity, as well as household membership. This varied perspective of the family allows for a better understanding of psychosocial variables that relate to health such as marriage and family function/dysfunction, family supports and conflicts, demographics, household composition, positive and negative life events, and the timing of these events, health issues, and psychosocial/behavioral components such as alcohol or drug use, depression, and suicide.[11] The genogram is not limited by genetic attributes of first and second degree relatives; it allows for the depiction of household members, conflicted and supportive relationships, and partners who may or may not be household members. It may also portray marriage, divorce, separation, widowhood; and through analysis, family life transitions and family crises.[12] Ideally, the genogram is compiled by the healthcare provider. This approach has more positive associations with health outcomes than those completed by patients or office staff.[13]

Genograms may be constructed by hand or by one of the new computer-based approaches. Constructing the genogram during a patient interview need not take long. Most can be sketched out in a 10- to 15-minute portion of the patient visit.[13] Instruction on how to diagram a family using a genogram can easily be found in a variety of texts, articles, and Web sites.[5,11]

With the patient, the provider can begin to sketch out the family, clarifying the meaning of each symbol. As the provider extends questioning beyond the immediate family and as the diagram of the family begins to take stage of the patient and

the reason for shape, the patient can observe the mapping and develop insights into his/her background. Questions should be nonjudgmental[14] and open-ended.

Begin by asking about first-degree relatives then move to siblings, partner (as opposed to "spouse"), children, and then to second-degree relatives such as grandparents, aunts, uncles, and cousins. When asking about each of these family members, determine their age or year of birth, health status, and the year and cause of death for those who are deceased. All genograms are at least three generations. Determining which generations to include is up to the provider and may be based on the age and life stage of the patient and the reason for the visit (primary care versus prenatal or preconceptual visit). Bennett[5] recommends a five-generation genogram for elders to include parents, grandparents, siblings, children, and grandchildren. If conditions present that have a strong genetic component, probes about other family members with the same diagnosis and the severity of the illness may be helpful. Information about household members and ethnicity of each grandparent in addition to immigration history are also important.

Once all essential family members have been added to the genogram, a list of illnesses and health issues that are pertinent can be reviewed with the caveat, "I am going to ask about a number of conditions that often run in families. Does anyone in your family or household have any of the following?" With each positive response, the age of diagnosis, the degree of severity, and the date and age of death should be noted.

With respect to a history of cancer, heart disease, and dementia, age of diagnosis is especially important. For example, with certain cancers, such as breast cancer, and cardiovascular conditions, such as myocardial infarction, earlier age at diagnosis increases the probability that the illness may have a hereditary component.[5,15]

The list of illnesses should be tailored with sensitivity to those that are more or less common in certain ethnic groups. For example, asking about sickle cell disease is important in persons of African descent, anemias in persons of Mediterranean descent, skin cancers in persons of northern European descent, and Tay-Sachs disease in persons of Ashkenazi Jewish descent. Noting the ethnic background for each grandparent of the index case is key as some groups have a higher prevalence of certain mutations.[10] Conditions that relate to environmental exposure or infectious diseases, serious illnesses, social, or lifestyle issues of household members should also be included. Examples are: lead poisoning in siblings of children, and illicit drug use, smoking, and tuberculosis in household members. The interview may be wrapped up with a final question such as, "Are there any illnesses or conditions that run in your family?"

Analysis of the Genogram

The genogram allows providers to quickly capture the gestalt of the family. Analyses include assessing for family structure, size, developmental stage, (childbearing or retirement for example), patterns of physical and psychosocial illnesses, and disability, family transitions and life events that may lead to possible

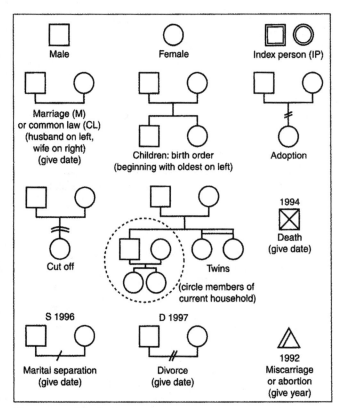

Genogram Symbols

From: Weber J, Kelley J. *Health Assessment in Nursing,* 2nd ed. Philadelphia, Pa.: Lippincott Williams & Wilkins; 2003.

stressors (recent birth or death, multiple life events occurring simultaneously, unemployment, and caregiving of members with disabilities), signs of individual and family dysfunction, and issues surrounding parenting and partnering.

Once the family history is revealed on the genogram, treatment options can be individualized and may include counseling relative to lifestyle, surveillance for health issues and diseases, and prophylactic medical measures, surgical intervention, or genetic testing.[2]

The genogram allows providers to quickly capture the gestalt of the family.

The genogram should be dated and kept in a designated location that is easily retrieved in the medical record.[13] Because family health issues are not static, it should be reviewed and updated with each visit by asking if there have been any changes in the health of family members in the interim.

As Thanksgiving approaches, providers can talk to their patients about family history. A variety of government-sponsored Web sites are now available to assist with this initiative (for example, My Family Health Portrait at http://www.hhs.gov/familyhistory). This tool can be easily downloaded on the computer and once completed by the patient, can be printed and brought to the practice for the next visit. A similar Web site, http://www.ama-assn.org/ama/pub/category/13333.html provides an adult family history questionnaire, and a pediatric genetics form is available at http://www.ama-assn.org/ama/pub/category/13334.html.

References

1. United States Department of Health and Human Services. U.S. Surgeon General's Family History Initiative. Available at: http://www.hhs.gov/familyhistory. Accessed September 25, 2006.

2. Yoon PW, Scheuner MT, Gwinn M, et al. Awareness of family health history as a risk factor for disease—United States. *MMWR*. 2004;53(440):1044–1047.

3. Yoon PW, Scheuner M. Genomics and Population Health: United States 2003, Chapter 6: The Family History Public Health Initiative. Available at: http://www.cdc.gov/genomics/activities/ogdp/200/chap06.htm. Accessed September 25, 2006.

4. Medalie JH, Zyzanski SJ, Goodwin MA, Stange KC. Two physician styles of focusing on the family: Their relation to patient outcomes and process of care. J Fam *Pract.* 2000;49(3):209–215.

5. Bennett RL. *The practical guide to the genetic family history.* New York: Wiley-Liss; 1999.

6. Ruenson B, Asberg M. Family history of suicide among suicide victims. *Am J Psych.* 2003;160(8):1525–1526.

7. Salo JA, Soisalon-Soininen S, Bondestam S, Mattila PS. Familial occurrence of abdominal aortic aneurysm. *Ann Intern Med.* 1999;130(8):637–642.

8. Huang W, Qiu G. AOPE genotype, family history of dementia, and Alzheimer disease risk: A 6-year follow-up study. *Arch Neurol.* 2004;61(12):1930–1934.

9. Okamoto K, Hoirsawa R, Kawamura T, et al. Family history and risk of subarachnoid hemorrhage. *Stroke.* 2003;34(2):422–426.

10. Loescher LJ. The family history component of cancer genetic risk counseling. *Cancer Nursing.* 1999;22(l):96–102.

11. McGoiderick M, Gerson R, Snellenberger S. *Genograms: Assessment and Intervention.* New York: W.W. Norton & Co.; 1999.

12. Herth KA. The root of it all: genograms as a nursing assessment tool. J *Gerontol Nurs.* 1989;15(12):32–37.

13. Bender PL. Genetic Family History Assessment. *AACN Clinical Issues.* 1998;9(4):483–490.

14. American Medical Association. Family Medical History in Disease Prevention. Available at: http://www.ama-assn.org/amal/pub/upload/mm/464/family_history02.pdf. Accessed September 25, 2006.

15. Murff H, Spigel DR, Syngal S. Does this patient have a family history of cancer? An evidence-based approach. *JAMA.* 2004;292(12):1480–1489.

Dr. Susan M. Reece is a professor in the Graduate Program in Nursing at the School of Health and Environment, University of Massachusetts, Lowell.

Get a Closer Look

12 Tips for Successful Family Interviews

IRA WOLFMAN

How do you get relatives talking? A good family history interview isn't easy to conduct. You need to combine the best attributes of caring friend, hard-nosed reporter, and sensitive psychologist. But do it well and you may be rewarded with wonderful stories.

Interviews are different from normal conversations. One person has a goal: to get information from another person (let's call him or her the "talker"). You want the talker to feel comfortable, but you also need to direct the conversation to the points you are interested in.

You also have to be flexible. Sometimes an unexpected topic can turn out to be wonderful. Other times you'll need to lead your talker back to the main point—without hurting his or her feelings. This can be difficult, but you will become better at it as you go along—practice will make you skilled. Be patient with yourself and expect some mistakes. To make things easier, keep these tips in mind:

1. Before any interview, give advance warning. Explain what you want to do, why you want to do it, and why the talker is important to you and your research. You can call or write a letter or e-mail. Here's an example of the kinds of things you should say:

Dear Aunt Gus:

I'm working on a history of our family, and it would be very helpful if I could sit down and talk with you. I'm particularly interested in your memories of my great-grandparents (your mother and father) and the family's early years in Minnesota. I'd also love to look at any old photographs or documents you have.

I won't need much more than an hour of your time and would like to hold our talk at your home. Any weekend day would be fine. Can you let me know a date that is convenient for you?

Thanks so much for your help.

By writing this letter, you've given your relative a chance to start thinking about the topics you're interested in, and you may have even jogged her memory. Of course, not all your relatives will be close by, and your arrangements may be more difficult than "any weekend day." That just makes your writing—and planning—even more important.

2. Prepare before your interview. Find out whatever you can about the talker *before* the interview. Where does she fit in the family? What documents might she have? What other genealogical jewels might she have?

Gather as much information as you can ahead of time about her relationship to everyone in your family. Your parents can probably help you with this.

3. Think out all your questions beforehand. Interviewing requires structure. Write your questions on a sheet of paper, organized by subject. One easy way to organize what you want to ask is by year: Start with your relative's earliest years and then move on from there.

"So, Aunt Gus, you lived in the house in a town outside Minneapolis till you were 10—about 1922, right? Then where did you move?" Or "You say Great-grandpa worked as a tailor in St. Paul. Did you ever visit his shop? Where was it? What years did he have the business there?" As this interviewer did, it's a good idea to summarize what you already know so that your subject can verify your facts. Then move on to a request for more detail.

Sometimes the simplest questions can hit the jackpot. I asked my great-uncle Max, "How old were you when you went from Poland to America?" I didn't get an answer; I got a story:

I must have been about 15 when I went to Warsaw to get a visa to emigrate. I got the visa, but then the counselor at the examination said, "Listen, boy, you are underage. You can't go without your father." He crossed out my stamp.

I went back to our town and told my father. He said, "Don't worry, we'll take care of that."

My father was a religious man, but he also knew how to get things done. He called a policeman from our town and asked him to make me older.

Ready, Set, Research . . . Your Family Tree

- Interview your parents about their family history. Practice interviewing with them.
- Make appointments to interview other family members.
- Prepare your questions. (For a list of good questions for family interviews, see www.workmen.com/familytree.)
- Type up your notes from interviews. Ask the relatives you interviewed to review them and correct or add to them.
- Write a thank-you note to every family member you interviewed.

I got new papers. Now I turned from 15 to 18 or 19. I went back to Warsaw, and I was able to leave. And on February 20, 1920, I took the boat Susquehanna *from Danzig to New York.*

Remember to also ask open-ended questions. "What do you remember most about the apartment on Division Street?" or "Tell me about your relationship with your brothers" may yield something unexpected and wonderful.

4. Bring a video or tape recorder if possible.
A small tape recorder usually doesn't disturb anyone, and it catches every bit of information, including the way your talkers sound and exactly how they answer questions. If you plan to videotape, be sure someone comes with you to run the camera. You need to focus on your talker.

5. In any case, bring a notebook and a pen.
Even if you have [an audio tape or video] recorder, always take handwritten notes. Recorders can break down.

During the interview, write down names and dates and double-check them with your subject. Facts are important, but the most important information your talkers offer are their stories. Try to capture the way they talk and their colorful expressions: "That ship was rolling on the ocean like a marble in your hand."

There's another good reason to bring pen and paper with you. You won't have to interrupt when you think of a question; just write a note to yourself so you'll remember to ask it at an appropriate time.

6. Start with easy, friendly questions.
Leave the more difficult or emotional material for later in the interview, after you've had time to gain your talker's trust. If things aren't going well, you may want to save those questions for another time.

It's also a good idea to begin with questions about the person you're interviewing. You may be more interested in a great-grandfather if he is the missing link in your family chart. But first get some background information about your talker—your aunt, for example. This serves two purposes. First, it lets her know she's important to you, that you care about her, and that her life is interesting, too. Second, as she talks, she may reveal some other information that you would never have known about otherwise.

7. Bring family photographs with you.
Look for photos, artwork, or documents that will help jog your subject's memory. Bring the pictures out and ask your talker to describe what's going on. "Do you remember when this was taken? Who are the people? What was the occasion? Who do you think took the picture?" You may be amazed at how much detail your relative will see in a photograph and also at the memories that come spilling forth.

8. Don't be afraid of silence.
You might feel uneasy and want to rush in with another question when your talker stops speaking. *Don't.* Silence is an important part of interviewing and can sometimes yield to interesting results. Because people often find silence uncomfortable, they often try to fill it if you don't—and in doing so, they may say something you might not have heard otherwise.

Sometimes silence is also necessary for gathering thoughts. Don't forget—you are asking your subjects to think back on things they may not have considered for years. Calling up these memories may spark other thoughts, too. Allow your subject time to ponder. You may be thrilled by what he or she remembers.

9. Ask the same question in different ways.
People don't know how much they know, and rephrasing a question can give you more information. This happens all the time. "I don't know," a relative will tell you, sometimes impatiently. They do know—they just don't know that they know. The most common version of this occurs when an interviewer asks, "What was your father's mother's name?" The relative answers, "I never knew her. I don't know." Then a few minutes later, in response to "Whom were you named after?" this answer comes; "My father's mother."

Try to find a couple of ways to ask important questions. You may feel like you're being repetitive, but you never can be sure what you will learn.

10. Be sensitive to what you discover.
Sometimes people become emotional talking about the past. They may remember long-dead relatives or once-forgotten tragedies. If your talker is upset by a memory, either remain silent or quietly ask, "Is it all right if we talk some more about this? Or would you rather not?" People frequently feel better when they talk about sad things; you should gently give your relative the *choice* of whether or not to go on.

11. Try not to interrupt.
If your talker strays from the subject, let him or her finish the story and then say, "Let's get back to Uncle Moe" or "You said something earlier about . . . " By not interrupting, you make the conversation friendlier, and the story may lead you to something you didn't expect.

Of course, there is always the exception to the rule. If a story goes on forever and seems useless, the best way to handle it may be to say, "Gee, Aunt Gus, could you hold the rest of that story for later? I'd like to get the facts out of the way and then come back to that."

12. Ask for songs, poems, unusual memories.
You may discover something wonderful when you ask your subject if she recalls the rhymes she used to recite while jumping rope as a little girl or the hymns she sang in church. Probe a little here—ask about childhood games and memories, smells and tastes and sounds.

Spirituality and Family Nursing
Spiritual Assessment and Interventions for Families

Ruth A. Tanyi MSN RN FNP-C APRN-BC

Introduction

In this paper, family spirituality is described as the search for meaning and purpose in life, meaningful relationships, individual family member spirituality, family values, beliefs, and practices, which may or may not be religiously based, and the ability to be transcendent (Sperry & Giblin 1996, Tanyi 2002). Family spirituality can be much broader than individual spirituality, as it encompasses individuals' distinct spirituality and that of the family unit. The broadness of this description is consistent with the multi-dimensional and ambiguous nature of spirituality.

The family is defined here as two or more individuals who call themselves a family and are bonded together emotionally. They may or may not be biologically related or share physical space. Family is further defined as a single unit with interconnected parts (Friedman 1998, Wegner & Alexander 1999).

Given the complex nature of spirituality, the intention in this paper is not to serve as a conclusive and definitive guide to spiritual assessment and interventions for families. Rather, a beginning guideline is proposed in order to better equip nurses to provide and improve spiritual care. In accordance with this era of modern nursing and increased discourse on spirituality, this paper introduces the category of spiritual *interpretation* to represent *diagnosis*. Finally, the paper contributes to the literature on family health nursing and spirituality.

Background

Despite the lack of consensual definition of spirituality (MacLaren 2004), its positive effect pervades health care and is evident in the nursing literature. Therefore, providing spiritual care will remain an invaluable part of nursing, as nurses work with humans who are spiritual beings. Spirituality and religion are sometimes used interchangeably, but the two concepts are different, thus warranting a distinction. Religion involves an organized entity with established rules, practices, beliefs, values, and boundaries about a Higher Power or God to which individuals should adhere (Thoresen 1999). On the contrary, spirituality has been described as a personal journey and defined as:

the personal search for meaning and purpose in life, which may or may not be related to religion. It entails connection to self-chosen and/or religious beliefs, values, and practices that give meaning to life, thereby inspiring and motivating individuals to achieve their optimal being. This connection brings faith, hope, peace, and empowerment. The results are joy, forgiveness of oneself and others, awareness and acceptance of hardship and mortality, a heightened sense of physical and emotional well-being, and the ability to transcend beyond the infirmities of existence (Tanyi 2002).

From the above definition, family spirituality may or may not be religiously based. While some families' spiritual orientation may involve religion, others may view spirituality as related to the universe, environment, or significant relationships. Families with an atheist or agnostic orientation may also be spiritual. Whatever the spiritual orientation, families' values, practices, beliefs are all part of their distinct spirituality, which may influence their functioning and help them manage crises (Walsh 1998).

The need to address family spirituality has been espoused by family health nursing writers (e.g. Friedman 1998, Wright & Leahey 2000). It is also clearly evident in the literature of various health professions, such as medicine (Maugans 1996, Walsh *et al.* 2002), clinical psychology (Frame 2000, Wolf & Stevens 2001), social work (Hodge 2000, 2001), and family therapy (Anderson & Worthen 1997, Rivett & Street 2001). While other disciplines such as social work and family therapy have several guidelines/strategies to assess family spirituality (e.g. Boyd-Franklin & Lockwood 1999, Frame 2000, Hodge 2000), there is a dearth of such guidelines in the family nursing and spirituality literature, in spite of the rhetoric to incorporate spirituality as part of total family assessment.

The majority of published guidelines in the nursing literature (e.g. Stoll 1979, Murray & Zentner 1989, Labun 1997) are predominately geared for assessing individual clients rather than families. They fail to distinguish between individual and family unit spirituality, or offer only brief discussions on family spirituality. Guidelines to assist the family health nurse with the spiritual dimension of care are timely and necessary in order to meet families' holistic needs.

It could be argued that family health nurses may still employ the same guidelines as nurses working with individual clients. To an extent this approach is appropriate, but may pave the way for potential problems, as nurses may focus on only the individual's spirituality, neglecting to discern the family's spirituality as a unit. Guidelines exclusively for the family would better equip nurses to consciously approach the spiritual dimension from both the individual and family perspectives. It would alleviate the frustration of sorting through volumes of literature not specifically germane to assessing family spirituality. It would help nurses recognize conflicts between individual and family spirituality, and the impact on the individual's health and family unit. Lastly, it would assist nurses to better organize spiritual data.

Spirituality: A Powerful Family Resource

A few published studies have examined spirituality as a family phenomenon. Electronic database searches of CI-NAHL, Psyc-INFO, MEDLINE/PubMed, and ProQuest, in addition to manual searches of family journals such as Marital and Family Therapy, Family Relations, Marriage and Family Counselling, and Family Process over the last three decades yielded few studies in this area. The scant published studies reviewed for this paper were conducted in various countries; however, two from the United Kingdom (UK), three from Canada, and the remainder from the United States of America (USA) were pertinent to the paper's focus. The ensuing section summarizes the studies that underscore the powerful effects of spirituality as an invaluable resource.

Spirituality can be expressed vertically via a relationship with God/Higher Power and/or horizontally via significant relationships with others or self (Stoll 1989). The families in the following studies expressed their spirituality both vertically, as they reported a relationship with God/Higher Power, and horizontally, because of significant relationships with family members and others.

Spirituality is an important factor in facilitating healthy marital and family functioning (Giblin 1996). Research shows that spouses' spiritual views and beliefs can decrease psychological stress and increase their sense of coherence (Mullen *et al*. 1993). A family's spirituality can assist in maintaining normalcy, cohesion, and resilience in the midst of crises (Beavers & Hampson 1990, Leis *et al*. 1997, Boyd-Franklin & Lockwood 1999). It can expedite positive adjustment to the loss of a family member (Richards & Folkman 1997, Handsley 2001, Walsh *et al*. 2002), ameliorate difficulties associated with disabilities (Treloar 2002), help foster a deeper meaning and purpose in positive family events such as childbirth (Callister *et al*.1999, Semenic *et al*. 2004), and contributes to satisfying, lasting marriages (Kaslow & Robison 1996).

Other findings show that families with strong spiritual orientations can effectively attenuate family caregivers' burdens (Pierce 2001, Theis *et al*. 2003). In single-parent families, spiritual rituals such as prayers have been shown to provide solace and unity (Moriarty & Wagner 2004). Kloosterhouse and Ames' (2002) study further highlights that families' spiritual beliefs and practices can strengthen them and provide hope, meaning and purpose in their lives when dealing with stressors.

Spiritual Assessment

The major goals of spiritual assessment are (1) to support and enhance families' spiritual well-being and development; (2) to discern spiritual distress and its effect on overall family health; and (3) to ascertain ways to incorporate family spirituality when providing care. To capture the essential elements of spirituality and organize the assessment, nurses can utilize the guideline in Table 1 to categorize the data according to: meaning and purpose, strengths, relationships, beliefs, individual member's spirituality, and family's preference for spiritual care.

The initial step of a thorough spiritual assessment and intervention requires that nurses be comfortable with the topic and develop a trusting relationship with the family (Maugans 1996). One cannot precisely gauge when a nurse should establish a trusting

Table 1 Guideline to Spiritual Assessment for Families

Meaning and purpose
Who or what does the family consider the most meaningful?
What gives the family meaning in their daily routines?
What gives the family peace, joy, and satisfaction?
Strengths
What gives the family strength?
What helps the family to deal with crises?
What does the family do in order to rebuild their strength?
Relationships
What do family members like about their family?
Does the family have a relationship with God/Higher Power, universe, or other? If yes, how do they describe it?
Is the family involved in community-based spiritual activities? If yes, which ones?
Beliefs
What are the family's beliefs? And what do these beliefs mean to their health?
Does the family practice rituals such as prayer, worship, or meditation?
Individual family member spirituality
How do family members express/describe their spirituality? And what does this mean to their health?
Are there conflicts between family members because of their spiritual views?
If yes, what is the impact, if any, on the individual and family's health?
Family's preference for spiritual care
How does the family describe/express their spiritual views?
Can the family give examples of how nurses can integrate their spiritual views when working with them?
Does the family consider anyone their spiritual leader? And if necessary, can the spiritual leader be contacted to assist with providing care to the family?

Sources: Fitchett (1993), Maugans (1996), Hodge (2000), McEvoy (2000), Wilkinson (2000), Tanyi (2002). These questions serve only as a guide to help nurses elicit spiritual information for each category. Nurses can, therefore, rephrase these questions according to the family's understanding and expressions of their spirituality.

relationship with a family as this depends on their interactions over a period of time. However, nurses' actions, such as displaying genuine caring and concern, respecting families' circumstances, and remaining non-judgemental can foster a healthy environment and expedite the development of a trusting relationship. In order to maintain the ethical aspects of spiritual care, nurses must remain open to families' spiritual beliefs and perspectives, never imposing their personal beliefs or values on families. They also must explain the purpose of the assessment, how the information is used, and obtain families' consent before consulting with spiritual leaders (Richards & Bergin 1997).

Before beginning the assessment, nurses must first attain family consent. Thereafter, the significance of spirituality in the family's lives must be ascertained (Table 1). Answers to the example questions in Table 1 would provide insight about the family's beliefs and strengths, and the influences of spirituality on their health. It would reveal the role of spirituality in family's abilities to seek meaning and purpose in their lives, and shed light on the family's sense of connectedness/disconnectedness, alerting nurses to potential sources of spiritual distress.

Although nurses should approach the family as a single unit, it is advantageous to collect data on each family member, as these data may reveal conflicts in spiritual views among family members, and the impact, if any, on the family unit and individuals' health. Family responses on how to incorporate spirituality in their care would also add understanding to their unique spiritual needs.

Additionally, genograms and ecomaps are visual diagrammatic tools that can be used to assess family spirituality. A genogram is a three-generation family tree, which depicts a family's history (Bowen 1980). Likewise, the spiritual genogram can be used to depict a three-generation picture of the family's spiritual journey. Any event the family describes as spiritual should be outlined in the genogram. The process of completing the genogram can serve as a reflective tool for family members to evaluate their spirituality, as they understand and perceive it. It can also help to clarify questions about the family's spirituality and to affirm their strengths (Massey & Adriana 1999, Hodge 2000, 2001). Ecomaps portray a family's relationship with external systems such as health care or government, and the impact of these systems on the family. Information from the ecomap would help nurses to organize the family spiritual history and address legitimate spiritual issues (Frame 2000).

Spiritual needs may be difficult to discern; hence, nurses should observe family members' non-verbal behaviours during the assessment. The home environment, including books or artwork, may also provide clues to family spirituality (Ross 1994).

Because spiritual distress may impede a family's ability to manage conflicts and have a devastating effect on their well–being, nurses must be astute in discerning it and intervening quickly and appropriately (Table 2). Spiritual distress should be suspected if the family expresses a sense of hopelessness, abandonment, inner conflicts about their beliefs, and questions the meaning of their existence (Wilkinson 2000).

Spiritual Interventions

The process of spiritual assessment is an effective intervention. It allows the family to openly discuss their spiritual strengths and legitimizes their abilities to manage life's challenges (Hodge

Table 2 Guideline to Spiritual Interventions for Families

Spiritual support

Be present and available to the family in a non-hurried manner

Respect the family's spiritual orientation and support their practices

Encourage and support comments that reflect the family's need for spiritual growth

Spiritual well-being

Support and encourage the family's use of spiritual resources as desired

Assist the family in locating spiritual groups and resources in their community

Support, acknowledge, and applaud verbalized comments of peace, harmony, and satisfaction with family circumstances and relationships

Encourage continual spiritual growth

Spiritual distress

Attempt to determine the reason(s) for the distress, and support the family's efforts to examine their beliefs and values

Acknowledge the family's position, but if necessary, obtain their consent to consult with a spiritual leader of their preference

Provide research-based evidence to the family about the positive impacts of spirituality on family health and functioning

Continue to display empathy, acceptance, kindness in a non-judgemental manner

Sources: Maugans (1996), Wilkinson (2000), Tanyi (2002).Due to the multi-dimensional and ambiguous nature of spirituality, the assessment and interventions may overlap into other categories. Nurses must, therefore, bear in mind each family's unique situation.

2000). Nurses can, therefore, encourage families to draw upon this strength to manage other problems. Following the assessment, nurses would formulate an appropriate interpretation to guide the interventions in Table 2.

The desired outcome for spiritual assessment and intervention is spiritual well-being. In this state, family members express satisfaction with their relationships, beliefs, circumstances, and display a strong sense of connectedness with each other, their God/Higher Power, universe, environment, and others (Wilkinson 2000). Evaluation criteria are verbalized comments from family members indicating (1) continuing spiritual growth; (2) feelings of connectedness and peace; (3) satisfaction with family circumstances, and improved sense of overall health and well-being.

Case Examples

The ensuing fictitious case studies exemplify certain potential components within a family unit to favour an interpretation of spiritual support, well-being, or distress. While there are many other potential spiritual interpretations, these cases only underscore the major ones. As families' circumstances change over time, spiritual interpretations are not permanent; they change to reflect a family's state at any given time. The cases further illustrate how to integrate spiritual assessment, interpret data and implement appropriate interventions.

The Ntuba Family

The Ntuba family consists of husband Henry, aged 50, wife Maggie aged 48, and Henry's brother Evan, aged 37. Evan has acute kidney failure. He undergoes haemodialysis 3 days per week and has recently tested positive for tuberculosis (TB). He does not have active TB, but takes TB prophylaxis treatments. After completing this treatment, he will receive a new kidney.

The nurse discerns that this family's spiritual orientation is religion based, Catholic, thus vertically connected to God. They report that God helps them deal with difficulties, such as Evan's health. They engage in weekly family prayer and attend church regularly. They believe God is in charge of their lives and Evan's health. This family displays a strong horizontal connection with one another, and they believe their purpose is to stay connected as a family unit. They deny any sense of anxiety about Evan's health, exhibiting a deep sense of strength and peace. Each family member's unique expression of spirituality is similar to other members (Augsberger 1986), and no conflicts are apparent. They agree that having a nurse who respects their spiritual views and prays for and with them is very important.

Upon collecting the information, nurses would organize and document the data under the Tables' headings. As an example, the Ntuba family's meaning and purpose is to stay connected; they believe in God; their strength comes from God; they have a strong horizontal relationship with each other and their church; no spiritual conflicts are present; and they prefer nurses to respect their spiritual views, and pray for and with them.

Nurses would then formulate the appropriate interpretation of continual spiritual well-being. This interpretation is appropriate for families that express satisfaction with their spiritual lives (Wilkinson 2000). In this case, the role of nurses is to encourage, acknowledge, and support the family in their spiritual journey, and incorporate the other interventions in Table 2.

The Ngoh Family

The Ngoh family consists of Martin, aged 48, his wife Anna, aged 46, their son Phil, aged 16, and daughter Amy, aged 18. Amy has hepatitis C, which she contracted following a blood transfusion. The nurse discovers that this has been a very close Protestant family. They usually resolved conflicts through open communication, Bible study, church attendance, and prayer. Their spirituality is religion based, and their belief and faith in God has given them strength to manage crises.

Since Amy's diagnosis of hepatitis C, the father has become withdrawn and openly verbalizes his anger towards God. He feels he is being punished and asks why God would allow such a thing to happen to their child and family. He no longer attends church or Bible studies and communicates less with his family. His behaviours have a negative impact on the family's health, creating tension in the household and destabilizing the family unit. The family prefers nurses to support their spirituality by displaying kindness, genuine caring and respect. With the exception of the father, family members share similarities in their spiritual views (Augsberger 1986).

In this case, nurses would document the appropriate interpretation of spiritual distress depicted by the father's vertical disconnectedness with God and horizontal disconnectedness with family members. The initial nursing intervention would be to acknowledge the family's situation in a non-judgemental manner, while gaining their trust. Thereafter, nurses would attempt to reach the father by reminding him how the family has effectively managed crises in the past through spiritual practices.

If nurses are unable to diffuse the distress or feel ill-equipped to handle the situation, they should ask the family's permission to initiate a spiritual referral from a spiritual leader of their choice. If the family rejects the nurse's initiation, the topic could be reintroduced at a later time. Nonetheless, nurses would continue to acknowledge and respect the family, while providing continual support, and implement the other interventions in Table 2.

The Wong Family

The Wong family consists of Paul, aged 67, who has Diabetes Mellitus type 2, his wife Mary, aged 64 and their daughter, Maggie, aged 21. Paul's laboratory tests are stable. However, nurses visit the family regularly for diabetic education and to monitor Paul's blood sugar levels, diet, and exercise. The nurse observes they are a spiritual family although they openly express their atheism. They have strong horizontal relationships with the external systems of health care, their neighbours, and extended family members; they show deep love and trust in one another. The vertical aspect of their spirituality is evident in their love for the universe; they often spend quiet moments enjoying nature. Faith in and commitment to all their vertical and horizontal relationships give them strength, enabling them to cope with Paul's diabetes.

This family's purpose is to remain supportive, connected, and loving to one another. They express inner peace and joy as a family unit. They want nurses to support their spirituality by showing genuine kindness while respecting their atheism. No

---

What Is Already Known about This Topic

- Because humans are spiritual beings, all families are spiritual; spirituality is a vital resource that helps families manage crises and maintain equilibrium.
- The need to address family spirituality is espoused in the literature.
- There is a lack of guidelines to assist nurses with spiritual assessment and interventions explicitly for families.

What This Paper Adds

- When considering family spirituality, it is important to recognize the uniqueness of each family member's spirituality.
- A guideline is proposed for spiritual assessment and interventions for families as a beginning solution to the lack of such guidelines.
- A call is issued to family nursing writers, clinicians, and researchers to develop this proposed guideline.

conflicts are noted, and family members share similar spiritual views (Augsberger 1986).

Although an atheist family, the Wongs clearly display a strong sense of spiritual well-being. They epitomize the concept that all families are spiritual, because humans are spiritual beings. They further exemplify that each family has spiritual needs (e g. respect and kindness from nurses) even when no crises are present, although the extent of needs would vary for every family and circumstance. In this situation, nurses would document the data, formulate an accurate interpretation of continual spiritual support, and then implement the interventions in Table 2.

Implications for Nursing Practice

After obtaining other healthcare information, the spiritual data should be collected next; this may be at the initial, second, or subsequent encounters with the family, provided a trusting relationship is established or beginning to be developed, and the family consents to it. The initial process of collecting healthcare data provides an excellent opportunity for nurses to introduce the spiritual aspect, because most healthcare history forms ask for religious affiliation. If the family is willing to discuss their religious affiliation, nurses may use this opportunity to broach the topic of spiritual assessment. The family's response will tell nurses either to continue or to abandon the topic (McEvoy 2000). If the family appears interested but reluctant, nurses should nurture a trusting relationship with the family during subsequent encounters before reintroducing the topic.

If the family agrees, nurses must first explain the purpose of the assessment and how the information would be used. A thorough family assessment requires that data be collected from each family member (Wright & Leahey 2000). If all family members are not present, data from those not available can be obtained later. If time does not allow nurses to complete the entire assessment, data from one category (e.g. beliefs) can be obtained, and the rest completed at subsequent visits.

While a lack of educational preparation and time constraints are cited as barriers to providing spiritual care (McSherry 1998), other research suggests that nurses do in fact attend to families' spiritual needs (Stiles 1990) regardless of these barriers. Therefore, Swinton's (2001) argument that the issue of time constraints may represent how nurses prioritizes care may be operative; especially for nurses who desire to provide spiritual care, and do not perceive it as a burden (Walter 2002). While educational preparation is beneficial, the initial step in providing spiritual care is being comfortable with the topic regardless of a formal education (Maugans 1996).

The ideal setting for using this guideline is families' homes, and so it is especially useful for family health nurses making home visits. However, the guideline is useful in almost all community settings, such as nursing homes and hospices, where nurses have frequent contact with families.

Patients with chronic illnesses are more likely to make frequent visits to their healthcare providers and develop trusting relationships with them; therefore, the guideline is also applicable for advanced practice nurses in clinic settings. In clinics, the guideline can be used during annual physicals, as more time is typically allotted for these visits. It is unlikely that nurses will meet the entire family during clinic visits. Nonetheless, the data can still be obtained and documented from one source, then expanded as nurses encounter other family members at different visits. This guideline would improve nurses' understanding of families' dynamics, and could reveal potential conflicts between spiritual beliefs and adherence to healthcare treatments; thus, it can be adapted to suit each family's unique needs.

Conclusion

Use of this guideline would improve nurses' understanding of family functioning, thereby enhancing communication and trust in nurses–family relationships. Spiritual care is ongoing with each family interaction, and spirituality is an important component of many families: its impact cannot be underestimated on the overall family health.

By attending to families' spiritual needs, nurses would be promoting a comprehensive and holistic approach to healthcare delivery. Not examining the spiritual dimension of families would be ignoring a vital aspect of their overall health. In essence, one cannot truly assess a family's health without examining its spirituality.

References

Anderson D. A. & Worthen D. (1997) Exploring a fourth dimension: spirituality as a resource for the couple therapist. *Journal of Marital and Family Therapy* 23(1), 3–12.

Augsberger D. (1986) *Pastoral Counseling Across Cultures.* Westminster, Philadelphia, PA.

Beavers W. R. & Hampson R. B. (1990) *Successful Families: Assessment and Intervention.* W. W. Norton, New York.

Bowen M. (1980) Key to the use of the genogram. In *The Family Life Cycle: A Framework for Family Therapy* (Carter E. A. & McGoldrick M., eds.), Gardner Press, New York, p. xxiii.

Boyd-Franklin N. & Lockwood T. W. (1999) Spirituality and religion: implications for psychotherapy with African American clients and families. In *Spiritual Resources in Family Therapy* (Walsh F., ed.), Guilford, New York, pp. 76–103.

Callister L. C., Semenic S. & Foster J. C. (1999) Cultural and spiritual meanings of Childbirth. *Journal of Holistic Nursing* 17(3), 280–295.

Fitchett G. (1993) *Assessing Spiritual Needs: A Guide to Caregivers.* Augsburg Fortress, Minneapolis, MN.

Frame M. W. (2000) The spiritual genogram in family therapy. *Journal of Marital and Family Therapy* 26(2), 211–216.

Friedman M. M. (1998) *Family Nursing: Research, Theory, and Practice,* 4th edn. Appleton & Lange, Stamford, CT.

Giblin P. (1996) Spirituality, marriage, and family. *The Family Journal: Counseling and Therapy for Couples and Families* 4(1), 46–52.

Handsley S. (2001) "But what about us?" The residual effect of sudden death on self identity and family relationships. *Mortality* 6(1), 9–29.

Hodge D. R. (2000) Spiritual ecomaps: a new diagrammatic tool for assessing marital and family spirituality. *Journal of Marital and Family Therapy* 26(2), 217–228.

Hodge D. R. (2001) Spiritual assessment: a review of major qualitative methods and a new framework for assessing spirituality. *Social Work* 46(3), 203–214.

Kaslow F. & Robison J. A. (1996) Long-term satisfying marriages: perceptions of contributing factors. *The American Journal of Family Therapy* 24(2), 153–170.

Kloosterhouse V. & Ames B. D. (2002) Families' use of religion/spirituality as a psychosoical resource. *Holistic Nursing Practice* 16(5), 61–76.

Labun E. (1997) Spiritual aspects of care. In *Psychiatry-Mental Health Nursing: Adaptation and Growth,* 4th edn (Labun E., ed.), Lippincott, Philadelphia, PA, pp. 159–170.

Leis A. M., Kristjanson L., Koop P. M. & Laizner A. (1997) Family health and the palliative trajectory: a cancer research agenda. *Journal of Cancer Prevention Control* 1(5), 352–360.

MacLaren J. (2004) A kaleidoscope of understanding: spiritual nursing in a multi-faith society. *Journal of Advanced Nursing* 45(5), 457–464.

Massey R. F. & Adriana B. D. (1999) Viewing the transactional dimensions of spirituality through family prisms. *Transactional Analysis Journal* 29(2), 115–129.

Maugans T. A. (1996) The spiritual history. *Archives of Family Medicine* 5, 11–16.

McEvoy M. (2000) An added dimension to the pediatric health maintenance visit: the spiritual history. *Journal of Pediatric Health Care* 14(5), 216–220.

McSherry W. (1998) Nurses' perceptions of spirituality and spiritual care. *Nursing Standard* 13(4), 36–40.

Moriarty P. H. & Wagner L. D. (2004) Family rituals that provide meaning for single-families. *Journal of Family Nursing* 10(2), 190–210.

Mullen P. M., Smith R. M. & Hill E. W. (1993) Sense of coherence as a mediator of stress for cancer patients and spouses. *Journal of Psychosocial Oncology* 11(3), 23–46.

Murray R. B. & Zentner J. P. (1989) *Nursing Assessment and Health Promotion Strategies Through the Life Span,* 4th edn. Appleton & Lange, Norwalk.

Pierce L. (2001) Caring and experiences of spirituality by urban caregivers of people with stroke in African American families. *Qualitative Health Research* 11(3), 339–352.

Richards P. S. & Bergin A. E. (1997) *A Spiritual Strategy for Counseling and Psychotherapy.* American Psychological Association, Washington, DC.

Richards T. A. & Folkman S. (1997) Spiritual aspects of loss at the time of a partner's death from AIDS. *Death Studies* 21(6), 527–552.

Rivett M. & Street E. (2001) Connection and themes of spirituality in family therapy. *Family Process* 40(4), 459–467.

Ross L. A. (1994) Spiritual aspect of nursing. *Journal of Advanced Nursing* 19(3), 439–447.

Semenic S. E., Callister L. C. & Feldman P. (2004) Giving Birth: The voices of Orthodox Jewish Women Living Canada. *Journal of Obstetric and Gynecology Neonatal Nursing* 33, 80–87.

Sperry L. & Giblin P. (1996) Marital and family therapy with religious persons. In *Religion and the Clinical Practice of Psychology* (Shafranske E. P., ed.), American Psychology Association, Washington, DC, pp. 511–532.

Stiles M. K. (1990) The shining stranger: nurse family spiritual relationships. *Cancer Nursing* 4(13), 235–245.

Stoll R. I. (1979) Guidelines of spiritual assessment. *American Journal of Nursing* 79(9), 1574–1577.

Stoll R. I. (1989) The essence of spirituality. In *Spiritual Dimension of Nursing Practice* (Carson V. B., ed), WB Saunders, Co., Philadelphia, PA, pp. 4–23.

Swinton J. (2001) *Spirituality and Mental Health Care: Rediscovering a 'Forgotten' Dimension.* Jessica Kingsley, London and Philadelphia, PA.

Tanyi R. A. (2002) Towards clarification of the meaning of spirituality: nursing theory and concept development or analysis. *Journal of Advanced Nursing* 39(5), 500–509.

Theis S. L., Biordi D. L., Coeling H., Nalepka C. & Miller B. (2003) Spirituality in caregiving and care receiving. *Holistic Nursing Practice* 17(1), 48–55.

Thoresen E. C. (1999) Spirituality and health: Is there a relationship? *Journal of Health Psychology* 4(3), 409–431.

Treloar L. L. (2002) Disability, spiritual beliefs and the church: The experience of adults with disabilities and family members. *Journal of Advanced Nursing* 40(5), 594–603.

Walsh F. (1998) Beliefs, spirituality, and transcendence: Key to family resilience. In *Re-Visioning Family Therapy: Race, Culture, and Gender in Family Resilience* (McGoldrick M., ed.), Guilford Press, New York, pp. 62–77.

Walsh K., King M., Jones L., Tookman A. & Blizard R. (2002) Spiritual beliefs may affect outcome of bereavement: Prospective study. British *Medical Journal* 324(7353), 1551–1558.

Walter T. (2002) Spirituality in palliative care: Opportunity or burden? *Palliative Care* 16(2), 133–139.

Wegner G. D. & Alexander R. J. (1999) *Readings in Family Nursing,* 2nd edn. Lippincott, Philadelphia, PA.

Wilkinson J. M. (2000) *Nursing Diagnosis Handbook with NIC Interventions and NIC Outcomes,* 7th edn. Prentice Hall Health, Upper Saddle River, NJ.

Wolf C. T. & Stevens P. (2001) Integrating religion and spirituality in marriage and family counseling. *Counseling and Values* 46(1), A66–A74.

Wright L. M. & Leahey M. (2000) *Nurses and Families: A Guide to Family Assessment and Intervention,* 3rd edn. F. A. Davis Co., Philadelphia, PA.

Correspondence: **RUTH A. TANYI,** Family Nurse Practioner, Prevention, Lifestyle and Wellness Services, PO Box 1185, Loma Linda, CA 92354, USA. E-mail: rtanyi@yahoo.com

Acknowledgements—The author would like to thank Jennifer L. Feeken and Mary Wittenbreer, librarians at Region's Hospital Medical Library, St Paul, MN, USA for their invaluable assistance during the literature search process for this article. Special thanks to Dr Werner, UWEC, WI and DeAnn Lancashire-Mabin, St Paul, MN for their proofreading assistance.

The Joy of Rituals
Simple Strategies for Strengthening Family Ties

Reading Bible stories before bedtime, sitting down to Sabbath dinner, and saying grace before each meal brings warmth and joy to many families. Now, researchers are discovering that such activities enhance child development as well.

Dawn Marie Barhyte

Rituals are repeated and shared activities that carry meaning and provide an emotional reward to family members. Although routines are also repetitious family behavior and vital to family life, they lack the symbolic content and compelling nature that rituals possess. Unlike rituals, routines are purely instrumental rather than symbolic; they are activities family members *have* to do rather than *want* to do.

Meg Cox, expert on rituals and author of *The Heart of a Family—Searching America for Traditions that Fulfill Us,* believes that a ritual is anything—big or small—that families perform together deliberately. She says they must be repetitious and provide some dramatic flourish that elevates the activity above the ordinary grind.

Even simple activities can be transformed into satisfying and memorable rituals, such as always singing a certain song whenever you give your child medicine, or declaring an evening study break for hot cocoa on cold winter weeknights. Cox writes, "The more we understand [rituals], the more their power will enrich our lives."

William J. Doherty, professor of family social science at the University of Minnesota, and author of *The Intentional Family* adds, "Children are natural ritualists. They crave connection and love predictability. Family rituals give children a sense of steady love and connection, and give order to their lives."

Shared Experience

Rituals are significant not so much for the act itself but for the results they yield; the sense of togetherness that grows out of shared experience and the feeling of rightness that comes from its repetition.

According to research, these repeated positive experiences form strong connections between neurons in the brain and foster a sense of security in children. They also help kids learn what to expect from their environment and how to understand the world around them.

Other studies have shown that young people who are best equipped to face the challenges of life and stay centered are those who feel close to their families. That closeness comes from the routine reassurances and shared experiences found in everyday rituals.

At one time or another, all families experience stress. Rituals have the capacity to provide stability even during trying times. Researchers have found that rituals are integral family resources that can act as a coping mechanism during those challenging moments. Professor Doherty adds that family rituals are what children can fall back on when under stress. He says that regular meals with parents provide emotional protection from every major risk factor.

Little Celebrations

When you think of family rituals, you probably picture the grand annual events such as Thanksgiving, Christmas, Hanukah, birthdays, weddings, or baby dedications. But you may want to consider adding some everyday rituals that can serve as glue that binds families together right in the midst of our harried lives. These common, often repeated happenings can become extraordinarily vital and act as a powerful buffer against this complex world. These rituals will build a bridge that connects the past to the future and allows children to pick up the torch and pass it on to the next generation.

According to Meg Cox, "Scientists tell us that many animals have rituals, and anthropologists report they haven't found any human societies without them, which alone is compelling evidence that rituals must be a human necessity."

Psychologists insist that rituals help us keep track of where we came from and essentially who we are. While this is key for all family members, it's profoundly significant for children who are forming their own identities. Rituals become a road map for kids, offering a comforting sense of predictability and order to life. When children have a clear sense of where they come from, they have a better sense of where they are going. Knowing what to do and being able to predict what comes next helps a boy or girl feel competent, and feeling competent is key to emotional well-being.

Grounded by Constancy

Children delight in rituals, look forward to them, learn from them, and feel comforted and grounded by their constancy. Positive family rituals leave indelible imprints on children's minds and form treasured memories ready to be passed on from generation to generation. For instance, knowing that every fall the family will load themselves into the minivan and go pumpkin or apple picking makes the season something to look forward to and savor.

Knowing that, each night, dad will talk to his child about his or her day and read a story at bedtime gives often-lonely children something to which they can look forward. In fact, developing a bedtime ritual is an excellent way to unwind and quietly embrace the day's happenings.

Whether it's reading a story, saying a prayer, or giving a hug and kiss, these nightly rituals offer security and comfort that fold gently into pleasant slumber.

The challenge, of course, lies in making the decision to create this time and saying no to any intrusions. With the myriad of demands on our time, it will require some effort. But the payoff will be well worth it.

Takes Work

Once you have good family rituals in place, keeping them alive takes work. If it's centered on a specific day, like Sabbath dinner, and you're not able to do it one week, don't let it slip away. Squeeze it in later in the week if you have to do so.

With some attentiveness, your family rituals will survive the demands of life and may endure for generations to come. Know that no matter what life brings, rituals will act as a safety net for your family members. Establishing your own distinctive activities now and faithfully repeating them will offer a much-needed

shelter in unsettling times. Rituals are like keepsakes that live in your heart.

Springboard for Action

If you are inspired but feel at a loss at the thought of starting your own family ritual, here are some ideas to use as a springboard for action.

- If you're like many families today and can't manage family dinners seven nights a week, try for **breakfasts together or special fruit-juice treats in the evening.** These relaxed moments of sharing nourishment and conversation provide a much-needed platform for reconnecting.
- Recognition night. A fun way to celebrate your child's achievements in the classroom or extracurricular activity is to serve an **"Honoree Dinner"** on a special plate reserved for that occasion with all the healthy foods they crave.
- Designate one night a week as **"Family Night"** created solely for family members to connect, interact, and communicate while having wholesome fun. One week you could play board games, another rent a DVD and serve popcorn, and yet another allow various family members to plan the meal and help cook it as a team.
- Hold an **"Unbirthday"** where you surprise your child by unexpectedly celebrating the fact that they exist. Include their favorite foods, a cake, and small tokens of affection.
- Create a **"Give a Helping Hand Day"** to help children cultivate altruism and focus on others less fortunate. As a family, participate in some community service like volunteering at a nursing home or soup kitchen, or collecting food for a local food pantry.

Life is hard. Rituals can help soften the edges and bring a sense of togetherness back into the lives of every family member. Why not start one today?

Freelance writer **DAWN MARIE BARHYTE** of Warwick, New York, is a stepmother of two and grandmother of six. She's a former junior volunteer coordinator at St. Anthony Community Hospital and teacher at the First Baptist Child Care Center.

Sustaining Resilient Families for Children in Primary Grades

JANICE PATTERSON AND LYNN KIRKLAND

The adversities that today's families face are well-documented and staggering (Children's Defense Fund, 2004). Even in the midst of tough times, however, many families are able to display resilience. Family resilience refers to the coping mechanisms the family uses as a functional unit to recover from life's setbacks. The purpose of this article is to provide parents and teachers with guidelines for creating resilient families, thereby helping primary-grade children withstand the challenges in their lives. In this article, we will consider what is known about family resilience, examine the role of protective factors and recovery processes, and suggest specific strategies that families and teachers can use to support resilience.

Family Resilience

Much of the work on family resilience is anchored in studies about the resilience of children. Werner and Smith (1982, 1992; Werner, 1984), authors of arguably the most important study on childhood resilience, spent 40 years studying children on the island of Kauai who were judged to be at risk of living in hardship. The children were born into poor, unskilled families, and were judged to be at risk based on their exposure before age 2 to at least four risk factors, such as serious health problems, familial alcoholism, mental illness, violence, and divorce. By age 18, about two-thirds of the children had fared poorly, as predicted by their at-risk status. The remaining one-third had developed into competent, confident, and caring young adults living productive lives, as rated on a variety of measures. In a follow-up study, the overwhelming majority of this group, now at age 40, were still living successful lives. In fact, many of them had outperformed Kauai citizens from more advantageous backgrounds. They were more likely to be stable in their marriages and fewer were unemployed. The key factors that promoted individual resilience were:

- Caring and support were provided by at least one adult who knew the child well and cared deeply about that child's well-being
- Positive expectations were articulated clearly for the child, and the support necessary to meet those expectations was provided

- Meaningful involvement and participation provided the child the opportunity to become involved in something she cared about and to contribute to the well-being of others

Although it is not impossible for an individual child from a non-resilient family to bounce back from adversity, the child's health and well-being is best supported if the family functions as a resilient unit. When a crisis upsets the life of a primary-grade child, the impact of that crisis on the child is determined largely by the extent to which the family's normal functioning is disrupted. Even when the child is not directly affected by a situation, he or she is touched by the changes in relationships that result from the changes or crises for others in the family.

As we reflect on the image of a resilient family, note how changes in society contribute to that image. Traditionally, the model of a resilient family, those who successfully navigated the ups and downs of life, was the image of a white, affluent, nuclear family led by the breadwinning father and a mother working as full-time homemaker. Enormous social changes in recent decades highlight the fact that resilient families can be non-white, upper or lower income, represent a variety of ethnic and cultural traditions, and include single parents, non-custodial parents, grandparents, stepparents, and same-gender parents. Changes in the definition of family are dynamic. In one landmark court decision supporting the rights of gay parents, the judge recognized changing definitions of "family" by acknowledging, "It is the totality of the relationship, as evidenced by the dedication, caring and self-sacrifice of the parties, which should, in the final analysis, control the definition of family" (quoted in Stacey, 1990, p. 4).

Protective and Recovery Factors

An understanding of family resilience incorporates research on *protective factors* and *recovery factors* (Cowan, Cowan, & Schultz, 1996; Garmezy & Rutter, 1983; Hawley & DeHaan, 1996; McCubbin, Thompson, Thompson, & McCubbin, 1992). Protective factors are behaviors that help give people strength in times of stress (Patterson, Patterson, & Collins, 2003). Examples of such factors include family celebrations, planned family time, consistent routines, and family traditions. In addition, family resilience can be sustained by maintaining open communication within the family and building a solid support network beyond the family.

Recovery factors refer to the family's ability to develop and use adaptation strategies when confronted with a crisis. Families can and do bounce back and adapt by changing their habits, their patterns of functioning, or the situation that has created the problem. Some evidence exists that there may be variation in the nature of the needed recovery factors, depending upon the situation. For instance, families having to deal with chronically ill children (e.g., cystic fibrosis) made use of the following strategies:

- *Family integration.* The mother's and father's optimism and efforts to keep the family together were important to the child's health.
- *Family support and esteem building.* The parents made concerted efforts to reach out to family, friends, and the larger community, thereby helping them to develop their self-esteem and self-confidence.
- *Family recreation orientation, control, and organization.* A family emphasis on active involvement in recreational and sporting activities is positively associated with improvements in the child's health. The greater the family's emphasis on control and family organization, rules, and procedures, the greater the improvement in the child's health.
- *Family optimism and mastery.* The greater the family's efforts to maintain a sense of optimism and order, the greater the improvement in the child's health. Furthering one's understanding and mastery of the health regimen necessary to promote the child's health helps the adaptation process (McCubbin & McCubbin, 1996).

During any family crisis, disruption in the daily routine exacerbates the chaos and confusion. Within the context of divorce, for instance, it is important for the family to establish and maintain routines that provide continuity of family connections, such as Sunday brunch with Dad. Research on children's positive adjustment following their parents' divorce shows that predictability and reliability of contact with the non-custodial parent is as important as the amount of contact (Hetherington & Kelly, 2002; Walsh, 1991). It is also clear that authoritative parenting, which combines warmth and control, is a significant positive protection against family stress that children may encounter (Hetherington & Kelly, 2002).

Strategies to Strengthen Family Resilience

Effective communication, including problem solving and affirmation, is a critical variable for family success in facing routine and extraordinary challenges. Contemporary lifestyles may allow little time for really listening to children, discussing their problems, and affirming their value to the family. A growing number of parents and teachers realize that communication is not something that can be left to chance; they plan for it.

One family reported on the "talk" that took place each night at the dinner table (Feiler, 2004). First, dinner was designated as a sacred time and attendance was mandatory. No television was allowed. Instead, they played a game, "Bad and Good," which began with a moderator asking each person, "What happened to you today that was bad?" Everyone had to respond; respect for others was supported by not allowing anyone to criticize, interrupt, or refute another person's bad experience. It was important that parents participated, to demonstrate that bad things happen to all of us on a daily basis and how we cope is what matters. Next, the rotating moderator asked each person, "What happened to you today that was good?" As family members reported their good stories, others affirmed them and good news begot good news. Primary-grade children in the family learned to celebrate successes. Of course, some events had both good and bad elements; as the family discussed what happened, children learned that everything doesn't fit neatly into good or bad categories. Variations on the theme might be such questions as, "What are you most afraid will happen to you?" or "If you could have one wish, what would it be?" or "What makes you feel really special?"

Problem solving can be nurtured in this context by asking everyone for thoughts on solving family problems. Our daily lives are inundated by e-mail, voice mail, computers, video games, iPods, and other diversions that can replace face-to-face communication, and so we must take conscious steps to let children know we are listening and care about them and their ideas.

These strategies are easily adapted to the classroom. Teachers routinely listen to children during community time, at meals, and in small groups, and can pose questions for all to answer. Class meetings also can provide many venues for children to discuss issues related to their lives and the lives of their families. As part of a class meeting, carefully selected articles from the newspaper can be used to initiate conversation about issues that relate to the lives of the children in the class. For example, children can consider alternative ways of dealing with problems other than those exhibited by individuals acting unlawfully within the local community. As part of routine class meetings, children utilize problems that arise throughout the day in play situations in the classroom, coming up with appropriate resolutions. For example, if a problem has arisen on the playground between children, offering the opportunity for children to defend their position, as well as hear the positions of others, helps them to consider other people and become less egocentric in their reasoning. Hearing others' perspectives encourages the moral development of the child (Piaget, 1997) and encourages flexible thinking, which builds a child's resilience, both individually and within the family.

It is also important that parents and teachers teach children how to ask for help when they need it. One of the biggest predictors of resilience in the Kauai study mentioned earlier in this article was that children knew how to ask for help. We cannot assume that every child (or adult) will, or knows how to, ask for needed help. Today's society places a high value on independent action and neglects teaching collaboration. Parents and teachers can guide children in forming questions and in practicing their help-seeking skills (e.g., "Where would you go if no one was home when you came home after school?").

Within the classroom, teachers can use the writing workshop process to help children write about issues that trouble them. For instance, one teacher found it helpful to encourage a student, from a military family about to relocate, to draft a paper about her fears of moving to a new school. Through the writing and subsequent conferencing that preceded the final draft, the teacher and parent learned that the child's greatest fear was not having someone to sit with at lunch. The parent and teacher in the new school were able to find a "lunch mate" and thus eased the transition. A variation on the writing conference is to establish dialogue journals so that the student is writing to the teacher or parent and the adult responds in writing. Some children will write about fears that are difficult to verbalize.

Another important strategy is to strive to maintain an optimistic outlook, even when the going gets rough. The family that expects to prevail in times of crisis very often will prevail. An orientation toward such hardiness is reflected in the work of Steve and Sybil Wolin, who speak of "survivor's pride"—the deep self-respect that comes from knowing you were challenged and that you prevailed. Children who grew up in families that were *not* resilient and later compared notes reported very similar family experiences, as identified below:

- We rarely celebrated holidays.
- They [parents] hardly ever came to a soccer game, a school play, or a community picnic.
- There were no regular mealtimes.
- They forgot my birthday.
- The house was a pigsty.
- No one had a good word for me; nothing I ever did was right.
- They were always fighting with each other, tearing each other apart in front of us, as if we didn't exist. (Wolin & Wolin, 1993, p. 27)

If we turn this list around, we can see the practices of resilient families for primary-grade children. They *do* celebrate holidays and attend soccer games, school plays, and community picnics as a family. They make time for regular mealtimes and birthday celebrations. The house is clean enough to be functional and pleasant. Love and affirmation are given freely and parental conflict is minimized in front of children. Within the classroom, through conversations, parent meetings, and written communication, teachers can emphasize to parents the importance of participation in these activities as resilience-building strategies.

Importance of Family Traditions and Routines

A family that promotes its own resilience with these strategies takes deliberate steps in building the resilience of the family unit for all members, including the primary-grade child.

The family values traditions, saves mementos, and tells stories about family heroes. Conducting these activities within the family promotes pride in the family heritage and also can provide a link to the present. If the family reflects on the struggles immigrant parents faced in coming to a new country and the strategies they used to survive, the current move across town takes on a different perspective. Children in resilient families see themselves as part of the family unit and take pride in finding ways to contribute to the family's strength. Effective communication and family optimism work to create a resilient family that considers itself to be healthy and is reflected in such statements as:

- We are a good family.
- Home is a safe, welcoming place.
- We have a past that is a source of strength and we have good, sound values that guide our future.
- We are known and respected in the community.
- We like each other.
- Our blood runs thick; we will always be there for one another. (Wolin & Wolin, 1993, p. 40)

Without a doubt, a variety of challenges and crises can tax even the strongest family. Such situations call for all family members to pull together and use their collective strength (all of us are stronger than one of us) to weather the challenge. An attitude of family resilience gives the family a sense of its own competence and control over the outcome.

Deliberately structuring family time and rituals is another important strategy for strengthening resilience in families. Every family has a routine, even if it is one of chaos. Resilient families take control of the routine for the purpose of establishing predictability and stability—critical elements to family balance. Although sometimes difficult to establish, this strategy can make a difference in how the child copes with new events. For instance, a 7-year-old girl was confused by where she was to go each day after school and began crying every morning, saying, "I don't know where to go today." The mother and teacher combined forces to develop a routine in which the mother sent the teacher each Monday a list of where the child was to go every day of the week. She also tucked a note in the child's lunch box that said, "Today, you go to Brownies in the gym after school." The mother used a combination of words and picture symbols to be sure the child understood the message; thus, a stabilizing routine was established.

Family Communication with Children's Literature

Family mealtimes are important venues for communication, as mentioned earlier. They also serve the function of reinforcing family routine. Spending quality time together, including just "hanging out," is important for building family resilience. Family time together does not need to involve money or extensive time commitments. Playing board games or reading together can provide routine and meaning to family relationships.

Children's literature can be used at home or as part of classroom curricula to initiate caring and conversation related to issues that children and families face. When parents and teachers sit and read with children, caring for that child is reinforced and the child feels valued. Discussions of book characters and plots provide meaningful and relevant ways for children to consider the lives of others and begin to look at ways of dealing with problems they face. Resilience in children is promoted through time spent with a caring adult and their participation in retellings and creative dramatizations of story plots.

Table 1 lists examples of good books that promote resilience in primary-grade children. These books were selected because they address, either directly or indirectly, elements of resilience or strategies for strengthening the skills of resilience. For instance, in *Wemberly Worried* (2000), Henkes writes of Wemberly, the little mouse, who worries about everything, especially her first day of school. As Wemberly struggles not to worry, she taps into some basic resilience-building strategies (e.g., telling adults you're worried, finding a friend to share your worries, and building on your strengths by successfully navigating the first day of school and returning for another day). In Faith Ringgold's *Tar Beach* (1991), Cassie Louise Lightfoot, an African American 8-year-old growing up in Harlem in 1939, demonstrates how believing good things will happen and drawing on the love of friends and family can promote a feeling of pride. Critical elements in building resilience include a belief in a positive future and support from a loving community.

Another example of the power of these books is drawn from *Amazing Grace* (Hoffman, 1991). Grace is an African American girl who loves stories and regularly adopts the roles and identities of strong, problem-solving characters, such as Joan of Arc, Hiawatha, and Anansi the Spider, in the plays she writes herself. Grace's grandmother takes her to see a famous black ballerina to encourage her to do "anything she can imagine." That role model encourages Grace to work hard and ultimately achieve her dream of performing the role of Peter Pan in the class play. Grace demonstrates problem-solving skills, emulates successful positive role models, and maintains perseverance—all foundational traits in building resilience.

The literature on individual and family resilience underscores the importance of building strategies to secure a network of social support. Such support begins with a loving relationship between one child and one adult (generally, a parent). Family therapists have likened the resilient family to open systems with clear, yet permeable boundaries, similar to a living cell (Beavers & Hampson, 1993; Satir, 1988; Walsh, 1998; Whitaker & Keith, 1981).

Boundaries are important for the child and an authoritative parent earns the respect that comes from predictability; "no" means no. Inconsistent reinforcement of family rules undermines trust within the family and is not healthy. In fact, Hetherington and Kelly (2002, p. 130), in their studies of divorcing families, reported that "children of authoritative parents emerged from divorce as the most socially responsible, least troubled and highest-achieving children." Parents building resilient families ask their children for help in maintaining the household.

Examples include setting the table, mowing the lawn, washing dishes, and caring for a younger sibling, all of which can contribute to the resilience, maturity, and competency of a child. Age-appropriate chores are an important aspect of building children's resilience and sense of self-worth.

Family and Community

Resilient families have strength and integrity in their interactions within the family and also know when to reach outside the family circle for satisfying relationships. In an ideal world, the family of a primary-grade child is actively engaged in the broader community and relates to the community and each other with hope and optimism. Family members go out into the community and bring strength and new learnings back into the family circle.

There is a practical element to having relationships outside the family. Other connections can provide information, concrete services, support, companionship, and even respite from difficult situations. A family's sense of security can be enhanced by meaningful relationships with others. Community activities, including involvement in school and extracurricular activities, foster family well-being. Regular participation in sports leagues, faith-based activities, and parent-teacher organizations can bolster protective and recovery processes for the family. Research suggests that there is a highly protective element in belonging to a group and having regular social activity. This is particularly true for those in isolation and depression (Walsh, 1998b).

Because extended family is too often far away or unavailable for other reasons, it is important that families establish connections to meet their life circumstances. In the armed forces, families regularly share meals and child care in support of each other. Some families turn to older people in the community to provide "family" contact and meaningful activities with children at home or school. Both children and elders benefit in these situations. Also, multifamily groups band together in other ways to support single parents or families coping with a chronic illness, and such support can be vital in managing chronic stress or crises.

Conclusion

In this article, we have presented guidelines for creating and sustaining resilient families for primary-grade children and offered strategies for developing effective communication and building an attitude of family hardiness or resilience. We suggested promoting the value of family time, authoritative parenting, routine, and the importance of social support. We offer this work with the caveat that family resilience is an emerging field and we have only touched the surface.

Yet, our research and conversations with teachers, parents, and other child care providers have convinced us that teachers can take particular steps to support children and their families. Work with school administrators to develop sessions for parents on building family resilience during the critical primary-grade years. Invite children to talk about their experiences and say

Table 1   Resilience-Building Books for Primary-Grade Children

Andreae, G. (1999). *Giraffes can't dance.* New York: Orchard Books.

Bottner, B. (1992). *Bootsie Barker bites.* New York: G. P. Putnam Sons.

Bradby, M. (1995). *More than anything else.* New York: Orchard Books.

Brimner, L. D. (2002). *The littlest wolf.* New York: HarperCollins.

Burningham, J. (1987). *John Patrick Norman McHennessy—The boy who was always late.* New York: The Trumpet Club.

Burton, V. L. (1943). *Katy and the big snow.* Boston: Houghton Mifflin.

Cannon, J. (1993). *Stellaluna.* Orlando, FL: Harcourt Brace & Company.

Cannon, J. (2000). *Crickwing.* San Diego, CA: Harcourt.

Carle, E. (1999). *The very clumsy click beetle.* New York: Philomel Books.

Clifton, L. (1983). *Everett Anderson's goodbye.* New York: Henry Holt and Company.

Couric, K. (2000). *The brand new kid.* New York: Doubleday.

Giovanni, N. (2005). *Rosa.* New York: Henry Holt & Co.

Havill, J. (1995). *Jamaica's blue marker.* New York: Houghton Mifflin.

Heard, G. (2002). *This place I know: Poems of comfort.* Cambridge, MA: Candlewick Press.

Henkes, K. (2000). *Wemberly worried.* Hong Kong: Greenwillow Books.

Hoffman, M. (1991). *Amazing Grace.* Boston: Houghton Mifflin.

Juster, N. (2005). *The hello, goodbye window.* New York: Hyperion Books for Children.

Kraus, R. (1971). *Leo, the late bloomer.* New York: Windmill Books.

Kroll, V. (1997). *Butterfly boy.* Honesdale, PA: Boyds Mills Press.

Lester, H. (1999). *Hooway for Wodney Wat.* New York: Scholastic Books.

Lithgow, J. (2000). *The remarkable Farkle McBride.* New York: Simon & Schuster.

McKissack, P. (1986). *Flossie and the fox.* New York: Scholastic Books.

Mora, P. (2005). *Doña Flor: A tall tale about a giant woman with a great big heart.* New York: Alfred A. Knopf.

Moss, S. (1995). *Peter's painting.* Greenvale, NY: MONDO Publishing.

Piper, W. (1986). *The little engine that could.* New York: Platt & Munk.

Puttock, S. (2001). *A story for hippo: A book about loss.* New York: Scholastic Press.

Ringgold, F. (1991). *Tar beach.* New York: Scholastic Books.

Salley, C. (2002). *Epossumondas.* San Diego, CA: Harcourt.

Seskin, S., & Shamblin, A. (2002). *Don't laugh at me.* Berkeley, CA: Tricycle Press.

Taback, S. (1999). *Joseph had a little overcoat.* New York: Scholastic.

Tafuri, N. (2000). *Will you be my friend?* New York: Scholastic.

Tompert, A. (1993). *Just a little bit.* Boston: Houghton Mifflin.

Wyeth, S. D. (1998). *Something beautiful.* New York: Dragonfly Books.

---

what they believe makes them "bounce back" when bad things happen. Get parents and others involved by creating informational programs and materials about the importance of family resilience. Together, we must do all we can to help families and their children develop and nourish their resilience.

References

Beavers, W. R., & Hampson, R. B. (1990). *Successful families: Assessment and intervention.* New York: Norton.

Children's Defense Fund. (2004). *The state of America's children 2004: A continuing portrait of inequality fifty years after Brown v. Board of Education.* Retrieved August 14, 2004, from www.childrensdefense.org/pressreleases/040713.asp

Cowan, P. A., Cowan, C. P., & Schulz, M. S. (1996). Thinking about risk and resilience in families. In M. Hetherington & E. A. Blechman (Eds.), *Stress, coping and resilience in children and families.* Mahwah, NJ: Erlbaum.

Feiler, B. (2004, August 15). A game that gets parents and kids talking. *Parade.*

Garmezy, N., & Rutter, M. (Eds.). (1983). *Stress, coping and development in children.* New York: McGraw-Hill.

Hawley, D. R., & DeHaan, L. (1996). Toward a definition of family resilience: Integrating life-span and family perspectives. *Family Process, 35,* 283–298.

Hetherington, E., & Kelly, J. (2002). *For better or for worse: Divorce reconsidered.* New York: W. W. Norton & Co.

McCubbin, H. I., & McCubbin, M. A. (1996). Resilient families, competencies, supports and coping over the life cycle. In L. Sawyers (Ed.), *Faith and families.* Philadelphia: Geneva Press.

McCubbin, H. I., Thompson, E. A., Thompson, A. I., & McCubbin, M. A. (1992). Family schema, paradigms, and paradigm shifts: Components and processes of appraisal in family adaptation to crises. In A. P. Turnbull, J. M. Patterson, S. K. Bahr, D. L. Murphy, J. Marquis, & M. Blue-Banning (Eds.), *Cognitive coping research in developmental disabilities.* Baltimore: Paul H. Brookes.

Patterson, J. L., Patterson, J. H., & Collins, L. (2002). *Bouncing back: How your school can succeed in the face of adversity.* Larchmont, NY: Eye on Education Press.

Piaget, J. (1997). *The moral judgment of the child.* New York: Simon & Schuster.

Satir, V. (1988). *Within our reach: Breaking the cycle of disadvantage.* New York: Anchor.

Stacey, J. (1990). *Brave new families: Stories of domestic upheaval in late twentieth century America.* New York: Basic Books.

Walsh, F. (1991). Promoting healthy functioning in divorced and remarried families. In A. Gurman & D. Kniskern (Eds.), *Handbook of family therapy.* New York: Brunner/Mazel.

Walsh, F. (1998a). *Strengthening family resilience.* New York: The Guilford Press.

Walsh, F. (1998b). Families in later life: Challenges and opportunities. In B. Carter & M. McGoldrick (Eds.), *The expanded family life cycle.* Needham Heights, MA: Allyn & Bacon.

Werner, E. (1984). Resilient children. *Young Children, 68*(72).

Werner, E. E., & Smith, R. S. (1982). *Vulnerable but invincible: A longitudinal study of resilient children and youth.* New York: Adams, Bannister, Cox.

Werner, E. E., & Smith, R. S. (1992). *Overcoming the odds: High risk children from birth to adulthood.* New York: Cornell University Press.

Whitaker, C., & Keith, D. (1981). Symbolic-experiential family therapy. In A. S. Gurman & D. Kniskern (Eds.), *Handbook of family therapy.* New York: Brunner/Mazel.

Wolin, S., & Wolin, S. (1993). *The resilient self: How survivors of troubled families rise above adversity.* New York: Villard.

JANICE PATTERSON is Associate Professor, Education Department, and **LYNN KIRKLAND** is Associate Professor, Education Department, University of Alabama-Birmingham.

The Consumer Crunch

Recession or not, American families will be forced to tighten their belts.

MICHAEL MANDEL

The long-awaited, long-feared consumer crunch may finally be here. That might not mean an economywide recession, but the pain for American households will be deep. In recent years the U.S. mostly has seen narrowly focused downturns, where a few sectors are hit hard while the rest of the economy and financial markets remain relatively unscathed. In the dot-com bust of 2001, for example, tech companies and stocks took it on the chin, while consumer spending and borrowing sailed through without a pause. This time the positions will be reversed, as consumers tank while much of the corporate sector stays on track. It's been a glorious run for the consumer. In the past 25 years, Americans have kept shopping through good times and bad. In every quarter except one since 1981, consumer spending rose over the previous year, adjusted for inflation. The exception was the first quarter of 1991, and even then the decrease was a mild 0.4% dip. The main fuel for the spending was easy access to credit. Banks and other financial institutions were willing to lend households ever increasing amounts of money. Any particular individual might default, but in the aggregate, loans to consumers were viewed as low-risk and profitable.

The subprime crisis, however, marks the beginning of the end for the long consumer borrow-and-buy boom. The financial sector, wrestling with hundreds of billions in losses, can no longer treat consumers as a safe bet. Already, standards for real estate lending have been raised, including those for jumbo mortgages for high-end houses. Credit cards are still widely available, but it may only be a matter of time before issuers get tougher.

What comes next could be scary—the largest pullback in consumer spending in decades, perhaps as much as $200 billion to $300 billion, or 2%–3% of personal income. Reduced access to credit will combine with falling real estate values to hit poor and rich alike. "We're in uncharted territory," says David Rosenberg, chief North American economist at Merrill Lynch, who's forecasting a mild drop in consumer spending in the first half of 2008. "It's pretty rare we go through such a pronounced tightening in credit standards."

Don't expect the spending to come to a screeching halt, however. Remember the stock market peak in early 2000? It wasn't until a year later that tech spending fell off the cliff and the sector didn't hit bottom until 2003. The same delayed impact holds true here. The latest retail sales numbers, which showed a soft 0.2% gain in October, suggest that spending may hold up through this holiday season.

Next year, though, will be much tougher. The consumer slump may be deep and long-lasting, and the political implications could be enormous. "There's growing evidence that the economy will become a dominant, if not the dominant issue of 2008," says independent pollster John Zogby. "It's even to the point where the numbers of people who say Iraq is the No. 1 issue are starting to decline."

Wide-Open Credit Window

Truth is, economists have been complaining about excessive borrowing and spending since the early 1980s. Journalists began writing about consumers being "tapped out," "profligate," and "spendthrift." Magazines and newspapers regularly ran stories about debt-ridden Americans not being able to buy holiday presents for their kids.

But no matter how many times economists predicted the demise of the consumer, the spending continued. The latest data from the Bureau of Economic Analysis show that the personal savings rate—the share of income left after consumption—fell from 12% in 1981 to just over zero today. And debt service, which is the share of income going to principal and interest on debt, kept rising. Those numbers aren't dead-on accurate: The data has been revised endlessly, and the BEA includes outlays on higher education as consumption rather than saving, which would seem odd to families who have socked away thousands of dollars for college.

But the story line is clear. Consumers' outlays have outpaced the growth of their income for a long time. Lenders learned how to judge risk and expand the pool of potential borrowers—and the party was on. "The most important factor has been that it is easier to borrow," says Christopher D. Carroll, a Johns Hopkins University economist.

The subprime crisis marks the beginning of the end for the long borrow-and-buy boom. Banks can no longer treat consumers as a safe bet.

While many companies struggled in the 2001 recession and afterward, American consumers just kept borrowing. "In 2001–02, the credit window was open for anyone who had a pulse," says Merrill's Rosenberg.

Fewer Trips to the Mall?

Not this time, though. "The consumer is retrenching, big-time," says Richard Hastings, economic adviser to the Federation of Credit & Financial Professionals. "It's starting to get to the point where people are achieving levels of debt that are getting uncomfortable."

The question, though, is just how much consumers will restrain their free-spending ways. Research by economist Carroll suggests that every $1 decline in house prices lops about 9¢ off of spending. The current value of residential housing is about $21 trillion, according to the Federal Reserve. So if home prices fall by 10%, as many people expect, that would lead to roughly a $200 billion hit to spending over the next couple of years. A 15% tumble in home prices would produce a $300 billion pullback in spending, or about 3% of personal income.

That accords well with calculations by BEA economists. They figure that households took out $340 billion in cash from mortgage and home-equity financing in 2006. That source of funding could largely disappear over the next couple of years.

Three percent—that doesn't sound like a lot. Look a little closer, though, and it's a bigger hit than it seems. The reason is that much of what the government counts as consumer spending is not directly controlled by households. For example, the $1.7 trillion in medical costs is counted as consumer spending, but 85% of that is spent by the government and health insurers, not individuals. And $1.5 trillion in "housing services" is listed as part of consumer spending, but for homeowners it really just represents the value of living in a home rather than any spending they can change. It's mainly a bookkeeping convention, not a real outlay.

A big pullback in spending may not lead to a recession. These days when Americans buy fewer clothes, the pain is felt overseas.

So that 2%–3% decline in income directly hits the wallet and the discretionary purchases that households actually control. One logical place for cutbacks is apparel. Autos will be hit. Another target could be luxury items, a surprisingly big part of discretionary spending. Pamela N. Danziger, president of Unity Marketing in Stevens, Pa., conducts a quarterly online survey of adults earning $75,000 a year and up. She found that people who make more than $150,000 have been unaffected, but the rest are cutting back on luxury goods such as fashion accessories. "They are taking a very cautious attitude," says Danziger.

A Lift from Exports

Will the consumer crunch spread to the rest of the economy? Conventional wisdom is that consumer spending makes up 70% of gross domestic product. While technically true, that figure is deceptive, because so much of what Americans buy these days is made overseas. Compared with the early 1980s, which was the last time consumers cut back, much more of what Americans buy is made abroad. Today, imports of consumer goods and autos run about $740 billion a year. That's fully one-third of consumer spending on goods outside of food and energy. As a result, most of the spending cutbacks won't cost Americans their factory jobs—those factory jobs have mostly fled offshore anyway. Workshop China, in contrast, will get hurt.

What's more, it's still a low-rate world for most nonfinancial corporations, which have access to relatively cheap funds for expansion and capital investment. Asia and Europe are continuing to expand, with German and French growth accelerating in the third quarter. Exports of aircraft and other big items are likely to rise, too, supplying the U.S. economy with an extra lift. In other words, globalization has made consumers less central to the American economy.

Still, the consumer recession will hit some parts of the economy harder than others. Particularly at risk are retailers, who have already seen sharp declines in their stock prices since the extent of the subprime crisis became clear. Nordstrom shares, for example, fell from 52 in September to as low as 32 before rebounding. On Nov. 14, Macy's cut its sales forecast for the fourth quarter, sending its stock down to $28 a share from $43 in July. "Retailers are looking to pare inventories," says Rosenberg.

Not everyone thinks American shoppers are tapped out. Consumers have about $4 trillion in unused borrowing capacity on their credit cards, enough to keep spending afloat, points out Stuart A. Feldstein, president of SMR Research in Hackettstown, N.J., which studies consumer loan markets.

But executives from Capital One Financial, Bank of America, Discover Card, Washington Mutual, and others have told investors in recent conference calls that they are using more caution in extending credit. Chief Financial Officer Gary L. Perlin of Capital One, the nation's No. 5 card issuer, says he believes last year's historically low defaults by credit-card holders were partly driven by the real estate boom, particularly in previously hot housing markets such as Arizona, California, and Florida. Those benefits also have seemed to run out. As a result, says Perlin, Capital One is tightening lending standards and limiting credit lines.

More rate cuts by the Fed can cushion the impact of the consumer cutbacks but not avert them altogether. It's best to think of this as the end of a long-term spending and borrowing bubble, where the role of policy is to keep the inevitable adjustment from turning into panic. "The Fed's job is to keep us all calm and reasoned," says Carroll.

Everyone now seems to be coming up with remedies. At a Nov. 8 congressional hearing, Fed Chairman Ben Bernanke suggested legislation that would temporarily add liquidity to the jumbo loan market. And the possibility of a consumer slump already has Presidential candidates and their staffs looking ahead. "Potentially, the next subprime crisis is the issue of credit-card debt," says Austan D. Goolsbee, economic adviser to Democratic hopeful Barack Obama and a professor at the University of Chicago Graduate School of Business. The Illinois senator's view, says Goolsbee, is that the U.S. needs to improve oversight in the credit-card market. Republican candidate Mitt Romney suggests eliminating taxes on savings and investment by low- and middle-class families, a move that could help make up for a tougher credit environment.

The politicians can say what they want. Recession or no, Americans had better get ready to tighten their belts.

With Peter Coy in New York and Dawn Kopecki and Jane Saseen in Washington.

Sparking Interest in Nature— Family Style

DONNA J. SATTERLEE AND GRACE D. CORMONS

"Daddy, come and look! There's a lizard on Tsara's jeans." Luís and his family are exploring the woods on a typical Family Learning/ Family Fun (FLFF) Day with the SPARK program. SPARK (Shore People Advancing Readiness for Knowledge) is a nature-based program designed to advance literacy and environmental knowledge in a rural Virginia county that has long been combating generational poverty and low literacy.

SPARK engages children between the ages of 3 and 7 and their families in nature learning. The program is a collaboration between the Adult Education Program at Eastern Shore Community College in Melfa, Virginia, and the Accomack County Schools, with support funds from Even Start and Title 1.

The SPARK program has grown from serving 25 families in 1998 to involving more than 200 today from a broad range of ethnic, economic, and educational backgrounds. Its purpose is to encourage and teach parents how to become involved in their children's education. To achieve this goal, we provide experiential learning activities by using nature as an outdoor classroom and the main learning theme.

How the Program Works

Principals at various schools encourage children and families to participate in the program. They invite SPARK staff to recruit at PTA and open house meetings and to set up SPARK bulletin boards. Teachers send home enrollment forms with pre-K and kindergarten students. Many teachers enroll their own children when they see that SPARK opens a whole new world for participating families. Parents and children spend more quality time together as they are introduced to new topics to learn about and new places to go, and to having fun.

Program participants receive weekly packets of reader-friendly, nature-oriented materials. Ideally, SPARK instructors explain the packets individually to participating parents (or grandparents, aunts, uncles), who pick up the materials at the elementary schools or, in some cases, their workplaces.

Typical packets may include live pussy willow branches and directions for rooting, a lesson on leaf identification and counting, or phonemic awareness activities using an alphabet series based on wildlife found on the Eastern Shore of Virginia. The program encourages parents to set aside time once a week to relax and enjoy doing SPARK activities with their children. The packet activities encourage the families to explore outdoors and document what they see.

The SPARK program is constantly evolving because of its focus on nature, which is ever changing.

The learning packets introduce families and children to new concepts and information relevant to the nature studies in upcoming outdoor trips, called FLFF Days. These outings are held two Saturdays and one Sunday per month. Families visit different ecosystems on Virginia's Eastern Shore. For some outings we use school buses, and for others families get there on their own.

SPARK Kids books are an important program resource. They feature photos of the families currently involved in the program during FLFF Day outings.

SPARK staff write one new book each year to record the nature field study trips. The books capture the story of families' discoveries and learning through easy-to-read captions and on-site photos. Eight different books exist to date and are enthusiastically used as learning tools by SPARK families, the Accomack County schools, and the general public.

Like the learning packets, the books are written in vocabulary-enhancing text that describes the photos in succinct, simple wording. Bilingual (Spanish and English) books and packets are used by speakers of Spanish to learn English and by speakers of English to learn Spanish.

Photo Books Are Preparatory Resources

The SPARK Kids photo books, along with the weekly packets, provide background information about the program's planned activities. For example, after reading "SPARK Kids in the Woods," we take the families on a hike through a local woodland, where they find many of the plants and animals described and illustrated in the book: daddy longlegs, lizards, squirrels, and woodpeckers, along with a variety of fall foliage, lichens on trees, or conical ant lion pits in sandy, sunny spots.

As part of the learning experience, the children and adults collect various natural items that we help them learn to identify before using in a follow-up art project. We often enhance the nature-based learning with relevant children's literature. For example, preceding a woods walk, the leader reads to the children *The Teddy Bears' Picnic,* by Jimmy Kennedy. During the walk the children miraculously discover teddy bears (thanks to our magical preplacement) having a picnic in the woods!

Another time we visit a marsh after an introductory reading of the "SPARK Kids in the Marsh" book and the families' preview of their resource packets. Together with the families we look for the fiddler crabs, periwinkles, marsh grass, mussels, and egrets that are shown in the book. The children catch killifish in small nets.

A favorite destination each spring is Sparky's farm. Families observe trees budding, geese nesting, and other spring events. The children can feed the chickens, hold a chick, pet a rabbit, milk a goat or cow, ride a horse, and get to know many of the other farm animals. In addition they may hunt for arthropods in the farm's fields, after seeing and reading about them in "SPARK Kids Find Arthropods." At the end of the day on the farm, families learn about echoes when they "meet" (hear) Echo in the woods.

Nature—An Ever-Evolving Program

The SPARK program is constantly evolving because of its focus on nature, which is ever changing. We continually adjust the materials according to what is happening at the time, often writing new text on the spot. For example, one fall there were many large, very hairy woolly bear caterpillars, and we wrote a woolly bear story and accompanying activity sheets. This is one way we keep the spark in SPARK.

We often enhance the nature-based learning with relevant children's literature.

Learning Skills and Having Fun

Another important facet of the program is exposing families to planning and organizational skills that they can use to be more effectively and efficiently involved in their children's education. To this end, we include date reminders in the packets and follow up with phone calls just before events. We provide a monthly events calendar as well as frequent newsletters for families. Our program planning emphasizes to the children and the adults that they need to prepare for trips by wearing suitable clothing, which usually means clothes they do not mind getting dirty.

Sparky the Blue Crab, our cartoon mascot, contributes to the success of the program. The blue crab is closely identified with Virginia's Eastern Shore. Sparky appears in the SPARK books and on stickers, T-shirts, flyers, materials packets, the events calendar, and the banner we use to welcome families to the program. The children love Sparky and often mimic him as he reads, asks questions, and investigates. Sparky helps to create a clublike atmosphere, giving a sense of belonging to all involved. As program incentives, participants receive Sparky stickers for completing activities in their packets and Sparky T-shirts for frequent attendance.

Trusting Staff and Program Quality

Another important program aspect is the trust and confidence families develop toward staff and the program activities. They count on us to interpret messages from the schools, lend a book, answer nature questions

Starting a Family Nature Program

Creating the Program

- Find an individual dedicated to child and adult learning, who is knowledgeable of natural history, enthusiastic about implementing a program, and prepared to try various ways to make it work.
- Locate a reliable assistant who shares a like passion for nature and learning.
- Have a mission/philosophy/goal and a name. Choose something that will identify the group and help create a club atmosphere. Identify an appropriate animal mascot for your area, such as a lizard for the desert, and find an artist who can draw it in a way that is appealing to children.
- Decide which is appropriate: to write your own curriculum or purchase a published nature-based curriculum.
- Get to know well the natural environment in your area, locating good places to explore with families. Remember, even small city parks offer many interesting plants and animals; children are fascinated with insects and tiny flowers; pigeons and sparrows can teach valuable lessons in natural history.
- Arrange for a place to meet families and distribute materials, for example, a preschool or Head Start center, public school, church, workplace, or library.
- Begin with program activities that take advantage of the best time of the year for doing things outdoors—in most areas, spring and fall.
- Find funding. Much can be done with volunteers, a copy machine, and an attitude that it is fun to "make do" with what is at hand. Local service clubs may donate funds, and individuals in the community may contribute to your program, especially if you ask for support for a particular trip or to put together a book. Check https://grants.gov for grants, or contact your local Community Foundation.

- Consider collaborative agreements with the school district for providing a parent-school connection. Check out adult education programs. Try the county Extension agency or other existing organizations in your community. Asking and networking often will solve a problem.
- Obtain transportation if needed by writing grants, connecting with the school for buses, car pooling, or using public or private transportation.

Leading the Sessions

- Get permission slips, release forms, and emergency contact numbers for everyone involved, including staff.
- Meet with adults in person to explain the weekly materials, which they then use with their children.
- Model healthful living. Include exercise as part of the program—taking a walk, for example, is essential for looking at things. Provide nutritious snacks.
- Take photos on Family Learning/Family Fun days to give to participants, use in a newsletter, send to the local paper, or put together to create resource books.

Working with Families

- Start small, ideally with 20 to 25 families you know well, who trust you and will bring others into the program.
- Involve parents, both physically and mentally, in all aspects of the program. Emphasize that it is a family program, not just for children. Require parents or other family adults to attend outings with the children.
- Communicate regularly with participants. Keep adults involved, interested, and connected through phone calls or e-mails that help all families stay in the loop.
- Respect parents and anticipate their possible reactions to materials (as "hard to read" and so on) or to field trips (like "Will we get dirty?" and so on).

thoroughly and carefully, or rescue a bird from a crab trap. To foster trust building, SPARK staff plan activities in advance. The result is that families are comfortable doing things they have never done before, such as wading through waist-deep water to reach an island or trudging through smelly mud to observe fiddler crabs. We are always amazed at how willingly and thoroughly our family participants immerse themselves (often literally!) in the activities.

One especially pleasing program outcome is the unusually high rate of participation by fathers. We believe that this is likely due to the outdoor focus of the program and having a male staff member who often leads FLFF Day events and makes fathers feel welcome.

Families are comfortable doing things they have never done before, such as wading through waist-deep water to reach an island or trudging through smelly mud to observe fiddler crabs.

Conclusion

Children, adults, and families, from a variety of backgrounds, find nature fascinating. Because most people don't know very much about nature, everyone is on a level playing field. The exposure to something new and interesting serves as a common denominator that brings

Nature Activities for Families

Nature occurs almost anywhere. There are many ways families can explore nature. Start by sampling some of the following:

1. Find wildflowers and insects along roadsides, on lawns, and in local parks. Through car, bus, and train windows, watch for birds flying high in the sky or perching on telephone wires. On neighborhood walks, spy birds in trees, shrubs, and on lawns around houses. Playgrounds are good places for observing nature too.

2. Choose an object in nature that you regularly see (like a tree or a cactus) and start a back-and-forth family exchange of observations on its size, structure, movement, color, texture, and so on. Use all five senses to study natural objects. Don't forget to smell and touch, and if you know something is safe (like a wild blackberry), taste it. Draw and photograph your chosen subject at different seasons and as it grows. Compare photos to identify changes you notice. Study your subject in relation to other similar things in nature that you see, and discuss similarities and differences.

3. Visit a nature preserve. Find out (from friends or on the Internet) the names of nearby state parks or a national park or wildlife refuge you can visit as a family.

4. Learn about local organizations such as a bird club or find an active member of the community who can help you discover nature. Check your local library for publications from groups like the National Wildlife Federation and the National Audubon Society or visit the Web sites of The Nature Conservancy or other organizations.

5. Try some simple experiments like the following: fill up a large, clear plastic jar with rain or pond water and see how it changes each week. First, you may see green algae growing on the inside of the jar, and then you may discover tiny mosquito larvae wriggling around in the water. They will grow and change (you can cover the top of the jar with a piece of old panty hose to keep adult mosquitoes from exiting and biting anyone!).

6. Look around and use your imagination to find meaningful things to observe, learn from, and share with children. You might share what you did by writing about it in your local newspaper, neighborhood Listserv, or a school or nature organization newsletter.

7. Examine the weeds in a vacant lot, a small edge of woods, a yard with trees, a public park, a log or rock to look under, an overlooked corner of a school yard, a stream/creek/pond or somewhere where there is water occasionally and that is safe. Any places where small creatures and plants can live offer lessons waiting to be learned.

8. Grow things yourselves. For example, plant the seeds from apples and oranges in pots.

---

everyone together. Watching program participants easily establishing a cooperative and amiable network among themselves and with one another's children is rewarding.

Exposure to something new and interesting serves as a common denominator that brings everyone together.

We value our staff, who include individuals with knowledge and understanding of early childhood development. They model effective parenting behavior, including positive interactions and investigative behaviors, and they expertly use the natural environment. These aspects contribute to a successful program and support the SPARK philosophy that "learning is fun."

Last, there is a very positive, important corollary to the SPARK program that is part of the plan: families can learn to become good stewards of the environment, helping to assure the very survival of our planet in the future.

Donna J. Satterlee, MEd, is a full-time lecturer with the Department of Human Ecology at the University of Maryland Eastern Shore in Princess Anne, Maryland, and a child development specialist at the Eastern Shore Community College in Melfa, Virginia. She has 18 years experience as an educator focusing on experiential learning. djsatterlee@umes.edu **Grace D. Cormons**, BA, is the family learning instructor at Virginia's Eastern Shore Community College. Grace started teaching children and adults about nature at the American Museum of Natural History in New York City. She originated the SPARK program and gives presentations at national conferences. gcormons@es.vscc.edu

Test-Your-Knowledge Form

We encourage you to photocopy and use this page as a tool to assess how the articles in *Annual Editions* expand on the information in your textbook. By reflecting on the articles you will gain enhanced text information. You can also access this useful form on a product's book support Web site at *http://www.mhcls.com/online/*.

NAME: DATE:

_____

TITLE AND NUMBER OF ARTICLE:

_____

BRIEFLY STATE THE MAIN IDEA OF THIS ARTICLE:

_____

LIST THREE IMPORTANT FACTS THAT THE AUTHOR USES TO SUPPORT THE MAIN IDEA:

_____

WHAT INFORMATION OR IDEAS DISCUSSED IN THIS ARTICLE ARE ALSO DISCUSSED IN YOUR TEXTBOOK OR OTHER READINGS THAT YOU HAVE DONE? LIST THE TEXTBOOK CHAPTERS AND PAGE NUMBERS:

_____

LIST ANY EXAMPLES OF BIAS OR FAULTY REASONING THAT YOU FOUND IN THE ARTICLE:

_____

LIST ANY NEW TERMS/CONCEPTS THAT WERE DISCUSSED IN THE ARTICLE, AND WRITE A SHORT DEFINITION:

We Want Your Advice

ANNUAL EDITIONS revisions depend on two major opinion sources: one is our Advisory Board, listed in the front of this volume, which works with us in scanning the thousands of articles published in the public press each year; the other is you—the person actually using the book. Please help us and the users of the next edition by completing the prepaid article rating form on this page and returning it to us. Thank you for your help!

ANNUAL EDITIONS: The Family 09/10

ARTICLE RATING FORM

Here is an opportunity for you to have direct input into the next revision of this volume.
We would like you to rate each of the articles listed below, using the following scale:

1. **Excellent: should definitely be retained**
2. **Above average: should probably be retained**
3. **Below average: should probably be deleted**
4. **Poor: should definitely be deleted**

Your ratings will play a vital part in the next revision.
Please mail this prepaid form to us as soon as possible.
Thanks for your help!

RATING	ARTICLE	RATING	ARTICLE
	1. Marriage and Family in the Scandinavian Experience		25. Aging Japanese Pen Messages to Posterity
	2. Interracial Families		26. Recognizing Domestic Partner Abuse
	3. Children as a Public Good		27. The Myths and Truths of Family Abduction
	4. This Thing Called Love		28. Children of Alcoholics
	5. Pillow Talk		29. My Cheatin' Heart
	6. How to Talk about Sex		30. Love but Don't Touch
	7. On-Again, Off-Again		31. Is This Man Cheating on His Wife?
	8. A New Fertility Factor		32. Becoming Financial Grown-Ups
	9. Starting the Good Life in the Womb		33. Making Time for Family Time
	10. Breeder Reaction		34. Partners Face Cancer Together
	11. Adopting a New American Family		35. A Guide for Caregivers
	12. Free As a Bird and Loving It		36. Caring for the Caregiver
	13. Gay Marriage Lite		37. Bereavement after Caregiving
	14. Two Mommies and a Daddy		38. Terrorism, Trauma, and Children
	15. Marriage at First Sight		39. A Divided House
	16. Couple Therapy		40. Civil Wars
	17. Kaleidoscope of Parenting Cultures		41. Stepfamily Success Depends on Ingredients
	18. Do We Need a Law to Prohibit Spanking?		42. The 3rd National Family History Initiative
	19. Prickly Père		43. Get a Closer Look
	20. When Parents Hover Over Kids' Job Search		44. Spirituality and Family Nursing
	21. Last Hope in a Weak Economy?		45. The Joy of Rituals
	22. Being a Sibling		46. Sustaining Resilient Families for Children in Primary Grades
	23. Aunties and Uncles		47. The Consumer Crunch
	24. Roles of American Indian Grandparents in Times of Cultural Crisis		48. Sparking Interest in Nature—Family Style

BUSINESS REPLY MAIL
FIRST CLASS MAIL PERMIT NO. 551 DUBUQUE IA

POSTAGE WILL BE PAID BY ADDRESSEE

McGraw-Hill Contemporary Learning Series
501 BELL STREET
DUBUQUE, IA 52001

ABOUT YOU

Name   Date
_____

Are you a teacher? ❏ A student? ❏
Your school's name
_____

Department
_____

Address   City   State   Zip
_____

School telephone #
_____

YOUR COMMENTS ARE IMPORTANT TO US!

Please fill in the following information:
For which course did you use this book?
_____

Did you use a text with this ANNUAL EDITION? ❏ yes ❏ no
What was the title of the text?
_____

What are your general reactions to the Annual Editions concept?
_____

Have you read any pertinent articles recently that you think should be included in the next edition? Explain.
_____

Are there any articles that you feel should be replaced in the next edition? Why?
_____

Are there any World Wide Web sites that you feel should be included in the next edition? Please annotate.
_____

May we contact you for editorial input? ❏ yes ❏ no
May we quote your comments? ❏ yes ❏ no